Lecture Notes in Computer Science 4744

Commenced Publication in 1973
Founding and Former Series Editors:
Gerhard Goos, Juris Hartmanis, and Jan van Leeuwen

T0223197

Yvonne de Kort   Wijnand IJsselsteijn
Cees Midden   Berry Eggen   B.J. Fogg (Eds.)

Persuasive Technology

Second International Conference
on Persuasive Technology, PERSUASIVE 2007
Palo Alto, CA, USA, April 26-27, 2007
Revised Selected Papers

 Springer

Volume Editors

Yvonne de Kort
Wijnand IJsselsteijn
Cees Midden
Eindhoven University of Technology
Technology Management
PO Box 513, 5600 MB Eindhoven, The Netherlands
E-mail: {y.a.w.d.kort, w.a.ijsselsteijn, c.j.h.midden}@tue.nl

Berry Eggen
Eindhoven University of Technology
Industrial Design
PO Box 513, 5600 MB Eindhoven, The Netherlands
E-mail: j.h.eggen@tue.nl

B.J. Fogg
Stanford University
Persuasive Technology Lab
Box 20456 Stanford, CA 94309, USA
E-mail: bjfogg@stanford.edu

Library of Congress Control Number: 2007941160

CR Subject Classification (1998): H.5, H.1, J.3-4, K.4.1, I.6, I.2.0, I.2.6

LNCS Sublibrary: SL 3 – Information Systems and Application, incl. Internet/Web and HCI

ISSN   0302-9743
ISBN-10   3-540-77005-4 Springer Berlin Heidelberg New York
ISBN-13   978-3-540-77005-3 Springer Berlin Heidelberg New York

Springer is a part of Springer Science+Business Media

springer.com

© Springer-Verlag Berlin Heidelberg 2007

Typesetting: Camera-ready by author, data conversion by Scientific Publishing Services, Chennai, India
Printed on acid-free paper   SPIN: 12196791   06/3180   5 4 3 2 1 0

Preface

Persuasive technology is the general class of technologies that purposefully apply psychological principles of persuasion – principles of credibility, trust, reciprocity, authority and the like – in interactive media, in the service of changing their users' attitudes and behavior.

Only one year ago, in 2006, the first international conference in this area, PERSUASIVE 2006 was hosted in Eindhoven. The conference was entirely geared towards communicating the progress made in the area of persuasive technology, and towards presenting recent results in theory, design, technology and evaluation. It brought together a wide range of research fields, including social psychology, HCI, computer science, industrial design, engineering, game design, communication science, and human factors, and the formula worked: plans for a follow-up were made immediately upon its conclusion.

PERSUASIVE 2007, the second international conference on persuasive technology, was hosted by Stanford University, April 26–27. The program featured a large number of presentations, both oral and in poster format, on new findings, new conceptualizations and designs, and new reflections on persuasion through technology. Sponsored by the National Science Foundation, this conference featured the best new insights into how video games, mobile phone applications, and Web sites can be designed to motivate and influence people.

PERSUASIVE 2007 topped its predecessor in bringing together almost 200 people interested in how computers can change people's beliefs and behaviors. The Stanford team introduced an innovative – captivating – format for the conference. During the two days, 38 researchers each talked for 10 minutes – sharp – which resulted in a fast, stimulating program with sufficient amounts of open time for questions and discussion. The keynote speakers, Clifford Nass, Jeremy Bailenson, and Karen Pryor, each brought a surprising perspective to persuasive technology.

The PERSUASIVE 2007 proceedings contain only accepted and presented full and short papers. They are listed under the 13 themes they were also grouped in during the conference. The papers were selected from the large collection of submitted papers through a carefully conducted review process, using blind peer-review. We are greatly indebted to the members of the Programe Committee for their excellent work in reviewing the submitted papers and selecting the best papers for presentation at the conference and inclusion in the current volume of the LNCS.

PERSUASIVE 2007 was another landmark in captology. Never before have so many people gathered to share so many new ideas on this topic. We thank all those who helped make PERSUASIVE 2007 a success, and we look forward to next year's event in Europe.

July 2007

Yvonne de Kort
Wijnand IJsselsteijn
Cees Midden
Berry Eggen
B.J. Fogg

Organization

Organizing Committee PERSUASIVE 2007

Programe Chair

B.J. Fogg (Stanford University)

Associate Chair

Brian Ong (Stanford University)
Dennis Bills (Stanford University)
Nadja Blagojevic (Stanford University)
Dean Eckles (Stanford University)
Berry Eggen (Eindhoven University of Technology)
Wijnand IJsselsteijn (Eindhoven University of Technology)
Yvonne de Kort (Eindhoven University of Technology)
Cees Midden (Eindhoven University of Technology)
Kim Reeves (Stanford University)

Sponsoring Organization

National Science Foundation (NSF)

Scientific Review Committee

Cees Midden, Ph.D. (Chair)
Yvonne de Kort, Ph.D.
Wijnand IJsselsteijn, Ph.D.
Berry Eggen, Ph.D.
B.J. Fogg, Ph.D.

Reviewers

Richard Adler - Institute for the Future, USA
Mariano Alcañiz - Polytechnic University of Valencia, Spain
Chika Ando - Adobe Systems
Bernardine Atkinson - Charles Darwin University, Northern Territory, Australia
Jeremy Bailenson - Stanford University, USA
Daniel Berdichevsky - DemiDec Resources, USA
Peter Boland - BeWell Mobile Technology, Inc., USA

Don Bouwhuis - Eindhoven University of Technology, Netherlands
Cheryl Bracken - Cleveland State University, USA
Jared Braiterman - jaredRESEARCH, USA
Angela Brooker - Stanford University, USA
Erik Damen - Pam pv, Netherlands
David Danielson - Stanford University, USA
Arie Dijkstra - Groningen University, Netherlands
Kees Dorst - TU/e, Netherlands; University of Technology, Sydney
Berry Eggen - Eindhoven University of Technology, Netherlands
Felix Eschenburg - University of Cologne, Germany
Arnout Fischer - Wageningen University, Netherlands
B.J. Fogg - Stanford University, USA
Robert Gable - Claremont Graduate University, USA
Luciano Gamberini - University of Padua, Italy
Antal Haans - Eindhoven University of Technology, Netherlands
Curt Haugtvedt - Ohio State University, USA
Jettie Hoonhout - Philips Research, Netherlands
Wijnand IJsselsteijn - Eindhoven University of Technology, Netherlands
Aditya Johri - Stanford University, USA
Alex Kass - Accenture Technology Labs, USA
Yvonne de Kort - Eindhoven University of Technology, Netherlands
Dale Larson - Donor Digital, USA
Fred Leach - Stanford University, USA
Craig Lefebvre - Lefebvre Consulting Group
Debra Lieberman - University of California, Santa Barbara, USA
Panos Markopoulos - Eindhoven University of Technology, Netherlands
Judith Masthoff - University of Aberdeen, Scotland, UK
Teddy McCalley - Eindhoven University of Technology, Netherlands
Jeffrey McCandless - NASA, USA
Cees Midden - Eindhoven University of Technology, Netherlands
Harri Oinas-Kukkonen - University of Oulu, Finland
Kevin Patrick - University of California San Diego, USA
Johan Redström - Interactive Institute Stockholm, Sweden
Boris de Ruyter - Philips Research, Netherlands
Timo Saari - Temple Univeristy, USA
Ramit Sethi - Stanford University, USA
Anna Spagnolli - University of Padua, Italy
Mirjana Spasojevic - Nokia Research Center, USA
Jason Tester - Institute for the Future, USA
Harm van Essen - Eindhoven University of Technology, Netherlands
Iris van Rooij - Eindhoven University of Technology, Netherlands
Peter-Paul Verbeek - Twente University, Netherlands
Peter de Vries - Twente University, Netherlands
Stephan Wensveen - Eindhoven University of Technology, Netherlands
Joyce Westerink - Philips Research, Netherlands
Martijn Willemsen - Eindhoven University of Technology, Netherlands
Ruud Zaalberg - Eindhoven University of Technology, Netherlands

This conference was supported, in part, by the National Science Foundation under award IIS-0732353.

Table of Contents

Technology That Motivates Health Behavior

Persuading People with Video Games

New Form Factors for Persuasive Technology

Surrounded by High-Tech Persuasion

Controlling People by Using Digital Punishment

Technology That Motivates Groups to Unify

How Peers Influence You Online

New Insights Into Web Persuasion

Persuasive Agents on the Screen

Using Digital Images to Persuade

Persuasion Via Mobile Phones

Insights Into Persuasion Principles

Perspectives on Persuasive Technology

Persuasion, Task Interruption and Health Regimen Adherence

Timothy Bickmore, Daniel Mauer, Francisco Crespo, and Thomas Brown

College of Computer and Information Science, Northeastern University
Boston, Massachusetts, USA
{bickmore,daniel,crespof}@ccs.neu.edu, brown.tho@neu.edu
http://www.ccs.neu.edu/research/rag

Abstract. Cueing strategies, such as real-time reminders, are among the most effective methods of persuading individuals to perform healthy behaviors such as taking their medication and exercising. However, these reminders often represent a task interruption for users who are engaged in work activities. This paper presents the results of a study which explores strategies for interrupting users at work to perform a healthy behavior, in which the primary outcome of interest is long-term adherence to a desired health behavior change regimen. We find that the degree of perceived politeness of interruptions is positively correlated with predicted long-term adherence, but negatively correlated with short-term compliance. We also find that, among several interruption coordination strategies previously explored in the literature, empathic interruptions are superior overall in gaining both short-term compliance and long-term adherence.

Keywords: Interruption, relational agent, embodied conversational agent, politeness, health compliance, mobile computing.

1 Introduction

Poor lifestyle health behaviors, such as lack of physical activity and unhealthy dietary habits, are among the leading causes of death and chronic disease in the United States [21]. In addition, adherence to prescribed treatments — such as medication regimens — is estimated to average only 50%, and represents another significant source of morbidity, mortality and healthcare cost to the nation [12]. Each of these large classes of health behavior problems have been the targets of numerous technology-based interventions in recent years.

One of the simplest such interventions is a reminder system that alerts users when it is time to engage in a healthy behavior, such as going for a walk or taking medication. Timed reminders are examples of "cueing" or "stimulus control" processes, which involve changing an individual's environment so that it presents a conditional stimulus to perform a desired health behavior (e.g., keeping a gym bag by the door as a physical reminder to work out). It has been shown that such techniques have been used by most individuals who have successfully changed their health behavior [23].

Y. de Kort et al. (Eds.): PERSUASIVE 2007, LNCS 4744, pp. 1–11, 2007.

For users who happen to be sitting idly when these alerts are triggered, the reminders may result in a relatively high compliance rate. However, as many recent studies in task interruption have shown, responsiveness to an interruption (in this case, compliance with the recommended health behavior) depends crucially on what the user is doing at the time the interruption presents itself [14] in addition to many other factors such as the emotional state of the user [15] and the modality of the interruption [1].

We are developing a mobile, PDA-based health advisor that is able to provide real-time reminders and con-versational counseling to help users change their health behavior (Fig. 1) [2,3]. In this effort, we are exploring dif-ferent interruption modali-ties and strategies that can be used by the advisor to persuade users to perform a healthy behavior while they are work-ing at routine office tasks. We are particularly interested in maximizing *long-term* adher-ence, summed over weeks or months of regular use. A very insistent or annoying inter-ruption may be effective at gaining compliance in the short term, but individuals may be likely to use the device less fre-quently (or discontinue use altogether), resulting in an overall loss of adherence. On the other hand, an extremely polite inter-ruption may have the inverse

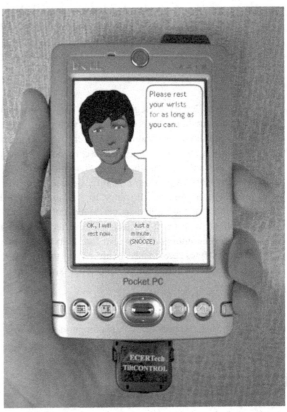

Fig. 1. PDA and Relational Agent Interface

effect: it may not be very effective at gaining compliance at any particular moment (e.g., if the user is engrossed in a task), though individuals may be more likely to continue use of the device over time. Thus, we hypothesize a curvilinear relationship between the perceived "politeness" of interruption strategies and health behavior adherence, holding all other factors constant.

While we plan to conduct a longitudinal study of the PDA-based advisor, we chose first to conduct short-term studies of interruptions so that we could explore as many design options as possible. Consequently, we used self-reported "desire to continue use" as a proxy for long-term adherence. While the validity of this measure with respect to actual long-term use needs to be established, there is an analogue in the study of human relationships, in which self-reported relational commitment has been found to be one of the best predictors for relationship longevity [4].

In the remainder of this paper we first present a review of related work in task interruption and health behavior promotion, followed by a description of the PDA platform used in our intervention work. We then describe the experimental setup used in the current effort, followed by a detailed description of the study we conducted. We conclude with a discussion of the study results and their implications and future research directions.

2 Related Work

Although there is a significant and growing literature on technologies to promote health behavior change, very few of these technologies involve real-time interventions. One notable exception is a body of research on reminder systems for individuals with cognitive impairment using pagers [13] and PDAs [17].

Several systems have also been developed to provide older adults with real-time reminders to perform various activities of daily living (including medication taking). The ILSA system used automated phone to calls to provide real-time reminders to older adults living alone, but the calls were not always effective and users did not like them [11]. Pollack *et al.* developed the AutoMinder system, which could reason about whether, when and how to give a reminder based on a deep understanding of the tasks involved and the user's schedule (e.g., "If you take your medicine now, I won't have to interrupt you during your favorite TV show later") [22]. Preliminary evaluation indicated that acceptance among older adult users was high, although results of any efficacy evaluations have not been reported.

2.1 Real-Time Health Behavior Compliance Studies

Goetz, *et al*, evaluated user compliance to the requests of a "nurse" robot to perform exercise [10]. The robot was controlled by a confederate ("wizard of oz") and spoke using synthetic speech. Study subjects performed more exercise when the robot was "serious" (emphasizing the importance of exercise) than when it was "playful" (.telling jokes and making fun of exercise).

The Breakaway system used an ambient display to provide real-time feedback to users when they had been seated at work for too long, in an attempt to get them to go for periodic walks [16]. Unfortunately, the system was only evaluated with a single user and only anecdotal results were reported.

2.2 Task Interruption Studies

There has been considerable research done in the area of task interruption of computer users in recent years. Much of this work is primarily concerned with the impact of interruptions on task performance, while our focus is primarily on user responsiveness to the interruption.

Gillie and Broadbent [9] showed that even a very short interruption can be significantly disruptive and affect task performance, and Cutrell *et al.* [7] found that even an *ignored* interruption can negatively affect performance.

A number of studies have shown that, in terms of supporting human performance of all kinds, negotiation-based methods in which users are alerted that there is a notification, but are able to control whether or when the full content of the notification is displayed, are preferable to simpler models in which the full notification is delivered immediately [19,20,24]. Czerwinski *et al.* also found that delivering a pre-interruption warning prior to the delivery of the content of the interruption can also have a significant positive effect on performance [8].

Arroyo, *et al.* found that different interface modalities (e.g. heat, light, sound, odor) carry varying degrees of "disruptiveness" [1]. However, they did not investigate different stimuli within a modality (e.g., multiple sounds), nor did they measure short or long-term compliance to an interruption-based request.

There is also evidence that the use of empathy in interruptions can create a more positive user experience. Liu and Picard presented a wearable system that periodically interrupted users and asked them (via text-based prompts) to annotate whether or not this was a good time to interrupt, and to specify their current stress level and activity [18]. The use of empathic language in the system prompt was varied within subjects, who showed (via self-report) significantly higher desire to continue using the empathic version of the system. Additionally, subjects perceived a lower frequency of interruptions when using the empathic system. However, they also did not investigate the impact of empathic interruption on compliance, or compare their approach to other interruption coordination strategies (users were required to either acknowledge an interruption or cancel it immediately).

3   Experimental Platform

We have developed a general purpose social agent interface for use on handheld computers (see Fig. 1). The animated agent appears in a fixed close-up shot, and is capable of a range of nonverbal conversational behavior, including facial displays of emotion, head nods, eye gaze movement, eyebrow raises, posture shifts and "visemes" (mouth shapes corresponding to phonemes). These behaviors are synchronized in real time with agent output utterances. Agent utterances are displayed in a text balloon rather than using speech, to avoid privacy issues. The words in the agent utterance are individually highlighted at normal speaking speed and the nonverbal behavior displayed in synchrony. User inputs are constrained to multiple choice selections and time-of-day specifications at the bottom of the display.

Interaction dialogues are scripted in an XML-based state-transition network, which allows for rapid development and modification of dialogues. Scripts consist primarily of agent utterances (written in plain text), the allowed user responses to each agent utterance, and instructions for state transitions based on these responses and other system events (timers, sensor input, etc.).

Once a script is written, it is preprocessed using the BEAT text-to-embodied-speech engine [6], which automatically adds specifications for agent nonverbal behavior. In addition, each word of each utterance is processed by a viseme generator (based on the freeTTS text-to-speech engine [25]) that provides the appropriate sequence of mouth shapes the agent must form in order to give the appearance of uttering that word.

Interruption behavior can be very flexibly defined, since the scripting language supports a variety of wait states and state transitions conditioned on events. During specified wait states, the PDA's display shuts off, and the interface remains dormant until some condition is met. Example conditions include specific times of day, changes in user behavior as measured by sensor input, or other factors. The particular modality of an interruption can consist of various combinations of audio tones and/or visual cues presented on an arbitrarily complex schedule. User failure to respond to an interruption (or any agent utterance) can also be handled in a flexible manner.

The architecture of the run-time system on the handheld is shown in Fig. 2. The actions of the system are primarily controlled by a finite state machine, which is built at run time according to the XML script. The Agent/Interface module comprises the relational agent itself (graphics, animations, audio, etc.), as well as areas for text output and user input in the form of clickable buttons which effect state transitions. During time periods in which the script does not explicitly specify agent actions, the idle action system takes over control of the agent, randomly performing various idle behaviors (eye blinks, posture shifts, etc.).

The run-time software was developed entirely in Macromedia Flash, and we are using Dell Axim X30 Pocket PC computers for development and experimentation.

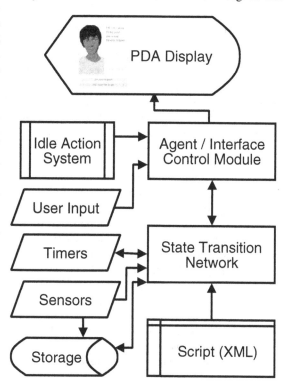

Fig. 2. Run-time System Architecture

4 Experimental Method

We conducted a study to evaluate our hypothesis about the relationship between politeness of interruption and compliance, holding as many factors constant as possible. To do this, we evaluated the impact of a range of audio alert tones that were pre-selected to vary in perceived politeness. We used "wrist rests" as the health behavior to be promoted (secondary task), and web searching and typing answers to questions on a desktop computer as the representative primary task.

4.1 Experimental Design

The study is a four treatment, randomized, within-subjects design experiment, in which the sound used to signal the start of the interruption is varied between treatments (AUDIO1-AUDIO4), with the order of presentation completely counterbalanced. Each interruption strategy was evaluated using a different PDA that was presented to the user as a "different advisor agent," with the agent having a different physical appearance and name. The order of presentation of interruption methods was counterbalanced, but with a fixed order of characters and quiz questions so that different interruption methods were presented with different questions and characters for each subject.

4.2 Procedure

Subjects were initially told that they would be testing a health advisor who will help people "avoid repetitive stress injuries, such as carpal tunnel syndrome" by reminding them to take occasional breaks when they are working at a desktop computer. Following instruction on the primary task, subjects were told how to interact with the agent on the PDA, and then were told "When the advisor wants to talk to you, the PDA will make a sound. When you hear this, you should talk to the advisor."

At the start of every session the experimenter would tell subjects "Remember, we are keeping track of how many questions you answer and we will review your performance with you at the end of the study." Importantly, however, the experimenter never said anything about whether the subject should follow the advisor's instructions or anything about the importance of wrist rests or whether the subject should take rests or not. The experimenter telling subjects the importance of the primary task together with the advisor telling subjects the importance of wrist rests set up a dilemma for subjects that could often be visibly observed in their behavior following each interruption (e.g., false starts at task resumption, throwing hands in the air, rolling eyes, facial display of exasperation, etc).

The duration of each primary task session is approximately 10 minutes, with the interruptions timed to occur at fixed intervals, so that there are always exactly two interruption events per primary task session. Because there are only a small number of brief inter-primary-task time intervals, most interruptions occur while subjects are in the middle of performing a primary task.

4.3 Apparatus

Study subjects were seated at a desktop (primary task) computer with 17" color monitor, keyboard and mouse (see Fig. 3). The PDA with the wrist-rest advisor agent was placed on the desk just to the left or right of the keyboard, at each subject's discretion. Three video cameras (overhead, left and right frontal), audio, and the computer screen video were continuously recorded during the study for subsequent analysis.

There was one program always running on the primary task computer that sequentially posed questions to subjects during each session and provided them with a text box within which they had to type their response. A web browser, pre-loaded to a search engine page, was open on the desktop at the start of each session as well, and subjects were encouraged to use the search engine to help them answer the questions. The program prevented users from pasting text; attempts to do so would produce a dialog box telling them they had to answer "in their own words". The program also presented a "DONE" button that subjects were instructed to push once they had finished answering the question. If subjects pushed this button before they had typed 40 words, another dialog box informed them how many more words they needed before their answer would be considered complete. Once they successfully finished a question, an audio tone was sounded and they were presented with the next question. At the end of the session (normally 10 minutes) a different tone was sounded and a dialog box appeared informing them that "TIME IS UP" for the primary task. Questions for the primary task program were designed to be answerable in 3-5 minutes; data from the study indicated that subjects actually took on average 3.2 (SD 1.2) minutes, and answered 2.0 (SD 1.13) questions per session, using an average of 59.4 (SD 14.2) words per answer. Sample questions are "Describe some of the features of HD DVDs." and "What is the greenhouse effect?".

Four PDAs were running the agent software described above, with four different female characters, each with a unique name and appearance. For each of the four conditions evaluated in each study, an introduction and interruption script was written. In the introduction script the character introduces itself, tells the subject a fact about upper body musculoskeletal disorders and/or how to prevent them, a statement about the importance of taking frequent wrist rests when working at a computer, and a farewell, lasting six turns of dialogue. The interruption scripts vary by study condition, but always end with the agent saying "Please rest your wrists for as long as you can." The only allowed user response is

Fig. 3. Experimental Setup

"OK, I'll rest now". After the user selects this response, the PDA display turns off until the next interruption.

4.4 Selection of Stimulus Alert Sounds

Four alert sounds were selected for use in the study, which varied from very polite (AUDIO1, a subtle "ping") to very impolite (AUDIO4, a loud klaxon). Selection was performed by first identifying 210 candidate sounds on the Internet using the FindSound.com search engine with keywords "alarm", "beep", "phone", "alert" and "chimes", and only selecting relatively brief sounds (< 5sec) of high quality. This list was manually reduced to 128 sounds by removal of clips we felt were duplicates. The resulting sounds were rated by seven members of our research group on a 7-point, "polite" to "annoying" scale, and four sounds that evenly spanned the range of averaged scores were selected for use in the study.

4.5 Measures

Self-report. Following each condition, subjects were asked to rate the wrist-rest agent on the self-report scales shown in Table 1, covering various ratings of the agent as well as 'desire to continue' using the agent.

Table 1. Self-Report Measures for Rating Interruption Methods

Measure	Question	Anchor 1	Anchor 7
POLITE	How polite was the advisor?	not polite	extremely
ANNOYING	How annoying was the advisor?	not annoying	intolerable
CONTINUE	How much would you like to continue working with the advisor?	not at all	very much

Compliance Behavior. Durations of all wrist rests taken by subjects were measured based on analysis of recorded video. Rest duration was coded from the time a subject acknowledged an interruption ("OK, I'll rest now.") until they returned to work on the primary task. This second 'end of rest' time involved subjective judgment, since subjects exhibited a wide range of behavior that could be interpreted as resting. Consequently, a coding manual was written and rest times were coded in parallel by two judges, with an overall inter-rater reliability of 0.99 (using SPSS single measure intraclass correlation coefficient), and final values taken as the average of the scores by each judge.

Primary Task Impact. Productivity on the primary task was assessed by the number of questions completed per primary task session (TASKS).

4.6 Participants

Twenty-nine subjects participated in the study: 52% female, 83% students, aged 18-30. Computer, web and search engine experience was fairly high (5.3, 5.6, 6.0 respectively on 1='never used one' to 7='expert' scales), but they had less experience using PDAs (2.4 on the same scale). The average wrist-rest behavior stage of change (adapted from [23]) was 'preparation', but subjects spanned the entire scale from ' pre-contemplation' to 'maintenance'.

4.7 Results

Comparison among study conditions was performed using repeated measure ANOVAs in SPSS.

Results are shown in Table 2. Most differences across conditions are highly significant (Fig. 4). Subjects did perceive a significant difference in politeness/ annoyingness across conditions (manipulation check). LSD post hoc analysis indicated significant differences among all pairs of conditions except for AUDIO1 and AUDIO2.

Desire to continue using the advisor varied directly with politeness ratings, confirming part of our hypothesis. Post hoc analyses indicated significant differences between AUDIO4 and the other conditions, but not among any other pairs of conditions.

Table 2. Study Results, Mean(SD)

Measure	AUDIO1	AUDIO2	AUDIO3	AUDIO4	Sig.
POLITE	6.54(1.63)	6.23(1.58)	4.96(2.09)	3.89(2.66)	p<.001
ANNOYING	2.48(1.76)	1.84(0.85)	2.96(2.09)	5.40(2.77)	p<.001
CONTINUE	5.00(2.51)	5.04(2.46)	4.39(2.30)	3.08(2.40)	p<.001
REST 1	15.30(3.06)	16.16(3.12)	17.02(3.29)	17.78(3.71)	n.s.
REST 2	16.79(3.08)	17.76(3.41)	16.52(3.57)	10.25(2.62)	p<.05
TASKS	3.69(1.29)	3.45(1.15)	3.38(1.02)	3.38 (1.12)	n.s.

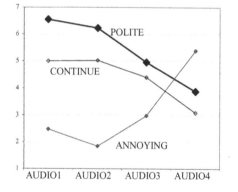

Fig. 4. Self-Report Measures

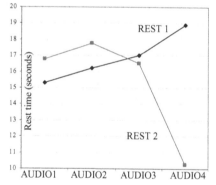

Fig. 5. Compliance(Rest Times)

Fig. 5 shows short-term compliance behavior (rest time) for the two interruptions in each evaluation session. Rest time following initial exposure to each stimulus sound (REST 1) did appear to vary according to our hypothesis (subjects rested longer for more annoying sounds), but this variation was not significant. By the second exposure to each stimulus sound (REST 2), the hypothesized longitudinal effects were already visible, with a curvilinear relationship between politeness and compliance, and the most annoying sound resulting in the shortest rest time. Post hoc analyses on REST2 indicated significant differences between AUDIO4 and the other conditions, but not among any other pairs of conditions.

There were no significant effects of perceived politeness on primary task performance.

5 Conclusion

Overall, our hypotheses regarding the relationship between politeness and compliance were supported. We were surprised to find that compliance would drop off so quickly with a very annoying interruption, but this was further confirmed by video analysis showing several subjects shutting off the second exposure AUDIO4 alarm with a disgusted expression and continuing to work without stopping. In sum, this study indicates that an appropriate level of politeness must be used when interrupting and persuading users in order to maximize long-term effectiveness.

Future Directions

There are many interesting directions of future research in this area. Our next study involves manipulation of the perceived social distance between the user and advisor. Following Brown & Levinson's theory of politeness [5], we expect this to moderate the relationship between politeness and compliance, such that as familiarity grows, users are more accepting of less polite forms of interruption. Our planned field study of the Just-in-Time advisor agent will also provide feedback on the long-term efficacy of the interruption strategy we finally implement for the system. Finally, techniques from studies such as this on the *best way* to interrupt someone should be combined with techniques for determining the *best time* to interrupt someone (e.g., [14]) to design systems that have the overall best chance of promoting long-term health behavior regimen adherence.

Acknowledgments. Thanks to the other members of the Relational Agents Group for the help on this project, and to Jennifer Smith for her many helpful comments on this paper. This work was supported by NIH National Library of Medicine grant R21LM008553.

References

1. Arroyo, E., Selker, T., Stouffs, A.: Interruptions as multimodal outputs: which are the less disruptive? In: 4th IEEE International Conference on Multimodal Interfaces, pp. 479–482. IEEE, Los Alamitos (2002)
2. Bickmore, T., Mauer, D.: Modalities for Building Relationships with Handheld Computer Agents. In: ACM SIGCHI Conference on Human Factors in Computing Systems (CHI) (2006)
3. Bickmore, T., Gruber, A., Intille, S., Mauer, D.: A Handheld Animated Advisor for Physical Activity Promotion. In: American Medical Informatics Association Annual Symposium (2006)
4. Brehm, S.: Intimate Relationships. McGraw-Hill, New York (1992)
5. Brown, P., Levinson, S.C.: Politeness: Some universals in language usage. Cambridge University Press, Cambridge (1987)

6. Cassell, J., Vilhjálmsson, H., Bickmore, T.: BEAT: The Behavior Expression Animation Toolkit. In: SIGGRAPH '01, pp. 477–486 (2001)
7. Cutrell, E., Czerwinski, M., Horvitz, E.: Notification, Disruption, and Memory: Effects of Messaging Interruptions on Memory and Performance. In: INTERACT'01, pp. 263–269 (2001)
8. Czerwinski, M., S, C., Schumacher, B.: The effects of warnings and display similarities on interruption in multitasking environments. SIGCHI Bulletin 23(4), 38–39 (1991)
9. Gillie, T., Broadbent, D.: What makes interruptions disruptive? A study of length, similarity and complexity. Psychological Research 50(1), 243–250 (1989)
10. Goetz, J., Kiesler, S., Powers, A.: Matching robot appearance and behavior to tasks to improve human-robot cooperation. In: Proceedings of the 12th IEEE Workshop on Robot and Human Interactive Communication. RO-MAN 2003, IEEE Computer Society Press, Los Alamitos (2003)
11. Haigh, K., Kiff, L., Ho, G.: The Independent LifeStyle AssistantTM (I.L.S.A.): Lessons Learned. Assistive Technology 18, 87–106 (2006)
12. Haynes, R., McDonald, H., Garg, A.: Helping Patients Follow Prescribed Treatment. JAMA 288(22), 2880–2883 (2006)
13. Hersh, N., Treadgold, L.: Neuropage: The rehabilitation of memory dysfunction by prosthetic memory and cueing. NeuroRehabilitation 4, 187–197 (1994)
14. Ho, J., Intille, S.S.: Using Context-Aware Computing to Reduce the Perceived Burden of Interruptions from Mobile Devices. In: CHI (2005)
15. Hudson, J.M., Christensen, J., Kellogg, W.A., Erickson, T.: I'd Be Overwhelmed, but It's Just One More Thing to Do: Availability and Interruption in Research Management, 97–104 (2002)
16. Jafarinaimi, N., Forlizzi, J., Hurst, A., Zimmerman, J.: Breakaway: An Ambient Display Designed to Change Human Behavior. In: CHI 2005, pp. 1945–1948 (2005)
17. Kim, H., Burke, D., Dowds, M., Robinson Boone, K., Park, G.: Electronic Memory Aids for Outpatient Brain Injury: Follow-up Findings. Brain Injury 14(2), 187–196 (2000)
18. Liu, K., Picard, R.: Embedded Empathy in Continuous, Interactive Health Assessment. In: CHI Workshop on HCI Challenges in Health Assessment (2005)
19. McFarlane, D.C.: Comparison of Four Primary Methods for Coordinating the Interruption of People in Human-Computer Interaction. Human-Computer Interaction 17(1), 63–139 (2002)
20. McFarlane, D.C., Latorella, K.A.: Coordinating the Interruption of People in Human-Computer Interaction. In: IFIP TC.13 International Conference on Human-Computer Interaction, pp. 295–303 (1999)
21. Mokdad, A.H., Marks, J.S., Stroup, D., Gerberding, J.: Actual causes of death in the United States, 2000. JAMA 291, 1238–1245 (2004)
22. Pollack, M.E., Brown, L., Colbry, D., McCarthy, C.E., Orosz, C., Peintner, B., Ramakrishnan, S., Tsamardinos, I.: An Intelligent Cognitive Orthotic System for People with Memory Impairment. Robotics and Autonomous Systems 44, 273–282 (2003)
23. Prochaska, J., Marcus, B.: The Transtheoretical Model: Applications to Exercise. In: Dishman, R. (ed.) Advances in Exercise Adherence, Human Kinetics, Champaign, IL, pp. 161–180 (1994)
24. Robertson, T.J., Prabhakararao, S., Burnett, M., Cook, C., Ruthruff, J.R., Beckwith, L., Phalgune, A.: Impact of interruption style on end-user debugging CHI, pp. 287–294 (2004)
25. Walker, W., Lamere, P., Kwok, P.: freeTTS opensource repository (2006), http://freetts.sourceforge.net/

Promoting Physical Activity Through Internet: A Persuasive Technology View

Weimo Zhu

Department of Kinesiology & Community Health
University of Illinois at Urbana-Champaign
205 Freer Hall, MC-052, Urbana, IL 61801, U.S.A.
weimozhu@uiuc.edu

Abstract. Participation in regular physical activity (PA) is critical to sustaining good health. While a few attempts have been made to use internet-based interventions to promote PA, no system review has been conducted in determining the effectiveness of the intervention. The purpose of this study was to conduct a review under the framework of persuasive technology (PT). Based on a comprehensive of literature search, nice experimental studies were identified and evaluated using the PT functional triad defined by Fogg in 2003[1]. It was found that only two studies led to short-term impact in promoting PA and, furthermore, two studies have found that the intervention based traditional print materials worked better. From a perspective of PT, none of the studies designed its intervention based on the framework of captology and few took full advantages of PT functions. Designing new-generation, PT based internet intervention and examining related human factors are urgently needed.

1 Introduction

1.1 Physical Activity and Public Health

The past two decades have seen an increased interest and understanding in the association between physical activity (PA) and health. Considerable evidence has been accumulated to support the hypothesis that a moderate level of PA reduces the risks of coronary heart disease and virtually all causes of mortality [2,3]. The American Heart Association has named physical inactivity a major risk factor for coronary heart disease, joining the more established risk factors of hypertension, smoking, and an adverse blood lipid profile [4]. Evidence has also accumulated linking physical inactivity to an increased risk for other chronic conditions, including stroke [5], cancer [6], non-insulin dependent diabetes [7], and osteoporosis [8]. While the health benefits of PA have been well documented, more than 60% of Americans do not get adequate PA. Because of the importance of PA and lack of participation, great efforts have been made to identify major factors that determine people's PA behavior and develop methods to promote PA on a large scale. As an example, numerical health behavior theories have been developed to explain the relationships between PA behavior and its correlates. Health belief model, transtheoretical (or stage of change) model and social cognitive theory are just a few examples [9,10].

Y. de Kort et al. (Eds.): PERSUASIVE 2007, LNCS 4744, pp. 12–17, 2007.
© Springer-Verlag Berlin Heidelberg 2007

Because studies and interventions based on these theories/models have not produced impressive or long-term increases in PA on a large scale [11], researchers started to explore other, more effective, models/methods. PA promotion based on persuasive technology appears to have great potential/promise in effectively promoting PA on a large scale.

1.2 Persuasive Technology for PA Promotion

Persuasion is one of the most effective tools to help change others' attitudes or behaviors [12]. Using available present-day technology to assist persuasion is almost as effective as persuasion itself [1]. The first major breakthrough in this relationship was the technology that allowed easier production and distribution of books, flyers, pamphlets, billboards and other forms of written and visual communication. With the introduction and advances of computers and other new technologies, persuasion based on technology is getting smarter. As a result, technology-centered persuasion is rapidly developing. Dr. B.J. Fogg [1] of Stanford University introduced the term persuasive technology, which he defined as "a computing system, device, or application intentionally designed to change a person's attitude or behavior in a predetermined way." He coined the term "Captology," which he derived as a partial acronym for Computers As Persuasive Technologies (CAPT-ology), for this area of study. It is expected that persuasive technology will become a major research area in behavior change. Persuasive technology itself is not unknown to the field of physical activity research and promotion. Two examples that have been around for a long time are pedometers and heart rater monitors. Very recently, internet-, GPS/GIS-, cellphone-, and multisensor-based technologies have been used as persuasive technology for physical activity promotion. Devices such as Nike+iPod shoes and Dance Dance Revolution (DDR) have gained the attention of the media and the public.

1.3 Research Needs

Most of the above efforts and products, however, were not developed and evaluated under the framework of captology, or in this case physical activity persuasive technology (PAPT). Although some design requirements were proposed for PA promotion technologies [13], critical questions such as "What are the critical characteristics of PAPT?" "Which (or which set of) persuasive strategy/PT is the most effective in PA promotion?" "What ethical issues are in PAPT?" "How should PAPT be developed for subgroups, especially those with health disparities?" have yet to be addressed. Thus, there is an urgent research needs to address these questions. In addition, how to evaluate PAPT under the framework of captology is still unknown.

1.4 Purpose

The purpose of this study was to conduct a comprehensive literature search to identify internet based PA promotion studies, one of the fastest developed areas in PA promotion, and evaluate them under the framework of PT.

2   Method

2.1   Literature Search

A comprehensive literature was conducted in several PA related databases, including Sport Discus, ERIC, PsycLIT, or MEDLINE, as well as in Google. The key words used in search included "Internet/E-mail/Web-Based Physical Activity/Exercise Intervention/Promotion." Cross-reference searches were further followed based on the identified studies. Only experimental studies were included in the final evaluation of this study.

2.2   Evaluation/Data Analysis

The quality of identified studies was evaluated and coded using a procedure employed in meta-analysis [14]. The studies were then coded using the Functional Triad defined by Fogg [1]:

1. PT as tools: A = Reduction, B = Tunneling, C = Tailoring, D = Intervening, E = Self-monitoring, F = Surveillance, G = Conditioning; H = Other;
2. PT as media/Simulation: A = Cause-and-effect, B = Environment, and C = Object, D = Other;
3. PT as social actors: A = Physical cues, B = Psychological cues, C = Influencing through language, D = Social dynamic, E = Adopting social roles, F = Social cues/handle with care, G = Other;
4. PT as other.

Coded data were then analyzed statistically and summarized accordingly.

3   Results and Discussion

A total of 27 studies were identified based on the search. Among them, nine focused on promoting PA and these studies [15-23] were included in this study (see Table 1). Overall, internet-based PA intervention has not brought in significant impact on promoting PA. Among nine studies, only one study [22] showed that the internet intervention group significantly improved the moderate PA minutes at the 1-month assessment, but the difference disappeared at the 3-month assessment. Another study [23] showed that the internet-based individually tailored intervention encouraged more participants to meet recommended PA than the control group, but no group difference was found in terms of total amount of PA participation measured by an activity monitor. In fact, when comparing with the print-material intervention groups, the internet based intervention groups did poorly in both studies with such a comparison [19,21].

There are many factors that may be related to the finding that internet based intervention has showed no or only short-term impact on PA promotion. Age groups employed and associated computer literacy in these studies, for example, may be a factor. Among nine studies reported, only two groups employed young age females participants and the rest seven studies all employed participants of 40 years or older. It is not clear if these middle-age or older participants' computer literacy was proficient enough to perform daily or regular internet tasks associated with the intervention.

Table 1. Summary of identified internet-based PA intervention studies

Author /Year	N	Age	Gender	Internet Used	Length of study	Design	Behavior Theory	Major finding
Kosma et al. (2005)	75	38.75±8.86 yr.	72% female	Web	4 weeks	Experiment/control	Stage	No different
Leslie et al. (2004)	327 (250 finished follow; 152 visited cite	42 yr. (mean)	50% each gender	E-mail/Web	8 weeks	Follow-up	Stage	Limited website engagement
Rydell et al. (2005)	194 (5 and 6 grades)	10 - 12 yr.	girls	Web/E-mail	2 yr.	Follow-up	Social Cognitive	Limited website engagement
McKay et al. 2001	78 (38 intervention and 40 control)	52.3 yr.	53% female	Web	8 weeks	Experiment/control	Social-ecological	No different; use down with time
Marks et al. (2006)	319 (web = 181, print = 178)	web = 12.2 yr; print = 12.1 yr.	girls	Web/Print	2 weeks	Follow-up	Social Cognitive	Print is better
Spittaels et al. (2006)	526 (e-mail-174; tailored=175; no-tailored=177)	39.5 yr	30.6% female	E-mail/Web	6 month	Follow-up	Stage	no difference; more use in tailor
Marshall et al. (2003)	655 (web = 327; print = 328)	43 yr	50 female	Web/E-mail	8 weeks	Experiment /control	Stage	no difference; print is better
Napolitano et al. (2003)	65 (30 intervention 35 control)	42.8 yr	56 females (86%)	E-mail/Web	1/3 months	intervention/ wait-list c	Social Cognitive/ Stage	difference in 1 month; not 3
Berg et al. (2006)	160 (IT = 82; GT = 78)	49 yr	no reported	E-mail/Web	3,6,9,12 months	Experiment /control		more exer in IT group, no diff total PA

Note: yr. = year; IT = individualized training; GT = general training; Stage = Stages of Change; exer = exercise.

The web design, especially in terms of using its PT function, is likely another major factor. None of the studies designed their websites under the framework of captology (see Table 2). Although the judgment is based on the description of the design and function of the web in these studies, the rating based on Fogg's function triad is interesting. In most cases, both web and e-mail are used in designing the intervention and most of them (7 of 9, 77.78%) are connected with an existing behavior theory (Social Cognitive = 4, 44.44%; Stages of Change = 5, 55.56%; and Social-Ecological = 1, 11.11%). Only limited PT functions were employed in these web designs. For PT as a tool, only one study employed three functions simultaneously, six employed two, and three employed one. The most commonly used tool function is tailoring (7 of 18, 38.89%), following by tunneling (5 of 18, 27.78%), intervening (3 of 18, 16.67%), self-monitoring (2 of 18, 11.11%) and other (1 of 18, 5.56%). For PT as a media, only two of nice studies employed web as "environmental simulation," but at a very simple level. Finally, for PT as a social actor, except for one study using PT as a "psychological cue," all studies used PT as an "adopting social roles" (either a consultant or coach or trainer). Employ more functions of PT in designing more effective web intervention and determine related human-interaction factors are clearly the focus of study in order to use internet to promote PA at a large scale.

Finally, it should point out that only the information in published studies was examined and evaluated. Other important PT features, such as interface and usability of the interventions, were not available for the evaluation. Future study should also include these features into the design and evaluation consideration.

Table 2. Functional triads employed in the studies

Author/Year	Tools	Media	Social A
Kosma et al. (2005)	D		E
Leslie et al. (2004)	C,E		E
Rydell et al. (2005)	H (information)	B	E
McKay et al. 2001)	C,D,E		E
Marks et al. (2006)	D	B	E
Spittaels et al. (2006)	B,C		E,B
Marshall et al. (2003)	B,C		E
Napolitano et al. (2003)	B,C		E
Berg et al. (2006)	B,C		E

Note: See 2.2 for the meaning of coding categories (e.g., "D" in PT as Tools = Intervening).

4 Conclusion

In summary, although internet has been shown a useful meaning in behavioral changes in other areas, such as weight control and fruit and vegetable consumption, identified studies have not shown the effectiveness of internet based invention in promoting PA. Designing internet invention based on the framework of captology and determining key persuasive strategies that are useful for promoting PA at large scale should be the future research focus.

Reference

1. Fogg, B.J.: Persuasive technology: Using computers to change what we think and do. Morgan Kaufmann Publishers, New York (2003)
2. Blair, S.N., Kampert, J.B., Kohl, H.W., Barlow, C.E., Macera, C.A., Paffenbarger, R.S., Gibbons, L.W.: Influences on cardiorespiratory fitness and other precursors on cardiovascular disease and all-cause mortality in men and women. J. Am. Med. Assoc. 276(3), 205–210 (1996)
3. Manson, J.E., Hu, F.B., Rich-Edwards, J.W.: A prospective study of walking as compared with vigorous exercise in the prevention of coronary heart disease in women. New England Journal of Medicine 341, 650–658 (1999)
4. Fletcher, G.F., Blair, S.N., Blumenthal, J., Caspersen, C., Chaitman, B., Epstein, S.: Statement on exercise: Benefits and recommendation for physical activity programs for all Americans: A statement for health professionals by the committee on exercise and cardiac rehabilitation of the council on clinical cardiology, American Heart Association. Circulation 86(1), 340–344 (1992)
5. Hu, F.B., Stampfer, M.J., Colditz, G.A., Ascherio, A., Rexrode, K.M., Willett, W.C.: Physical activity and risk for stroke in women. J. Am. Med. Assoc. 283(22), 2961–2967 (2000)
6. Verloop, J., Rookus, R.A., van der Kooy, K., van Leeuwen, F.E.: Physical activity and breast cancer risk in women aged 20-54 years. J. Nat. Cancer Institute 92(2), 128–135 (2000)

7. Brancati, F.L., Kao, W.H.L., Folsom, A.R., Watson, R.L., Szklo, M.: Incident type 2 diabetes mellitus in African American and white adults: The atherosclerosis risk in communities study. J. Am. Med. Assoc. 283(17), 2253–2259 (2000)

8. Milgrom, C., Finestone, A., Simkin, A., Ekenman, I., Mendelson, S., Millgram, M.: In vivo strain measurements to evaluate the strengthening potential of exercises on the tibial bone. J. Bone and Joint Surg (Br) 82-B, 591–594 (2000)

9. Glanz, K., Lewis, F.M., Rimer, B.K.: Health behavior and health education: Theory, research, and practice, 2nd edn. Jossey-Bass Publishers, San Francisco, CA (1997)

10. Elder, P.J.: Behavior change & public health in the developing world. Sage, Thousand Oaks, CA (2001)

11. Dishman, R.K., Sallis, J.F.: Determinants and interventions for physical activity and exercise. Human Kinetics, Champaign, IL (1994)

12. O'Keefe, D.J.: Persuasion theory and research (2nd. Sage Publications, Thousand Oaks, CA (2002)

13. Consolvo, S., Everitt, K., Smith, I., Landay, J.A.: Design requirements for technologies that encourage physical activity. In: CHI 2006 Proceedings: Designing for Tangible Interactions, pp. 457–466. ACM, Montreal, Canada (2006)

14. Thomas, J.R., Nelson, J.K., Silverman, S.: Research methods in physical activity, 5th edn. Human Kinetics, Champaign, IL (2005)

15. Kosma, M., Cardinal, B.J., Mccubbin, J.A.: A pilot study of a web-based physical activity motivational program for adults with physical disabilities. Disability & Rehabilitation 27(23), 1435–1442 (2005)

16. Leslie, E., Marshall, A.L., Owen, N., Bauman, A.: Engagement and retention of participants in a physical activity website. Prev. Med. 40(1), 54–59 (2004)

17. Rydell, S.A., French, S.A., Fulkerson, J.A., Neumark-Sztainer, D., Gerlach, A.F., Story, M., Christopherson, K.K.: Use of a web-based component of a nutrition and physical activity behavioral intervention with girl scouts. J. Am. Diet Assoc. 105, 1447–1450 (2005)

18. McKay, H.G., King, D., Eakin, E.G., Steeley, J.R., Glasgow, R.E.: The diabetes network internet-based physical activity intervention. Diabetes Care 24, 1328–1334 (2001)

19. Marks, J.T., Compbell, M.K., Ward, D.S., Ribisl, K.M., Wildemuth, B.M., Symons, M.J.: A comparison of web and print media for physical activity promotion among adolescent girls. Journal of Adolescent Health 39, 96–104 (2006)

20. Spittaels, H., Bourdeaudhuij, I., De., B.J., Vandelanotte, C.: Effectiveness of an online computer-tailored physical activity intervention in a real-life setting. In: Health Education Research: Theory & Practice (in press)

21. Marshall, A.L., Leslie, E.R., Bauman, A.E., Marcus, B.H., Owen, N.: Print versus website physical activity programs: A randomized trial. Am. J. Prev. Med. 25(2), 88–94 (2003)

22. Napolitano, M.A., Fotheringham, M., Tate, D., Sciamanna, C., Leslie, E., Owen, N., Bauman, A., Marcus, B.: Evaluation of an internet-based physical activity intervention: A preliminary investigation. Annals of Behavioral Medicine 25(2), 92–99 (2003)

23. van Berg, M.H., Ronday, H.K., Peeters, A.J., le Cessie, S., van der Giesen, F.J., Breedveld, F.C., Vlieland, V.: Using internet technology to deliver a home-based physical activity intervention for patients with rheumatoid arthritis: A randomized controlled trial. Arthritis & Rheumatism (Arthritis Care & Research) 55(6), 935–945 (2006)

Digital Therapy: The Coming Together of Psychology and Technology Can Create a New Generation of Programs for More Sustainable Behavioral Change

Pål Kraft[1], Harald Schjelderup-Lund[2], and Håvar Brendryen[1]

[1,2] Department of Psychology, University of Oslo, P.O. Box 1094 Blindern, 0317, Norway
[2] Changetech AS, Gaustadallèen 21, 0349 Oslo, Norway
pal.kraft@psykologi.uio.no

Abstract. By mapping critical psychological processes involved in an attempt at behavioral change, we can design digital programs to deliver specific cognitive therapy at the right moments, increasing the probability of successful behavioral change in a variety of domains. This breakthrough, named Digital Therapy, has been proven in random clinical trials to be a cost-effective way for people to achieve lasting behavioral change, with the help of modern psychological science, but without seeing a therapist.

Keywords: Digital Therapy, Digital Therapy Developer, Behavior Change, Chronology of Change, Self-Regulation, Cognitive Therapy.

1 Introduction

When people try to quit smoking, drink less, lose weight, exercise more, adhere to their medication, and other such behavioral modifications, the outcome is dependent on a series of psychological processes. Many people fail to maintain the change long term because they are incapable of managing these processes. Changetech is a company that is staffed by experts in psychology, technology and communications, and which collaborates closely with the University of Oslo. By combining modern cognitive therapy with the latest tools for interactive digital communication, Changetech has developed a brand new method to design more effective behavior change programs. This method is called Digital Therapy, and it represents the coming together of psychology and technology. The programs designed represent a breakthrough within the area of behavioral change, and allow people to benefit from the efficacy of modern psychological therapy, without seeing a therapist.

Changetech has developed a construction tool called Digital Therapy Developer (DTD). DTD was constructed to make it possible to design behavioral change programs on an industrial scale. DTD consists of a development unit and an operating unit that interacts with a technological platform used by the program owner to distribute the program. The main advantages of the DTD are as follows.

- It allows a more structured and shorter planning period.
- People with little domain knowledge can develop programs.

Y. de Kort et al. (Eds.): PERSUASIVE 2007, LNCS 4744, pp. 18–23, 2007.

- A shorter overall production time is needed.
- The development tools are directly linked with end-user technological platforms.
- All developments are made on the same development platform.

With Digital Therapy from Changetech based on the mapping of psychological processes and their chronology, people can get day-by-day therapy throughout the behavioral change period. This method can be used in a variety of fields where people need to change their behavior. This can be at their own initiative, such as weight reduction, stopping smoking, alcohol reduction and so on, but also in areas where behavioral change is recommended for medical or psychological reasons such as elevated levels of cholesterol, diabetes, asthma and after heart or cancer surgery.

2 The "Psychological Chronology" of Self- and Behavioral Change

Large proportions of the population are motivated to stop smoking, lose weight, get more physically active, control their drinking, stop gambling, and to pursue other such changes in behavior. In psychological terms, people often have the intention to change [1]. However, motivation or good intentions do not by themselves guarantee long-term goal attainment. On the contrary, intentions to change one's lifestyle are seldom successful [2]. Going from motivation to long-term change requires that one enters a volitional phase in which the intended change must be planned, initiated and maintained [3]. Whereas attempting to change requires motivation, staying on track requires self-regulation [4]. The inability to maintain the new behavior represents a self-regulation failure, i.e., an inability to exert self-control and acting in a way that runs counter to the person's long-term goals. In short, all successful change needs two ingredients: motivation and self-regulation. While motivation is more important early and late in a change attempt, i.e., in the deliberative states, self-regulation is a key factor in the volitional states of the change chronology. This is where technology and psychology have the possibility of coming together in e-Health interventions. In fact, there is an extremely promising fit between the multifaceted successful change process and characteristics of digital media (e.g., interactivity, individualization, presence and availability, persistence, reduction, tunneling, etc.). For an overview, see [5].

It takes time to change one's habits or personal characteristics. For example, people who quit smoking are at substantial risk of relapse for at least one year after quitting. However, the magnitude and nature of the relapse forces vary considerably along the timeline of the change attempt. Hence, stopping smoking (and the same goes for every change process) has a certain "psychological chronology", i.e., the timeline of the change is characterized by different psychological processes having varying importance throughout the change process. In fact, many self- and behavioral change processes to some extent reflect a generic core of "psychological processes", e.g., losing weight, coping with a disease, or recovering from depression. Albeit each type of change has a unique psychological make up (and there are individual variations within one type of change as well), many changes also seem to share some core characteristics as far as the "psychological chronology" of the change is concerned. Thus, over different types of changes some psychological processes, i.e., predictors of successful goal attainment, seem to be more important relatively early in the change sequence, while other processes or predictors seem to be more important later in the change sequence. This is exactly what is reflected in many of the "change" and "phase" models of behavioral change that have been proposed in social- and health psychology during the past few decades, and this insight allows us to model the psychological chronology of the core ingredients of successful behavioral change.

In essence, personalized, interactive, digital media makes tailoring and individualization possible, that is, by providing information relevant to the phase of the change process that the individual client is in. Individualization can be achieved by designing a program that reflects the "psychological chronology" of the change timeline, but also by including feedback systems to ensure individualization of the change program. By collecting information throughout the change process, individualization is made possible. Hence, the amount of information, help and support that the client receives can be reduced and be more focused to the specific needs of the client. In other words, one can capitalize on the principle of reduction [5]. Reduction technologies make target behaviors easier to achieve by breaking a complex activity into more manageable steps, and providing only task-relevant pieces of information. For example, complex goals may be broken down into specific subgoals or behaviors that may foster successful goal attainment. Additionally, and perhaps more importantly, the reduction implies that the information that the client needs during the change process is broken down into chunks that are presented to the client at the relevant time, stage, phase or even situation in the change process. Hence, this will increase the client's perceived utility of the program, a key factor for the use of any kind of media or communication channel. Also, since the content appears relevant and useful to the user, the likelihood of elaborated information processing will be increased.

Having modeled the "psychological chronology" of the change process that the client goes through, a natural next step is to lead the client through a predetermined sequence of intervention components, step by step. To some extent, this resembles the idea behind what has been called tunneling [5]. For the client, tunneling makes it easier to go through a process. He or she is not introduced to a web-based help-yourself library of information, but is instead "led by the hand" through the change process. The client enters the tunnel (i.e., starts the program) when they initiate the change attempt. By entering the tunnel they give away a certain level of self-determination in that information and activities are presented to him/her in a predetermined sequence. However, the principles of reduction and tunneling ensure that the client is led through a predetermined change sequence and receives the most appropriate information, support and therapy at the right time.

3   The Digital Therapy Developer (DTD)—A Construction Tool

Based on the above ideas, we have created a construction tool, called the Digital Therapy Developer (DTD), which can be utilized to design individualized intervention programs that are delivered by means of interactive, digital media (the web, cell phone, PDA, mp3 player, etc.). The DTD is a *construction tool*. More precisely, DTD is a tool suite for designing interventions, and combines psychological know-how with digital communication technologies. Our core idea was to digitalize and industrialize the construction of interventions aimed at supporting psychological and behavioral change through the support of a "digital therapist".

The DTD provides an environment for designing digital health behavior interventions (e.g., alcohol use, smoking cessation, dieting, exercise), health problems (e.g., depressed mood, tinnitus, sleeping problems), individual changes and transitions (e.g., divorce, retirement, unemployment, pregnancy), patient support (e.g., adherence to medication and health promoting lifestyles), and rehabilitation (e.g., heart and cancer rehabilitation). DTD contains: (i) a basis of psychological theory and research giving a point of departure for the construction of psychological interventions; (ii) a careful selection of intervention and therapeutic principles; (iii) a carefully selected set of core predictors for successful change; and (iv) a set of evidence-based therapeutic tactics and techniques. In other words, DTD bridges psychological theory and research with practical interventions and procedures, all in the service of supporting successful change. Hence, DTD contains tools that provide an environment for: (i) defining the chronological nature (phases and timeline) of the relevant change process; and (ii) linking specific therapeutic techniques (which reflect the specific predictors of specific changes) with relevant digital communication tools. Consequently, DTD is a support system for managing the psychological predictors and relevant therapies in an operative environment. In effect, this is done by the construction of *intervents*. Each intervent represents an intervention element, which: (i) is based on and reflects psychological theory and research; (ii) is constructed according to accepted principles of psychological therapy; (iii) reflects a specific predictor of successful change; (iv) is launched according to a reasoned chronology of the change process; and (v) is distributed via appropriate digital, interactive media.

A central premise for making DTD has been the fact that individual change processes in different behavioral domains share some communality. For example, different types of changes seem to reflect some communality as far as the phases and chronology of change are concerned. Additionally, a successful outcome of different change processes seems (to some extent) to be predicted by a set of common antecedents or predictors. The generic chronology and core predictors of much individual change have been incorporated into DTD. However, importantly, the total set of predictors and underlying processes of change in one specific (behavioral) domain are not totally identical with those in a different domain. Consequently, although many types of changes share some communality, every domain of change also has a certain amount of uniqueness and a set of specific predictors of outcome that are not common or shared with other types of change. This reasoning supports the notion that intervention programs that are produced to help people change, can contain both a *generic* component and a *domain-specific* component. DTD is a tool for constructing the generic components; i.e., the basis of numerous domain-specific applications. Consequently, when applied within a specific domain of (behavioral) change, the core of DTD must be *supplemented* by the construction of domain-specific elements; a unique set of predictors for successful change within the specific domain addressed. Furthermore, a domain-specific application (a "skin") must always be added to DTD (the "backbone" of the intervention) in order to represent a complete domain-specific intervention.

Broadly, three "layers" of psychological insights are reflected in DTD. The first layer represents a selection of psychological theories and research that identifies and explains *basic mechanisms* involved in successful individual change. The second layer contains a selection of *general psychological intervention techniques, therapies and procedures*, which are based on the more general theoretical insights. Finally, the third layer contains a set of processes and predictors related to successful change. These processes and predictors, organized in a reasoned and explicit chronological order, are deducted from the two "layers" described above, and reflect more specific factors that may promote or hinder successful change. They have all been described in psychological research as predictors of sustainable individual change. Importantly, these predictors are utilized for constructing specified and detailed intervention components, called *intervents*, which are delivered by means of digital media. To the end user, an intervent appears to resemble a communication message. Importantly, however, each intervent is *based* on and reflects psychological theory and research; is *constructed* according to accepted principles in (for example) cognitive therapy; *reflects* a specific predictor of successful change; is *delivered* through interactive, digital media at a carefully selected *time point* of the change process; and is *individualized* to the needs of the specific client going through the change process. Hence, messages that are distributed to end users do not only carry information. Rather, they reflect theoretical reasoning, clinical expertise, the chronology of change, the characteristics of the digital channel through which the message is distributed, and are individualized to the specific needs of the end user.

4 Happy Ending—The First Practical Application of DTD

The team behind Changetech has recently developed a program for smoking cessation, delivered by means of the web, E-mail, and cell phone (Interactive Voice Response and Short Message Service). Adaptations of this program are now being launched worldwide in combination with quit-smoking medicines provided by Pfizer Inc. (Champix/Chantix) and Johnson & Johnson (Nicorette). The program, called Happy Ending (HE), has been evaluated in two randomized clinical trials (RCTs). In both RCTs, motivated smokers were randomized to receive either HE or a control intervention (a self-help booklet). In study 1 (n=396), both interventions were combined with the supplement of nicotine replacement therapy (NRT), whereas in study 2 (n=290), NRT was neither offered to nor intended to be used by the quitters. Abstinence (abstinent over the previous seven days) was based on self-reports and assessed at 1, 3, and 6 months. The intention-to-treat principle was applied, and nonresponders were counted as smokers. Both studies revealed a significant and substantial treatment effect of HE on both short- and long-term abstinence (odds ratios varied between 2.01 and 3.46). For both intervention conditions, higher abstinence rates were observed in study 1, while higher effect sizes of the treatment conditions were observed in study 2. In conclusion, both trials demonstrated the benefit of HE as compared to a self-help booklet. Moreover, the effect of HE was very favorable when compared with other digital smoking-cessation programs that have been described in the literature.

5 Conclusions

By mapping the critical psychological processes that arise throughout a behavioral change attempt, Changetech can design digital programs that deliver specific cognitive therapy at the right time, increasing the probability of successful behavioral change in a variety of domains. This breakthrough, named Digital Therapy, has been proven in RCTs to be a cost-effective way for people to achieve lasting behavioral change, with the help of modern psychological science, but without seeing a therapist. Changetech has developed a construction tool denoted Digital Therapy Developer (DTD) that makes it possible to design behavioral change programs on an industrial scale. The DTD consists of a development unit and an operating unit that interact with a technological platform used by the program owner to distribute the program.

References

1. Fishbein, M., Ajzen, I.: Understanding Attitudes and Predicting Social Behavior. Prentice Hall, Englewood Cliffs, New Jersey (1980)
2. Sutton, S.R.: The Past Predicts the Future: Interpreting Behaviour-behaviour Relationships in Social-psychological Models of Health Behaviors. In: Rutter, D.R., Quine, L. (eds.) Social Psychology and Health: European perspectives, pp. 47–70. Avebury Publishers, Aldershot, England (1994)
3. Gollwitzer, P.: Action Phases and Mindsets. In: Higgins, E.T., Sorrentino, J.R.M. (eds.) The Handbook of Motivation and Cognition, Guilford, New York, vol. 2, pp. 53–92 (1990)
4. Baumeister, R.F., Heatherton, T.F.: Self-regulation Failure: An Overview. Psychological Inquiry 1, 1–15 (1996)
5. Fogg, T.J.: Persuasive Technology. Using Computers to Change What We Think and Do. Morgan Kaufman Publishers, Boston (2003)

Designing Persuasion: Health Technology for Low-Income African American Communities

Andrea Grimes and Rebecca E. Grinter

College of Computing, Georgia Institute of Technology, Atlanta, GA
{agrimes,beki}@cc.gatech.edu

Abstract. In the United States, African Americans face a disproportionate amount of diet-related health problems. For example, African American adults are 1.6 times more likely to have diabetes than their Caucasian counterparts. Individuals in low-income communities may face a greater risk because they typically have less access to healthy foods. Due to the significant diet-related problems within the African American community, public health researchers call for approaches to health promotion that take into account the relationship between culture and dietary habits. In this paper, we discuss three important considerations for the design of technologies that address the diet-related health disparities in low-income African American communities. These considerations include designing for cultural relevancy, modeling health behavior, and encouraging healthy behavior through the use of social psychological theories of persuasion. We use a game design example to illustrate how each of these considerations can be incorporated into the development of new technology.

Keywords: Culture, Health, Low-Income, Nutrition, Persuasive Technology.

1 Introduction

The United States faces a serious crisis as rates of diet-related diseases such as obesity continue to rise. Today 65% of people 20 and older are either overweight or obese [8]. This statistic reflects an increase of over 75% in obesity prevalence since 1991. While these statistics are sobering, the issue becomes even more alarming when looking at the disproportionate amount of diet-related health problems in minority groups such as the African American community. In 2002 the heart disease related mortality rate for African Americans was 30% higher than that of Caucasians [16]. In addition, African American adults are 1.6 times more likely to have diabetes than their Caucasian counterparts [16]. While these statistics reflect an aggregate of income levels, low-income African Americans may be even more at-risk than those with higher income levels. For example, low-income communities typically have less access to healthy foods and may be more accepting of overweight [13, 18]. Because of the disproportionate amount of diet-related diseases that exist within the African American community, public health researchers advocate the development of programs and services that take into account the ways that dietary habits are tied to aspects of culture [1, 3]. These *culturally relevant* interventions should account for the beliefs, norms, behaviors and challenges that exist within a particular cultural

Y. de Kort et al. (Eds.): PERSUASIVE 2007, LNCS 4744, pp. 24–35, 2007.

group [23]. Accounting for these cultural factors can help researchers address health issues in a way that is sensitive to the existing values and practices of a community.

While many culturally targeted approaches to health issues have resulted in programmatic efforts (*e.g.* church-based educational campaigns), few have leveraged the possibilities that technology may afford. Yet, given the nature of the challenge—to promote better dietary patterns—the use of persuasive technology is a promising approach. Technologies designed to persuade individuals to live healthier lifestyles can take the form of tools (*e.g.* by monitoring blood sugar levels), media (*e.g.* by simulating the effects of smoking), or social actors (*e.g.* by rewarding positive behaviors) [7]. Furthermore, there is a growing body of research in the field of Human-Computer Interaction (HCI) to address health, such as work being done on physical fitness [5]. Still, even given this research, few projects have accounted for the relationship between culture and health in technology design. To design a technology that is effective at encouraging a specific cultural group to develop healthy dietary habits, we argue that there are three critical questions to consider:

1. What aspects of culture should be considered in the design?
2. How can theories of health behavior be incorporated into the design?
3. How can social psychological theories of persuasion be used to design technology that encourages healthy behavior?

While each of these considerations by themselves is not novel, the explicit use of the three together in an effort to create persuasive health technology is rarely done. We argue that each of these considerations represents a critical aspect of designing technologies to promote health in specific cultural contexts. In this paper we provide justification for this argument through a discussion of literature from the domains of public health, health behavior theory, and social psychological persuasion theory. We focus our discussion on low-income African American communities, a segment of the population that faces a disproportionate amount of diet-related disease. In addition, we illustrate how each of the three considerations that we propose can be reflected in technology design by describing a hypothetical game in which the goal is to promote healthy dietary habits among low-income African Americans.

To begin, we first provide an overview of the mechanics of the hypothetical game. Following this overview, we describe the public health literature that advocates designing culturally relevant health interventions. Next, we discuss health behavior theory and its importance for designing technology that reflects an understanding of individuals' dietary habits and beliefs. Finally, we describe persuasion theory and how it can be leveraged to design technologies that encourage individuals to develop healthy dietary habits.

2 An Illustration: OrderUP!

Games are becoming a popular way of persuading individuals to engage in healthy behavior (*e.g.* see [7]). They provide an entertaining medium through which issues such as health can be addressed. Because games are a promising way of addressing health issues, we use a hypothetical game to illustrate the three design considerations that we propose in this paper.

Imagine a game, which we will call OrderUP!, in which the user plays the role of a restaurant owner. To begin with, he or she chooses what to include on the restaurant's menu from an assortment of items representing varying degrees of healthfulness (*e.g.* steamed vegetables, apple pie). After the player makes his or her selections, the main portion of game play begins and customers start entering the restaurant. Each customer asks the player for a recommendation of what to order. The player must decide what to serve the customer, taking into consideration any health conditions that he or she may have (some customers will have conditions such as diabetes). In easier levels of the game, the players are provided with hints that will help them understand how to make healthy selections. The game includes a fixed set of customers that come into the restaurant and the goal of the game is to serve the customers a balanced set of foods, allowing them to maintain a high health level. Players receive points for serving customers quickly and keeping their health levels high. Players lose points when their service is slow and when they serve too many unhealthy foods. Players win the game by reaching a certain point level within the specified time limit.

We will refer back to OrderUP! throughout the paper. We now turn to a discussion of the first of the three considerations that we argue are critical in designing persuasive health technology for low-income African American communities.

3 Designing for Cultural Relevancy

3.1 Nutrition in African American Communities

As noted previously, African Americans are a segment of the population that experiences a disproportionate amount of diet-related diseases, motivating numerous researchers to call for culturally relevant interventions [1, 3]. Our operational definition of cultural relevancy is adapted slightly from that of Williams, *et al.* [23]: we argue that cultural relevancy may be achieved when interventions designed for a specific group reflect an understanding of the group's particular needs, beliefs, norms, and behaviors. This is not to say that any intervention that sets out to incorporate these cultural dimensions will automatically be successful. Rather, we argue that an understanding of these dimensions will increase the likelihood that the intervention is culturally meaningful to the target population. In the context of designing persuasive health interventions, this point is critical because programs and technologies that do not take into account the cultural aspects of health may be unsuccessful in persuading individuals to develop positive habits [23].

Airhihenbuwa *et al.* [1] suggest that foods, their flavors, and the way that they are prepared may be utilized to maintain group identity or preserve traditions. Because of this relationship between food and culture, they conclude that it is important to design health interventions that are culturally relevant and sensitive to existing practices. The authors conducted focus groups to examine the cultural aspects of eating among African American residents of Pennsylvania. Their study participants felt that the African American community has some culturally distinct eating traditions, and older participants expressed a preference for eating at home because in the past they had experienced discrimination in restaurants. This study provides examples of eating habits being affected by culture and identifies aspects of culture that should be accounted for in health interventions.

Kreuter & Hughton [12] identified four dimensions of culture which they argue are related to health behaviors: religiosity (*e.g.* prayer), collectivism (emphasis is placed on the group rather than the individual), racial pride (*e.g.* participating in traditional practices), and time orientation (tendency to respond to consequences that are immediate or further in the future). The authors used these dimensions to tailor a cancer prevention program for African American women. In their previous work, the authors found these dimensions to be measurable, correlated with health related behaviors and common amongst urban African Americans [11]. Their work has also shown the importance of using theories of health behavior in conjunction with cultural tailoring to design effective interventions [12].

Stolley & Fitzgibbon [21] also developed a culturally tailored program; theirs was aimed at obesity prevention among low-income African American mothers and their daughters. The researchers made their program culturally relevant in a number of ways, for example, by addressing the common food preparation methods of their participants and the accessibility of healthy foods in the community. Stolley & Fitzgibbon tested the effectiveness of their program using an experimental study. After going through the program, the treatment group consumed significantly less saturated fat and calories from fat than participants in the control group.

For the purposes of designing culturally relevant health technologies for low-income African Americans, the studies described here illuminate three important aspects of culture. First, they illustrate the importance of *identifying common health attitudes and behaviors within the culture*. For example, Stolley & Fitzgibbon [21] studied common food preferences and preparation practices and designed their obesity prevention program to reflect an understanding of these attitudes and behaviors. While we discuss modeling individual health behavior in more detail later in this paper, here we would like to highlight the importance of examining the shared attitudes and behaviors that exist within the culture. For technology designers, understanding culturally perpetuated health behaviors may allow the designed application to be made relevant for a range of individuals within a culture.

Stolley & Fitzgibbon [21] also show the importance of creating interventions that are reflective of the *environmental effects on healthy eating*. For example, these researchers took into account the limited availability of healthy foods in their target neighborhoods While Stolley & Fitzgibbon focused on the effects of the physical environment on health, the social world is another important aspect of environmental effects on health. The importance of the social environment is exemplified in the cultural dimensions that Kreuter & Hughton [12] use to design health interventions, particularly the notion of collectivism. For technology designers, the lesson to be learned here is that to create technology that is effective at helping users practice healthy eating habits, it is critical to take into account the context in which they have to make their health decisions. This requires a thorough examination of how the physical and social environment affects the target community's ability and motivation to engage in healthy behaviors.

In their obesity prevention program for low-income African Americans, Stolley & Fitzgibbon [21] taught their participants how to engage in healthier behaviors while accounting for their existing physical and social environment (*e.g.* how to make healthy choices at local food markets). Thus, the authors provided *culturally relevant behavioral modification suggestions* and in so doing contributed to the improved health of their participants. For technology designers, this point implies that care must be taken to incorporate culturally relevant behavioral modification suggestions in applications that are targeted toward specific cultural groups.

The studies described here provide useful insight into designing culturally relevant health programs, but only a few studies of this type exist. That is, while many researchers have conducted formative work in which they conclude that designing culturally relevant health interventions is important, few have actually tested the effectiveness of such approaches [12]. Consequently, there are only a few studies that provide evidence for how such interventions should be implemented. Thus the design considerations that we propose in this paper can be seen as a contribution because not only do they add to the limited work on culturally relevant health interventions but they also represent an attempt to use technology to address health disparities.

3.2 OrderUP!: Designing Collectivism

Understanding how to design for cultural relevancy represents the first consideration that we argue should be made when creating persuasive health technology for low-income African American communities. In the preceding section we presented evidence that making health interventions culturally relevant is critical to influencing health behavior change. To explore how to design culturally relevant technology, we now refer back to the hypothetical game we introduced earlier in this paper. Recall that in OrderUP! the player assumes the role of a restaurant owner who is responsible for keeping customers healthy. This game can account for culture by using the concept of collectivism which, as noted above, has been shown to be a valued cultural construct within the African American community [12]. In collectivist cultures, the emphasis is placed on the group rather than the individual. Thus, individuals may feel particularly compelled to advocate for the health of their community members. For example, Kreuter *et al.* [12] find that in a collectivist culture, individuals often tend to the needs of family members before their own. Collectivism could be incorporated into OrderUP! by making each of the customers that enters the restaurant a type of person that the player is likely to interact with in their everyday lives (*e.g.* sisters, church members, etc.). By having each customer be identified by their relation to the player, they will not simply be generic aspects of the game but may instead invoke collectivist feelings within the player. That is, since the customers represent members of the player's family and community, players may feel a greater responsibility to make healthy recommendations. Furthermore, stimulating feelings of collectivism may help the players feel more culturally connected to the game and thus make them feel that what they learn through the game is relevant to their own lives.

This example of the inclusion of collectivism is just one way that technology can be designed to address health problems in a culturally meaningful way. To learn whether or not the stimulation of collectivist feelings in the game would translate to behavioral changes in real life, researchers could conduct a study where behaviors pre- and post-game play are compared. In the next section we discuss the second consideration that should be made when designing culturally relevant health technologies: how to model individual health behavior.

4 Modeling Health Behavior

Much of the formative research into designing new technology begins with studies of human life (*e.g.* behaviors and activities) that will affect how the new technology will be used, reacted to, or appropriated [20]. Indeed, though many technology researchers use methods such as ethnography to study human behavior, it is not always clear how to reflect the study results in the design of new technology [6]. Theories can help scaffold this process by providing ways to map results from empirical studies of human behavior to resulting system design requirements. For example, Nardi *et al.* [14] used activity theory (an approach which studies the mind "within the context of human interaction with the world" [10]) as a framework for studying social networks in the workplace and the implications that they have for technology design. In the domain of health technology, we argue that such theoretical scaffolding can come in the form of health behavior and persuasion theory. While we detail persuasion theory later in this paper, in this section we overview three health behavior theories: the Transtheoretical Model, Social Cognitive Theory and the Health Belief Model. Each of these theories is uniquely useful for developing health technologies for low-income African American communities. After this overview, we provide examples of how health behavior theories can be incorporated into aspects of the OrderUP! game.

4.1 Theories of Health Behavior

Redding, *et al.* [17] state that the Transtheoretical Model (TTM) conceptualizes the change of unhealthy behaviors as a process, not a discrete event. Furthermore, TTM describes the various "stages of change" that occur as people modify their health behaviors. The stages of change most commonly used by researchers include: *precontemplation* (no intention to change behavior), *contemplation* (thinking about changing), *preparation* (committed to modifying behavior soon), *action* (behavior has recently been changed), and *maintenance* (behavior has become a habit). In addition to these stages of change, TTM also describes "processes of change" which refer to the emotional, behavioral, cognitive, and interpersonal techniques that are used to change unhealthy behaviors by helping people progress through the stages of change. Examples of such processes include consciousness raising, that is, learning ways to engage in behavior change. TTM has been used successfully in a variety of empirical studies and within diverse populations, including low-income communities [3] .

Social Cognitive Theory (SCT) takes a holistic view of health behavior by accounting for individual, social and environmental factors [2]. Reciprocal determinism is the foundational principle of SCT and it describes the ongoing interaction that exists between the environment, the individual, and the individual's behavior. This principle resonates with the public health argument for culturally targeted interventions. As we discussed earlier, the physical and social environments represent important aspects of culture that should be taken into consideration when attempting to develop culturally targeted health programs and technologies.

The Health Belief Model (HBM) states that the likelihood that a person will take steps to prevent illness is dependent upon four perceptions: *perceived susceptibility* (their belief that they are vulnerable to the illness), *perceived severity* (the effects of the illness will be serious), *perceived effectiveness* (the preventative action will effectively prevent the illness), and *perceived cost* (the benefits of reducing the risk of illness outweigh the cost of engaging in the preventative behavior) [17]. The HBM may be an especially useful model for low-income communities because it explicitly addresses the notion of the perceived cost of eating healthy foods. This is a concern that may arise for any individual, but in particular a person with limited financial resources may view it as an insurmountable barrier.

4.2 OrderUP!: Accounting for Health Behavior Theory in Design

Modeling health behavior is the second consideration that we propose for designing culturally relevant health technology. As noted previously, the TTM has been used successfully in health programs designed for low-income populations and this demonstrated effectiveness makes it a promising theory to use in the design of technologies for low-income African American communities. One way that the TTM can be used in technology design is in identifying the target user groups and the subsequent processes of change that need to be supported. For example, OrderUP! could target individuals who are currently in the precontemplative stage identified by TTM. By restricting the target user group to individuals in this stage, the designers of the game would also be able to identify the processes of change that could help users move from the precontemplative to contemplative stage.

The TTM states that for individuals in the precontemplative stage to progress to later stages of change, an important processes of change is consciousness raising (*i.e.,* learning how to engage in healthy behaviors). The designers of OrderUP! could target this process through the use of informative tips throughout the game. For example, recall that at the beginning of the game, players decide what to include on their restaurant's menu. The healthier the food options on their menu, the better the player's chances are to score points. The game designers could give players suggestions for choosing healthy items for their menu which would serve the dual purpose of teaching them how to gain points in the game and also how to make healthy dietary choices in their everyday lives.

In addition to TTM, the Health Behavior Model (HBM) and Social Cognitive Theory (SCT) could be incorporated into health technologies. For example, in OrderUP! players decide what foods will be served at their restaurant, thereby creating the environment for the game characters. This environment has an effect on customer health – the more healthy foods there are to choose from (*environmental influence*), the greater the likelihood that players will serve healthy foods (*behavioral response*), and consequently customers will be more likely to stay healthy. This game design reflects the SCT focus on the relationship between the environment and behavior (reciprocal determinism, described above), thus giving players a vivid picture of how environments can support or inhibit healthy behaviors.

If a player continually serves customers unhealthy foods, the customers' health levels will decrease. Therefore, the HBM concept of perceived severity is targeted because players will see that the behavior of eating poorly has negative consequences (as manifested by the decrease of the customers' health levels). In addition, game designers can target the extent to which a player believes that engaging in healthy behavior is effective (what HBM calls "perceived effectiveness") because the player has the chance to see that they can improve the health levels of the customers by making simple changes to the foods served.

5 Encouraging Healthy Behavior

We have discussed different ways of modeling health behavior, which is an important part of understanding how to motivate people to change problem behaviors. Another component is the process of persuasion. Chaiken *et al.* [4] define persuasion as the study of "the variables and processes that govern the formation and change of attitudes". In the following sections we overview three areas of social psychological persuasion research which have implications for the design of health technologies within low-income African American communities: attitudinal advocacy, message-based persuasion and issue framing.

5.1 Methods of Persuasion

Attitudinal Advocacy. Research on attitudinal advocacy looks at how individuals' attitudes change as a result of engaging in a behavior [4]. For example, when someone voices support for a position, even if he or she does not initially agree with that position, the person may come to believe it simply as a result of vocally supporting it. This phenomenon was initially examined in research on role-playing. In this type of research, subjects are presented with a position on an issue and are then asked to advocate support for that position [4]. For example, Janis and King [9] conducted an experiment in which subjects both advocated an opinion on an issue and watched someone else advocate a position on two different issues. Their results showed that when subjects advocated an opinion themselves (through role playing), they were persuaded more than when they listened to others support positions.

Persuasion Through Messages. In addition to attitudinal advocacy, persuasion research has examined how an individual's attitudes can be affected by verbal messages presented by others. According to Chaiken *et al.* [4], up to the 1980s, most research in this area focused on how individuals engage in systematic, controlled processing of the persuasive elements of a message. Since the 1980s however, dual-process theories of persuasion have gained increasing popularity. Such theories account for systematic as well as more automatic cognitive processing. For example, the Elaboration Likelihood Model describes the central and peripheral routes to persuasion where the central route consists of thinking about the content of the message and the peripheral route is an automatic approach to information processing [15]. This model posits that attitudes changed via the central route are more persistent and predictive of behavior than those changed via the peripheral route. This is because the central route allows for cognitive elaboration, the process in which an individual evaluates and reacts to a message's arguments.

Issue Framing. In addition to message-based persuasion, issue framing is a related strategy in which certain aspects of an issue are emphasized more than other aspects [24]. Typically, message-based persuasion takes an *intraattitudinal* approach by describing the attributes of a single attitude object. Contrastingly, issue-framed approaches are *interattitudinal* in nature because they describe aspects of an attitude object (*e.g.* consequences) in the context of another attitude object. Prospect theory argues that the way a message is framed affects how people respond to the issue at hand [22]. Gain-framed messages emphasize the potential benefits of an issue, or behavior whereas loss-framed messages highlight the potential cost of not engaging in the behavior. In terms of health communication strategies, this theory provides a framework for understanding how to effectively structure messages and influence behavior change [19]. Rothman & Salovey [19] found that loss-framed messages are more effective at promoting disease detection behaviors (*e.g.* monthly breast exams to detect cancer) and gain-framed messages are more effective at promoting preventative behaviors (*e.g.* eating a high fiber diet to raise good cholesterol levels).

5.2 OrderUP!: Implications for Persuasive Design

Using persuasion theory to encourage healthy behavior is the final consideration that we argue is important for designing culturally relevant technology for health promotion. We have highlighted three methods of persuading: attitudinal advocacy, message-based persuasion and issue framing. While this is not an exhaustive list of approaches, each of these methods can be leveraged to create technologies in which the goal is to persuade individuals to engage in healthy dietary habits. The domain of persuasive technology research provides promising case studies of technologies being used to persuade individuals to engage in healthy behavior. For example, Fogg [7] describes Nintendo's Pocket Pikachu toy as a technology that persuades individuals to walk more. However, we argue here not only for the design of technologies that persuade, but technologies that persuade in a culturally meaningful way.

While changing individuals' attitudes does not guarantee a change in behavior, it is an important step towards behavior change. As noted above, research on attitudinal advocacy has found that role-playing is an effective way of helping people change their attitudes [9]. In OrderUP!, the basic premise of the game leverages the concept of attitudinal advocacy by allowing individuals to play the role of restaurant owner. In order to win the game, this role requires users to advocate healthy choices to their customers. Through this advocacy players may come to believe that the suggestions they make are legitimate ones that should be integrated in their own lives. Furthermore, this type of advocacy also draws upon the concept of collectivism (because game players are responsible for the health of other community members), which has been shown to be an important dimension of African American culture.

Designers of the game could also incorporate research on persuasive message framing into the development of the game hints. For example, designers could experiment with using gain versus loss-framed messages to create hints that provide players with suggestions for serving their customers healthy foods. The Elaboration Likelihood Model (ELM) could also be utilized in the game design. Recall that the ELM states that attitude change that occurs through the central route to persuasion is more likely to be persistent. To this end, in OrderUP! a screen could be displayed at the end of each round that allows players to reflect on the decisions they made during the game. This pause in game play would allow players to engage in more controlled processing which may not occur while they are serving customers (due to how quickly they have to serve customers).

6 Discussion

Researchers are becoming increasingly interested in the use of technology to persuade individuals to change their attitudes and behaviors [5]. B.J. Fogg [7] coined the term captology to describe the study of computers as persuasive technology and he states that captology addresses the "design, research, and analysis of interactive computing products created for the purpose of changing people's attitudes or behaviors". Though Fogg lays out a conceptual foundation for designing persuasive technology, the field is quite new and thus much of the development of persuasive technologies has been done with an implicit rather than explicit use of theories of persuasion. In addition, Fogg's framework is broad, encompassing persuasive technologies in a range of domains, from environmental conservation to education [7]. Thus, the ideas that we have presented in this paper contribute to the emerging field of persuasive technology by identifying three important considerations for the design of technologies to promote healthy dietary habits in low-income African American communities.

There is much left to be done in the area of persuasive health technology both from the public health and Human-Computer Interaction (HCI) perspectives. Both fields have a lot to offer one another: within public health there exist a number of theories of health behavior and strategies for health communication that can help HCI researchers design more theoretically sound applications. Conversely, HCI research can help public health researchers leverage, in a user-centered way, the vast range of technological possibilities that exist. The sharing of ideas, theories, and empirical data between the fields of public health and HCI may be stimulated as more research on health technology begins to take account the relationship between culture and health and the implications this has for the design of new applications.

7 Conclusion

In this paper we described three important considerations for creating technology to address nutrition within low-income African-American communities: designing for cultural relevancy, modeling health behavior, and encouraging healthy behaviors through persuasion. While we do not argue that these are the only considerations that should be made, we do suggest that they are fundamental areas of research that should be incorporated into the design of technologies for health promotion. While some of the points we have made here could apply to the design of health technologies for other communities, our goal was not to present an exhaustive framework, but rather to address the concerns of one specific population that experiences a disproportionate amount of diet-related disease. Furthermore, because eating is a culturally situated activity it is important to consider individual cultural groups when designing technologies to promote healthy dietary habits.

Our goal in this paper has not been to promote gross generalizations about the eating habits of a specific culture, but rather to advocate for the focused study of the diet-related health disparities that exist within specific cultural groups. The public health community has advocated for such an approach for years because of the wide gap that exists between the health of the minority and majority populations in the United States. The point is not to ignore the rest of the American population, but rather to add to the existing research on health more specialized studies of how to address health problems within specific cultural groups. Research into the relationship between culture and nutrition can serve as the foundation for the design of new technologies to promote healthy eating practices and this in turn may reduce the amount of diet-related health problems that exist within minority communities.

Acknowledgements. We thank the National Science Foundation for their Graduate Research Fellowship support. We also thank REACH for Wellness Atlanta for their continued support of our research.

References

1. Airhihenbuwa, C.O., Kumanyika, S.: Cultural Aspects of African American Eating Patterns. Ethnicity & Health 1(3), 245–260 (1996)
2. Bandura, A.: Health Promotion by Social Cognitive Means. Health Education & Behavior 31(2), 143–164 (2004)
3. Campbell, M.K., Honess-Morreale, L., Farrell, D., Carbone, E., Brasure, M.: A tailored multimedia nutrition education pilot program for low-income women receiving food assistance. Health Education Research 14(2), 257–267 (1999)
4. Chaiken, S., Wood, W., Eagly, A.H.: Principles of Persuasion, in Social Psychology: Handbook of Basic Principles. In: Higgins, E.T., Kruglanski, A.W. (eds.), pp. 702–742. The Guilford Press, New York (1996)
5. Consolvo, S., Everitt, K., Landay, J.A.: Design Requirements for Technologies that Encourage Physical Activity. In: CHI (2006)
6. Dourish, P.: Implications for Design. In: CHI (2006)
7. Fogg, B.J.: Persuasive Technology: Using Computers to Change What We Think and Do. Morgan Kaufmann Publishers, San Francisco (2003)
8. American Heart Association and the Robert Wood Johnson Foundation, A Nation at Risk: Obesity in the United States (2005)
9. Janis, I.L., King, B.T.: The influence of role playing on opinion change. Journal of Abnormal Psychology 49(2), 211–218 (1954)
10. Kaptelinin, V., Nardi, B.A., Macaulay, C.: Methods & tools: The activity checklist: a tool for representing the "space" of context. Interactions~6(4), 27--39 (1999)
11. Kreuter, M.W., Steger-May, K., Bobra, S., Booker, A., Holt, C.L., Skinner, C.S., et al.: Sociocultural characteristics and responses to cancer education materials among African American women. Cancer Control 10(5), 69–80 (2003)
12. Kreuter, M.W., Haughton, L.T.: Integrating Culture Into Health Information for African American Women. American Behavioral Scientist 49(6), 794–811 (2006)
13. Morland, K., Wing, S., Roux, A.D., Poole, C.: Neighborhood characteristics associated with the location of food stores and food service places. American Journal of Preventive Medicine 22(1), 23–29 (2001)
14. Nardi, B.A., Whittaker, S., Schwarz, H.: NetWORKers and their Activity in Intensional Networks. Computer Supported Cooperative Work 11, 205–242 (2002)
15. Petty, R.E.C., J., T.: The elaboration likelihood model of persuasion. In: Berkowitz, L. (ed.) Advances in experimental social psychology, pp. 123–205. Academic Press, San Diego, CA (1986)
16. Centers for Diseases Control and Prevention, Racial and Ethnic Approaches to Community Health (REACH) 2010: Addressing Disparities in Health (2006)

17. Redding, C.A., Rossi, J.S., Rossi, S.R., Velicer, W.F., Prochaska, J.O.: Health Behavior Models. The Intl. Electronic Journal of Health Education 3, 180–193 (2000)
18. Resnicow, K., Yaroch, A.L., Davis, A., Wang, D.T., Carter, S., Slaughter, L., Coleman, D., Baranowski, T.: GO GIRLS!: Results From a Nutrition and Physical Activity Program for Low-Income Overweight African American Adolescent Females. Health Education & Behavior 27(5), 616–631 (2000)
19. Rothman, A.J., Salovey, P.: Shaping perceptions to motivate healthy behavior: The role of message framing. Psychological Bulletin 121, 3–19 (1997)
20. Salvador, T., Bell, G., Anderson, K.: Design Ethnography. Design Management Journal (1999)
21. Stolley, M.R., Fitzgibbon, M.L.: Effects of an Obesity Prevention Program on the Eating Behavior of African American Mothers and Daughters. Health Education & Behavior 24(2), 152–164 (1997)
22. Tversky, A., Kahneman, D.: The Framing of Decisions and the Psychology of Choice. Science 211(4481), 453–458 (1981)
23. Williams, J.H., Auslander, W.F., de Groot, M., Robinson, A.D., Houston, C., Haire-Joshu, D.: Cultural Relevancy of a Diabetes Prevention Nutrition Program for African American Women. Health Promotion Practice 7(1), 56–67 (2006)
24. Wood, W.: Attitude Change: Persuasion and Social Influence. Annual Review of Psychology (51), 539–570 (2000)

Fine Tuning the Persuasion in Persuasive Games

Rilla Khaled[1], Pippin Barr[1], James Noble[1], Ronald Fischer[1],
and Robert Biddle[2]

[1] Victoria University of Wellington,
Wellington, New Zealand
{rkhaled,chikken,kjx}@mcs.vuw.ac.nz, ronald.fischer@vuw.ac.nz
[2] Carleton University,
Ottawa, Canada
robert_biddle@carleton.ca

Abstract. Persuasive games are a relatively new phenomenon, and hold promise as effective vehicles for persuasion. As yet, however, there are few set rules guiding how to design persuasive games to be interesting, compelling, and effective. Furthermore, little theory exists that guides their development from a persuasive technology (PT) perspective. The results of a recent pilot test on *Smoke?*, our persuasive game about smoking cessation, highlighted several design issues related to persuasive games in general. In this paper we discuss some of those issues, contextualizing them in terms of B J Fogg's PT strategies, in order to both explain underlying forces, and point towards potential design solutions. The five issues we discuss are: *managing player attention, balancing "replayability" with reality, player control vs. system control, identity issues*, and *target audience*.

1 Introduction

Persuasive games are a relatively new phenomenon, and have been shown to be an effective means of message promotion, both in the realms of advertising [1,2], and as tools for promoting health and well-being [3]. But the youth of persuasive games as a genre means that there are few helpful rules guiding how to design persuasive games to be interesting, compelling, and effective, especially from the theoretical perspective of persuasive technology (PT).

As part of a larger research project concerning culture and PT, we decided to use games as a platform for exploration [4]. In accordance with our research objectives, we developed two prototypes of a persuasive game, *Smoke?*, about smoking cessation. An important design goal for *Smoke?* is to persuade people who are contemplating quitting smoking, or have recently quit smoking, that quitting permanently will be beneficial. *Smoke?* can be classified as a simulation game, and presents six weeks of the life of a main character, MC (either male or female), who has decided to quit smoking. It includes events that are typical of smokers attempting to quit, as drawn from the literature on smoking cessation [5]. Throughout the game, the player must decide what course of action MC is to take next, including who MC talks to, who MC attempts to maintain relationships with, how

Y. de Kort et al. (Eds.): PERSUASIVE 2007, LNCS 4744, pp. 36–47, 2007.
© Springer-Verlag Berlin Heidelberg 2007

MC spends his free time, and how MC handles smoking cravings. The game cannot be won or lost: at the end of game play, players are instead presented with an outcome for MC's smoking status after a year, reflecting the decisions the player made for MC. Figure 1 shows a screenshot from *Smoke?*.

We decided to perform an evaluation on an initial version of *Smoke?* to help identify any obviously problematic features in need of addressing in future development iterations. In this paper we share our reflections on some of the findings of the evaluation. We present our findings in five categories: *managing player attention, balancing "replayability" with reality* (by "replay", we mean "undo/redo"), *player control vs. system control, identity issues,* and *target audience*. In line with the discussion of the issues as they presented themselves in the game, we propose ways to explain the issues in terms of B J Fogg's PT strategies [6].

The relationship between video games and persuasion is largely acknowledged by Fogg in the context of a behaviouristic perspective [6]. In fact, within the game studies literature this has been taken somewhat further, and research has focused on issues such as ethics [7], ideology [8], and rhetoric [9]. Within our own research group, work exists in specifically considering the relationship between a game's interface and the values it may interactively project to the user [10]. In this paper, we attempt to focus more on the particular applications of Fogg's persuasive strategies within a video game design, rather than considering the general persuasiveness of game design itself. We are aware that this focus may limit the innovation of the solutions we suggest, since the strategies are abstractions of existing design solutions for PTs, as opposed to games. Nonetheless, there is still significant benefit to studying persuasive games from a PT perspective, as we believe the strategies highlight the existence of interesting tensions and potential solutions. From a more high-level perspective, research of this type helps establish necessary connections between the PT and the game studies literature.

2   Findings from an Evaluation of *Smoke?*

To obtain external perspectives on *Smoke?*, we had a diverse group of people play it. They included high school and university students, alongside smoking cessation advisors and experts. The group also included representatives of the Toihuarewa, our university's academic forum for Maori, the indigenous people of New Zealand. The feedback was obtained through observation of play, guided free-form discussion, and in some cases, written reports. After analysing the participant feedback, certain issues regarding the design of persuasive games in general emerged.

We have categorised our reflections on the feedback into five groups: *managing player attention, balancing "replayability" with reality, player control vs. system control, identity issues,* and *target audience*. Discussion for each of these commences by describing the issues as encountered in the game, then we reformulate the problems in terms of known PT strategies. The strategies we refer

Fig. 1. A screenshot from *Smoke?*

to in this section include *reduction*, simplifying away certain details to make users notice other details more, *tunnelling*, leading users through a predetermined sequence of events to facilitate certain behaviour, *customisation*, providing users with personally relevant information to increase interest, *self monitoring*, informing users about aspects of their own progress to motivate a behavioural or attitudinal change, *suggestion*, intervening at the "right time" to motivate a user to react in a particular way, and *conditioning*, using operant conditioning to reinforce target behaviours when they occur [6].

2.1 Managing Player Attention

In practise. Score bars and screens are commonplace in the average digital game. The first version of our game featured a status screen, as seen in figure 2, that charted eight continuously changing aspects of MC's health and well-being. We thought it was important to supply this information to players, as an integral part of learning about smoking cessation is understanding the effects of smoking on health and well-being. The status screen was designed like a browser "tab", and could be viewed at any point during play. The status screen components were also summarised as an overall well-being score in a mini status summary window in the lower right-hand corner of the screen. Our evaluation

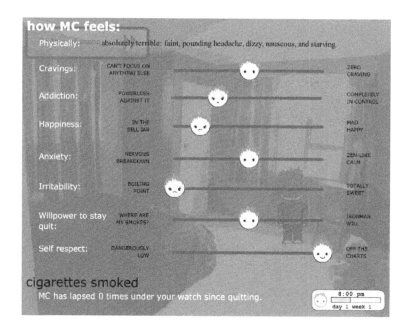

Fig. 2. The initial version of the status screen

participants brought to our attention a couple of serious issues with the status screen, however. One participant claimed that there were too many aspects to keep track of, and felt cognitively overloaded. Other participants observed that they hardly ever referred to the status screen. Since we believed that there was important information present in the status screen, we have since redesigned it to report on only five elements, as in figure 3. In addition, we modified the mini status summary window to provide more specific, rather than generalised information. Finally, we are also considering tying in incentives for more regular status checking, for example, by decreasing MC's "anxiety" aspect as a reward.

In theory. The issue we just described can be recast as a tension between several, vying PT strategies: *reduction* and *tunnelling* versus *conditioning*, *self monitoring* and *suggestion*. Linear narratives are an application of *reduction* and *tunnelling*, where narrators essentially control what their audience pays attention to, and, to some extent, how they arrive at particular understandings. Games with clearly defined narratives thus employ *reduction* and *tunnelling*, in that players' paths are predetermined, and their attention is being focused upon particular game elements. Score and status screens, on the other hand, can be considered as a co-operation between *conditioning*, *suggestion*, and *self monitoring*, in the following way. Changes in score, as related to progress, are presented as *conditioning* feedback to players. Since players are responsible for their game progress, this information then facilitates both *suggestion*, and *self monitoring*, i.e. suggesting ways that they might want to improve game performance.

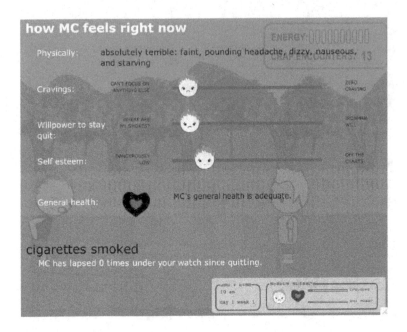

Fig. 3. A revised version of the status screen

That several of our participants were more interested in progressing along the narrative path of the game than checking the status page is evidence that we had indeed succeeded in tunnelling their attention. We had succeeded to the extent that we were failing to draw their attention to other feedback information; and thus losing valuable opportunities to point out how game performance could be improved. The forces of *reduction-tunnelling* and *conditioning-suggestion-self monitoring* clearly need to be balanced: players should be interested enough in the game narrative to continue progressing, but also remain aware enough of feedback information, such that they are willing to pay attention to suggestions about performance improvement. Equally, once they have noted the suggestion, players should be able to smoothly transition back into the world of the game narrative in order to apply it. The participant who commented about feeling overloaded with status information is another indication that we had not achieved a workable balance between the strategies. In terms of a cost-benefit analysis, comprehending the status information was causing a cognitive processing overhead that was deemed too costly, and our participant was unable to smoothly transition back into the game narrative. *Reduction* is one way to lessen the perceived cost. Our decision to remove some status information was made on the basis of whether we thought it was related enough to the game narrative to actually serve as a narrative progression in itself. In this way, we tried to facilitate smooth transitions back into game narrative as well. The introduction of incentives is another typical way of balancing a cost-benefit ratio, as it adds extra benefits [11]. In the context of PT, this is known as the *reciprocation principle* [12], and in our game it would translate as the offer of rewards for checking status. With a simulation, however, we need to take care that we do not add too many artificial motivators, otherwise we run the risk of the simulation having little basis in reality.

2.2   Balancing "Replayability" with Reality

In practise. Part of the power of simulation lies in the ability to represent real world cause-and-effect relationships [6]. With certain phenomena, the causality chain may be at least a few links long. In the first iteration of game design, we decided not to allow players to partially replay portions of the game, believing that it might interfere with messages we were trying to communicate about various consequences of smoking. One of our evaluation participants, however, expressed that she would have liked to have been able to replay certain parts of the game, in order to be able to "fix" unintentional choices she had made for MC that resulted in game outcomes she had hoped to avoid. She claimed that playing the game all the way through to achieve a sub-optimal outcome was disenchanting, and made her feel like "giving up". Nowadays, digital games typically do allow some amount of replayability, therefore players are likely to expect a "replay" option during play. Failure to find this feature led to frustration for the participant, which in turn had the detrimental consequence of her paying less attention to the game message. At the same time, we were concerned that adding "replay" would confuse the game narrative, in that cause-and-effect chains would be far less obvious, and the intended learning outcomes might become ambiguous. We have since decided to introduce "replay" to some parts of the game, but intend to experiment with its placement to identify where it seems crucial, and where it can be omitted.

In theory. The aforementioned scenario relates to a tension between *reduction* and *tunnelling* on one side, and *conditioning* on the other. Cause-and-effect simulations are closely linked to the concept of narrative, and therefore relate to *reduction* and *tunnelling*, in that the attention of users is directed along specific paths to prompt particular understandings of phenomena. Replay points, which can be likened to tunnel exit points, can also be construed as tools players use to improve their chances of obtaining positive feedback, and in this way, relate to *conditioning*. In the quest for maximising positive feedback then, players seek out ways to redo actions they have decided were not beneficial. They seek a tunnel exit point, such that they can re-enter the tunnel, having optimised a prior game state, which may lead to receiving more positive feedback.

The first version of the game made use of tunnelling with no exit points. When tunnels of this nature are short, users are less likely to notice that they are being tunnelled, and therefore less likely to become frustrated at not being able to "exit" the tunnel. Our game, however, featured long tunnels, which were necessary for illustrating real relationships between smoking, health, and social situations. Failing to find a replay point, the participant, whose experience we recounted previously, quickly became frustrated at not being able to exit the tunnels. Given her intentions for achieving an optimum outcome, she felt that she had been denied hypothetical positive feedback, and so felt disillusioned with the sub-optimal outcome she believed she unjustly received at the end of the game. To avoid this situation, an obvious remedy is to introduce tunnel exit points. But too many exit points means that the benefits of tunnelling are reduced, as it becomes unclear as to where tunnels begin, how players reached their outcome, and consequentially what interpretations they take away from it. Additionally, in real life, as in true simulation, there is no "undo/redo" option. Adding "replay" is therefore a concession to players' desires for maximising potential positive feedback, as well as exploring unreality. In turn, this can detract from the original goal of modelling the real world. Addition of "replay" throughout the game is therefore a careful balancing act between providing enough exit points such that players are able to immediately address particular types of feedback information, while providing few enough exits such that overall paths are still discernible, and enough semblance to reality is maintained.

2.3   Player Control vs. System Control

In practise. Digital games by necessity should facilitate player activity. Given our developmental time and budget constraints, we designed our prototypes such that parts of the game play concentrated on simulation, while others were dominated by system-led progression of game narrative. Several participants commented that they would have liked to have been able to complete other

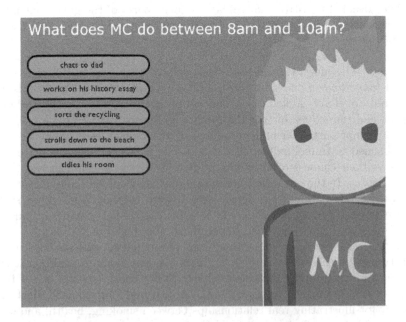

Fig. 4. The initial version of the random activity selection screen

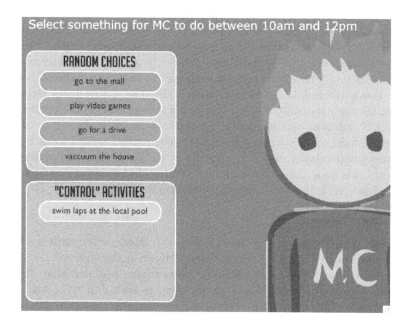

Fig. 5. The revised version of the random activity selection screen

activities in the game world that were not available. For example, some of the participants said they would have liked to have been able to take MC shopping for clothes, and not just groceries, which was all the game supported. In a related vein, a central component of our game design was the idea of random mood shifters, which players must use to specify how MC fills particular blocks of time, as in figure 4. The outcome of the random activity on MC's mood is unpredictable, and only gets revealed to players after the choice has been made. We believed this had parallels with the experience of quitting in the real world, where many aspects of life are out of personal control. Yet some of the participants were frustrated that they were not in control of every aspect of MC's state. To some extent, this is an issue that technology users are always likely to encounter. All the same, we are redesigning our game prototypes to contain clearer descriptions of what actions can be completed, and indications for where MC is not strictly under the control of players, as in figure 5.

In theory. The frustration users felt at not being able to complete or control particular activities in the game world may be related to the *customisation* strategy. *Smoke?* features certain affordances of customisation: for example, players can choose who MC talks to, how MC interacts with them, and what MC does to manage his cravings. We wanted players to control particular aspects of their game experience, because we wanted them to "generate" their own outcome. When people believe that information is particularly relevant to them, they tend to find it more persuasive [6,13]. But perhaps what happened as a consequence is that some of our participants interpreted these real affordances of customisation as pointers to other perceived, but non-existent affordances of customisation, and the mismatch between expectation and reality led to frustration. Facilitating further customisation by implementing and supporting a greater range of player activity is one solution to this problem. At the same time, however, there is a trade-off between customisation and simulation. Customisation is about supporting user intent and generating user-specific content or experiences; it is essentially about emphasising uniqueness. Simulation, on the other hand, typically describes known cause-and-effect relationships, or known relationships between particular entities; it is about emphasising predictability and sameness. As in earlier discussions, perhaps the resolution to this issue lies in balancing the desires of players for customisation, with our wishes as designers to control simulation information.

2.4   Identity Issues

In practise. The beginning of *Smoke?* features an introduction sequence where players are informed that they are to "guide MC to make choices" for the six weeks of game time. Discussion with the participants revealed that different participants had quite varied ideas about their relationship with MC as an avatar. A couple of the younger participants described this relationship as one of friendship, i.e. they thought of MC as a friend who they were helping. An older participant described feeling responsible for MC, and felt worried and guilty when MC started to suffer from craving-induced shaking. Another participant described how she played the game by identifying as MC. Yet another viewpoint shared was that during play, the participant was attempting to "get into MC's head". At several points during the game this participant even asked out loud, "What would MC do?" It seems reasonable to assume that players' conceptions of their relationships with the avatar may well have an effect on how the game content is understood and internalised. For example, if players feel responsible for MC, and view MC as dependent on their help, then it seems feasible that in the event of MC's success or failure, they may feel motivated to learn how to increase MC's chances of staying quit. In turn, they have a greater chance of internalising generalised knowledge about quitting behaviour. On the other hand, if players view MC as an entirely independent, preformed entity, then it is ambiguous as to whether they would be willing to explore how to reach a quit state for MC. In corollary, these players may miss out on valuable information about the consequences of different actions. To prompt a more dependency/responsibility view of the player-avatar relationship, we have added more language cues to different parts of the game reminding players of how we would like them to view MC.

In theory. The issue of how players perceive the player-avatar relationship relates to *customisation* and *self monitoring*. *Customisation* is partly about making users believe that that they are able to self-identify with content they view. The participant who asked "What would MC do?" clearly did not feel that MC was customised to be like her. In fact, her question leads us to believe that she was almost trying to customise *herself* to be more like MC. As discussed earlier, increased customisation leads to players paying more attention to outcomes.

Maintaining player interest through an increased level of player-avatar identification is important for a couple of reasons. Firstly, it increases the likelihood that players are internalising information presented in the game, which is a key objective for any persuasive game. But secondly, the identification with the avatar can lead to a form of interest and motivation similar to that which drives *self monitoring*. Once self monitoring becomes established as a motivational driver, players are more likely to be open to experimenting with ways of pushing MC in different directions, and thus likely to learn a lot more from the experience of play. As discussed previously, however, support for total customisation in *Smoke?* is not possible for a number of reasons. Nonetheless, alerting players to some ways in which they can customise MC, or do have control over MC, may lead to greater self-identification, and accordingly, some of its associated benefits.

2.5   Target Audience

In practise. As designers of PTs for health and well-being, typically we seem to assume that as long as we believe what we have designed is beneficial, the end product will also be beneficial. One of the senior cessation experts who looked at the game commented that quite young players who had never smoked might be misled about the easiness of quitting based on what they experienced during the game. We had not foreseen the game as potentially being detrimental, because we had not considered how audiences of different levels of maturity and life experience might perceive it. Short of not allowing people who are "too young" to play the game, there seems to be no simple workaround to this issue, but it appears worthy of bearing in mind.

In theory. As in *identity issues, customisation*, or its lack thereof, plays a role here. When people believe they are receiving customised information, they tend to believe it more, even though it might not actually be tailored towards them [6]. In the hypothetical case that younger players did play the game, they may believe they are creating customised experiences that relate to their own lives. But our game was not intended for them as players, so it was not a context of interpretation that we planned for. This could lead to the young players taking away spurious understandings of the game's persuasive content, additionally compounded by a belief that the game applies to their lives. This scenario seemingly points to a need to explicitly clarify, when designing customisable products, the range of people that the customisation extends to, and that the persuasive messages may be less relevant for anyone not falling within this group.

3   Conclusions

The recent emergence of persuasive games means that there still remain many unanswered questions regarding how to design them to be effective and compelling. Additionally, little research has focused on designing persuasive games from the theoretical standpoint of PT. The results of a recent pilot test on *Smoke?*, our persuasive game about smoking cessation, highlighted several issues related to persuasive games in general.

One such issue was that of needing to find a way of presenting useful information in a manner that does not cause cognitive overload, and that players feel compelled to pay attention to. Another concern is striking a workable balance between allowing players to replay game segments while still making overall narrative cause-and-effect chains obvious. Players were also on occasion confused as to where they were in control as compared to where progress was system-determined. Additionally, they sometimes had expectations about being able to complete certain activities that the game did not support. An interesting issue that could impact on how persuasive information is interpreted and eventually applied relates to how players perceive their relationship with the avatar: a dependency/responsibility-driven view of the relationship might be more conducive to information internalisation than an independence relationship. A final observation we reported on was that it is important to remember the target audience of any persuasive game, because showing the game to a non-target audience may result in detrimental misinterpretation of information.

In line with our discussion of the evaluation findings, we reflected on how the issues can be observed in terms of PT strategies. This theoretical reformulation has led us to identify several recurring themes that seem generally applicable to the design of persuasive games. One such theme is the notion that *customisation*, which is often sought by players, does not directly support *simulation*. Yet players seem naturally drawn to content that they believe is customised. For the purpose of attracting and maintaining player attention, it seems in our best interests to at least partially support customisation, even though it may not necessarily enhance the accuracy of our simulation information. Another theme is the observation that certain groupings of strategies naturally lend themselves towards particular tasks. *Reduction* and *tunnelling* support story-telling, cause-and-effect simulation, and generally drawing the player into the game world. In contrast, *self monitoring*, *suggestion* and *conditioning* operate synergistically to interrupt players from their current course of action to show them why they may want to modify their actions, and how they might go about it. Meanwhile, *customisation* is a powerful tool for maintaining player interest. A final, almost "meta" theme, is the idea of balance. While some PT strategies work together harmoniously, it is not always a case of "the more, the merrier", as certain strategies practically work at cross-purposes. When using conflicting strategies together in persuasive games, we need to consider some of the various trade-offs that their coexistence will engender, as persuasion is a phenomenon that can always benefit from some fine tuning.

References

1. Nelson, M.R., Keum, H., Yaros, R.A.: Advertainment or Adcreep? Game Players Attitudes toward Advertising and Product Placements in Computer Games. Journal of Interactive Advertising 5 (2004)
2. Deal, D.: The ability of online branded games to build brand equity. In: Proceedings of the Digital Games Research Association 2nd International Conference (2005)

3. Slater, S.G.: New Technology Device: Glucoboy, for Disease Management of Diabetic Children and Adolescents. Health Care Management & Practice 17, 246–247 (2005)
4. Khaled, R., Barr, P., Fischer, R., Biddle, R., Noble, J.: Factoring culture into the design of a persuasive game. In: Proceedings of OzCHI 2006 (2006)
5. U.S. Department of Health and Human Services: You Can Quit Smoking (2000), http://www.surgeongeneral.gov/tobacco/quits.pdf
6. Fogg, B.J.: Persuasive Technology: Using Computers to Change What We Think and Do. Morgan Kaufmann, San Francisco (2003)
7. Sicart, M.: The ethics of computer game design. In: Proceedings of DIGRA2005, Simon Frasier University, Burnaby, BC, Canada (CD–ROM) (2005)
8. Garite, M.: The ideology of interactivity (or video games and taylorization of leisure) (CD Rom). In: Copier, M., Raessens, J. (eds.) Level Up Conference Proceedings, University of Utrecht, Utrecht (2003)
9. Davidson, D.: The rhetoric of gameplay (Last accessed 1 April, 2007), Available online at http://waxebb.com/writings/gamerhet.html
10. Barr, P., Biddle, R., Noble, J.: Videogame values: Human-computer interaction and games. Interacting With Computers (2006)
11. Cialdini, R.B.: Interpersonal influence. In: Brock, T.C., (ed.): Persuasion: Psychological Insights and Perspectives. Allyn and Beacon, 195 – 217 (1994)
12. Reeves, B., Nass, C.: The Media Equation: How People Treat Computers, Television, and New Media Like Real People and Places. University of Chicago Press (1996)
13. Petty, R.E., Cacioppo, J.T., Strathman, A.J., Priester, J.R.: To Think Or Not To Think. In: Brock, T.C., (ed.): Persuasion: Psychological Insights and Perspectives. Allyn and Beacon, 113 – 147 (1994)

Captivating Patterns – A First Validation

Sabine Niebuhr[1,2] and Daniel Kerkow[2]

[1] Technische Universität Kaiserslautern
Software Engineering Research Group (AG SE)
Gottlieb-Daimler-Straße
67663 Kaiserslautern, Germany
Sabine.Niebuhr@informatik.uni-kl.de
[2] Fraunhofer Institute for Experimental Software Engineering
Fraunhofer Platz 1
67663 Kaiserslautern, Germany
Daniel.Kerkow@iese.fraunhofer.de

Abstract. Is it possible to motivate users of an application through software elements? Is it also possible to do so for business applications? Having a long lasting, monotone, little challenging work task does not motivate users a lot in continuing a task, especially if this task comes up regularly, like typing numbers or addresses. We found software patterns - design recommendations – that keep a user working on such a task. We validated one of them in an experiment and found out that it is possible to motivate users through captivating software elements.

Keywords: Motivation, pattern, status display, business application.

1 Introduction

Software has taken over many of our tasks – but is this really good news? On the one hand, it is beneficial to get more support in difficult tasks. But on the other hand, this might lead to a worst case scenario with unwanted effects, where a computer is doing our work and we end up supporting the software in steps it is not able to do. Because the computer is doing the intelligent work, our task might get more simple and monotone.

Imagine an employee doing quality assurance: His supervisor has assigned him to the boring task of proofreading scanned addresses. Now look at the way in which the employee will most probably perform this task. He will take breaks, drink coffee, think about sports, his next trip, or the last evening with friends. Research has taught us the unavoidable nature of this behavior in certain moods [1]. On the other side, there is the supervisor of the organization the employee is working for: He would like him to work on the given task in a concentrated and effective manner. How can the supervisor motivate the employee to do so? He can promise him better tasks in the future; he can promise him a higher salary or other extrinsic incentives. He can observe the user and put him under pressure. He can remind the user in regular intervals to perform his task. There are many possibilities for extrinsic and intrinsic motivation in working contexts [2,3,4,5,6,7]. Without them, an employee will zone out, will turn away from his task from time to time.

Y. de Kort et al. (Eds.): PERSUASIVE 2007, LNCS 4744, pp. 48–54, 2007.
© Springer-Verlag Berlin Heidelberg 2007

The question now is: Can we change the employee's attitude in such a way that he will take this task as a challenge? Can we change the employee's attitude in such a way that he is motivated to perform this task – although it is monotone, boring, long lasting? Can we change his behavior in such a way that he will work with concentration on this task, without noticing distractions? And the most challenging question is: Can we cause this motivation through software elements?

Following the idea of persuasive and motivational technology [8,9], our goal is to inject motivational elements into business software. Therefore, we identify interaction patterns to engage the user's experience, to motivate the user in his tasks and motivate him in adapting the business goals of his organization, or in finding new goals that could help the organization in competition with other organizations. We did some research, found approaches and wrote them down in software interaction patterns (like Tidwell [10]). Exemplarily, we tested the effect of one pattern to ensure that we are going the right way[1].

In the following, we describe one of the patterns we analyzed, the changes that were necessary until this example pattern was consciously perceived by the users, and the experiment we designed to find out if it had the expected motivational effect. We also describe the outcomes of the experiment and our further steps.

2 Captivating Patterns

What was our approach to the motivation problem? As a first step, we decided to identify patterns. Patterns capture approved methods for recurring problems. So we wanted to learn from disciplines that have a long tradition of developing motivating software and that are really successful in this area, namely game design and e-learning [11]. In both disciplines, developers have to capture the attention of their users with their software, because it is used voluntarily. Especially in game design, developers fascinate users in such a way that they play a game for a whole night, for weeks, or even for months. Therefore, we try to apply this knowledge in business application design.

Furthermore, we looked into existing usability pattern languages for detecting patterns. As a result, some of our patterns are specialized from the existing usability pattern "Status Display" by Jennifer Tidwell [10]. Tidwell's intention was to keep the user informed about things that are transparent for the user. We want to remind the user of goals or tasks that become transparent because they move out of the user's mind. We specialized this pattern in order to apply it to business applications and working situations. One example of this specialized pattern is the Task Status Display.

Another source are existing psychological theories dealing with motivational effects. One of these theories that fits to the task status display is the goal setting theory [2]. The intention of this theory is that goals should be set, and they should be set as specific and challenging goals. These goals lead to higher performance. The important thing in this theory is how to define the term specific and how to define the term challenging; both correlate with the complexity of the given task. Nevertheless,

---

[1] Context is the FUN-project (fun of use for business applications; www.fun-of-use.de), a research project supported by the German government (BMBF).

this theory can be applied to single persons, different task types, and different cultures [12], which makes it interesting for our patterns.

The desired effect of our patterns is motivation or engagement. We combined the existing Pattern Status Display, the knowledge from e-learning and game design, and the psychological theories, and were able to write down this knowledge in our pattern Task Status Display.

The Pattern Task Status Display

You as a user might face a monotone, simple, or long lasting task. You do not work on it very fast because you are distracted by many other things not concerning this task. We as developers want to motivate you to work on your task with concentration – as fast as possible or as attentively as possible. A solution for this problem is described in our pattern Task Status Display: it shows you the goal you have to achieve. The solution is to show to which extent you have reached the goal and what has to be done yet.

It is a specialized Status Display and we think this works because it sets a specific goal for the user. It depicts a more or less complex task in single steps, making progress visible. We give feedback, which gives the user information about what he has already achieved and how he can adjust his performance, if necessary. This feedback is another important factor [2]. By looking at the given information, the user sees which specific goals he has already achieved, which keeps him motivated or increases his motivation. The desired effect for the Task Status Display is to keep motivation up, especially during these boring, long lasting tasks.

Our intention is now to change the user's attitude towards such a task by adding a Task Status Display into the business application he uses. We try to change his behavior in such a way that he remains concentrated during work. The user will not turn off, but will keep on working with concentration on his task, as depicted in Figure 1. You can see at the top of the picture that the user gets distracted at the circles, because his motivation becomes low during his task. At the bottom of the picture you can see that the motivation is kept at a higher level by the Task Status Display in order to avoid the distraction.

Implementing a status display can happen in different ways. As in the real world, the work progress can be derived from different things. If your task is washing dishes, you can see your progress in a decreasing heap of dirty dishes. If you are doing a

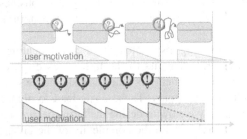

Fig. 1. The user's focus with, respectively without, Task Status Display

puzzle, you see the progress in a growing picture. This aspect captures the direction of the progress: You can use increasing numbers for showing the work that has been done until this moment. You can draw decreasing numbers to show how much still has to be done. Finally, you can combine both approaches and depict how much has been done and how much is still left. Another possibility is to show the task state or the performance state compared with other users doing the same or nearly the same task. You find this in game design in high score lists. These lists could be about personal values, for example how I performed the same task before. These lists can also show relations to other users, to best marks, or something similar. Implemented, these lists have an appearance similar to a traffic light, a tachometer, or a scale.

3   Experimental Validation of the Task Status Display Pattern

A simple, boring task, which can be supported by a status display, is adding addresses to a database. In most organizations, customer addresses are stored in a database – and an employee has to type in these data. Therefore, we set up a simple input mask for an address database and implemented the task status display pattern. In a first approach, we just drew a big stack of business cards, and for every entered address, one card disappeared from the top of the stack. However, the pattern did not work: the stack was too huge and no real progress could be noticed. So we put our business cards into smaller stacks, and the actual stack was drawn bigger, as depicted in figure 2. Additionally, the disappearance of the card was emphasized by a looping animation of the card.

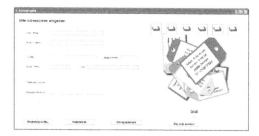

Fig. 2. Screenshot of the first test application with implemented Task Status Display

Now the disappearing cards were noticed, but not felt as motivation. To focus the user's attention on the disappearing cards, we put the pictures between the input mask and the button for saving. This status display shows 10 address cards lying horizontally in a row – after each database input, one address disappears (see Figure 3 (a)). Below this line, small card stacks are shown – if the card line above the stacks is empty, the active card stack disappears, and the next card stack gets activated.

3.1   Experimental Design

For proving the effect in an experiment, our hypothesis was derived from the desired effect of the Task Status Pattern: We claim that a user works with more concentration on a given task if he gets information about the state of the task, where his goal is pointed out, the steps for reaching this goal are clear, and the direction (reaching or departing to/from the goal). Therefore, the number of distractions should be smaller when using the application with Task Status Display.

H: #Distractions(Task Status Display) < #Distractions()

For the validation of this hypothesis and the Task Status Display, we asked 14 test persons (11male, 3 female; 12 students, 2 without employment; age between 20 and 33) to fill a database with 40 addresses in a time period of 1 hour and 15 minutes. They had a special input mask for their task. Six persons had a mask with a Task Status Display as depicted in (a) in Figure 3. Eight participants had a simpler task without a Task Status Display (see Figure 3 (b)). The test persons were assigned randomly to their group.

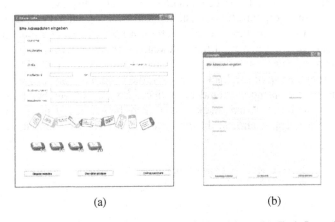

(a)   (b)

Fig. 3. The final test application with (a), respectively without (b), Task Status Display

A PDF file containing the addresses to be entered as scanned business cards was sent to a Google mail account. The starting screen of Google was customized in a way to seduce users to distract themselves: at the top left edge, there was a widget for the mails. Around this widget, we arranged some games like Pacman, Tetris, and Sudoku. For people who do not like playing games, we added a widget with the latest news. During the experiment's introduction, we pointed out that there is enough time to take breaks and that these widgets could be used to start surfing the web or for playing.

While a test person performed the task of entering addresses, we took the screen signal and stored the test person's actions in a video file. Thus, we were able to observe how many breaks a test person took and what he did during this time. Comparing the number of breaks the test persons took while performing their task with and without Task Status Display will help us prove our hypothesis.

3.2 First Results of Recent Experiments

Although all test persons described the task of adding addresses to a database as a simple, boring task, there were differences in their behavior: No test person

Table 1. Number of distractions among the participants

	No breaks	One or more breaks	N
with pattern	6	0	6
without pattern	3	5	8

performing the task with the Task Status Display (with pattern) took any break or got distracted from his task. Of the test persons performing the task without a Task Status Display (without pattern) three did not take any break, four took one or more breaks (compare Table 1). A first analysis (Mann-Whitney-U-Test: $n_1=8$; $n_2=6$; $U=39.0$) supports our hypothesis with a one-tailed significance of $p=0.030$.

Asked whether anything caught the test person's eye, test persons with the Task Status Display application described the disappearing address cards and that they felt motivated going on with typing addresses to clear all cards. Test persons performing the task without Task Status Display used the given possibilities of reading news, playing Pacman, solving a Sudoku puzzle, or reading emails. They were distracted by the different possibilities of activities that seem to be more interesting than adding addresses to a database. So looking at this result, we could say – although this statement is limited due to the small sample and the laboratory situation – that this motivation could be engaged through the Task Status Display, a captivating pattern.

4 Consequences and Further Work

We found some patterns that promise to motivate users to keep on working on simple, monotone, recurring tasks. We tested one of these patterns, the Task Status Display, in a small application and could observe that we do change the user's behavior by implementing this pattern.

In our next steps, we will apply this and other patterns we discovered in existing business applications of our project partners. We will validate their effects in a laboratory environment as well as in real working situations.

Maybe we will manage to transform dull working situations into challenging and motivating ones.

Acknowledgments. This work is supported by the German Federal Ministry of Education and Research (BMBF) within the project FUN (Grant: 01 IS E06 A).

References

1. Hassenzahl, M., Kekez, R., Burmester, M.: The importance of a software's pragmatic quality depends on usage modes. In: Luczak, H., Cakir, A.E., Cakir, G. (eds.) Proceedings of the 6th international conference on Work With Display Units (WWDU 2002), ERGONOMIC Institut für Arbeits- und Sozialforschung, Berlin, pp. 275–276 (2002)
2. Locke, E.A., Latham, G.P.: A theory of goal setting and task performance. Prentice Hall, Englewood Cliffs (1990)
3. Spreitzer, G.M.: Psychological Empowerment in the workplace: Dimensions, measurement, and validation. Academy of Management Journal 38, 1442–1465 (1995)

4. Steers, R.M., Porter, L.W.: Motivation and work behavior. McGraw-Hill, New York (1991)
5. Herzberg, F.: The motivation of work. John Wiley & Sons Inc., Chichester (1959)
6. House, R., Herzbergś, W.L.: Dual factor Theory of Job Satisfaction and Motivation: A Review of Evidence and a Criticism. Personnel Psychology 20, 369–389 (1967)
7. Weiner, B.: An attributional theory of motivation and emotion. Springer, New York (1986)
8. Fogg, B.J.: Persuasive Technology. In: Fogg, B.J. (ed.) Using Computers to Change What We Think and Do., Morgan Kaufmann Publishers, Inc., Amsterdam, Elsevier (2003)
9. Millard, N., Hole, L., Crowle, S.: Smiling Through: Motivation At The User Interface. HCI (1), 824–828 (1999)
10. Tidwell, J.: Common ground: A Pattern Language for Human-Computer Interface Design
11. von Ahn, L.: Games with a Purpose. In: Computer, vol. 39(6), pp. 92–94. IEEE Computer Society Press, Los Alamitos (2006)
12. Latham, G.P., Lee, T.W.: Goal setting. In: Locke, E.A. (ed.) Generalizing from laboratory to field settings, Lexington Books, pp. 101–117 (1986)

Promoting New Patterns in Household Energy Consumption with Pervasive Learning Games

Magnus Bang, Anton Gustafsson, and Cecilia Katzeff

Interactive Institute, Eskilstuna, Sweden
{magnus.bang,anton.gustafsson,cecilia.katzeff}@tii.se

Abstract. Engaging computer games can be used to change energy consumption patterns in the home. PowerAgent is a pervasive game for Java-enabled mobile phones that is designed to influence everyday activities and use of electricity in the domestic setting. PowerAgent is connected to the household's automatic electricity meter reading equipment via the cell network, and this setup makes it possible to use actual consumption data in the game. In this paper, we present a two-level model for cognitive and behavior learning, and we discuss the properties of PowerAgent in relation to the underlying situated learning, social learning, and persuasive technology components that we have included in the game.

1 Introduction

Computer games have been used as educational tools for over two decades. However, the efficacy of this learning and behavior-modifying approach has been criticized on several accounts. For example, researchers are questioning whether students can actually use the knowledge they acquire in simulation games and apply it to real-world tasks (e.g., generalization and transfer of knowledge) [1,2]. Moreover, traditional interactive games seem to result in shallow learning. This problem has to do with difficulties in conveying deeper meaning, as well as the underlying learning models in the expeditious interactive games [3]. Modern theories on learning have also criticized the notion of knowledge transfer. Instead, researchers emphasize the importance of *relevant and authentic real-world tasks* in learning, and they discuss the social aspects of education, including mediation of skills via peer interactions [4,5]. Among others, Brown and colleagues [4] have stated that learners actively construct knowledge, and that it is built on previous experience of real-world tasks. Studies in the field of persuasive technology have also highlighted the role of social aspects such as peer group pressure [6,7].

Advances in augmented reality and ubiquitous computing show promise, and new computer games in this area have the potential to turn ordinary surroundings into sophisticated learning environments. Pervasive games constitute a relatively new class of computer games that extend the gaming experience to the real world [8]. In these games, the players are framed by real-life surroundings and interact with computer-enhanced objects. This approach has attractive properties from the perspective of

Y. de Kort et al. (Eds.): PERSUASIVE 2007, LNCS 4744, pp. 55–63, 2007.

learning and behavioral modification: learners do not have to rely on simulation, and tasks can be trained in the real environment, which might reduce problems with knowledge transfer.

According to Thomas [9], pervasive learning games are important primarily because they entail social processes that connect learners with communities of devices, people, and real learning situations. We are exploring this new game approach to target energy-use behaviors in the home. The hypothesis underlying our work is that persuasive games have the potential to strengthen situated learning and promote behavioral changes by reframing familiar activity and social systems.

Few pervasive games have been developed for the purpose of learning [ibid.]. Furthermore, to our knowledge, no games in this genre have been described that promote behavioral changes aimed at altering energy usage patterns. In this paper, we present PowerAgent, a pervasive learning game for teenagers designed to encourage more efficient energy use in the home. To strengthen the learning and persuasion components, PowerAgent has been constructed from the perspectives of situated learning [5] and social learning theory[1] [10,11], and it also makes use of persuasive technology methods [6]. We begin by discussing the area of pervasive gaming and summarizing research on pervasive learning games. Thereafter, we present the theoretical foundation on which our game rests. The main part of the text covers the design of the game, or, more correctly, how the micro-social activity system is re-shaped by the game. Lastly, we consider aspects of the design of pervasive learning games from the standpoint of behavioral and persuasion technology.

2 Pervasive Gaming and Learning

Pervasive games belong to a rather heterogeneous category of such entertainment that includes location-based games, urban mobile games, cross-media or hybrid games, immersive games, urban super-hero games, and alternative reality games [9]. The main feature that distinguishes pervasive games from traditional simulation games is that they extend the gaming experience to the physical world [8]. Consequently, there is no need for developers to simulate a game world such as that in the Sims [12]; instead, the approach involves overlay of game scenarios onto real world objects and environments (cf., augmented reality). Typically, the games utilize technologies like ad hoc computer networks and satellite positioning to link and track devices and users in the physical surroundings. Special interfaces such as displays and cameras are frequently used to superimpose the virtual game world and its tasks onto everyday physical artifacts and spaces. BotFighters [13] was an early location-based game on mobile phones, the mission of which was to find and defeat other players' bots out on the streets. By comparison, the goal of the modern pervasive game called Epidemic Menace [14] is to seek out and destroy viruses that invade different physical locations. To enhance the gaming experience, Epidemic Menace includes a set of special interfaces and physical props, such as mobile phones, mobile-augmented reality systems, physical game boards, and special communication stations.

---

[1] In 2001, Bandura renamed social learning theory (SLT) social cognitive theory to emphasize the cognitive aspects of learning and behavior modification.

Pervasive games are particularly interesting when considered from the perspective of persuasive technology and learning. Researchers such as Sotamaa [15] have argued that a fundamental trait of pervasive games is that they alter the social landscape. A possible consequence of blurring the distinction between different social landscapes is that the internal social rules of a game can have an influence on previously established activity rules. That is, activities in the game have the potential to be learned and transferred to related off-game activities. Of interest in this discussion are the four tenets of pervasive learning games suggested by Thomas [9]: community, autonomy, locationality, and relationality:

- **Community:** Pervasive learning is a social process that connects learning to communities of devices, people, and situations that can also include other pervasive learning situations. Learning in such environments are mediated by peers in the game community.

- **Autonomy:** Gamers direct learning experiences themselves and are in control of their learning processes.

- **Locationality:** Learning occurs at places and at times that are relevant for the learner.

- **Relationality:** Learners construct meaningful and relevant learning situations to which they can relate. Learning familiar concepts within their own personal environment allows them to better understand the implications of what they have learned, and this facilitates the construction of meaning.

Before we describe the PowerAgent game, it is appropriate to discuss underlying theories of learning that are related to our design.

Modern theories of learning seem to involve a consensus of major standpoints. First, as pointed out above, the learner is regarded as an active constructor of meaning, which is a view of learning emphasized within constructivist theory [16]. Second, learning is regarded as a social process; just as the physical world is shared by all of us, we also share an understanding of it [17]. Learning is a process that is in progress not only in the individual learners, but also in the culture of the learners [5]. For example, according to ideas of situated learning [4] and distributed cognition [18], knowledge exists not only within individuals, but also in the discourse among those persons, their interconnecting social relations, and the physical artifacts they employ, as well as the theories, models, and methods they use to produce supporting tools.

Social learning theory (SLT) is related to the above-mentioned perspectives,[2] in particular situated action [10]. SLT is especially attractive for the purpose of persuasive game design, because it can provide principles to guide that process. For instance, SLT includes behavioral reinforcers such as positive feedback, which is very

---

[2] Situated learning, situated action theory, distributed cognition, and social learning theory share several assumptions about how learning is achieved. However, it should also be said that there are significant divergences on some issues, particularly in terms of the feedback components and modeling that are not addressed in the situated theories.

common in interactive games, and such notions are outside the scope of the situated learning theories. The power of SLT lies in that it explains human behavior as an *interaction process* between cognitive, behavioral, and social/environmental components.

The basic tenet of SLT is the importance of observing and modeling: people learn by *observing the behavior of others* and by watching the outcome of actions (cf., vicarious learning). The outcome of observations can be in the form of cognitive learning alone, and it can also entail changes in behavior. The learnt is subsequently reinforced by several factors. For example, imitating the model can result in being accepted in the social group from which the model originated. Compliments and praise from people that back such behavior also reinforce the modeled behavior. Vicarious reinforcements, that is, when the model is being reinforced and that is observed by the learner, can increase the response and thus be regarded as yet another form of reinforcement.

According to Bandura, there can be two models, one that is symbolic and one that is live. The latter refers to a person who demonstrates behavior in the real world, and the former can be a person portrayed in a medium such as television and computer programs. It should also be noted that the maximum level of observational learning is achieved when the modeled behavior is *symbolically* rehearsed and the behaviors are subsequently enacted and rehearsed in the real world. Moreover, symbolic coding by use of words, labels, and images can further strengthen retention of behaviors.

3   PowerAgent

PowerAgent is a pervasive game for teenagers designed to have a positive influence on everyday energy consumption behavior in the home. It can be seen as a hybrid pervasive game, because it makes use of several media components—both traditional gaming and pervasive mechanisms—to support both cognitive and behavioral learning. A key design goal was to foster social interactions with peers that are playing the game and also with family members that becomes entangled indirectly in the game due to its pervasive social nature. PowerAgent is shown in Figure 1.

3.1 Game Scenario

The person playing PowerAgent has the role of a secret agent, and the mobile phone is the main agent tool. Via the phone, the boss, the mysterious Mr. Q, gives the player special missions to save the planet from the energy crisis. These are divided into training missions and real-world tasks. The training missions are played on the cell phone and these precede the actual real-world missions in the home. This training element is in the form of a traditional *platform game* characterized by jumping/climbing to and from suspended platforms (cf., Super Mario Bros.), which is done to catch batteries. Every battery contains a suggestion on how to act in order to be energy efficient in the upcoming real-world task, and it also holds information on how to influence family members.

Fig. 1. The PowerAgent game

For example, the tips for the cooking food mission can be the following: "Use the microwave oven instead of the ordinary oven, use the water boiler to heat water instead of putting the kettle on the stove, and tell everyone that you love food cooked in the microwave."

All real-world missions are focused on saving electricity in the home, particularly in conjunction with everyday activities. Typical missions include (1) adjusting the heating in the house, (2) washing clothes, (3) cooking food, (4) switching off all stand-by appliances, and (5) minimizing the total household energy use for a day. Hence, the goal is to figure out how to reduce energy consumption while performing the mission assigned by Mr. Q. The mobile phone is connected to special equipment in the home that measures the use of electricity and heat water during the missions. In this way, it is possible for us to provide feedback on the success of the missions and reinforce behaviors that are appropriate from the standpoint of energy conservation.

PowerAgent is normally played by two teams with five members each. The real-world tasks are done individually at home, but at the end of each mission the results from all team members are summarized and compared with the results of the competing team (see Fig. 3g). We included the competition factor to create engaged coherent social teams that work together to win. A special mobile chat is also available to the agent to share tips on how to carry out the missions with other team members.

3.2 System and Infrastructure

To monitor electricity consumption, PowerAgent makes use of existing automatic meter reading (AMR) systems in the players' homes. Basically, the AMR systems are connected to the residential central fuse hubs and provide consumption data automatically to the servers at the power companies via a computer network.

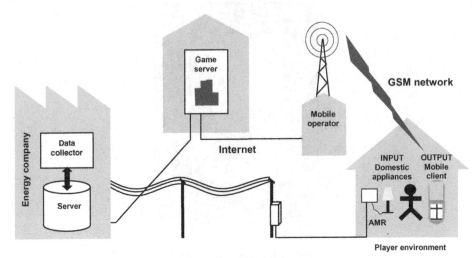

Fig. 2. Infrastructure of PowerAgent

A set of collector daemons relays this information to a central game server that processes and normalizes the data for the game so that all players have the same chance of winning.[3] Figure 2 shows the infrastructure of the game.

Unfortunately, a deficiency in our prototype is that the data can be delayed up to 12 hours in the power grid due to the underlying implementation of the AMR databases. This means that even though we can monitor each player's consumption on an hourly basis in most cases, the full results might not be accessible until next day. It was necessary to design the game based on those limitations.

The mobile game client that accesses the energy statistics is implemented in Java for SonyEricsson K750 mobiles, and the central game server is implemented in Python. An additional Java-based chat server is also provided in the system to support in-game communication among players.

3.3 Playing the Game

Before the beginning of a mission, the game client asks the user to logon to the Agent Network (Fig. 3a). Once logged on, the player is directed to headquarters where Mr. Q is waiting (Fig. 3b). Mr. Q. gives his mission directives verbally, and a countdown clock is started in the background (Fig. 3b). This counter indicates the time remaining until the real-world mission starts at home.

Agent logons are usually requested at 4 PM, so that the players can prepare and practice for the upcoming tasks. An important part of the preparations is the above-mentioned platform game in which the player can find clues with important information about how to get the best results during the upcoming real-world mission (Fig. 3, d and e).

---

[3] We had to normalize the energy consumption data, because different households use different means of heating, which could have a negative impact on the outcome for some players.

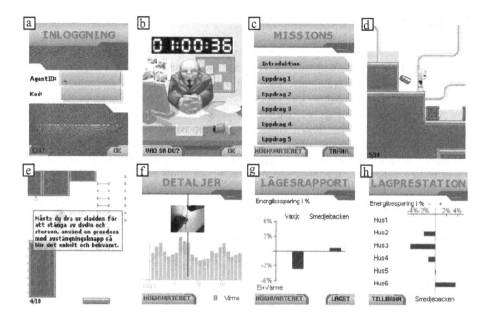

Fig. 3. Screenshots from the PowerAgent

Preparations can also include getting the family to participate in the game session and starting to turn off energy-consuming devices in the home. Other measures can be to check the Internet for information on how to be energy efficient in relation to the specific task. In addition, the player can browse Mr. Q's office when he is not there to access crucial information and chat with other team players.

A typical real-world mission will last for 24–48 hours, and during the mission the mobile phone notifies the user if something important happens in the game, such as when a sub-task starts or when there is new information available. If the mission lasts for 24 hours or longer, a partial result is presented halfway through the mission. Once a partial or a final result is available, the user is notified and asked to logon to the agent network. Then the player again meets Mr. Q, who provides feedback on both the individual player's work and on the team results. The player can also view individual and team performance statistics (Fig. 3, f, g and h).

Every real agent records his or her mission carefully. Hence, an important task for the energy agent is to document the conservation actions made in their homes. They are using the camera in the mobile phone for this purpose. These pictures are time stamped, mapped to the consumption data, and presented on a timeline after the end of the mission (Fig. 3f). In this way, the pictures serve as reminders of the actions and enable players to get feedback as to whether the things they have done had any effect on the electricity consumption.

4 Discussion

Traditional simulation games for learning have been questioned regarding whether learners are really able to generalize knowledge they acquire in a virtual game world and apply it to real life situations. This is a phenomenon referred to as knowledge transfer, and it is of central interest to researchers in pedagogical psychology. However, when performing the learning tasks in the real world, such as in the PowerAgent game, the mentioned uncertainty becomes, as we shall demonstrate, at least partially obsolete. The question here is not whether the game provides a sufficiently accurate simulation of the real world, but rather if the game supports both cognitive and behavioral learning, and if the acquired knowledge can be remembered and applied in similar situations.

Bandura has suggested that the highest level of learning can be achieved if the modeled behavior can first be symbolically (i.e., cognitively) *organized and rehearsed* and then *overtly enacted* [10; cf., 19]. We have attempted to make use of a similar two-stage model in PowerAgent. Essentially, PowerAgent can be looked upon as a hybrid game, since it has both virtual and pervasive gaming parts. The underlying idea is to let the users first play a simulation (platform) game on the phone to symbolically learn wanted behaviors, and then let them enact and rehearse these behaviors at home in the family context (the real-world tasks). Thus, in the real missions, the gamers can test the behaviors and get both direct and social feedback on their actions.

The first version of the game—the one presented in this paper—is limited in that the platform game does not show people performing the target behaviors (i.e., modeling via observation). Hence, the platform part of the game could probably be improved significantly by also allowing the players to catch "batteries" that contain video snippets of people illustrating proper energy conservation behaviors to support observational learning and cognitive modeling. Nevertheless, after conclusion of the platform game (using the model available in the present version), we deliberately provide time to prepare for and reflect on the upcoming real-world task. Being able to rehearse game scenarios and create strategies to solve problems are crucial factors that strengthen cognitive learning and lead to a positive outcome that reinforces the target behaviors [10].

We have also included a text chat function to support knowledge sharing among team members, which agrees with the situated learning theories that emphasize social collaboration to solve tasks. Further improvement might be achieved by including the means for video chatting or attaching movies clips in which gamers show each other how they deal with their missions, and that could strengthen social learning and peer modeling. We are currently performing a pilot study of the game at two sites in Scandinavia. Our goal is to investigate the concepts and the playability and to determine how we should empirically evaluate the cognitive and behavioral learning components.

5 Conclusion

In this paper, we present PowerAgent, a pervasive game designed to have a positive influence on energy consumption behaviors and activity patterns in the home. The principles underlying the design of the game were derived from situated learning and social learning theory. We believe that the two-stage model for learning, in which gamers observe target behaviors in a simulation game and subsequently enact these behaviors in the real world, is a promising persuasion strategy for future pervasive learning games.

Acknowledgements. The research was funded by the Swedish Energy Agency. The authors would like to thank Växjö Energi AB, Smedjebacken Energi & Vatten, and Mobile Interaction, Stockholm, Sweden.

References

1. Mayer, R.E. and Wittrock, M.C., Problem-solving transfer. I.D.C. Berliner & R.C. Calfee (Eds.), Handbook of educational psychology. Macmillan Library Reference USA, Prentice Hall International, New York, N.Y.
2. Gee, J.P.: What video games have to teach us about learning and literacy. Palgrave Macmillan, New York (2003)
3. Ramsden, P.: Student Learning Research: Retrospect and Prospect. Higher Education Research and Development 4(1), 51–69 (1985)
4. Brown, J.S., Collins, A., Duguid, P.: Situated cognition and the culture of learning. Educational Researcher, 32–42 (January-February, 1989)
5. Lave, J., Wenger, E.: Situated learning: Legitimate peripheral participation. Cambridge University Press (1991)
6. Fogg, B.J.: Persuasive Technology, Using Computers to Change What People Think and Do. Morgan Kaufman Publishers, San Francisco (2003)
7. de Vries, P.: Social presence as a conduit to the social dimensions of online trust. In: IJsselsteijn, W., de Kort, Y., Midden, C., Eggen, B., van den Hoven, E. (eds.) PERSUA-SIVE 2006. LNCS, vol. 3962, pp. 55–59. Springer, Heidelberg (2006)
8. Magerkurth, C., Cheok, A., Mandryk, R.L., Nilsen, T.: Pervasive games: bringing computer entertainment back to the real world. Computers and Entertainment 3(3), 4 (2005)
9. Thomas, S.: Pervasive learning games: Explorations of hybrid educational gamescapes. Simulation & Gaming 37(1), 41–55 (2006)
10. Bandura, A.: Social learning theory. general Learning press, New York (1977)
11. Bandura, A.: Social Cognitive Theory: An agentic perspective. Annual Review of Psychology 52, 1–26 (2001)
12. Electronic Arts Incorporated. Available at http://thesims.ea.com/
13. Botfighters. Last visited (September 30, 2005), http://www.botfighters.com
14. Lindt, I., Ohlenburg, J., Pankoke-Babatz, U., Prinz, W., Ghellal, S.: Combining Multiple Gaming Interfaces in Epidemic Menace. In: Conference on Human Factors in Computing Systems (CHI 2006), Montreal, Canada, April 24-27 (2006)
15. Sotamaa, O.: All The World's A Botfighter Stage: Notes on Location-based Multi-player Gaming. In: Mäyrä, F. (ed.) Computer Games and Digital Cultures: Conference Proceeding. Studies in Information Sciences, University of Tampere, pp. 35–44 (2002)

iParrot: Towards Designing a Persuasive Agent for Energy Conservation

Abdullah Al Mahmud[1], Pavan Dadlani[1], Omar Mubin[1], Suleman Shahid[1],
Cees Midden[2], and Oliver Moran[1]

[1] User-System Interaction, [2] Department of Human-Technology Interaction
Eindhoven University of Technology
P.O. Box 513, 5600 MB Eindhoven, The Netherlands
{A.Al-Mahmud,P.M.Dadlani,O.Mubin,S.Shahid,
C.J.H.Midden,O.P.Moran}@tm.tue.nl

Abstract. Computational agents can motivate people to change their behaviour towards energy use in a home setting. In this paper, we investigate the design and evaluation of the iParrot, an intelligent agent that helps to persuade family members to conserve energy in their home. The iParrot was designed as a concept in the form of a video prototype with two conditions. The results from the evaluation show that people will comply with the advice from such an agent for energy conservation if the agent is friendlier. Moreover, participants were able to distinctly perceive the friendliness level for both conditions.

1 Introduction

Energy conservation is a crucial and critical issue in today's modern society. Due to the improper management of electrical appliances in households, substantial energy is being wasted. Research results show that energy consumption in households is increasing day by day and changes in human behaviour are needed to save energy rather than just depending on technology. A behavioural coaching mechanism may help family members to change their behaviour towards energy saving. Persuasive technology has been deployed to motivate people to help them in behavioural change. For instance, direct feedback on energy conservation at home can help in a positive behavioural change [3, 4]. Even computer games have been used to grow environmental awareness and to enhance energy usage patterns [1].

Our goal is to design a persuasive agent that can encourage energy conservation in a home setting by offering feedback, advice, praise, and providing incentives. The feedback will be given in such a way that users perceive it to be supportive rather than dominating or possessive (controlling). Hence, characteristics of the agent are important prior to deploying it for persuasive means. There are factors that might influence the development of a successful user-agent relationship, for instance the agent's attractiveness, perceived competence, types of messages, persistency, etc. It is important to investigate the effect of user-agent interaction especially when the relationship is established for persuasive purposes.

A life-like embodied agent can help to change people's attitudes and behaviours [3]. Life-like agents can be seen as social actors [5] and consequently persuasion

Y. de Kort et al. (Eds.): PERSUASIVE 2007, LNCS 4744, pp. 64–67, 2007.

theories [8] were used in designing our persuasive agent: the iParrot. In this study, we wanted to investigate whether and under which conditions a user would comply and rely on the advice of the social agent. In particular, we focused on the role of friendliness of the agent.

2 Experiment

Participants. In total we had 30 participants (18 male and 12 female) divided equally over each condition. The participants were recruited through our personal network and email listing.

Design. The experiment was conducted as a simple two conditions between participants design. The friendliness of the iParrot (personality of the agent) was hence the independent variable. The main hypotheses were: (1) energy conservation advice from the iParrot agent seen as friendly will be rated more trustworthy than an unfriendly agent, and (2) energy conservation advice from the iParrot seen as competent will result in better compliance than an incompetent agent. For the experiment, we used two different variants of the video, which characterized our independent variable. We also wanted to explore gender effects, if any, and hence this outlined our second independent variable. In order to evaluate and measure trust and friendliness of the iParrot, a questionnaire was adapted from the scales (7-point Likert) devised by Warner and Sugarman [6]. The items from the questionnaire were also embedded with some dummy items. Besides a quantitative question (one 7-point item - 'I will comply with such a robot/agent'), a qualitative comment question was added to determine the compliance of the subjects with the iParrot's personality.

Procedure. The experiment was conducted either online or in a laboratory setting. In the second case, the facilitator welcomed the participant in the laboratory and left the laboratory before the participant started the experiment. For both cases a set of instructions was outlined, which the subjects read carefully before starting out with the experiment. Moreover, for both cases the video was shown on the online YouTube interface [7]. Each participant was given a particular type of video to view (each video lasted for approximately 5 minutes), followed by the questionnaire.

Apparatus and Materials. The videos were role-plays simulated by the researchers. The iParrot was a paper mock-up of a parrot and was depicted as the social agent. For both videos the scenarios and storyline used were identical, however, the personality of the iParrot was varied distinctly with regards to its friendliness.

Each video consisted of three scenes, each scene dealt with a different aspect related to energy conservation. The storyline was built around a character who owned the iParrot. The first scene portrayed the character leaving a television on standby mode and leaving the room. The second scene illustrated a similar situation, in which the character was shown to go for a nap leaving a laptop on standby mode. In the third scene, a conversation was demonstrated between the iParrot and the character regarding a competition related to energy conservation amongst the neighbourhood, in which the iParrot was shown to congratulate the character on being victorious in the competition. For each video type, the personality of the iParrot was modified. For Video A the iParrot was portrayed as a highly persistent agent (via various means) and at the same time having a rather annoying voice of a parrot. For example, in the case of the first scene, the iParrot would simply repeat what was being shown on the television, even though the television was on standby mode. The character was shown not to pay heed; the iParrot would then call on the character's cell phone and repeat the feed from the television on the phone. For the second scene the iParrot would generate the sound of typing on a keyboard in order to emphasize its persistence. For the last scene, the voice of the iParrot was the major persistent element. For Video B the iParrot was brought forward as more soft, calm (in voice), and less persistent. It did not employ the use of any of the drastic measures used in Video A.

3 Results and Discussion

Firstly, in order to adjudicate if the subjects understood and comprehended the difference between the two video conditions we performed a simple t-test comparison of means of the Unfriendly-Friendly item in the questionnaire. A significant difference was found between the two means of the item from the questionnaire scale (t (-2.046) =-1.054, p=.05). This confirmed that the participants in fact did perceive the difference with respect to friendliness between the two video scenarios (item mean of unfriendly video = 4.18, item mean of friendly video = 5.23).

The second part of our results evaluated the effect of gender as the second independent variable in our study. An Analysis of Variance (ANOVA) was executed in which gender and video type were the independent variables, and Unfriendly–Friendly, Untrustworthy–Trustworthy, and Perceived Competence were the measurements. Perceived Competence was taken as the mean of the following three items from the questionnaire: Ignorant–Knowledgeable, Irresponsible–Responsible and Unintelligent–Intelligent, (Cronbach Alpha = 0.709). Gender was found to have a significant influence on Perceived Competence (F (1.772) = 5.487, p = .027). The same setup was repeated for a user's compliance with the advice of the iParrot. Both gender and video type were found to have a significant effect on the willingness to comply with the iParrot, (F (11.416) = 4.293, p = .048) and (F (13.974) = 5.255, p = .030), respectively.

Lastly, we conducted a correlation analysis between our two dependent variables: Unfriendly–Friendly and Untrustworthy–Trustworthy; a relationship that extended from our hypothesis. A significant correlation was observed between the two variables (r = 0.530, p = .003). This ascertained the fact that the two main elements of our study, i.e. friendliness and trust, were significantly correlated and that subjects tended to trust an agent that was more friendly. Our quantitative results indicate that friendliness and trust indeed had an influence on people's willingness to comply with a social agent. Firstly, subjects did perceive the subtle difference between levels of friendliness, and secondly, they exhibited a tendency to comply with a rather friendlier agent. Therefore, we conclude that persuasiveness could have a cause-effect relationship with friendliness. By designing a friendly agent, indirectly, persuasiveness can be achieved. Gender was an interesting result: males tended to comply with the iParrot agent significantly more often than females (compliance mean of males = 4.56, compliance mean of females = 3.58).

During the laboratory experiments and online surveys, we extracted several valuable comments from the participants. Nearly all subjects appreciated the motivation of the design and expressed awareness towards energy conservation. Subjects stated a willingness to comply with the advice from such a parrot but they did not wish for it to be too dominant. From the qualitative remarks, we ascertained that the voice of the iParrot (or any social agent for that matter) is an important factor, as participants commented that the voice of the iParrot should be more cordial. There was also a suggestion from various participants that the iParrot might be useful for handicapped people. As an assistant, the iParrot played the role of parents according to some of the respondents. Respondents had mixed reactions about switching the iParrot off. Generally, if the iParrot would show an unfriendly and annoying behaviour, people would tend to switch it off more often. Others commented that the iParrot should interpret and identify the mood and context of the owner and switch itself off automatically. One suggestion was the inclusion of a snoozing function rather than switching the iParrot off.

The results from this study were obtained from a limited number of participants. However, the conclusions from this study suggest that there is potential in the deployment of a social agent in order to assist and persuade humans in energy conservation. Future exploration would be along the lines of building a more tangible and functional prototype of the iParrot and testing other persuasive factors such as trust and value similarity of the agent.

References

1. Bang, M., Torstensson, C., Katzeff, C.: The PowerHouse: A persuasive computer game designed to raise awareness of domestic energy consumption. In: IJsselsteijn, W. A, de Kort, Y.A.W., Midden, C.J.H., Eggen, B., van den Hoven, E.A.W.H. (eds.) PERSUASIVE 2006. LNCS, vol. 3962, pp. 123–132. Springer, Heidelberg (2006)
2. Fogg, B.J.: Persuasive Technology: Using Computers to Change What We Think and Do. Morgan Kaufmann Publishers, San Francisco (2003)
3. McCalley, T., Kaiser, F., Midden, C.J.H., Keser, M., Teunissen, M.: Persuasive appliances: Goal priming and behavioural response to product-integrated energy feedback. In: IJsselsteijn, W.A., de Kort, Y.A.W, Midden, C.J.H, Eggen, j.H, van den Hoven, E.A.W.H. (eds.) PERSUASIVE 2006. LNCS, vol. 3962, pp. 45–49. Springer, Heidelberg (2006)
4. McCalley, L.T., Midden, C.J.H.: Energy conservation through product-integrated feedback: The roles of goal-setting and social orientation. Journal of Economic Psychology 23-5, 589–603 (2002)
5. Reeves, B., Nass, C.: The Media Equation: How people treat computers, television, and new media like real people and places. Cambridge University Press, New York (1996)
6. Warner, R.M., Sugarman, D.B.: Attributes of Personality Based on Physical Appearance, Speech, and Handwriting. Journal of Personality and Social Psychology 50-4, 792–799 (1996)
7. YouTube. http://www.youtube.com/
8. Zimbardo, P.G., Leippe, M.R.: The Psychology of Attitude Change and Social Influence. McGraw-Hill, New York (1991)

The Pet Plant: Developing an Inanimate Emotionally Interactive Tool for the Elderly

Teddy McCalley and Alain Mertens

Human-Technology Interaction, Technical University Eindhoven, P.O. Box 513, IPO 1.32
5600 MB Eindhoven, The Netherlands
l.t.mccalley@tm.tue.nl

Abstract. The development of an interactive "pet" house plant could provide the same positive health support functions as a robotic pet, and with fewer problems, if it could be shown that an emotional attachment with a human was possible. This required that an inanimate living artifact (the plant) along with its pot, be accepted as stimulating emergent emotion. An experiment comparing an interactive, apparently aware, plant with a control was conducted in three retirement homes. Individuals were found to attribute emotions to the interactive plant that increased if the plant was described as having a character similar to that of the user. Results of the study support the conclusion that interactive plants have potential for further development as supportive companions to the elderly.

Keywords: Persuasive technology, emergent emotion, interactive technology, robotic pet, elderly, health, restorative.

1 Introduction

The study has been designed to explore whether the development of an interactive "pet" house plant that can generate an emotional attachment with a human is feasible. This study is part of a series designed to explore how emotional attachment to a living, but inanimate, artifact develops through human-object interaction. Psychological and physical factors that the human perceives as emotion and thereby motivates an individual to interact with a living, but immobile, objects are explored through a working prototype. The interactive plant is intended as a substitute for a companion animal (pet) in order to alleviate boredom, loneliness, stress and inactivity in residents of elderly care facilities where pets are not allowed. (In fact, the plant itself is not programmed to interact, but the pot, which is viewed as part of the potted house plant.) Robotic animal pets are currently being tested for therapeutic effects and have shown some promise [1], however there are some possible negative ethical, social and cultural aspects to their use that an interactive plant might avoid, or at least minimize. These are discussed in a later section.

Y. de Kort et al. (Eds.): PERSUASIVE 2007, LNCS 4744, pp. 68–79, 2007.
© Springer-Verlag Berlin Heidelberg 2007

2 Background

2.1 Emergent Emotion

According to several researchers in the field of interactive robotics [2], human beings subjectively attribute emotions to machines that respond to their environment in ways that the humans can interpret according to their own emotional responses. [3] gives the example of a simple mobile robot with two light sensors. In one case the robot senses a light source straight ahead and moves towards it until it collides with the source. In another case, the light source is not directly ahead of the robot so the robot turns towards the light source and continues towards it until it collides again. In this case the action can be interpreted by a human observer as aggressive - the robot "sees" an object and "attacks" it. In the first case, the human observer might see the robot as being stupid. Thus, both intelligence and emotions are subjectively attributed by the observer. This attribution of emotions to robotic behavior is referred to as emergent emotion.

2.2 Building a Relationship

Emergent emotion refers to the emotions and social characteristics a human attributes to the machine because of the machine's behavior. How the human reacts in return forms the other side of a dyadic relationship. The attribution of emotion prompts social responses by the human to the machine that is viewed by the human as a social actor [4] According to Bickmore and Picard [5], a relationship does not reside in one partner or the other, but in the pair's own unique pattern of interaction. This interaction can take several forms as there is no one definition of relationship. The forms of support that relationships can provide, and are of import to this study, include emotional support, attachment, feedback, self-esteem, and opportunities to nurture [6].

Physical embodiment and tactile interaction is also crucial to the building of a relationship between a human and a social agent (social robot) [7]. Lee et al. [7] conducted two experiments that compared social agents appearing on a computer screen with their robotic counterparts and found that the physical presence of the agent enhances its social presence as long as the participant is allowed to touch it. Experiment 2 also showed that the more lonely a person feels, the more intense the feeling of social presence when interacting with the social agent.

2.3 Robotic Pets

It is well established in the medical community that stress can lead to risk factors of heart failure. Recent research has proven that having a pet can reduce these risk factors in non-institutionalized older people by triggering feelings of relaxation, restfulness, reduced loneliness, and a lowering of blood pressure and cholesterol [8-10]. Unfortunately, because of hygienic aspects, physical hindrance, allergy, or fear for the concerns of other residents, pets are not usually allowed in elderly care facilities. Robot pets have therefore been developed in an attempt to substitute for real animals with some success. According to [11], a soft seal robot was successfully used to improve the mood of elderly people visiting a day service care center. Nonetheless, robot pets remain, on the whole, expensive and mechanically more complex and artificial as compared to the proposed pet plant. It is the artificiality that brings up ethical questions. According to an article by MacDonald [12], some experts see the use of robotic pets as cheap and inappropriate substitutes for necessary human interaction. Furthermore, one of the elderly interviewed for the MacDonald [12] article admitted to talking to the robot even when it was turned off. Although the comment was intended as amusing, many an elderly person has been threatened with loss of rights or institutionalization for less in some cultures.

Although solutions can probably be found for the above criticisms of robotic pets, the pet plant certainly holds some advantages. The pet plant is a living thing that does need care and is not artificial, and can also serve the function of a normal house plant. If, for some reason, the plant dies, it can be replaced easily as it is the pot that is interactive. Furthermore, the interactive pot needs far less electronics than a robot and is therefore less expensive and a plant cannot get underfoot. As plants are an acceptable part of most decors, it is doubtful that the pet plant will be seen as a substitute for human interaction, but more as a beneficially enhanced old friend. In fact, in some cultures, as in the U.S., talking or playing classical music to one's plant is acceptable behavior.

2.4 Therapeutic Plants

Research has long shown that plants can have restorative effects on humans. There is also research that suggests that plants too might offer some of the same benefits of pets, just through their presence. For example, a study by Lohr et al. [13] has shown that in office settings the presence of plants contributes to lower work-related stress, lower blood pressure, more relaxed muscles, and improved work efficiency and self-reported attentiveness. Shibata et. al [14] also reported that the presence of plants in a work environment enhanced performance on an associative task thereby suggesting that the presence of leafy plants also increased creative work performance.

Two studies described by Kaplan [15] show strong links to view content. The conclusion of the first study is that people with nature views showed greater job satisfaction and experienced fewer illnesses. The second study, held among 615 office employees, proved that those with a nature view felt less frustrated and more patient. They also found their job more challenging, were more enthusiastic and satisfied with their lives and experienced an overall better health. In addition, Laumann, et al. [16] conclude from their own studies that subjects watching a video depicting a natural environment had a significantly longer cardiac inter-beat interval compared to the baseline than subjects watching an urban environment on video. The video depicting natural environments had a relaxing effect on autonomic functions. In addition, Ulrich [17] reported that hospital patients with views of natural scenery recovered faster than ones with a view of brick buildings.

3 The Pet Plant

Taking into account the positive aspects of plants and the pros and cons of robotic pets, a hybrid between the two seems a logical step to take. Computational artifacts that are interpreted as social actors can take on any number of embodiments such as handheld electronics, clothing, jewelry, as well as the more familiar robotics and embodied software agents. It is our belief that movement of an object is not necessary for human attribution of emotions to occur. For example, people tend to like computers more when the computers match their personality [5]. Fogg and Nass [18] have also shown that the effects of flattery from computers are the same as from humans. This implies a perceived emotional interaction between the machine and the human.

Fogg [19] lists five types of social cues for persuasive social actors: physical, psychological, language, social dynamics, and social roles. Of these, the pet plant prototype was designed to incorporate the latter four. 1) Psychological: The major psychological social cue chosen for the plant was similarity. Both Norman [20] and Fogg [19] cite similarity as one of the strongest personality traits with studies showing that people are more persuaded by computing technology products that they perceive as being similar to them in some way [19]. The means by which the pet plant could be made similar was to give it a "birth certificate" describing personality traits it was "born" with. 2) Language: According to Nass et al. [21] praise from a computer can produce the same effect as praise from humans. By offering praise via symbols the Pet Plant might make the user more open to persuasion. Light intensity in the pot was the "language" used to communicate the need for, and appreciation of, attention. 3) Social dynamics: According to [22] the rule of reciprocity is a universal concept. Fogg [19] describes research showing that people feel the need to reciprocate when technology has done them a favor, the same as if the technology was a person. It was therefore anticipated that if the plant was seen to help its user to relax, the user would feel the need to reciprocate, thereby setting up an emotional relationship. 4) Social roles: Fogg [19] also states that people who perceive a technology as being an authority are more susceptible to persuasion by that technology. Thus the plant was designed to have the social role of a pet. When people have the plant as pet, it was expected that they would respond to the plant as a pet as long as it was able to respond to them in return. The plant was also designed to respond to touch, allowing for a physical interaction shown to enhance social presence as described by Lee et al. [7]. This sort of physical interaction via touch is different from the physical social cues, such as facial expression, outlined by Fogg [19]. The main hypothesis to be tested was as follows:

H 1: Do people attribute more emotions to the pet plant than to a plant that does not respond to human presence or action?

As Fogg [19] stated, "A computer's persuasiveness is stronger when it has a greater similarity with its user." Therefore, we chose to additionally investigate if the same principle applied to the pet plant. This resulted in two sub-hypotheses:

H 1a: Do people attribute more emotions to the pet plant if it has characteristics similar to the user?

H 1b: Do people like the pet plant more if it has similar characteristics?

4 Method

4.1 Participants

Participants were 62 residents of three retirement homes in the region of Eindhoven, The Netherlands, ranging in age from 66 to 89 years (mean age = 78.4).

4.2 Design

The experiment had four conditions: (1) personality – matched (2) personality - unmatched (3) responsive (no definite personality) (4) random response (control). Each group had a minimum of 13 participants. Six persons who were neither definitely introvert nor extrovert according to the personality test (see below) and could thus not be used for either personality test group were randomly but evenly distributed into the two remaining groups as extra participants. Their data was used only for the overall analysis of whether or not the control condition group was different from the responsive plant groups, as described later.

4.3 Procedure

The experiment took place in the common 'living' room area of each retirement facility where a small portion had been partitioned off for the study. The total procedure consisted of three parts: a pre-user test questionnaire, interactive experiment, and a post-user test questionnaire. The four experimental conditions were as follows:

Control Plant: blinked and changed light intensity in a random fashion. Which color it blinked or intensified was also random. This means that it did not respond to human presence or actions (in a coherent fashion).

Light Plant: (Figure 1) responded to touch (intensity of the green LEDs increases gradually as subjects hold the plant pot), speech (green LEDs blink according to the volume of the subject's voice) and touching its leaves (same as touching the plant pot, but also the red LEDs intensify gradually; creating a 'blush'). As the subjects stop touching the pet plant, the light intensity diminished gradually to its original state.

Similar Plant and Dissimilar Plant: were basically the same as the Light Plant. However they conveyed a certain character (extrovert or introvert) through a birth certificate that was presented to the subjects before they engaged in interaction with the plant. In this condition the pet plant was either similar or dissimilar to the subjects. The subject was aware of the character of the plant because the pet plant had a birth certificate attached. The plant's characteristics were based on the traits defined by Monson et al. [23]. The extrovert plant had the following traits; outgoing, sociable, energetic, confident, talkative, dominant and enthusiastic. The extrovert plant is confident and relaxed in social situations and rarely has trouble making conversations with others. The introvert plant is shy, timid, reserved, quiet, distant, submissive and retiring. The introvert plant is awkward and not at ease in social situations and is not adept in making good conversations with others.

Participants were first told about possible advantages of caring for both pets and plants, and that these two are combined in the pet plant because it is not always possible to keep real animals in retirement homes. When the subject agreed to join the experiment, they first filled in a questionnaire. This questionnaire consisted of a list of general questions (name, gender etc.) and a list of questions with regard to the degree the subject is extrovert or introvert as described by Monson et al. [23]. The answers to the questions were bipolar. When the average score of this questionnaire was below or equal to 2.5, the participant was scored as introvert. When the average score was

Fig. 1. The Pet Plant as it appears in a resting state

equal or higher than 3.5, the participant was scored as extravert. When the score was between 2.5 and 3.5, the participant was labeled as being neutral and added as extra participants to groups 1 and 2 so as not to make them feel unacceptable. (The participants labeled neutral were excluded from the statistical analyses comparing the similar and dissimilar groups.)

Participants were randomly assigned to one of four conditions. In case of conditions three and four, participants were instructed to read the matching birth certificate before engaging interaction with the pet plant. The experiment consisted of three small tasks which were explained to each participant by someone of the experiment staff (because elderly people have difficulty reading or hearing sometimes). Subjects had to perform the following tasks: holding the plant pot, touching the leaves, and having a conversation with the plant. The prototype's behavior was controlled using a Wizard of Oz setup. This means that the plant did not respond by itself, but was controlled from a distance by one of the experiment staff through two hidden dials. The plant's behavior however remained consequent.

After the participants had successfully performed the tasks they were asked to fill in the post-user test questionnaire. The goal of this questionnaire was to find out if people attribute emotions to the pet plant and if similarity is of any importance in their judgment of the pet plant. To find out whether people attribute emotions to the pet plant, and to find out if they experience emotions when interacting with the pet plant, one has to measure the covert responses. Covert responses were measured by self reports of thought, feelings, needs and desires [24]. The participants in the pet plant experiment had to fill in a self-report in the form of a questionnaire (Table 1). A part of the questionnaire was based on the questionnaire used by Nass, et al. [21]. Nass, et al. [21] asked participants about team relationship, similarity to computer, cooperativeness, openness to influence, information quality, friendliness of information and behavioral conformity. The questionnaire used in the pet plant experiment uses similarity to the plant, information quality and behavioral conformity. Respondents responded to the statement by choosing one of the five alternatives as proposed by Likert [25].

Two pilot studies had earlier been conducted to check for errors in the design of the experiment. Participants were students at the Eindhoven University of Technology. The current experiment setup resulted from these two studies.

5 Results

Using Factor Analysis, questions 7 through 12 were used to establish the dependent variable, attributed emotion (Cronbach's Alpha .90). ANOVA was used to test whether there was a difference between the control plant and the three other plant conditions using the responsive plant and the responsive plant with a similar or dissimilar personality description. Hypothesis 1 was confirmed. With an alpha level of .05 set for all analyses, the effect of attributed emotion was statistically significant, $F (5, 52) = 9.0$, $p = .000$. The effect of the plant's similarity to the user (Hypothesis 1a) was tested using post hoc analysis (LSD). All responsive conditions were significantly different from the control (Figure 2) but not from each other and therefore Hypothesis 1a was rejected.

Table 1.

Questions
1. I feel like I want to give the plant attention.
2. I find the plant fun/pleasing.
3. I would be sad if the plant died.
4. The plant amuses me.
5. The plant makes me feel good.
6. I have the feeling that the plant has the same character as I do.
7. I have the feeling that the plant reacts to my presence.
8. I have the feeling that the plant understands me.
9. I have the feeling that the longs for attention.
10. I have the feeling that the plant likes to receive attention.
11. I have the feeling that the plant recognizes me.
12. I have the feeling that the plant is disappointed when it doesn't get attention.

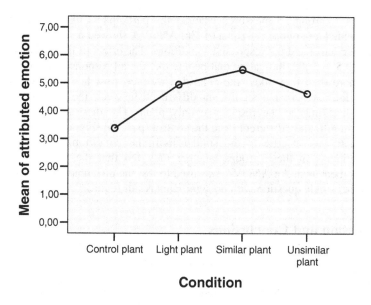

Fig. 2. All responsive plant conditions were significantly different from the control plant ($p = .005$, $p = .000$, $p = .03$, respectively)

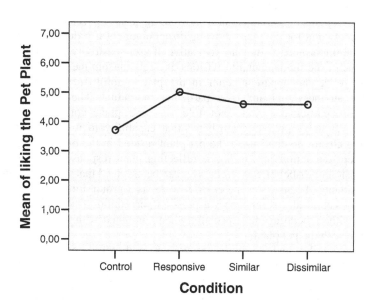

Fig. 3. The responsive plant conditions, light plant and similar plant were significantly different from the control plant ($p = .002$, $p = .03$, respectively) but the difference between the control and the dissimilar plant did not reach significance ($p = .06$)

Questions 1 through 5 measured whether the participants liked the plant. Factor Analysis yielded a Cronbach's Alpha 0f .86. ANOVA showed a significant difference between the control and the responsive conditions. The effect of liking was significant $F (3, 53) = 3.5$, $p = .02$, indicating that people like the all responsive conditions of the pet plant more than they liked the control. However, post hoc comparisons of the conditions did not reveal a significant difference between the plant conditions of similar or dissimilar to the responsive only plant. The dissimilar plant was only marginally significantly different from the control ($p = .06$) (Figure 3).

Question 6 was specific to the similar/dissimilar conditions reported later and asked participants in these groups whether they felt that the plant had the same character as their own. An ANOVA was used to test the difference between these two groups on this single question with no significant result found.

6 Discussion and Conclusions

The focus of this project was to discover whether a therapeutic pet plant that generates attribution of emotions is feasible. A prototype was built that allowed for basic interactions with humans, based on their presence and actions (touch and speech) and was used in a series of user tests. The dependent variable, attributed emotion, designed to test whether the user attributes emotion to the plant, was found to be highly significant leading to the acceptance of the main hypothesis that participants attributed emotion to the responsive pet plant. Looking at the questions forming the dependent variable, those attributing a strong desire of the plant for getting attention and for the plant showing disappointment if it does not get attention, are of special importance as they are indicative of user sensitivity to an opportunity to nurture – one of the fundamental provisions of a relationship mentioned earlier [5,6]. The others reflect an apparent belief in the plant's ability to recognize both the presence of an individual and of a particular individual. The latter is especially interesting as participants were not told that the plant could recognize them specifically yet they apparently attributed that capability to it. This suggests that, although the electronic controls of the pet plant resided in the pot, participants were able to accept the actions of the pot as reflecting plant response. It is possible that their suspension of disbelief was strong as it can be assumed that the participants, who were all residents of homes for the elderly, were, as a group, lonely. This loneliness, as shown by Lee et al. [7], enhances a person's perception of social presence when interacting with a social agent, especially when combined with tactile interaction as was the case with the pet plant.

When the similar and dissimilar groups were directly compared on whether participants recognized their own characteristics in the plant as, described in the attached personality descriptions ("birth certificates"), they were not found to be significantly different. It was thus not surprising those participants who had interacted with a pet plant having a birth certificate that described personality traits similar to their own did not attribute more power of personal recognition to the plant or ability to the plant for understanding the user. Nonetheless, the post hoc comparisons of the dependent variable of likeability of the plant (that was significant overall) showed that only the plainly responsive plant and the plant similar to participants were significantly different from the control group. The dissimilar group was not significantly different from the control regarding likeability. This suggests that perhaps the method of making the plant similar to the participants was not adequate and thus did not awaken strong enough feelings to clearly support earlier findings such as those of Fogg [19]. However, the fact that the similar group was significantly different from the control in this respect does point in the direction of support for individuals preferring social actors that they consider to be like themselves. Certainly further research is needed to clarify this issue and perhaps identify particular contexts where similarity is of particular importance.

Taking into consideration the overall results of the study, the initial prototype of the pet plant successfully evidenced emergent emotion leading us to conclude that interactive plants can have potential to further development to serve as supportive companions. Bickmore and Picard [5] state that even routine interactions, such as the ones with the current prototype, can been seen as contributing to a relationship that does not reside in one partner or the other, but in the pair's unique pattern of interaction. A unique pattern of interaction calls for a prototype that has emotional behavior and recognizes (patterns in) the care giver's behavior.

The current prototype is not skilled enough for this sort of recognition; it is therefore recommended that other projects are initialized to develop the pet plant further. Once it has these skills we can talk of a matured and stronger concept, which has great potential of being an alternative to animal pets. Of course the term 'pet' can be put into a broader perspective, since advanced technology allows them to become actively involved in daily life in numerous ways. Think for instance of a personal coach that motivates people to become more active. Or what about a pet plant that makes elderly feel more secure. Both might improve the overall quality of life.

Further recommendations are a series of long-term user tests to investigate how a plant-human relationship develops over time. Repetitiveness and boredom are also of interest. Other issues include investigation of ethical objections regarding 'social' technologies, and the boundaries, and contextual influences on the boundaries, of human acceptance of advice from the pet plant as well as from any other interactive artifact serving as a social actor.

Acknowledgements

The authors wish to thank students Annet Zaagman, Harm Wijnja, Marijke Vos and Xandra Bronckers for their invaluable assistance with piloting and data collection and all subjects who kindly volunteered for the study.

References

1. Wada, K., Shibata, T., Saita, T., Tanie, K.: Analysis of factors that bring mental effects to elderly people in robot assisted activity. IEEE/RSJ International Conference on Intelligent Robots and Systems 2, 1152–1157 (2002)
2. Kriglstein, S., Wallner, G.: HOMIE: An artificial companion for elderly people. In: Proceedings, CHI 2005, Portland, Oregon, USA, April 2-7, pp. 2094–2098 (2005)

3. Shibata, T., Tashima, T., Tanie, K.: Emergence of emotional behavior through physical interactionbetween human and robot. In: R Proceedings, IEEE International Conference on Dept. of Robot, Detroit, MI, USA, May 10-15, pp. 2868–2873 (1999)

4. Nass, C., Moon, Y.: Machines and mindlessness: Social responses to computers. Journal of Social Issues 56(1), 81–103 (2000)

5. Bickmore, T.W., Picard, R.W.: Establishing and maintaining long-term human-computer relationships. ACM Transactions on Computer-Human Interaction 12(2), 293–327 (2005)

6. Berscheid, E., Reis, H.T.: Attraction and close relationships. In: Gilbert, D.T., Fiske, S.T., Lindzey, G. (eds.) The Handbook of Social Psychology, 4th edn., pp. 193–281. McGraw-Hill, New York (1998)

7. Lee, K.M., Jung, Y., Kim, J., Kim, S.R.: Are physically embodied social agents better than disembodied social agents?: The effects of physical embodiment, tactile interaction, and peoples' loneliness in human-robot interaction. International Journal of Human-Computer Studies 64, 962–973 (2006)

8. Raina, P., Waltner-Toews, D., Bonnett, B., Woodward, C., Abernathy, T.: Influence of companion animals on the physical and psychological health of older people: An analysis of a one-year longitudinal study. Journal of the American Geriatric Society 47(3), 323–329 (1999)

9. Beck, A.M., Meyers, N.M.: Health enhancement and companion animal ownership. Annual Review of Public Health 17, 247–257 (1996)

10. Vormbrock, J.K., Grossberg, J.M.: Cardiovascular effects of human-pet dog interactions. Journal of Behavioral Medicine 11(5), 509–517 (1988)

11. Shibata, T., Wada, K., Tanie, K.: Tabulation and analysis of questionnaire results of subjective evaluation of seal robot in Japan, U.K., Sweden and Italy. Intelligent Syst. Inst., Nat. Inst. of Adv. Ind. Sci. & Technol., Tsukuba, Japan.This paper appears In: R, 2004. Proceedings. ICRA '04. 2004 IEEE International Conference on Robotics and Automation, April 26-May 1, vol.2, pp. 1387–1392 (2004)

12. MacDonald, J.: The Christian Science Monitor (February 5, 2004), www.aaai.org/AITopics/html/video.html

13. Lohr, V.I., Pearson-Mims, C.H., Goodwin, G.K.: Interior plants may improve worker productivity and reduce stress in a windowless environment. J. Environmental Horticulture 14, 97–100 (1996)

14. Shibata, S., Suzuki, N.: Effects of the foliage plant on task performance and mood. Journal of Environmental Psychology 22, 265–272 (2002)

15. Kaplan, R.: The nature of the view from home. Environment and Behavior 4, 507–542 (2001)

16. Laumann, K., Gärlin, T., Stormark, K.M.: Selective attention and heart rate responses to natural and urban environments. Journal of Environmental Psychology 23, 125–134 (2003)

17. Ulrich, R.S.: View through a window may influence recovery from surgery. Science 224, 420–421 (1984)

18. Fogg, B.J., Nass, C.: Silicon sycophants: the effects of computers that flatter. International Journal of Human-Computer Studies 46, 551–561 (1997)

19. Fogg, B.J.: Persuasive Technology: Using Computers to Change What we Think and Do. Amsterdam, Morgan Kaufmann (2002)

20. Norman, W.T.: Toward an adequate taxonomy of personality attributes: Replicated factor structure in peer nomination personality ratings. Journal of Abnormal and Social Psychology 66, 574–583 (1963)

21. Nass, C., Fogg, B.J., Moon, Y.: Can computers be teammates? International Journal of Human-Computer Studies 45, 669–678 (1996)

22. Gouldner, A.W.: The norm of reciprocity: A preliminary statement. American Sociological Review 25, 161–1778 (1960)
23. Monson, et al.: In: Ajzen, I., Milton-Keynes (eds.) Attitudes, Personality and Behavior, Open University Press, England (1982)
24. Ajzen, I.: In: Milton-Keynes (ed.) Attitudes, personality and behavior, Open University Press, England (2005)
25. Likert, R.: A Technique for the Measurement of Attitudes. Archives of Psychology 140, 55 (1932)

Distributed User Experience in Persuasive Technology Environments

Katarina Segerståhl and Harri Oinas-Kukkonen

Department of Information Processing Science, University of Oulu,
Linnanmaa, FIN-90570 Oulu, Finland
{Katarina.Segerstahl,Harri.Oinas-Kukkonen}@oulu.fi

Abstract. An increasing number of persuasive technology systems consist of multiple devices that enable efficient just-in-time interaction with the user. Developing multi-device systems to support a human activity bring about new challenges for interaction and user experience design. The main challenge identified in this paper is the successful designing of coherent user experience, which may improve user acceptance and have a positive effect on the overall persuasiveness of the system. This paper analyses a multi-device heart-rate monitoring environment to illustrate the target of our research. We propose the notion of *distributed user experience* as a key concept for studying the design of efficient persuasive technology systems consisting of multiple devices.

Keywords: Distributed user experience, distributed user interface, heart-rate monitoring, multi-device systems, persuasive technology.

1 Introduction

Computing is shifting from the traditional desktop environment towards a network of increasingly distributed interactive devices [15]. Instead of monolithic *all-power-in-one* devices, computing products of the future will more likely support multi-device environments constituting an ambient infrastructure, mobile and stationary devices and wearables. The devices will have specific roles and functions in holistic systems that require interconnectivity, wireless connections and consistency. Recent developments in nomadic computing have resulted in various multi-device systems and distributed user interfaces [9], [14], [15]. Systems of these kinds have also emerged in the context of persuasive technology. Lyytinen and Yoo [10] define several approaches and research questions for studying this, which they call nomadic computing. Among the key research questions related to individual-level services are how to design and integrate sets of personalized mobile services that support users' task execution in multiple social and physical contexts, and how to understand usability in mobile contexts populated by a variety of devices.

Persuasive technology is designed with the intent to change a particular aspect of human behaviour in a predefined way [4], [5]. One of the most important current targets for persuasive technology is the promoting of healthy behaviour [6]. According to the World Health Organization [19], one of the major risk factors for health is the lack of physical activity. The focus of this study is on multi-device

Y. de Kort et al. (Eds.): PERSUASIVE 2007, LNCS 4744, pp. 80–91, 2007.

systems that support and motivate physical activity. Examples of such systems include:

- The *Nike + iPod* system, which uses music to motivate running. The system consists of a portable mp3 player, a running sensor and a Web service to support follow-up activities.
- The *Nokia 5500 Sport Phone,* a mobile phone managed with a PC application which is designed for sports enthusiasts, to support exercising tasks.
- The *Polar heart rate monitoring systems,* which are designed to support physical exercising and consist of a wrist unit, a mobile application and a PC application or Web service.

A multi-device system enables the optimal configuration of interaction devices for each major task context and a suite of technology that interacts with the user throughout the activity. We define *distributed user experience (DUX)* as covering the user's overall experience of interaction with a system consisting of two or more devices or interfaces for carrying out the user's intended tasks. This paper aims at identifying the key aspects of a distributed user experience in multi-device persuasive technology environments that support physical activity. The problem is addressed in terms of the following research questions:

1. How does a coherent distributed user experience promote persuasive interaction throughout a human activity?
2. What are the main challenges in providing a coherent distributed user experience?

The next section will discuss the conceptual background for a distributed user experience, section three will describe an exploratory case study consisting of multi-device persuasive systems known as the Polar F55 fitness system and Polar RS800sd training system, and the final section will summarize the main findings, draw conclusions and discuss future research.

2 Conceptual Background

Model-based support for designing distributed user interfaces or multi-device systems has been studied mainly from a technology point of view [3], [14], [15] whereas here we put more emphasis on the user experience and concentrate on how to enhance the persuasiveness of multi-device systems. The ways in which a user perceives interactions with the system and experiences different persuasive strategies may vary with the task context and with time, but an understanding of the overall user experience may contribute to better design. When studying user experience it becomes very important to obtain an understanding of the main concepts related to users' goals and expectations, which are closely related to the activities that they carry out [20]. Work and activity are concepts that appear in slightly different contexts in the literature. Welie & Veer [18] define *work* as the overall concept, whereas Kaptelinin et al. [7] refer to Activity Theory and define the main unit of analysis as *activity.* Activity consists of a subject, an object (goal, motive), artifacts (tools) and sociocultural rules. *Actions* are processes that need to be carried out in order to reach *goals* that direct the activity. In this paper actions and their goals are referred to as *tasks,* which is a common approach in the HCI literature. An activity and its tasks can be carried out within different temporal or physical contexts, constituting different task sets [7], [9]. The operational level is considered to be the lowest level of activity. Operations define the way in which a task is performed [7]. In the context of persuasive technology we perceive the operational level as the behaviour that is the object of persuasive intents. By mediating tasks within human activity, persuasive technology aims at changing the operational level in such a way that it modifies the behaviour to support the overall activity.

2.1 Multi-device Systems

An *integrative perspectives* approach, proposed by Kuutti and Bannon [8], is presented for investigating the concept of user interface. Based on conceptual and theoretical research into information systems, they identify three levels of abstraction for an interface: the work process or use situation level, the conceptual level and the technological level. One interpretation on the work process level is that "the interface is the system", while on the conceptual level the interface can be defined as "something that must be understood and mastered in order to use the system meaningfully for some purpose in some definite situation". The conceptual level implies the requirements for semantic coherence in the interface. The technological level can be seen as the configuration of interaction resources and devices.

In this paper we choose to adopt this integrative perspectives approach, which implies that despite multiple devices, contexts and tasks, the user interacts with a single interface (a system) that is designed to support a specific activity. A distributed user interface is an optimal configuration of interaction devices for supporting a specific activity and its tasks. An interaction device may be a desktop computer, a mobile phone, a personal digital assistant (PDA), or a wearable such as a heart rate monitor [17]. Although the performance of the overall activity is supported by several devices, user experience of the system should be perceived as a whole.

2.2 Distributed User Experience

Technology acceptance researchers have traditionally focused on a system's capability to help the user to achieve his/her goals, and have regarded an information system as acceptable simply if it is used, or if there is an intention to use it. However, to gain a deeper understanding of user experience the traditional focus should be broadened to cover aspects such as aesthetics, pleasure, affection and emotions, which have an impact on the overall experience [11]. It is also important to recognize that persuasive intents and strategies are rather sensitive to how people perceive them. If the user experience in a persuasive technology environment is disturbed, it is reasonable to assume that the efficiency of persuasion may suffer [20].

Csikszentmihalyi [2] suggests that a key concept in the study of user experience is *flow*. This is described as the optimal experience. The term originates from psychology, but it has also been applied in information systems research to study user experience [2], [13]. According to Csikszentmihalyi, flow is a mental state of operation in which the person is fully immersed in what he or she is doing, characterized by a feeling of energized focus, full involvement and success in the process concerned. An important prerequisite for experiencing a state of flow is a perceived congruency of skills and challenges that rises above a critical threshold. Oinas-Kukkonen [13] has defined flow in the context of web information systems as an optimal experience that can be predicted by using the key aspects constituting it, such as user's skills and perceived challenges, which can be kept above a critical threshold with the help of a proper set of system features. In multi-device environments the challenges for users' skills become more diverse as the mastering of different interaction devices is needed. Challenges in perceiving information in varying formats (different sizes, colours, and symbols vs. text depending on the resources) within the different contexts of the activity may also have an unpredictable impact on user experience.

To clarify the contents and relations of the concepts discussed here, we present a figure describing aspects of distributed user experience (see Figure 1). The different layers provide perspectives that can be adopted for analysing factors that may have an impact on user experience, such as goals, expectations, emotions and skills [11], [20], [13]. The analysis may be structured by recognising three layers, which are (from top to bottom) human activity, context and technology. The human activity layer represents tasks and task sets that can be identified within various contexts (social, physical or chronological), and the context layer is connected to the technology layer, which represents the distribution of interaction devices in relation to the activity. Both the activity and the overall user experience are temporally structured (from left to right). Learning, changes in behaviour or attitudes and overall user acceptance can be analysed from a temporal point of view.

Some studies have addressed the user experience in multi-device environments. Trimeche et al. [16] discuss the enhancement of end-user experience in a multi-device ecosystem, but our approach differs from theirs in that it is specialized to the kind of distributed user experience that mediates a holistic activity in the context of persuasive technology. Distributed user experience means the user's experience (attitudes, emotions and affect) upon interacting with a technology environment that

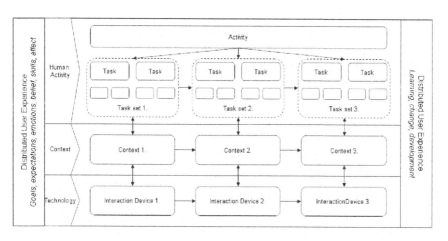

Fig. 1. Main perspectives for analysing a DUX

consists of multiple interaction devices. This interaction takes place within an activity that is temporally and contextually distributed and therefore initially motivates a multi-device approach for full support.

Persuasion, training and experience are important factors in the way users perceive technology and accept innovations [20]. How to support users' adoption of information technology in the first place and in the long term is an important aspect to consider in the context of user experience. When designing persuasive technology, strategies need to be considered at two levels. The primary level is how to persuade the user to accept the technological innovation, and only after that do the persuasive strategies used in human-system interaction become relevant [20].

2.3 Persuasive Technology

Persuasion is a social influence mechanism, or a form of interaction that aims at changing the way people think or behave [5], [20]. The persuasive technology paradigm is important for defining the interaction structures of systems supporting a healthy lifestyle. Fogg [4] lists the key terms and concepts of persuasive technology as: (1) an attempt to change attitudes or behaviour or both without coercion or deception, (2) a focus on human computer interaction, (3) a focus on planned persuasive effects, (4) a focus on endogenous or 'built-in' persuasive intent, which means that a system is intentionally designed to persuade, and (5) persuasion that may take place at either the macro or the micro level.

Some key persuasion principles have been suggested by Fogg [4]: reduction, tunnelling, tailoring, suggestion, self-monitoring, surveillance and conditioning. These principles are referred to further in this paper and will therefore be explained briefly at this point. *Reduction* means using technology to simplify complex tasks. The aim of this strategy is to make the desired behaviour more tempting by making it easier for the user. *Tunnelling* means guiding the user by leading him/her through a predefined sequence of actions. This strategy will be demonstrated in the next section on cases. *Tailoring* means using personalized and individually relevant information to change attitudes or behaviour or both. Tailoring has been acknowledged as one of the most potential persuasive strategies in e-commerce and it will also come up in our discussion on further research. *Suggestion* is an efficient principle in persuasion, although it is somewhat difficult to apply. Successful suggestion requires intervening in the activity at 'opportune moments', which means interacting with the user at the right time and in the right context and place. *Self-monitoring* is allowing people to monitor themselves and learn from information on their actions in order to change their behaviour. *Surveillance* technology is based on the overt monitoring of other people's behaviour, and *conditioning* means using the principles of operant conditioning to change behaviour. An interesting example of persuasion regarding the two final strategies is rewarding. This can roughly be identified as an act containing the principles of operant conditioning and as an act based on surveillance. Surveillance and conditioning are both strategies containing an extrinsically motivating emphasis, which is to some extent contradictory to the idea of persuasion and intrinsically motivated actions.

Social persuasion is another important factor in motivating healthy behaviour. Healthy lifestyles are strongly promoted in the media, education, leisure and health care sectors. Activities are usually linked to influential social factors such as being part of a group or collectivity (fitness club, weight watching group, school etc.), which often creates peer pressure and motivating or discouraging interactions. It is important to identify the impact of these social factors on user experiences in order to understand the nature of health-related information systems in a broader context.

3   Case: The Polar RS800sd and F55 Training Systems

Our case is based on the Polar RS800sd training system and the Polar F55 fitness system which are both designed to support the activity of physical exercising. The heart-rate monitor is traditionally perceived as a single device that provides feedback during physical activity. In our approach, this technology is viewed as a multi-device information system that is designed to interact with the user before, during and after physical activity (see Figure 2).

Fig. 2. An example of a multi-device system consisting of a wearable monitor (wrist unit), the desktop environment (a Web service and/or PC application) and a mobile application

3.1   The System Environment

The main characteristics of the activity and system environment may be outlined as planning, exercising and follow-up or analysis. The *planning tasks* usually take place at home, at a fixed workstation or on a laptop. Planning is supported by a Web service and PC software which can be used for the more complex tasks. It is important that the devices used *during exercise* should be small, unobtrusive, light-weight, portable and highly durable. During exercise, the wrist units and/or the mobile application provide feedback and guidance in performance. *Follow-up* is carried out at different levels. The user can view his/her performance on the wrist unit immediately after the exercise, and exercises can also be viewed with a mobile phone, which allows more graphics and space for information displays than the wrist unit. Detailed analysis can be carried out using the Web service or PC software, which provide the widest range of resources regarding the display, memory, graphical user interface and connectivity. The basic persuasive strategy that both of the following systems are based on is *self-monitoring*. Monitoring, documenting and visualizing progress and performance are important aspects in motivating and supporting goal-oriented exercising activities.

Suggestion For Exercise. The persuasive strategy of *suggestion* can be identified in the *event* and *trophy* features of the wrist units. These features are intended to be suggestive in the sense that they offer the user a reminder, a motivation for exercising in contexts other than exercise. In the RS800sd the user can specify an event that he/she is aiming at with the activity, which is then displayed on the wrist unit while it is being used as a wrist watch (see Figure 3, left). The trophy (see Figure 3, right) in the F55 is a reward that is granted to the user after he/she has reached his/her personal training targets.

Fig. 3. The event (*left*) and trophy (*right*) are displayed on the wrist unit when it is used in the watch mode to remind the user of his/her motivation for the overall activity

When used as a watch logo, the trophy may be perceived as a suggestive element, but rewarding by means of the trophy can also be identified as an act reflecting the classic principles of operant conditioning. Collecting information regarding the user's exercising and using it as a reward can also be seen as a form of surveillance. The rewarding feature, the trophy in this case, is difficult to identify with only one persuasive strategy as outlined by Fogg [4].

Supporting Planning Tasks. Supporting planning tasks by providing tools for generating fitness programmes or for planning complex interval exercises can be considered an application of the *reduction* principle. The computer environment enables the use of colours and graphs for visualizing exercise plans and training programmes. Visualization in this case means formulating a graphical presentation or image of a process or object which helps to conceptualize the task at hand. (See Figure 4)

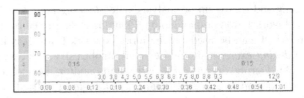

Fig. 4. Visualization of an interval-based exercise planned in the PC application

A personalized fitness programme can be generated based on the user's current fitness level and his/her personal targets. Offering the user a customized training programme is an application of the persuasion principle of *tailoring*. In the Web service the user can modify the programme, change exercising days and specific exercise targets and plan his/her own exercises, which is simultaneously both an indication of the limitations of 'tailored' programmes and a reference to the reduction strategy.

Guidance Throughout Exercise. The user is instructed in several ways during exercising, e.g. to slow down if his/her heart rate or speed rises above a predefined limit. The wrist unit provides feedback that corresponds to the targets defined by the fitness programme or the planned interval exercises. Guidance can also be based on the *OwnZone* feature, which measures and analyses the user's heart rate variability at the beginning of the exercise and suggests suitable limits for the exercise. This is an interesting example of the use of physiological information in *tailoring*. The wrist unit and the mobile application include a weight training programme which is a series of movements presented in a recommended order of performance. Guiding the user through the exercises can be identified as *tunnelling* in terms of persuasive technology (see Figure 5).

Fig. 5. Monitor displays (RS800sd) during exercises present context-sensitive information such as heart rate, speed, phase number, number of repeats, start, stop and duration

Self-Monitoring and Follow-Up. After the exercise the user can view summaries of his/her performance on the wrist unit. In order to proceed with more detailed analysis and more complex follow-up tasks, the exercise data need to be transferred to the Web service or the PC software. Various reports can be generated from exercise data collected over time. Supporting follow-up and detailed analysis is an important part of the overall activity, as planning and future exercising is often based on previous performance.

3.2 Persuasive Technology and DUX

We summarize our case and the aspects of DUX in table 1. The structure of the activity is presented as planning, training and follow-up. The context can be interpreted diagonally as a combination of the activity phase and the corresponding interaction device presented in the technology column on the left. The contents of the table presents the role of persuasive strategies in relation to the different aspects or perspectives of DUX.

Three things can be deduced from this table: (1) the different interaction devices play specific roles at different phases in the activity, (2) their functionalities are also partially overlapping in relation to the activity phases, and (3) persuasive strategies are used in all the devices that constitute the technology-supported training environment. When designing the systems described in our case, system-level usability studies were carried out. The test scenarios were designed to simulate the total work flow across task contexts and devices in order to collect information on the overall usability of the system.

Table 1. Description of the Polar training systems and the relations of the interaction devices, features and main phases to the contexts of the overall activity

	Planning	Training	Follow-up
	Reduction: Fitness programme or detailed planning (F55) Complex exercises (RS800sd)		*Self-monitoring:* Detailed analysis Training diary Progress (both)
	Reduction: fitness and strength training programmes	*Tunnelling*: workout instructions	*Self-monitoring:* Summaries of individual and weekly exercises
	Reduction: fitness and strength training programmes (F55), training programme, interval exercises (RS800sd) *Suggestion*: event display (RS800sd), trophy (F55)	*Tunnelling*: exercise and workout instructions	*Self-monitoring:* Exercise summary *Operant conditioning and/or surveillance*: reward, trophy (F55)

4 Findings and Discussion

In this section we discuss our main findings, which can be summarized as follows. (1) Technology may have higher requirements for user acceptance in multi-device environments than in environments consisting of a single interaction device or platform, which may result in distinct challenges for persuasion. (2) The semantic aspects of the user interface are of considerable importance in multi-device systems. Different interaction devices can be used to support the acceptance of other devices that co-exist within a system. (3) Multi-device environments may enable more efficient data gathering and personalization strategies and a higher level of tailoring, which may result in greater overall persuasiveness.

4.1 User Acceptance

Two main issues regarding the technological aspects of distributed user experience can be identified in our case. The first concerns data transfer from one interaction device to another, which is carried out via an infrared connection. This is one of the critical phases in terms of user experience, as it is vulnerable to multiple conflicts caused by human errors and technologically challenging events. Such conflicts include configuration of the infrared interface for the PC or laptop, mispositioning of the infrared interfaces in such a way that connectivity is disturbed (wrong distance or angle), or misunderstanding of the sequence of actions that the user is expected to perform in order to activate data transfer. A lack of continuity when switching contexts, such as conflicts in transferring tasks and data between devices, can detract from both task performance and user experience [9].

The second issue is related to the technical skills that the user must possess to benefit fully from the system. He/she needs to master the fundamentals of PC, Web and mobile device usage and to obtain an understanding of the interaction logic of the various software applications. It is possible to influence the interaction logic and semantics of applications that are operated with interaction devices, but the devices themselves remain a challenge. A comparative study of technology-mediated learning environments has suggested that learning results are weaker in an environment that is perceived as being technologically more challenging by the users [1]. Quite understandably user acceptance also plays a significant role in the efficiency of persuasion.

4.2 Semantic Coherence

The user needs to understand and interpret a great deal of information in order to obtain full benefit from systems. It was discovered in the usability studies that the visuals created in the PC environment have a significant impact on how the user perceives the information displayed by the wrist unit during exercise. Interpretation of the symbols and other information displayed on the wrist unit during exercise can be supported by introducing visual clues in the context of PC software usage (see Figure 4). This could help the user to link various pieces of information to the broader context of the tasks and activity and help in identifying the information on the displays. It was found that different interface devices can support the managing of information and interpretation processes at different phases of the activity.

Another important issue concerning the semantic coherence that contributes to user experience is that the symbols, terms and interaction logic should be as consistent as possible between interaction devices. An example of semantic inconsistency is the presentation of heart rate zones, which are presented horizontally in descending order in the PC software, whereas in the wrist unit they are presented on a vertical scale in ascending order. Despite the use of different interaction resources, the solutions should be designed on the basis of a single conceptualization, which can then be implemented in each device to the required extent.

4.3 Personalization

Our case study suggests that the tailored fitness programmes and rewarding strategies, although persuasive in terms of theoretical principles, are still in their early stages. The main issue affecting their long-term success is the inefficient utilization of data collection and personalization strategies. Also, if misused, the strategies incorporate a risk of having a counter-persuasive impact. According to Malhotra and Galletta [12], "The use of extrinsic rewards for what the user perceives as intrinsically satisfying behaviour may reduce motivation. Overemphasis on rewards and incentives may lead users to value the rewards more than the specific value created by system use". The following example gives some insight into the problems of extrinsic rewarding. Assume that the user has started to train for better physical condition using the Polar F55 system and the fitness programme as a support. He/she trains efficiently for the first period and is awarded the trophy. During the next period he/she keeps improving, but this time does not quite reach the targets set by the fitness programme due to injury or for some other reason, and does not get the trophy. Is this persuasive or not? In terms of flow theory this situation would be classified as one where the challenges are too high in relation to the user's skills, resulting in a sub-optimal user experience [1]. Multi-device systems enable usage data to be collected with different devices, at different phases and in different contexts of an activity, which may contribute to more efficient personalization and tailoring.

5 Conclusions

The coherence of distributed user experience in multi-device environments may be enhanced by concentrating on designing more seamless task transfer between devices, both technologically and semantically. Identification of the right interaction device for each task context and the designing of a 'systemic whole' may also contribute to a coherent user experience. Action taken with respect to these challenges may succeed in reducing the requirements for users' technical skills, increasing user acceptance and producing a positive impact on overall persuasiveness. A study of distributed user experience could contribute to obtaining knowledge of the efficiency and functionality of persuasive strategies throughout technology-mediated human activity and support the design of more efficient persuasive technology. This paper describes some of the challenges related to user experience in multi-device systems and gives us grounds for proposing distributed user experience as a key concept on which to base further studies.

Acknowledgments. We gratefully acknowledge Outi Hyyppä, Tanja Kalliojärvi, and Esa Tuulari for commenting the manuscript and Polar Electro for co-operation.

References

1. Alavi, M., Marakas, G.M., Yoo, Y.: A Comparative Study of Distributed Learning Environments on Learning Outcomes. Information Systems Research 13(4), 404–415 (2002)
2. Csikszentmihalyi, M.: Flow: The Psychology of Optimal Experience. Harper and Row, New York (1990)
3. Demeure, A., Calvary, G., Sottet, J-S., Vanderdonkt, J.: A Reference Model for Distributed User Interfaces. In: Proceedings of the Fourth International Workshop on Task Models and Diagrams (TAMODIA '05), Gdansk, Poland, September 26-27, pp. 79–86 (2005)
4. Fogg, B.J.: Persuasive Technology. Morgan Kaufmann Publishers, San Francisco (2003)
5. Harjumaa, M., Oinas-Kukkonen, H.: Persuasion Theories and IT Design. In: Proceedings of the Second International Conference on Persuasive Technology (Persuasive '07), Palo Alto, CA, US, April 26-27 (2007)
6. Intille, S.S.: A New Research Challenge: Persuasive Technology to Motivate Healthy Aging. IEEE Transactions on Information Technology in Biomedicine 8, 235–237 (2004)
7. Kaptellinin, V., Nardi, B., Macaulay, C.: The Activity Checklist: A Tool for Representing the "Space" of Context. Interactions 6(4), 27–39 (1999)
8. Kuutti, K., Bannon, L.J.: Searching For Unity Among Diversity: Exploring The "Interface" Concept. In: Proceedings of the SIGCHI Conference on Human Factors in Computing Systems (CHI'93), Amsterdam, The Netherlands, pp. 263–268 (May 1993)
9. Luyten, K., Vandervelpen, C., Coninx, K.: Task Modelling for Ambient Intelligent Environments: Design Support for Situated Task Executions. In: Proceedings of the Fourth International Workshop on Task Models and Diagrams (TAMODIA '05), Gdansk, Poland, September 26-27, pp. 87–94 (2005)

10. Lyytinen, K., Yoo, Y.: Research Commentary: The Next Wave of Nomadic Computing. Information Systems Research 13(4), 377–388 (2002)
11. Mahlke, S.: Understanding Users' Experience of Interaction. In: Proceedings of the Annual Conference on European Association of Cognitive Ergonomics (EACE '05), 1st edn., Chania, Greece, September 29 - October 1, pp. 251–254 (2005)
12. Malhotra, Y., Galletta, F.: Building Systems That Users Want to Use. Communications of the ACM 47(12), 89–94 (2004)
13. Oinas-Kukkonen, H.: Balancing the Vendor and Consumer Requirements for Electronic Shopping Systems. Information Technology and Management 1(1), 73–84 (2000)
14. Oliveira, R., Rocha, H.V.: Towards an Approach for Multi-Device Interface Design. Proceedings of the Eleventh Brazilian Symposium on Multimedia and the Web (WebMedia '05), Pocos de Caldas - Minas Gerais, Brazil, pp. 1–3 (December 5-7, 2005)
15. Savidis, A., Stephanidis, C.: Distributed Interface Bits: Dynamic Dialogue Composition from Ambient Computing Resources. Personal and Ubiquitous Computing 9(3), 142–168 (2005)
16. Trimeche, M., Suomela, R., Aaltonen, A., Lorho, G., Dossaji, T., Aarnio, T., Tuoriniemi, S.: Enhancing End-User Experience in a Multi-Device Ecosystem. In: Proceedings of the Fourth International Conference on Mobile and Ubiquitous Multimedia (MUM '05), Christchurch, New Zealand, December 8-10, pp. 19–25 (2005)
17. Vandervelpen, C., Coninx, K.: Towards Model-Based Design Support for Distributed User Interfaces. In: Proceedings of the Third Nordic Conference on Human-Computer Interaction (NordiCHI '04), Tampere, Finland, October 23-27, pp. 61–70 (2004)
18. Welie, M.v., Veer, v.d.G.C.: Groupware Task Analysis. In: Hollnagel, E. (ed.) Handbook of Cognitive Task Design, Lawrence Erlbaum Associates, New Jersey, US (2003)
19. World Health Organization: The World Health Organization warns of the rising threat of heart disease and stroke as overweight and obesity rapidly increase (13.10.2006), http://www.who.int/mediacentre/news/releases/2005/pr44/en/index.html
20. Xia, W., Lee, G.: The Influence of Persuasion, Training, and Experience on User Perceptions and Acceptance of IT Innovation. In: Proceedings of the Twenty-First International Conference on Information Systems, Brisbane, Queensland, Australia, pp. 371–384 (2000)

The PerCues Framework and Its Application for Sustainable Mobility

Wolfgang Reitberger, Bernd Ploderer, Christoph Obermair, and Manfred Tscheligi

ICT&S Center, University of Salzburg, Sigmund-Haffner-Gasse 18, 5020 Salzburg, Austria
{wolfgang.reitberger, bernd.ploderer, christoph.obermair,
manfred.tscheligi}@sbg.ac.at

Abstract. This paper presents a framework, design and study of an ambient persuasive interface. We introduce a novel framework of persuasive Cues in Ambient Intelligence (perCues). Based on this framework we designed an application for mobile devices. The application aims to persuade people to abstain from using their cars and to use public mass transportation instead in order to reduce emissions. It contains a bus schedule and information about the pollution status. We evaluated the application in two successive studies regarding user acceptance, opportune moments of use and persuasive effects. The perCues received a high acceptance due to its benefit for the users. The results confirm the importance of opportune moment and user acceptance for persuasion. The findings also indicate the persuasive potential of perCues.

1 Introduction and Background

We have developed and presented perCues [1, 2], a novel concept for persuasive Cues in Ambient Intelligence (AmI) [3, 4] environments. Our approach is based on the theory of Collective Intelligence (CI) [5] and its application on the design of AmI systems. From the perCues concept we derive a framework, which gives guidelines for the design of AmI applications that increase the collective intelligence of a target group. This goal is achieved by providing implicit and peripheral cues in the users' environment [6] to raise their awareness for certain aspects relevant for their group. These cues give additional information about the user's environment that would otherwise remain hidden from the user.

The application presented in this paper utilizes perCues as indicators about the environmental pollution state in a city. It is aimed at reducing emissions by fostering sustainable mobility behavior. We designed this application based on the perCues framework using a mobile platform as ambient display. We used the paratype method [7] to test this application before its actual implementation. The insights gained from this study serve as valuable input for the user-centered implementation of the envisioned application.

2 PerCues Framework and Application

The perCues framework [1, 2] is used to acquire the current group state, to determine a way to persuade the group members to achieve the desired group state, and finally

Y. de Kort et al. (Eds.): PERSUASIVE 2007, LNCS 4744, pp. 92–95, 2007.
© Springer-Verlag Berlin Heidelberg 2007

to present the necessary perCues to the group members. The process that underlies this framework consists of four steps that form a feedback loop (see Fig. 1).

Step 1 is to gather implicit input based on the collective group behavior and it's context. In step 2 the implicit output is inferred with the AmI system. Step 3 refers to the information of the group members by means of perCues. In step 4 the individual group members are aware of the state of the group and of the impact that their own actions and the behavior of the group as a whole have. To close the feedback loop, the updated group state serves again as input for the AmI system and a new cycle begins.

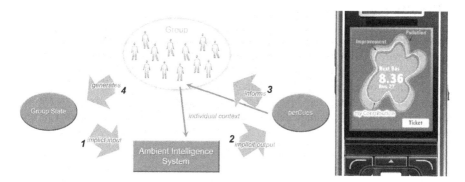

Fig. 1. The perCues framework and a perCues prototype for mobile devices to persuade people to use public mass transport

Based on the framework we designed an application prototype (see Fig. 1) using a mobile device. The prototype displays personalized bus and pollution information, such as the departure time of the next relevant bus and the decrease in emissions caused by taking the bus instead of using the car. Users of the application also see the impact that the actions of other users have on the environmental pollution.

3   Paratype Studies

We adapted the paratype method [7] to evaluate our prototypical application. A paratype consists of a survey and a low fidelity prototype. The prototype is shown to participants in real life situations and immediately followed by a survey. The study is conducted by a group of individuals called "proxies". They act on behalf of the researchers and ask people as they follow their daily activities. In this way proxies lead to a randomized and balanced sample, which is not directly related to the researchers' environment.

We conducted two successive paratype studies, both using the same procedure: We recruited proxies, advised them about the paratype and provided them with guidelines to ensure consistent paratype situations. We advised the proxies to ask only people who have access to public transport. Furthermore we advised them to ask people only in predefined situations. The paratype survey consisted of four parts: It started with an ex ante questionnaire evaluating the respondent's attitude towards transportation means. At the same time the proxy filled in a questionnaire to describe the sampling situation. Next the proxy introduced the basic concepts of the perCues prototype and the participant could examine it. Finally the participant rated its acceptance and persuasive potential in a questionnaire. In study 2 we revised this last part to evaluate whether the ratings were related to the individual benefit (bus information) or to the collective benefit (pollution information). Attitude, acceptance and persuasive potential were measured using multiple statements rated on a 5-option Likert scale, all other questions were multiple choice.

4   Results and Discussion

54 people participated in study 1 (35 female, 19 male) and 24 people in study 2 (13 female, 11 male). Study 1 spanned all age groups over 20, study 2 covered participants aged 20 to 49 years. The analysis showed no significant differences of any results between gender or age groups. 25 participants preferred driving a car, 10 taking a bus, and 43 walking or using the bike. Since many questions occur in both studies we present the results in a common section and indicate where results are related to only one of the studies.

4.1   User Acceptance

Participants reported a high acceptance of the perCues. We used ratings of statements on a 5 option scale, where 1 was "agree" and 5 "do not agree" to evaluate acceptance factors. The participants in both studies (n = 78) stated that the system would be easy to use (mean =2.0, SD =1.23). Furthermore the responses in study 1 (n = 54) indicate that users would like to use the perCues service (mean = 2.3, SD = 1.17). In study 2 (n = 24) we asked the participants whether they would like to use the system due to the information when the next bus leaves, or due to the pollution information. The participants rated the likeability of the bus information (mean =1.6, SD =0.97) significantly better (p < 0.001) than the pollution information (mean =3.0, SD =1.22). So bus information has proven its high individual benefit for the user. Thus it serves as a useful container for pollution information presented in the background.

4.2   Persuasive Potential

The survey results indicate potential persuasive effects of the perCues. Participants were asked to rate statements on a 5-option scale, where 1 was "very likely" and 5 "very unlikely". In study 1 (n = 54) we asked the participants whether the perCues have the potential to change their attitude towards public transport. The average rating of 2.6 (SD =1.28) indicates a rather positive potential.

In study 2 (n = 24) we tried to find out if the persuasive potential was contributed to the information when the next bus leaves, or to the pollution information. Figure 3 shows that the bus information was rated significantly (p < 0.05) better than the pollution information for attitude change (bus: mean =1.8, SD =0.88; pollution: mean = 2.6, SD = 1.32) and behavior change (bus: mean =2.1, SD =1.14; pollution: mean = 2.9, SD = 1.04). The interpretation is that the persuasion strategy of individual benefit (bus information) has more potential impact than the strategy of reasonable arguments (pollution information). Whereas our study already gives some insights about the persuasive potential of perCues these results cannot be interpreted as definitive proof that our application will lead to a change in user attitudes or behavior.

We also observed significant correlations between opportune moment and possible attitude change ($r = 0.49$, $p < 0.01$) and behavior change due to the perCues ($r = 0.43$, $p < 0.01$). This means that users who stated that it was an opportune moment for the perCues also reported a significantly higher persuasive potential. In line with [8] this finding proves that choosing the right moment of system usage has a strong impact on the persuasive effect. Recognizing this opportune moment based on user behavior is one of the major potentials of AmI technologies.

5 Conclusions

In this paper we presented a persuasive ambient application to foster the usage of public transportation. The results indicate the persuasive potentials of the perCues application and confirm our assumptions concerning the persuasive strategies derived from the perCues framework.

References

1. Tscheligi, M., Reitberger, W., Obermair, C., Ploderer, B.: perCues: Trails of persuasion for ambient intelligence. In: Proc. Persuasive 2006, pp. 203–206. Springer, Heidelberg (2006)
2. Obermair, C., Ploderer, B., Reitberger, W., Tscheligi, M.: Cues in the environment: a design principle for ambient intelligence. In: CHI 2006, pp. 1157–1162. ACM Press, New York (2006)
3. Aarts, E., Marzano, S.: The New Everyday: Views on Ambient Intelligence. 010 Publishers, Rotterdam (2003)
4. Weiser, M.: The computer for the 21st century. Scientific American, 94–104 (1991)
5. Lévy, P.: Collective Intelligence: Mankind's Emerging World in Cyberspace. Plenum Publishing Corp, Cambridge, MA (1997)
6. Schmidt, A.: Interactive context-aware systems interacting with ambient intelligence. In: Riva, G., Vatalaro, F., Davide, F., Alcañiz, M. (eds.) Ambient Intelligence, pp. 159–178. IOS Press, Amsterdam (2005)
7. Iachello, G., Truong, K.N., Abowd, G.D., Hayes, G.R., Stevens, M.: Prototyping and sampling experience to evaluate ubiquitous computing privacy in the real world. In: Proc. CHI 2006, pp. 1009–1018. ACM Press, New York (2006)
8. Fogg, B.J.: Persuasive technology using computers to change what we think and do. Morgan Kaufman, San Francisco, CA (2003)

Persuasive Technologies Should Be Boring

Conrad Wai and Pete Mortensen

Jump Associates LLC, 101 South Ellsworth Ave, Suite 600,
San Mateo, California, USA 94401
{Conrad,PeterM}@JumpAssociates.com

Abstract. New persuasive technologies often make the mistake of touting how
new and different they are from anything that came before. What they should
really be trying to do is mask any behavior change by making their interface
and interactions as familiar and mundane as possible. This lesson is illustrated
in a case study of the Nike + iPod, a revolutionary device that pretends to be
just a better way to go for a run while listening to music.

Keywords: Disruptive technology, design, Nike + iPod, adoption.

1 Introduction: Persuasive Technologies Can Learn From Disruptive Innovations

Persuasive technology is a new field, and many questions are as yet unanswered.
What will make people willing to use products designed to change their behavior?
Why are some persuasive products readily adopted while others languish? Those
interested in driving the adoption of persuasive technologies should study the
adoption of another set of inventions that encourage people to change their behavior –
if not always for direct social benefit. They're known as disruptive technologies,
challengers to an existing market or product category that reframe a given business
problem. As an example, the automobile dramatically changed transportation and
urban development. In this paper we'll draw a few lessons from such disruptors that
are crucial to the design of (more overtly) persuasive technologies, before diving
deeper into a case study of a persuasive product that has applied these principles
successfully – the Nike + iPod Sport Kit.

1.1 Successful Disruptive Technologies Often Take on Familiar Designs

Looking at the design of many successful disruptive products, a common theme runs
through: they're actually quite familiar. This seems counterintuitive – if you come up
with an amazing new way of doing something, it seems natural to make some bold
design statements about how radically new and different it is. But often the most
successful of these products actually take great steps to mask their novelty; their
designs recall a preexisting, well-understood technology [1]. The original cellular
phones looked like cordless telephones, which in turn looked like walkie-talkies.
Compact discs and laser discs mimic vinyl records to convey that they are media that
store entertainment. Interactions with the first Palm Pilot were designed to resemble
those of a pen-and-paper organizer in order to fit into people's existing context of use.

Y. de Kort et al. (Eds.): PERSUASIVE 2007, LNCS 4744, pp. 96–99, 2007.

Generally speaking, the bigger the behavior change a technology promises, the more familiar its design should be. Though not a universal requirement for success, familiarity can go some way in avoiding the adoption obstacles common to any discovery that demands people go about their lives in a different way. People are more likely to adopt a new technology if it is presented in a way that connects with the lives they already lead. This insight has profound implications for the design of persuasive technologies.

1.2 Persuasive Technologies That Embody Familiarity Are Often More Successful than Those That Try to Signal How New and Different They Are

Disruptive products necessitate a change in the way things are done. Persuasive technologies, by definition, are also trying to change behavior. Thus persuasive technologies, like disruptive ones, should attempt to take on familiarizing designs. To find their markets, these offerings should be designed to be as inconspicuous as possible at introduction. As Everett Rogers notes in *Diffusion of Innovations*, the key to driving mainstream adoption is fitting into what people already know and do – not emphasizing how different a new offering is [2]. Persuasive technologies that look and feel like existing products are less alien to customers. As a result, they don't depend on customers that are willing to step out of their comfort zones in order to succeed. They slot into people's existing routines. And they are understood as enhancements to existing activities, not as intentionally life-altering artifacts.

Let's dive deeper into an example of how downplaying disparities can actually lead to more profound changes in behavior.

2 Case Study: The Nike + iPod Sport Kit Gets It Right

One successful and instructive persuasive technology comes from the Nike + iPod product line, introduced in May 2006. The device has won wide recognition, including several year-end awards, and at Nike's earnings call on Dec. 22, 2006 the company credited the line for in part driving 10 percent sales growth [3]. The $30, two-piece kit is deceptively simple: it consists of a plain, rectangular receiver that clips on to the bottom of any iPod nano and a rounded transmitter that slips into running shoes. It promises to enhance the experience of running while listening to music. But underneath this unassuming promise lies a device capable of much more. It keeps track of distance covered in a work-out, time to complete individual goals and other fitness benchmarks. It can even give auditory directions for working out, filling the role of a virtual personal trainer.

In driving adoption, the Nike+ does three things very well, all of which could benefit any new persuasive technology: it uses a design that blends in with the iPod and running shoes, thereby framing itself in the familiar; it smoothes the change in people's behavior by promoting the best understood features first; finally, it invites comparison to less capable devices. By demonstrating how these principles work with the Nike+, we can show how they might be applied to other persuasive technologies.

2.1 Blend in by Adopting Familiar Forms and Frames

Design has the ability to make new and alien technologies familiar and comfortable. The Nike + iPod accomplishes this through the use of familiar forms and frames. The actual kit looks very much like other sports-branded consumer electronics equipment, including Nike's own MP3 players. More subtly, the device fits comfortably into the frame of going for a run while listening to music. The designers chose to make its components slot into some very well-understood pieces of technology: a portable music player and a pair of running shoes.

Nike's design team was very conscious to make the receiver small enough to blend in with the form of the iPod nano and to physically conceal the transmitter inside the sole of the line's associated shoes. Even once an owner begins to embrace the little box's ability to dynamically measure her fitness levels, her workout looks to the entire world like any normal exerciser wearing a set of headphones and stylish running shoes. On the inside, she might be listening to an inspiring coach's commands for greater fitness – on the outside, she looks like everyone else.

Another service that illustrates this principle is Bank of America's "Keep the Change" program, which encourages people to save by automatically rounding up any debit card purchase to the next whole dollar. This difference is added to the enrolled member's savings account. The bank provides an incentive to save by matching up to the first $250, but a second more subtle incentive is added by making the investment completely confidential and requiring no ongoing change in action. It's one thing to decide to put more money in your savings account. It's quite another to have a piece of software do it for you.

2.2 Emphasize Familiar Features First

Though the Nike + iPod is a sophisticated exercise tracking and motivational tool, Nike and Apple choose to downplay its powers. They focus instead on the potential for music to inspire athleticism, leaving the device's more ambitious capabilities to be discovered over time. The original press release for Nike+ quoted the company's CEO, Mark Parker: "Nike + iPod will change the way people run" [4]. The release backs up this claim by noting the device's ability to track distance, pace and calories burned – the same basic features of any pedometer or treadmill.

Nike and Apple gloss over the "virtual personal trainer" aspect, saying only: "A new Nike Sport Music section on the iTunes Music Store and a new nikeplus.com personal service site help maximize the Nike + iPod experience." They don't acknowledge how the experience might be "maximized" through the use of sport mixes. Nor does Nike declare that they have created "Coaching Mixes" that offer verbal instruction for specific fitness techniques. These features are de-emphasized, allowing people to discover additional abilities over time.

Another successful technology shows the value of playing up familiar features first. The TiVo Digital Video Recorder was marketed as a way for people to "simplify the increasingly complicated television experience," according to CEO Michael Ramsay [5]. Many early comments merely emphasized avoiding the need to find blank tapes for recordings. At most, the creators touched on the device's ability to recommend relevant programming, but only in reference to "personal taste," not through tracking of users' behavior. Had TiVo emphasized the box's ability to "read viewers' minds," it's entirely possible the company would never have gained the traction it needed to introduce increasingly disruptive and persuasive features to its customer base.

2.3 Choose Your Reference Point Carefully

The Nike + iPod is far from the first product that has attempted to motivate people to exercise more. Home exercise videos, countless websites and even a few video games all attempt to replicate the experience of working with a professional instructor [6]. Because these solutions mimic a real-life experience, they emphasize their artificial quality – and can remind people of how inadequate the digital device is to the task.

Subtly, the Nike + iPod is positioned to represent a better pedometer, not a cheap personal trainer. For $30, people can not only keep better track of their progress than most fitness computers could – they can also coordinate their work-outs with their music collections. By setting up favorable reference points, persuasive technologies can promote themselves as better versions of existing devices instead of poor replacements for professional services.

Another product illustrates the power of this principle. Intuit's Quicken software could be sold as a virtual accountant or financial manager. Instead, the company focuses on making the experience of balancing one's own checkbook simpler. By constantly referencing itself relative to the nightmare of balancing the books by hand, rather than as a poor man's accountant, Quicken has established a reputation with users as the most effective way to ensure that their spending is kept in check.

3 Conclusion: The Best Persuasive Technologies Downplay the Behavior Change They're Trying to Reinforce

The Nike + iPod is a great example of how to design a piece of persuasive technology. It gives us a concrete case from which to draw some broader lessons about how to design for persuasion. Other technologies would do well to emulate how the Nike + iPod presents an innocuous front, slots into existing activities, and messages augmentation instead of replacement. Conforming to people's routine and enhancing it goes a long way towards promoting adoption and use. Designing for familiarity is crucial when trying to persuade people to behave in unfamiliar ways.

References

1. Patnaik, D.: New Opportunities. In: Presented: IDSA: ROI, New York (December 12, 2006)
2. Rogers, E.P.: Diffusion of Innovations, 5th edn. Free Press, New York (2003)
3. Mahoney, S.: MediaPost's Marketing Daily. Nike's iPod Connection Pays, New York (2006)
4. Nike Inc. and Apple Computer Inc. Nike and Apple Team Up to Launch Nike + iPod (2006)
5. Swisher, K.: Wall Street Journal. On the Drawing Board: A Look At Some of the Latest Gizmos Being Readied For Market. Dow Jones, New York (1998)
6. Richards, S.: Wired Magazine. Games That Give You a Workout. Condenast New York (January 2005)

Electronic Monitoring of Offenders: Can a Wayward Technology Be Redeemed?

Robert S. Gable

School of Behavioral and Organizational Sciences, Claremont Graduate
University, 2738 Fulton Street, Berkeley, CA 94705, USA

Abstract. Electronic monitoring of offenders is being increasingly used as an
alternative to incarceration. Although surveillance and the threat of punishment
can temporarily suppress criminal behavior, this strategy has not reduced long-
term re-offending. An alternative use of monitoring technology would reward
prosocial behavior on a variable schedule. Miniature and inexpensive Bluetooth or
WiFi-enabled transceivers can electronically enrich designated environments in
order to encourage offenders to attend classes, arrive promptly at work, or make
appropriate decisions at critical choice-points in a crime-prone neighborhood.
Within the criminal justice system, only small, incremental changes can be
expected.

Keywords: Electronic monitoring, offenders, Bluetooth, WiFi, transceivers.

1 Introduction

Approximately two million offenders are incarcerated in state and federal prisons in
the United States at an estimated cost per inmate of $25,000 per year. In order to
reduce prison overcrowding and related costs, the courts have increasingly turned to
electronically-monitored home detention as a prison alternative.

The basic electronic monitoring (EM) system includes a radio transmitter in a
bracelet fastened around the offender's ankle with a tamper-proof strap. A stationary
receiver at the offender's residence is connected by land line or cellular phone
technology to a central monitoring center that is staffed by authorized correctional
agency personnel. The bracelet sends a regularly timed signal to the residential unit. If
the offender with the bracelet moves out-of-range (typically 80 meters) at designated
times, the receiver sends an alert message to the monitoring center. A second
generation EM system requires the offender to carry a tracking GPS unit in addition
to wearing the ankle bracelet. The tracking unit sends information regarding the
offender's location to the monitoring center.

The offender may be forbidden to enter certain locations (exclusion zones) where a
crime is likely to be committed. For example, in the case of domestic violence, the
offender might be forbidden to come within 100 meters of the victim's home. In GPS
configurations, corrections officers can have real-time Web access to visual maps of the
offender's movements.

Y. de Kort et al. (Eds.): PERSUASIVE 2007, LNCS 4744, pp. 100–104, 2007.

2 How Monitoring Began

The initial experiments with criminal offenders were conducted at Harvard University in the 1960s [1]. The goal was to establish a therapeutic relationship with a counselor in which the offender could be either rewarded or warned about activities that could positively or negatively impact rehabilitation. The experimental systems of the 1960s were expensive and cumbersome by contemporary standards, and in the words of Steve Mainprize [2, p. 6] "efforts to promote EM fell upon the shores of economic and technical impracticality."

In 1977, state district judge, Jack Love, noticed two items in a local Albuquerque, New Mexico, newspaper. The first was an article about an electronic identification tag, invented at the Los Alamos Scientific Laboratory. The tag was implanted under the skin of livestock. The second was a Spiderman cartoon wherein a villain clamped an I.D. bracelet on Spiderman that tracked movement. Judge Love subsequently convinced a technician to construct an anklet, and in 1983 three offenders were sentenced to wear the device as a condition of probation. This was the "live birth" of EM. Within six years, hundreds of units were being used in the United States. Today, an estimated 110,000 – 120,000 monitoring units are deployed on a daily basis in the U.S. Approximately 60,000 units are in use in England/Wales, Sweden and The Netherlands where EM is most widely accepted among the E.U. countries [3].

3 Contemporary Uses of Monitoring

Two groups of offenders are most often sentenced to EM. One group consists of high-risk offenders on parole. The surveillance capacity of EM provides a degree of public safety that is not present in typical community-based supervision. Monitored home detention is a logical transition from incarceration in prison to freedom in the community. Obviously, EM is not a physical deterrence because an offender, determined to commit a crime and willing to accept the consequences, can cut the ankle strap. Although tampering will immediately send an alert signal to the monitoring agency, a crime can be committed prior to the arrival of law enforcement personnel. At least 10 homicides have been committed while individuals were being monitored.

There are no credible studies showing that EM alone (i.e., without treatment) can reduce crime *after monitoring is terminated* [4]. Nonetheless, there is considerable enthusiasm for the use of EM by the general public. Voters in California and the legislators in six states have passed laws that mandate *lifetime* monitoring of some sex offenders.

A second group of offenders placed on EM includes low-risk individuals. Most often these offenders are non-violent repeat offenders for whom normal probation (e.g., "pay a fine and stay out of trouble") does not stop the offending behavior. DUI, minor drug offenses, shoplifting, and passing bad checks are typical violations. The more intensive EM community-based monitoring encourages offenders to stay in treatment programs and become more disciplined about meeting obligations of school or work.

A subcategory of low-risk offenders includes "white collar criminals" consisting of business executives, politicians, and other professionals who are sentenced to EM because it is more punitive than customary supervision in the community. The most visible example in the U.S. has been entrepreneur Martha Stewart. In 2005, after serving a five -month prison term, she was sentenced to five months of home confinement on her 153-acre estate. Martha was not a violent criminal from whom the public needed protection. Nor was her surveillance a means of motivating her to attend Alcoholic Anonymous, psychotherapy, or a job-training class. It was a lawyer-negotiated form of prison escape that satisfied the public's desire for retribution.

4 Misuses and Mistakes

Some professional guidelines for the use of EM have been developed [5], but their implementation has been slow or marginal. The following list of misuses and mistakes of EM is presented to illustrate the generally ineffective or haphazard application of this persuasive technology.

4.1 "Net-Widening"

A commonly stated purpose of EM is to provide an alternative to prison for persons who would otherwise be incarcerated. However, instead of diverting these would-be prisoners, individuals have often been sentenced to EM who would not have been be incarcerated for their offense, The clearest examples of such "net-widening" are instances where 13- or 14-year old teenagers are placed under monitored home detention for getting into a fight or using alcohol or other drugs [e.g., 6]. Similarly, parolees who would usually leave prison without restraint are put under surveillance for reasons of public relations (i.e., "the Martha Stewart effect").

4.2 Monitoring Persons Who Are Unable or Unwilling to Comply

Some individuals have cognitive or neurological problems that require on-going medication or other support. Time-limited EM is not an appropriate substitute. Other individuals may be severely addicted to a psychoactive substance or undergoing detoxification that prevents them from acting rationally.

Still other individuals do not find incarceration a particularly unpleasant experience compared to the hostility and dangerousness of the streets [7]. Hence, the threat of incarceration for violating EM rules does not act as a deterrent.

4.3 Use of Inappropriate Sanctions

Monitored surveillance often identifies many violations of probation or parole conditions that would normally go undetected. Fluctuations between law-abiding and criminal behavior is a natural learning process in the course of an offender's rehabilitation. Incarcerating a person for relapses not only interrupts a rehabilitation process but can actually increase the number of persons incarcerated (contrary to a stated goal of EM).

5 Effective Use of Electronic Monitoring

EM has unique capacities as a persuasive technology within the criminal justice system. Most obviously, it provides means of immediately delivering symbolic positive reinforcers for prosocial behaviors. Rewarding a socially desired behavior that is incompatible with the criminal behavior is a basic rehabilitation strategy. A research team in Utah County, Utah, gave cell phones to 150 offenders after they attended a six-week social skills class. An automated phone system sent recorded messages of support and encouragement at predetermined intervals during the day [8].

Rather than predetermined time-related contact, however, positive messages would likely have more impact if they were delivered in an unpredictable manner (i.e., on a variable-ratio/variable-interval schedule) contingent on desired behavior. For example, the present writer used a belt-mounted vibrating actuator to send a coded message to a probationer attending a job training class. The message indicated that he had become eligible to receive two tickets to a professional basketball game. Ideally, positive consequences should become psychologically associated with non-criminal, natural social settings.

Location-specific monitoring can allow real-time intervention during an offender's decision-making process. A critical choice-point might be, for instance, a bus stop where one bus takes the offender toward home; a different bus takes the offender toward a favorite video game arcade where illicit drugs are available. Gradually, the offender should practice making difficult decisions along a "digital pathway" without the aid of monitoring.

Advances in cellular and battery technology now enable the installation of a network of inexpensive transceivers in a neighborhood or city sector. Paulos and Goodman [9] attached low-power, 23mm diameter, encased processors to various objects (e.g., parking meters) in an urban area. A mobile version of the transceiver, each with a unique I.D. code, was clipped to a bag or hung from a belt. Each of the transceivers had short-range wireless connectivity (up to 30 meters), and was capable of recording the presence of a similar nearby device. Bluetooth or WiFi-enabled cell phones can support the same type of interaction. Thus, certain geographical areas can be "electronically enriched" for the potential rewarding of prsocial behavior.

For several decades, social psychologists have been measuring courteous, friendly, or helping behavior in various natural settings. One experimenter [10], walking with a clearly visible leg brace, dropped and unsuccessfully struggled to reach down for a pile of magazines. The proportion of pedestrians spontaneously offering assistance was observed. The prosocial behavior of offenders on EM could be reinforced by trained observers in specified public locations using interactive authentication devices without revealing their personal identity. Or offender information could be downloaded via cellular link to a central computer for later action. The technical configurations and behavioral examples presented in this paper are only general illustrations of the potential redirection of EM technology. Obviously, ethical and legal issues must be addressed; some of these were outlined early in the development of behavior modification technology [11].

6 Small Steps

The current punishment orientation of EM is not without merit—it does temporarily suppress unwanted behavior. This short-term benefit will be relinquished only when the long-term cost of its ineffective use becomes apparent. Three-year data on re-arrest rates should be incorporated into the operational strategies of correctional agencies In the meantime, the difficult and often frustrating work of correctional personnel should not be devalued. New persuasive technologies might be presented simply as tactical options.

Some correctional personnel will see how a redesign of EM can fulfill the need for long-term rehabilitation, and they will become early adopters. Implementation could begin unannounced (except for tacit support of a manager) in small, incremental steps with just one or two offenders. Flexibility and an experimental attitude will be useful attributes for overcoming expected organizational resistance. Later, a larger group of line-staff pragmatists (who tend to be risk averse but who perceive the advantage of a new technology) are likely to follow. This will be the beginning of a mass application of a positive persuasive technology and the redemption of today's punitive electronic monitoring.

References

1. Schwitzgebel, R.K., Schwitzgebel, R.L., Pahnke, W.N., Hurd, W.S.: A Program of Research in Behavioral Electronics. Behavioral Sci. 9, 233–238 (1964)
2. Mainprize, S.: Elective Affinities in the Engineering of Social Control: The Evolution of Electronic Monitoring. Electronic J. Sociology (1996), http://collection.nic-bnc.ca/100/201/ejofsociology/2003/ vo7n03/maimprize.html
3. Albrech, H-J.: Electronic Monitoring in Europe. Max Planck Society, Freiberg, Germany (2005)
4. Renzema, M., Mayo-Wilson, E.: Can Electronic Monitoring Reduce Crime for Moderate to High- risk Offenders? J. Experimental Criminology 1, 1–21 (2005)
5. Crowe, A.H.: Offender Supervision with Electronic Technology, American Probation and Parole Association, Lexington, Ky., U.S (2002)
6. Elliott, R.: Electronically Monitored Curfew for 10- to 15- Year Olds—Report of the Pilot. Occasional paper. Home Office London, U.K (2000)
7. Renzema, M.: How to Use Electronic Monitoring Intelligently in Pretrial Services. J. Offender Monitoring 18(4-6), 25–26 (2006)
8. Berraston, B.O., Cherrington, D.J.: Using Cell Phone Technology to Intervene in Delinquent Behaviors of Parolees: The Victory Seeker Program. In: Paper presented at Annual Meeting of the Society for Prevention Research, San Antonio, Texas (May 2006)
9. Paulos, E., Goodman, E.: The Familiar Stranger: Anxiety, Comfort, and Play in Public Places. In: Paper presented at Conference on Human Factors in Computing Systems., ienna, Austria, ACM, New York (April 2004)
10. Levine, R.V.: Measuring Helping Behavior Across Cultures. In: Lonner, W.J., Dinnel, D.L, Hayes, S.A, Sattler, D.H. (eds.) Online Readings in Psychology and Culture (Unit 15, chapter 9), Center for Cross-Cultural Research, Western Washington University, Bellingham, WA (2003)
11. Schwitzgebel, R.: Electronic Innovation in the Behavioral Sciences: A Call to Responsibility. Amer. Psychologist 22, 364–370 (1967)

Logical Modeling of Deceptive Negative Persuasion

Neil C. Rowe

U.S. Naval Postgraduate School, Code CS/Rp, 1411 Cunningham Road,
Monterey, CA 93943 USA
ncrowe at nps.edu

Abstract. It is often easier to persuade someone that something is impossible to do than that it is possible, since the absence of one necessary resource suffices. This makes lying a tempting tactic for negative persuasion. We consider the problem of finding convincing lies for it as one of maintaining consistency of a set of logical assertions; we can track that consistency with a computer program. We use an example of negative persuasion against electronic voting in elections, where automated analysis then suggests ways to prevent it.

Negative persuasion is convincing someone that a goal of theirs is impossible. Usually the persuader attempts to show that one or more necessary conditions on the goal cannot be achieved. Often these conditions concern needed resources. For instance, we can try to persuade someone to stop smoking by pointing out that a new tax on cigarettes makes them too expensive to afford.

Negative persuasion is so effective for motivation of people that there is a great temptation to lie to accomplish it. Lies can be more flexible than just denying a resource outright because they can provide excuses rather than just prohibitions. Our previous research investigated a wide spectrum of useful lies for defense of computer systems against attacks (Rowe and Rothstein, 2004) Computers can be excellent liars since they can be well prepared, think quickly, have a good memory, avoid feelings of guilt, and pretend effectively (Vrij, 2000). False excuses are good lies for computers since many features of cyberspace are hard to confirm. But convincing excuses must be consistent.

Our theory of deceptive negative persuasion addresses some goal resources that an agent wants to obtain (such as a vote in an election). A counteragent that controls the resources can try to interfere with agent plans by lying about secondary-resource availability in a "counterplan" (Carbonell, 1981). Denial of secondary resources can be more effective at foiling plans than denial of primary ones because (a) it is less suggestive of deliberate manipulation, and (b) it is less discouraging to more attempts of the same kind by the agent, thereby wasting more resources of the agent. We assume that the counteragent only wants to interfere with some kinds of agents, and will decide once they learn about the agent. To avoid contradicting themselves and revealing their deceptions, the counteragent should track the assertions it makes. Deceivers should conceal their deceptions because people can have emotional reactions to them and may engage in retaliatory or violent behavior.

Consistency can be maintained by tracking assertions about resources such as physical objects, data, credentials, authorizations, and knowledge. Most resources change status rarely; for instance, a working computer will be highly likely to be

Y. de Kort et al. (Eds.): PERSUASIVE 2007, LNCS 4744, pp. 105–108, 2007.
© Springer-Verlag Berlin Heidelberg 2007

working an hour later if it is still on. We propose six "facets" of status of each resource, in order of appearance: existence, authorization for use, intrinsic readiness for use, operability (functional correctness), compatibility with other resources, and reasonability of its parameters. When an agent successfully completes an action, this implies all the facets are valid for each input resource. But when an action fails, a particular facet can usually be blamed, and all subsequent facets are invalid. For instance, if a voting machine will not start up, then it cannot be operable or compatible with other resources. Inferences of facet invalidity also proceed upward from a part to a whole containing it, and inference of validity in the opposite direction. So if one page of a ballot does not work properly, the entire ballot does not work properly. Task-specific inferences can also apply; for instance, when voting machine is inoperable, it cannot produce ballots.

To thus do deceptive negative persuasion against an agent, the counteragent should choose some secondary resources necessary to their plan and some facets of those resources not yet described, and deny those resources by lying about the validity of the facets. A key issue is when to start deceiving. Although the deceivee must first be judged as worthy of deception, the longer the delay, the fewer possible resources on which to deceive without introducing inconsistencies. Deception should also be avoided at key agent actions (such when a voter submits a ballot) since then the link between them and deceptions is more obvious.

We can rate acceptable deceptions by the product of four factors in a form of Naive Bayes inference:

- The degree to which deception is appropriate (based on whether the interaction is seen as adversarial, as per our previously developed theory of suspiciousness);
- The reported prior likelihood of problems with the associated resource;
- Newness of the resource (making resource problems more plausible); and
- The reported prior likelihood of invalidity of the associated facet.

There are also several tactics for implementing deceptions, to provide variety:

- To deceive on existence, claim inability to find the resource.
- To deceive on authorization, deny outright that the agent is authorized to use the resource, or ask for additional passwords or codes that the agent does not possess.
- To deceive on readiness, issue an immediate error message on attempted use such as "cannot be opened" or a cryptic code string, or do nothing but say nothing.
- To deceive on operability, state that the resource isn't working, stop while using the resource with an error message, or appear never to terminate.
- To deceive on compatibility, pick another needed resource and cite a pair of allegedly incompatible attributes of the two.
- To deceive on moderation, cite a parameter limit that is exceeded.

Deceivees have options themselves in detecting and foiling deceptions, including thorough testing of automated systems against misuse, designing systems to log all events (especially unusual ones) so that deceptions can be detected and attributed later, asking probing questions to catch deceivers in inconsistencies, providing alternate resources for allegedly unavailable ones, and enforcing policies and laws against deceptive practices while ensuring that all potential deceivees know what they are.

Our previous work applied these ideas to the defense of a computer system from a network attack, by persuading the attacker that critical resources were not available to continue (Rowe, 2007). In the current work we studied an example of the reverse problem, of figuring how to thwart negative deception that tries to frustrate attempts to vote electronically. (Keyssar, 2000) recounts the tortured history of suffrage in the United States, which includes many methods of denial such as difficult registration sites, difficult registration hours, poll taxes, difficult required documents, difficult poll locations, ballot shortages, inadequate polling facilities, and lost ballots (Piven & Cloward, 1985). Electronic voting (Gritzalis, 2003) could provide more secure election management, but its implementation is difficult. Voting is an ideal target for negative deception because it is run by government bureaucracies with a reputation for frustrating inefficiency (Barton, 1980). We would like to provide systematic guidance for electoral commissions, watchdog groups, policies, and laws to safeguard the electoral process.

We implemented a Prolog program to model this problem using a two-agent model (voter and election commission). The process modeled is one where voters register to get a password, then use this password on election day to vote on machines at a polling place. The top-level goals for the voter were to submit a ballot and get it acknowledged; the top-level goals for the commission were to present a count of the vote and to correctly acknowledge that the vote of each voter was included in the total. We implemented a logical model of the voting process with formal definitions of 15 action types permitting a total of 35 distinct actions. The resources required were ballots, votes, voting machines, voting networks, counts, "logged-in" status, proofs of residency, proofs of age, passwords, registrars, knowledge of the locations of the registration office, the poll, and the information desk, and knowledge of the time of the election and when a voting machine was free. With some random choices included to model real-world uncertainty, the typical calculated voting plan had 38.2 steps. Here are example specifications for the act of person X marking document Y:

- Marking a ballot is done by a voter.
- Only documents can be marked.
- X should mark Y only when X wants Y marked.
- The preconditions on X marking Y are that X has Y, X sees Y, and X knows how to use the marking device.
- The normal postconditions are that X has marked Y.
- 10% of the time, marking fails and Y is "spoiled".
- Marking a ballot takes 10 minutes on the average.
- When several things can be marked, there is no preference of the order.

We rated plausible but consistent ways to falsely deny resources for a random voting plan. Our ratings method described above prefers deceptions that look like normal breakdowns of the voting process rather than a conspiracy to prevent voting which could cause public outcry. Here are the highest-rated deceptions found by our implementation; the full analysis found 116 deception opportunities. Ensuring logical consistency in deception means that each must be done with the first use of the resource and continued with every subsequent use of the resource.

- When the voter tries to vote page 1 of the ballot, abort execution with an error message about the ballot. [weight 0.129]
- When the voter tries to log in to the voting machine, refuse with an error message about invalid credentials. [weight 0.128]
- When the electoral commission tries to count the vote, abort with an error message saying the count is invalid. [weight 0.126]
- When the electoral commission tries to acknowledge a voter ballot, abort with an error message. [weight 0.126]
- When the voter tries to use a marker to mark their ballot, have this fail. [weight 0.125]

As mentioned, each of these can be implemented in several ways. For instance, the first deception could mean displaying an obviously damaged ballot image, having the machine crash (stop working), or having the machine wait forever without displaying.

Each of the ploys we have found (especially the high-rated ones) needs then to be addressed by specific planned countermeasures. For instance, voting machines should record all actions on them in a file on each machine, especially unusual actions such as ballot failure. Replacement voting machines or alternate procedures for obtaining voting credentials should be provided. Manipulation of voting counts could be reduced by requiring formal verification techniques on electoral software to show that it works correctly in all situations including with interruptions. Obstruction of legitimate voter registration attempts can be reduced by voters asking for precise legal justifications for obstructive behavior encountered, then checking these with independent authorities. Deception involving voter registration can be reduced by laws requiring the media to announce voter registration offices, and instituting penalties for deliberately disseminating incorrect information.

Acknowledgements. This work was supported by the National Science Foundation under the Cyber Trust Program. Opinions expressed are those of the author alone.

References

Barton, A.: A Diagnosis of Bureaucratic Maladies. In: Weiss, C., Barton, A. (eds.) Making Bureaucracies Work, pp. 27–36. Sage, Beverly Hills, California (1980)

Carbonell, J.: Counterplanning: A Strategy-Based Model of Adversary Planning in Real-World Situations. Artificial Intelligence 16, 295–329 (1981)

Gritzalis, D.: Secure Electronic Voting. Kluwer, Norwell, Massachusetts (2003)

Keyssar, A.: The Right to Vote: The Contested History of Democracy in the United States. Basic Books, New York (2000)

Piven, F., Cloward, R.: Prospects for Voter Registration Reform: A Report on the Experiences of the Human SERVE Campaign. Political Science 18(3), 582–593 (1985)

Rowe, N.: Finding Logically Consistent Resource-Deception Plans for Defense in Cyberspace. In: 3rd International Symposium on Security in Networks and Distributed Systems, Niagara Falls, Ontario, Canada (May 2007)

Rowe, N., Rothstein, H.: Two Taxonomies of Deception for Attacks on Information Systems. Journal of Information Warfare 3(2), 27–39 (2004)

Vrij, A.: Detecting Lies and Deceit: The Psychology of Lying and the Implications for Professional Practice. Wiley, Chichester, UK (2000)

Surveillance, Persuasion, and Panopticon

Julie Leth Jespersen, Anders Albrechtslund, Peter Øhrstrøm,
Per Hasle, and Jørgen Albretsen

Aalborg University, Denmark
{jlj2203,alb,poe,phasle,jalb}@hum.aau.dk

Abstract. The surveillance in public and private places, both physically and digitally, is increasing for different reasons. In this paper we intend to discuss surveillance and persuasive technology in an ethical perspective with an eye to its historical and cultural context. In section 1, we present some different tendencies of surveillance in society. In section 2, we elaborate on some important historical ideas on surveillance. In section 3, we consider the use of persuasive technology for surveillance purposes. In section 4, we discuss the development towards increasing surveillance in society, at work, in public places etc. In section 5, we draw up some ethical concerns on surveillance, and finally. In section 6, we discuss the question of a possible need for a public and democratic control of the use of surveillance technology.

Keywords: Captology, persuasive technologies, Panopticon, ethics, surveillance and democratic control.

1 Introduction

There is clearly an increasing interest in various forms of surveillance and information gathering activities. This tendency may be understood in terms of the Greek neologism 'Panopticon' ('pan' meaning 'everything' and 'opticon' meaning 'vision'), which was made famous by the British jurist and philosopher Jeremy Bentham (1748-1832). Panopticon was originally the name for a specific kind of prison (see below), but it has come to signify the wish or the will to let everything be seen and recorded. In modern society this desire seems to be very strong. All sorts of companies, organizations, and institutions want to store data about members, customers, patients etc. Such data are sometimes used for other purposes than those for which they were originally intended. Surveillance systems and IT systems are used to monitor people for different purposes – for instance the purpose of facilitating learning or daily work, or for security reasons.

Surveillance Tendencies

Since the introduction of computerized surveillance – also known as 'dataveillance' – in the latter part of the 20th century, we have witnessed an increase in monitoring practices in everyday life. Today, we are being monitored at home, at work and as consumers. Prevalent and emerging technologies such as closed-circuit television, electronic tagging and handheld computers contribute to the flow of private information in public

Y. de Kort et al. (Eds.): PERSUASIVE 2007, LNCS 4744, pp. 109–120, 2007.

space. These developments have led to what some people consider an erosion of civil rights and liberties, and a number of studies into this question have appeared. In the wake of the new surveillance technologies and the concern about their implications for the individual and society as a whole, surveillance studies have grown to be a broad field of research. The idea of the Panopticon has provided a metaphorical framework within which to discuss surveillance in a wide variety of contexts.

2 Surveillance in a Historical Perspective

The famous Panopticon building, 'the all-seeing place', was designed by Jeremy Bentham towards the end of the eighteenth century. It is a type of prison, also known as the 'Inspection House', whose construction enables an observer to watch all the prisoners without their knowledge.

Bentham is also known as a founding father of the ethical theory of utilitarianism, and it is in light of this theory that Panopticon should be understood. The basic principle of utilitarianism, according to which any moral behaviour is evaluated according to its utility, is realizeopd in the prison building, since the design facilitates effective surveillance and control with a minimum of human resources. Moreover, the aim is to punish effectively, but without undue human suffering, the punishment consisting in systematic confinement rather than physical torture. The development from physical torture to systematic confinement is by many considered a humanistic improvement in the history of punishment. This view has later been questioned by Michel Foucault (1926 - 1984), who in his influential book *Surveiller et punir* [7] argued that the change from physical torture to systematic confinement is not necessarily a humanistic improvement, but rather just a different way to exercise power.

For his day, Bentham was a controversial figure, and his prison design stirred attention. Bentham proposed a universal solution to the problems of his day: "Morals reformed - health preserved - industry invigorated instruction diffused - public burthens lightened - Economy seated, as it were, upon a rock - the Gordian knot of the Poor-Laws are not cut, but untied - all by a simple idea in Architecture!" [2 p. 31]

Not only would Panopticon solve the perennial problem of what to do with prisoners, the utilitarian architecture also provided answers to broader political questions. The prisons of this time were brutal, unsanitary, and overcrowded. Hence humanitarian improvements were on the political agenda, and in this context Bentham's prison building apparently offered a more humane alternative. Panopticon made it possible that prisoners could remain on British soil, rather than for instance being deported to Australia, which was not unusual at the time.

However, Bentham was unable to persuade the political establishment that the Panopticon would suffice. The decisive issue leading to the rejection of Bentham's plans was neither the prison design itself, nor its' underlying utilitarian ideas, but the other part of the project, namely the proposal that Panopticon should be open to private contractors. He imagined the prison as a private, profit-seeking enterprise, making money from the labour of the prisoners, and Bentham himself wanted to be the first contractor. The financial element coursed the project to be turned down, while the commercial gain from running prisons was considered inappropriate. The authority and control of prison labour was best kept in bureaucratic hands, and prisons should not meet economic criteria. Even though Panopticon was rejected by Bentham's fellow countrymen, his idea of such a prison has been very influential. This is among other things due to its effective application to most kinds of institutions where people are to be watched.

The prison was designed to have an inspection tower in the middle surrounded by a circular building with cells. The prison guard should be placed in the tower and the prisoners isolated in the cells, which should all be visible at any time from the tower in the middle. As much as possible of the cells should be made visible, whereas the tower is designed to make the guards inside the tower invisible from the cells, using screens and light as devices to hide the guard from the prisoners. The principle that the prisoners do not know whether they are being watched or not is essential to Panopticon. The prisoners have to presume that they are being watched all the time and must thus behave accordingly. Actually, this renders the guard dispensable, since the prisoners in a way have internalized the inspection by the guard. Thus the prisoner carries out his own surveillance. It should therefore be emphasized that Panopticon is not just the guard watching the prisoners. All personnel and all prisoners as well as the building, that is, the prison as a whole, make up the panoptic structure. An example blueprint can be seen in Figure 1.

Bentham was mainly occupied with prisons, but the utilitarian design could in principle be useful everywhere. Factories, military barracks, schools, and hospitals are institutions where the panoptic design would have obvious advantages. The specific prison design was never realized. Bentham had high hopes, but the utilitarian building was not to make him a wealthy man. Few prisons have been built with a direct influence from the Panopticon, but there are some, for example Eastern State

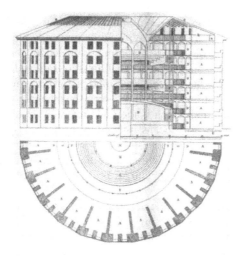

Fig. 1. Panopticon blueprint by Jeremy Bentham, 1791[15]

Penitentiary in Pennsylvania, USA. However, many prisons, factories, military barracks, schools, and hospitals all over the world may have been indirectly influenced by the panoptic principles from Bentham's prison design. As a proposal for a specific architecture the Panopticon is an idea of the past, but Panopticism, i.e. the underlying ideas, constitute a principle still at work today.

Bentham was declaredly a secular thinker. Like many other social thinkers of his time, he was occupied with providing an alternative to the theologically motivated ideas which still dominated society. Religion should be replaced with what he considered to be reason and rationality. Even so, there seem to be some religious undertones in Bentham's assumption that the constant gaze of the inspector will discourage prisoners from doing evil - and perhaps even remove the incentive to think about evil deeds. Since the constant gaze of the inspector can hardly be realized, because continuous supervision would be unpractical and expensive, Bentham comes up with the essential principle that the required supervision only needs to be in the minds of the observed. God's omnipresent eye is thus replaced by the internalization of the observer's potential gaze in the minds of the observed. Bentham rejected Christianity as a solution for social problems. Nevertheless, some of the useful social functions performed by Christianity could in his opinion with advantage be kept - just without its religious core. With the Panopticon, God's eye was thus transformed into a secular context [12 p. 599]. It is, however, clear that this kind of panoptic supervision is in fact qualitatively different from the divine omnipresence included in the Christian idea of an almighty, omnipresent, all-knowing, and all-loving God.

In his *Surveiller et punir* [7], Foucault discussed Bentham's ideas of Panopticon in the context of the European history of criminal law from medieval physical torture to modern day imprisonment. This history is a development leading from public, spectacular, and instantaneous punishment - e.g. the cutting off of limbs - to systematic confinement, putting away criminals into prisons for durations of months or years. Foucault described Panopticism as a new political anatomy, in which discipline replaces the earlier sovereign power (e.g. the king) that was manifested in pomp and circumstance. The sovereign was replaced by a more subtle and hidden authority. This new kind of authority exercised its power by objectifying the subjects which it desired to control, and by creating knowledge about them. Therefore, Panopticism implies a disciplinary power that aims to train and manipulate the body, and Panopticism thus has both a negative and a positive function. The negative function is to set up such limits as are necessary for maintaining discipline, and the positive one is the production which is the outcome of strict discipline. Disciplinary power comprises a series of means including drills, constant reports, testing, regulation, and not least surveillance. Among these means, surveillance plays a prominent part as a kind of 'visibility instrument' that ensures control of the individual. Disciplinary power thus mainly exercises its power through the gaze, more specifically the all-seeing eye.

The Panopticon was also a laboratory or a testing ground for social techniques. It could be used as a 'machine' to carry out experiments with the aim of altering behaviour, or of training or correcting individuals; to experiment with medicines and monitor their effects; to try out different punishments on prisoners, according to their crimes and character, and to seek the most effective ones; to teach different techniques simultaneously to workers in order to decide which is the best; to try out pedagogical experiments – in particular the well-debated problem of secluded education, by using orphans. [8 p. 3] To sum up the characteristics of Panopticism, at least five points can be made:

1. The observer is not visible from the position of the observed;
2. The observed subject is kept conscious of being visible (which together with the principle immediately above in some cases makes it possible to omit the actual surveillance);
3. Surveillance is made simple and straightforward. This means that most surveillance functions can be automated;
4. Surveillance is depersonalized, because the observer's identity is unimportant. The resulting anonymous character of power actually gives Panopticism a democratic dimension, since anybody can in principle perform the observation required;
5. Panoptic surveillance can be very useful for research on human behaviour, since it due to its practice of observing people allows systematic collection of data on human life.

Bentham's idea of the prison building Panopticon is really just the prototype of Panopticism, where discipline, normalization, and surveillance come together. This observation led Foucault to ask the polemic question, why factories, military barracks, schools, and hospitals have a striking resemblance to each other [7 p. 264]. Foucault's own answer was the contention that Panopticism has become general and is found everywhere. Hence, we live in a prison-like society founded on discipline and surveillance. The formation of this society stems from many historical processes, but it is a surveillance society and its purest form is the prison. Conceived in this way the Panopticon is not only a building. According to Foucault it is rather a schema which can be used for characterizing many aspects of society. In his own words it is "the diagram of a mechanism of power reduced to its ideal form" [8 p. 3]. Although Foucault's Panoptic interpretation of society has been widely criticised, it remains the preferred framework for discussing surveillance and an important inspiration within surveillance studies.

3   The Use of Persuasive Technologies for Surveillance

In his book *Persuasive technology – Using Computers to Change What We Think and Do*, B.J. Fogg gives a definition of surveillance technology, which is adapted to the context of persuasive technology: "… surveillance technology is defined as any computing technology that allows one party to monitor the behaviour of another to modify behaviour in a specific way." [6 p. 46] Fogg's discussion of surveillance presupposes that surveillance must be known by the person observed, who gives the input to the surveillance system in question. Output is sent to the observer, who then interacts with the person observed by either rewarding or punishing [6 p. 57 (Note 30)]. According to Fogg this feedback makes it reasonable to characterize the system as interactive.

Fogg explains the widespread use of surveillance with the observation that it works, that is, that surveillance usually yields the desired results. It has for a long time been a much researched topic within social psychology, and the conclusion from this research is that observation changes people's behaviours. Behaviour is changed when the observer is given the ability to reward or punish. This causes the observed subject to try to meet the expectations of the observer [6 p. 46]. Furthermore, the surveillance must be overt, since secret monitoring (covert surveillance) cannot be persuasive technology. However it must be admitted that the way the Panopticon was to be used implies a kind of surveillance which can also be viewed as Persuasive Technology, even though it is not a benign sort. In fact there is an interesting parallel between Foucault's discussion of the Panopticon and such a use of Persuasive Technology. In Foucault's terms the designer of (Panopticon-like) persuasive technologies may be viewed as an "inspector" whereas the user can be viewed as a prisoner caught in the framework of the system. Fogg suggests that companies, in order to motivate positively rather than punishing, should call their surveillance systems "incentive systems" or "incentive management technology" [6 p. 48].

In dealing with "Public Compliance without Private Acceptance", Fogg describes some further results of surveillance. People might accept surveillance while they are being observed and behave according to the relevant prescribed standards. When the monitoring stops, however, they may behave like before, except if they have private reasons for continuing the new behaviour. Fogg mentions ethical concerns in connection with the use of surveillance. He sees ethical questions arising in relation to the preservation of the individual's privacy and dignity [6 p. 49]. Furthermore, he thinks it makes a decisive difference *how* a system works and whether the intention is "…supportive or helpful rather than punitive" [6 p. 226].

This figure is based on Eric Neuenschwander and Daniel Berdichevsky's model [3 p. 55]. Eric Neuenschwander and Daniel Berdichevsky´s model differs from

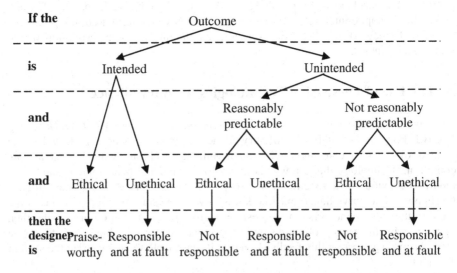

Fig. 2. Fogg's model of the ethical nature of persuasive technology [6 p. 227]

Fogg's on the case when the outcome is unintended, not reasonably predictable and unethical. In this case Eric Neuenschwander and Daniel Berdichevsky do not see the designer as responsible and at fault.The main criterion of Fogg's proposal for evaluating persuasive technology is indicated by the statement that "the ethical nature of persuasive technology can hinge on whether or not the outcome was intended" [6 p. 227]. Fogg puts forth a hierarchy of questions which in fact make up a decision tree or decision algorithm as depicted above.

Thus, for instance, one must ask as the first question whether the outcome of some use of a piece of persuasive technology was intended or not. Let us try to follow a path through the decision tree. If for instance the outcome was unintended, the next question should be whether it was reasonably predictable or not; if reasonably predictable, then it is time to evaluate whether the outcome was ethical, relative to the values and assumption underlying the particular analysis. If ethical, there is no special ethical value to attach to the designer(s) in question – they cannot be praised, since the positive outcome was not intended, but on the other hand there is no reason for a negative assessment either. If on the other hand the outcome was unethical, the designers are "responsible and at fault", since they ought to have foreseen the unethical effect (being in this case "reasonably predictable"). It should be clear how other paths through the decision tree can be followed [6 p. 227].

Fogg presents his version of a stakeholder analysis as a methodology for analyzing ethics [6 p. 233 f.]. In his analysis Fogg suggests that, like stakeholders, we focus on consequences, both gains and loses. To judge consequences one must also consider who gains the most and who loses the most. Having made our analysis we can then draw ethical conclusions by examining gains and losses in terms of a set of values. In this connection we must acknowledge the values and assumptions we bring into our analysis. This stakeholder analysis does not include the intentions behind the use of a technology, or the methods used to persuade.

Thus Fogg [6] raises various questions – and proposals – concerning the ethical dimension of persuasion and persuasive technology. It is acknowledged that there may be negative consequences of the use of surveillance technology. On the other hand we must keep in mind that surveillance seems to be very effective and useful when it comes to influencing people's behaviour.

It should be added that surveillance is in some cases aimed at behavioural patterns of groups rather than individuals. This kind of surveillance is more complicated, since it involves handling large collections of data in a specific manner. The kind of interactivity involved will also tend to be more complex. If for instance a relevant authority wants to confront a population group with the result of social surveillance (e.g. the drinking habits of young people) in order to obtain a certain change of the group's behaviour, this would presumably call for a sophisticated use of mass media.

4 Modern Surveillance Technology in a Social Perspective

In modern society the possibilities of monitoring people with the purpose of changing behaviour is growing – and hence the temptation to do so is growing, too. Below are listed a few examples of surveillance systems, all overt in some sense (the intention may be covert, but the surveillance as such is overt).

- Educational systems. Such systems may be designed and implemented with the purpose of educating staff, but may easily develop into a tool for seeing who improves his or her skills, and who does not.
- Accountancy systems. Basically, these are intended to make everybody's job easier. Data are formalized in a way that makes it possible for many systems to read and condition the data. But such systems are also potentially capable of registering if somebody makes a mistake, and to count the number of mistakes.
- Security systems. Such systems are installed in order to protect personnel. For instance, a small card with a chip and a pin-code can be used when entering and leaving all rooms. This also provides the management with the possibility of registering where all employees are at all times.

Such systems are all aimed at the behaviour of identifiable individuals. In other cases, however, the focus of the surveillance is rather on the collective behaviour pattern of specific groups in society. Here the surveillance will often be covert, i.e., not known by the persons being observed. This surveillance of various groups involves using various kinds of search strategies, statistics, and social sorting. In many cases data mining techniques could be utilized. Some algorithms for performing data mining are even classified as privacy preserving data mining (PPDM). They veil data in a given data set, typically extracted from databases, such that privacy is ensured while the veiled or aggregated data can be used as a reliable source for system administration, or indeed research. Even if the focus of surveillance is on social groups and not on individuals, researchers will in many cases be given access to sensitive personal and individual data. And this may of course be seen as a threat to the individual right to privacy. Philosophically, use of PPDM can be seen as a solution to the problem that from a societal point of view the argument "right to know" must be balanced by the individual's "right to private life".

Panoptic Sort and Social Sorting in Research on Personal Data

An increasing number of data describing different aspects of our personal activities are being stored in databases. Our search activities and various kinds of metadata related to what we consider to be our private writings and photos are continuously inspected and gathered for use in databases. In some cases, these databases can be accessed via the Internet. In fact, most of the databases on personal data may in a not too distant future be integrated into one comprehensive system. Information technology may in this way give rise to a new kind of Panopticism. This will obviously be very attractive from a research point of view – and so it may be for private purposes, for that matter. The new Panopticon will be the integrated system of all the personal databases to which the researcher is given access. Given the relevant political permission, the researcher may of course in principle use this new Panopticon as a laboratory – as suggested by Foucault in order to carry out social experiments. However, it is more likely that researchers will generally have to concentrate on observations rather than experiments, the latter being ethically and politically much more sensitive. But the researcher, like the Panopticon inspector, will be able to 'spy' on – or to put it more neutrally, to observe – all the individuals in the system in order to analyze and evaluate their behaviour in various ways.

From the perspective of the welfare of the persons being described, research on personal data may obviously in many cases be beneficial. However, in other cases people may find it problematic that somebody is carrying out research on their personal data and thereby providing results which may turn out to affect their lives. The results of this kind of research will inevitably be used in various kinds of decision making, notably and not least when employing personnel. One important problem has to do with the so-called 'panoptic sort', which is a concept Oscar Gandy introduced and described in *The Panoptic Sort: A Political Economy of Personal Information* (1993) [10] as well as in other works:

> The panoptic sort is a complex discriminatory technology. It is panoptic in that it considers all information about individual status and behaviour to be potentially useful in the production of intelligence about a person's economic value. It is discriminatory because it is used to sort people into categories based upon these estimates. [11 p. 133-34]

Usually, information is gathered in order to profile and categorize, and in this way people are included and excluded, qualified and disqualified, in all sorts of contexts. The panoptic sort is thus a pre-emptive means in the hands of governments and commercial enterprises. Gandy's primary concern back in 1993 seems to have been discriminatory practices related to consumer surveillance, using databases to target 'valuable' customers for further advertising, while undesired consumers are dismissed. In the light of the suicide attacks of September 11, 2001, on New York's Twin Towers and The Pentagon in Washington, D.C., the panoptic sort has become topical in the context of the so-called 'War on Terror'. All the suicide attackers were Muslims, and this fact could induce a panoptic sort profiling and categorizing of this group of people as potentially dangerous. This could in practice lead to wide discrimination in airports and at border crossings against the millions of people that fit this profile.

This leads to another point relating to the discriminatory technology of the panoptic sort, since profiling and categorizing is not only something that affects people at the individual level. David Lyon has described how surveillance goes beyond the individual realm to the social realm:

> [I] argue that there are dangers inherent in surveillance systems whose crucial coding mechanisms involve categories derived from stereotypical or prejudicial sources. Given that surveillance now touches all of us who live in technologically 'advanced' societies in the routine activities of everyday life, on the move as well as in fixed locations, the risks presented go well beyond anything that quests for 'privacy' or 'data protection' can cope with on their own. [13 p. 2]

Thus, discussions of surveillance in the context of research on personal data should not be limited to considerations of privacy – the observation that certain information due to its sensible and private nature should not be accessible without the consent of the relevant person(s). We must also be concerned with the super-individual level and include questions relating to the social justice of using information for research purposes. Similarly, we should be wary of prejudices which could be inherited in the way information has been gathered.

5 Modern Surveillance Technology in an Ethical Perspective

As mentioned above a distinction should be made between surveillance of the individual and surveillance of groups in society. However, in both cases there are important ethical problems to consider.

Individuals may be watched for security reasons. An example of this kind of surveillance could be digital surveillance, where the system registers the behaviour of the individual. This kind of surveillance is personalized and may imply, or utilize, various accusations concerning the individual (whether proved or not). Just for example, a store owner might video-tape a specific employee whom he suspects of stealing. This problem has prompted the invention of the cash register [14].

Mass surveillance targets groups or certain profiles, which can lead to discrimination of certain groups or people with certain traits. But it may also be justified and in fact necessary to make use of this surveillance technique, for instance to avoid terror activity.

Both kinds of surveillance raise concerns with respect to individual privacy and other civil liberties. On the other hand, surveillance can be seen as a form of persuasive design. If the individual is aware of being monitored he or she will be motivated to change behaviour to what is considered desirable according to society's norms. The same thing applies to group surveillance.

Surveillance of social groups is often carried out using various kinds of data mining, as mentioned earlier. The technique can popularly be defined as "the nontrivial extraction of implicit, previously unknown, and potentially useful information from data" or as "the science of extracting useful information from large data sets or databases" [16]. The purpose of data mining makes it applicable to behaviour patterns of selected social groups, especially when wishing to make general observations without giving researchers access to all individual data. In [4], [5] and [9] data mining and its privacy preserving potentials are discussed.

There is however one further question that applies to the ethics of persuasion and surveillance of individuals as well as groups. As argued by B.T.C. Atkinson [1] the intent of 'the persuader' should be made clear to whoever is exposed to the use of persuasive technology. If this condition is not fulfilled, the process should be characterized as manipulation. The view is that openness regarding the purpose of the technology employed could serve as a kind of 'ethical safeguard'. In relation to the use of surveillance technology for persuasion purposes this means that the people under observation, should be made aware of the intent of those conducting the surveillance. However, in many cases the purpose of surveillance is rather vague and general. When it comes to group surveillance, mass media will usually be involved when the result is communicated. We agree with this basic principle, but it must be admitted that it is difficult to make a clear distinction between the use of mass communication for persuasive purposes as opposed to the purpose of informing.

6   Conclusions and Further Perspectives

Surveillance makes it possible to change the behaviour of individuals – at least as long as they know they are being monitored. Surveillance may also influence the behaviour patterns of social groups, especially if the results of the surveillance studies are communicated in an adequate manner using mass media.

If one wants to limit surveillance involving private and ethically sensitive data, it may be required that access to the data is limited. All data may be depersonalized before they are used for research purposes. But such requirements may also make many important research projects very difficult or outright impossible to carry out. For this reason, it may be relevant to look for ethically acceptable alternatives to depersonalization and other requirements limiting research access to all relevant data. One obvious solution is to make use of privacy preserving data mining algorithms which make it possible to run the surveillance systems without human inspection of sensitive data. The appealing aspect of this approach is the fact that data need not be traced back to any individual. On the other hand, this makes an assessment of the correct use of the data with reference to ethical norms more important.

There is no reason to underplay the importance of developing good data mining algorithms, as long as this kind of computer based privacy preserving tools is not presented as the solution to all ethical problems of panoptic research and surveillance. The development of data mining algorithms is important as a possible way to ensure a high ethical standard in panoptic research and surveillance of personal data. But it is also clear that the use of such algorithms is not sufficient for that purpose. We also need some sort of public and democratic awareness and discussion of the values on which the data mining algorithms are based. Here the only acceptable solution seems to be some sort of control on the collection as well as the use of data in panoptic research and surveillance. This control should also include other aspects and problems such as social sorting by means of which can be disadvantageous for certain people in an unjust manner. Another potential problem, which calls for democratic awareness is data dredging, i.e.,"…the inappropriate (sometimes deliberately so) search for 'statistically significant' relationships in large quantities of data" [17].

Acknowledgements

We thank Mikkel Leth Jespersen for very useful comments on an earlier version of this paper. We also acknowledge the stimulus and support of the 'European project on delimiting the research concept and the research activities (EURECA)' sponsored by the European Commission, DG-Research, as part of the Science and Society research programme — 6th Framework.

References

1. Atkinson, B.: Captology: A Critical Review, In: IJsselsteijn, W., de Kort, Y., Midden, C., Eggen, B., van den Hoven, E. (eds.) PERSUASIVE 2006. LNCS, vol. 3962, pp. 171–182. Springer, Heidelberg (2006)
2. Bentham, J., Bozovic, M.: The Panopticon writings, London, New York, Verso (1995)

3. Berdichevsky, D., Neuenschwander, E.: Toward an ethics of persuasive technology. Communication of the ACM (1999)
4. Bertino, E., Nai Fovino, I., Parasiliti Provenza, L.: A Framework for Evaluating Privacy Preserving Data Mining Algorithms. Data Mining and Knowledge Discovery 11, 121–154 (2005)
5. Domingo-Ferrer, J., Torra, V.: Privacy in Data Mining. Data Mining and Knowledge Discovery 11, 117–119 (2005)
6. Fogg, B.J.: Persuasive technology – Using computers to change what we think and do. Morgan Kaufmann, San Francisco (2003)
7. Foucault, M.: Surveiller et punir: naissance de la prison, Paris, Gallimard (1975)
8. Foucault, M.: Discipline & Punish. Translated from the French by Alan Sheridan, 195–228 (1977), http://foucault.info/documents/disciplineAndPunish/foucault.disciplineAndPunish.panOpticism.html
9. Fule, P., Roddick, J.: Detecting Privacy and Ethical Sensitivity in Data Mining Results. In: Estivill-Castro, V. (ed.) Conferences in Research and Practice in Information Technology, Australian Computer Society, Inc. (2004)
10. Gandy, O.: The Panoptic Sort: A Political Economy of Personal Information. Westview Press (1993)
11. Gandy, O.: Coming to Terms with the Panoptic Sort. In: Lyon, D., Zureik, E. (eds.) Computers, Surveillance, and Privacy, Minneapolis University Press (1996)
12. Lyon, D.: Bentham's Panopticon: From Moral Architecture to Electronic Surveillance. Queen's Quarterly 98, 596–617 (1991)
13. Lyon, D.: Surveillance as Social Sorting: Privacy, Risk, and Digital Discrimination, Routledge (2003)
14. Quorion Data Systems (accessed March 28, 2007), www.quorion.de/Cash%20Registers/cash_register_history_types.htm
15. Wikipedia 2006a. Image: Panopticon (accessed March 9, 2006), available at the website http://en.wikipedia.org/wiki/Image:Panopticon.jpg
16. Wikipedia: 2006b. Data mining (accessed February 27, 2006), available at the website http://en.wikipedia.org/wiki/Data_mining
17. Wikipedia: 2007c. Data dredging (accessed January 30, 2007), available at the website http://en.wikipedia.org/wiki/Data_dredging

Support Services: Persuading Employees and Customers to Do what Is in the Community's Best Interest

Mark Brodie, Jennifer Lai, Jonathan Lenchner, William Luken, Kavitha Ranganathan, Jung-Mu Tang, and Maja Vukovic

IBM T.J. Watson Research Center, 19 Skyline Drive, Hawthorne, NY 10532
{mbrodie,jlai,lenchner,luan,wluken,kavithar,jmtang,
mvukovi}@us.ibm.com

Abstract. Getting workers to share knowledge in situations where "knowledge" is the primary asset making them valuable is a pressing problem in many organizations – leading to what we call "the knowledge worker's prisoner's dilemma." Interesting variants of this dilemma arise in the contexts of customer support and server system administration. We begin by describing some of the reasons why the uncooperative resolution of the dilemma is so detrimental from an organizational perspective. We then discuss a successful example of a cooperative resolution to the dilemma – the Open Source initiative. We articulate an ambitious long-term thesis regarding the electronic support ecosystem and then describe a multi-pronged approach for facilitating knowledge capture and sharing in the context of IBM's service industry, thereby facilitating a "win-win" or collaborative solution to the knowledge worker's prisoner's dilemma.

Keywords: knowledge sharing, prisoner's dilemma, collaboration, customer support, system administration.

1 Introduction: The Knowledge Worker's Prisoner's Dilemma

Asking workers to share their knowledge in situations where "knowledge" is the primary asset that makes them valuable is like asking taxpayers to spend their dollars to voluntarily contribute towards clean air. Everyone will benefit by contributing, but the person who will benefit the most is the one who does not make a contribution but benefits from the clean air others have paid for. Assuming that we all are rational human beings, it is not hard to see why no one would contribute to clean air and instead live in a polluted environment. Similarly, the worker who is able to zealously guard his or her knowledge but benefit from all the information contributed by workers to a centralized knowledge base has little incentive to contribute. Not only does he save the time and effort spent in sharing his knowledge but also preserves for himself the slice of knowledge that makes him highly valued and irreplaceable. In a competitive environment where workers value their time and jobs, it is again not hard to understand why a centralized knowledge base would lack viability despite the fact that if the collective knowledge and experiences of all the knowledge workers were pooled centrally and made accessible to all the players, everyone would benefit from the

Y. de Kort et al. (Eds.): PERSUASIVE 2007, LNCS 4744, pp. 121–124, 2007.

improved efficiency. This apparent paradox – where rationally behaving workers choose the sub-optimal path of non-cooperation is captured by the "Prisoners dilemma[1]".

2 The Open Source Analogy

One of the successful practices we can examine in an effort to escape the dilemma is open source software development. Open source has a simple philosophy that "when programmers can read, redistribute, and modify the source code for a piece of software, the software evolves. People improve it, people adapt it, people fix bugs ... at a speed that if one is used to the slow pace of conventional software development, seems astonishing [1]". Knowledge development shares common goals with software development such as the desire to create high quality content, a need for early error/ defect identification and fixes, and timely incorporation of new knowledge/features with up-to-date revisions. As such, knowledge development with broad participation from domain expert communities and the user communities can benefit from the open source philosophy and principles. User communities in open knowledge development play a more active and important role than in software development since users are the most likely ones to identify errors or shortcomings in existing knowledge documents and seek corrections, and/or identify the need for newly documented knowledge.

3 The Amazon/eBay Thesis and Its Extension to Support Services: The Support Ecosystem

Amazon Books and e-Bay are two prominent e-Commerce retailers that have succeeded in creating self-supporting e-Commerce infrastructures. These companies rely a great deal on user created content and are trusted reference sites when buying books or making auction purchases. From our perspective, the key elements provided by customers are the product reviews, vendor reviews, reviews of the reviews, and in effect the ratings of vendors and ratings of reviewers. The upshot is that because of all of the customer participation on these sites, each has become enormously credible.

Amazon and eBay have each managed to provide just the right incentives for their customers to share their knowledge and thus allow their sites to thrive. Our thesis is that the same can be done for electronic support. In other words, the most knowledgeable people about the typical company's products are not the manufacturers of the products, or the employees of the company, but rather the customers and users of the products, and so the optimal support structure is one in which the company simply facilitates customers helping customers, thereby relieving the company of amassing extremely expensive product expertise solely for the purpose of product support. Section 4 describes our modest steps towards realizing this vision of the company as facilitator of customers helping customers.

---

[1] The original conception of the "Prisoner's Dilemma" is credited to Merrill Flood and Melvin Dresher of RAND and its formalization is credited to the mathematician Albert Tucker. See [2] for details.

4   Components of Our Proposed Solution for Knowledge Acquisition and Management

Our approach for facilitating knowledge capture and sharing in the context of IBM's service industry is multi-pronged.

Firstly, our approach is based on *wiki-fying knowledge resources*, which enables maintaining up-to-date information at a minimal cost. Contrary to conventional knowledge management systems, which depend on knowledge producers to update and correct deficiencies in documents, our approach allows users to submit comments that become instantly visible to other users of the knowledge base. This objective may be accomplished through a wiki mechanism. This approach is most effective when there is no legacy knowledge base, or it is possible to replace a legacy knowledge base with a wiki-enabled data base containing wiki-enabled knowledge. In the case of an operational knowledge management system, it may be impossible to replace a legacy knowledge base with a wiki-compatible database. For incremental deployment, our system ensures that user comments only affect the presentation of the document. The legacy document stored in the knowledge base is not altered.

In parallel, our solution employs a *question-and-answer knowledge management system* – as opposed to a conventional knowledge management system, where all "knowledge" is contained in "knowledge documents", queries are ephemeral and mapped to documents upon search. The Q-and-A system contains a Question database (Q-base) and an Answer database (A-base). The A-base is equivalent to a conventional knowledge base except that we allow answer documents to be contributed by outside users, not necessarily official subject matter experts, in direct response to a specific question. The Q-base consists of records of every query submitted to the system. The contents of this database are generated by the users as they use the system. Any user can contribute a new question to the Q-base simply by asking a new question. If a submitted query has been submitted previously, or has high semantic affinity to a previous question, the system uses the experience from previous submissions to optimize the user's experience. If the query is not found in the Q-base, a new entry is added. After accumulating user experience for a period of time it becomes possible to anticipate the most common and most successful queries and answers, amongst other things making it possible to present a true and dynamic set of most frequently asked questions.

Furthermore, our approach enables *document and agent rating and ranking* for rating the efficacy of a document (knowledge slice) in the knowledge base as well as rating the contributors. Ranking/rating documents will help others locate useful slices – much like how a search engine ranks the results according to relevance. This ranking can either be done implicitly – by frequency of reference – or explicitly – by asking users to provide feedback on how useful a document was to them. The ratings of documents can then be used to rate/rank the contributor of the document. Providing workers with this opportunity to build their reputation not only fosters a sense of community but can also be used as the basis for a concrete reward structure.

In addition, our framework supports *real-time expertise sharing* to improve the efficiency of agent communication. The system is built on top of an existing instant messaging protocol and package and is available without the need to locate or install any additional software. In a first implementation we use the context of the current search or problem investigation to determine the subset of people with relevant expertise. Only "visible" experts are displayed on a given page. Visibility is defined by the person's willingness to be listed as available. The infrastructure for this tool, provides support for experts to control their visibility on the webpage, such as office hours, or how many simultaneous sessions they are willing to have open.

Another important component of our solution is *digital journaling* with blogIT. To facilitate the effective acquisition and sharing of information among system agents (up to 10% efficiency increase, according to initial tests), blogIT unifies multiple activity sources and depicts a comprehensive view of IT operations, including personal interactions and generated artifacts. blogIT is comprised of *data loggers*, which are responsible for automatic capture of problem-solving activities, *annotation tools*, which facilitate spontaneous recording and sharing of insights, and an *analytics engine*, which performs concept extraction from the archived multimodal data. blogIT integrates job ticket histories with other support activity such as email, chat sessions and phones calls into electronic chronicles, which can be illuminated with relevant documents, RSS feeds, images, and video clips. blogIT entries of resolution records can be reviewed by peers (other agents) for their usefulness and quality. The highest rated resolutions can then be incorporated into standard practices. By rating each other's problem resolution tickets, agents acquire a certain level of recognition and respect among each other as described in section (iii), giving an incentive for agents to provide additional and more precise feedback during *after call* activities.

5 Conclusion

We have described the knowledge worker's prisoner's dilemma and how it manifests itself in the contexts of customer support and server system administration. To address the dilemma, we have articulated an ambitious agenda regarding the support ecosystem, consisting of five lines of attack: (i) Wiki-fying knowledge resources, (ii) creating a Q-and-A based system that is stronger and more dynamic than the usual list of frequently asked questions, (iii) pervading document and agent rating and ranking across knowledge management systems, (iv) giving users real-time access just the right experts, and (v) giving those most pressed for time, a real-time assist to their process documentation via digital journaling. Our efforts to realize our ultimate agenda of simply facilitating customers helping customers are ongoing. For example, although we have succeeded in wiki-fying knowledge documents for use by call takers, this technology is yet to be put into the hands of end users. The same is true for real-time expertise sharing and digital journaling with blogIT, where we only have preliminary quantitative results pointing to the increased productivity of call center agents and server system administrators. In many cases, the full spectrum of the benefit is non-trivial to measure, but shall be the subject of our future work.

References

1. Open Source Initiative (OSI), http://www.opensource.org/index.php
2. Poundstone, W.: Prisoner's Dilemma. Doubleday, New York (1992)

Improving Cross-Cultural Communication Through Collaborative Technologies

Alyssa J. O'Brien, Christine Alfano, and Eva Magnusson

Stanford University, Örebro University

Abstract. The paper discusses an original research project in the area of education and cross-cultural rhetoric on the use of persuasive digital technologies to enable intercultural competencies among students and teachers across globally-distributed teams. The paper outlines the methodology for the research, including the use of video conferences, collaborative blogs, a project wiki, webforums, and Google documents, and presents the findings on how such information and communication technologies can influence people to approach cross-cultural communication with greater political understanding, ethical awareness, and intercultural competencies in order to bring about improved international and social relations. The paper presents statistical data pertaining to qualitative and quantitative assessment of project outcomes; it situates the project within current debates in intercultural communication and digital pedagogy; and it concludes with a projection on the scalability and sustainability of using computers to change human attitudes and behaviors in positive ways in an international context.

Keywords: education, trust, productivity, culture, social relationships, ethics, human attitudes, collaboration, international research, cross-cultural communication, and rhetorical theory.

1 Introduction

Through a Wallenberg Global Learning Network (WGLN) grant, our project aims to contribute new learning in the fields of education and cross-cultural rhetoric through application of persuasive digital technologies as the mode and apparatus for changing attitudes about cultures and for empowering users to develop intercultural competencies as a means for improving international relations, social relations, political understanding, and trust in educational and cultural exchanges. In this paper, we offer an international perspective on the use of persuasive technology in creating what in the literature is termed "intercultural competencies" among students and teachers across globally-distributed teams.

1.1 Overview and Research Goals

The past two decades have witnessed an explosion of interest in globalization, transnational studies, and cultural codes of communication and the concurrent scholarly attention to developing better methods of implementing technological tools in educational settings. Yet, a key problem remains: how best to use information and

Y. de Kort et al. (Eds.): PERSUASIVE 2007, LNCS 4744, pp. 125–131, 2007.

communication technologies (or ICTs) to offer students hands-on learning of transnational and intercultural differences. To address this problem, our WGLN project "Developing Intercultural Competencies through Collaborative Rhetoric" experimented with innovative uses of technology by bringing together students at Stanford and Örebro Universities in globally-distributed teams to analyze rhetorical artifacts (speeches, advertisements, architectural landmarks, representations of nationhood) with the aim of facilitating both practical and deep learning of effective cross-cultural communication skills and transnational cultural understanding.

In addition to this academic impetus, this project emerged to meet a very practical goal: how to prevent deep misunderstandings that can lead to conflagrations such as seen in the recent furor over a series of cartoons depicting the Prophet Muhammad; this incident focused worldwide attention not only on the power of images but also on the violence that can result from miscommunication stemming from narrow perspectives that fail to take into consideration intercultural contexts. Scholars Carl Lovitt and Dixie Goswami label this increasingly important skill intercultural competence and sensitivity. [1]

In such a globally connected world – where published words and images give rise to bombing and burnings – teachers need to know how to instruct students in intercultural rhetoric, that is, how to persuade people to understand the way in which others located in different global contexts perceive, analyze, and produce situated knowledge. By addressing this situation faced by academics and people in the field, this project aims to contribute both theoretical knowledge and a practical methodology for scalable implementation in other institutions as well as business and professional settings. Our larger goal is to build meta-knowledge about the critical role that intercultural competences and effective technologies solutions can play in global communication and international relations.

1.2 Intercultural Theory and Cross-Cultural Conflicts

Firstly, this project responds to debates within the field of intercultural theory about how best to approach developing sensitivity to and understanding of differently situated subject positions. The past decade's work in intercultural communication focused on emphasizing diversity and isolating differences; as researcher Dean Barnlund asked about the global village, "Will its residents be neighbors capable of respecting and utilizing their differences or clusters of strangers living in ghettos and united only in their antipathies for others?"[2] More recent scholarship in the field of intercultural communication, such as Fred Edmund Jandt's book, *Intercultural Communication: A Global Reader,* emerges from a sociological or cultural anthropological perspective and emphasizes deep immersion. However, while theorists such as David Vicor recommend learning "as much about another culture as possible" before initiating intercultural communication, this methodological approach to developing intercultural competencies leads to the pitfall that researchers Ronald Scollon and Suzanne Scollon describe as partial attention to specific cultural factors (such as ideology, discourse patterns, and facial features) at the expense of other interpersonal and cultural factors that influence the site of transnational exchange and understanding. [3]

Our project builds upon both this substantial body of research as well as upon rhetorical theory that offers ways of reading visual and verbal texts with attention to audience and cultural context. Thus, our approach relies on rhetorical theory, with its emphasis on audience, decorum, and doxa; we also build on digital technology and new media theory, building on scholarly advances in how individuals collaborate in multimedia modes across differences in abilities.

1.3 Information and Digital Technology Research

In addition, our project situates itself within new research in digital technologies for cross-cultural communication and international relations. Current work in intercultural theory, transnational studies, global rhetoric, and writing pedagogy all point to the need for new empirically tested practices and scholarly sound methods for developing solutions for how best to use information and communication technologies to offer students hands-on learning of transnational and intercultural differences.

Researchers such as Cynthia Selfe and Gail Hawisher [4] have called for studies on how technology can address global needs, and our research project attempts to explore the use of persuasive technologies for producing positive change in global worldviews, improved cross-cultural communication, and a deepened understanding of audience and context to facilitate improved international relations. To this end, we draw on the work of scholars such as Chris Abbott [5], who has argued persuasively for a reevaluation of the use of ICTs in the classroom based on their increasing prevalence as a mode of communication within an international context. In addition, our practical applications of ICT technologies in the classroom have been largely informed by scholars such as Robert Godwin-Jones [6], who argues that users increase their sense of personal accountability through engaging with a real audience via ICTs, and Ernst Bekkering and J.P. Shim, who theorize about how to optimize video conferencing interchanges to best facilitate the formation of strong working relationships [7]. Moreover, within the Wallenberg Hall Learning Network, the work of Renata Fructer on globally-distributed teams provided a foundation for our development of a protocol for small-group collaboration practices [8].

At its heart, therefore, this project builds on current scholarly literature and research to offer a model of pedagogical instruction and cross-cultural learning using ICTs to develop innovative classroom practices with persuasive, social end-goals. This project builds on the scholarly literature and previous research on digital technologies for collaborative global learning to present the design, implementation, and dissemination of a model for cross-cultural learning using persuasive digital technologies.

2 Methodology and Outcomes

2.1 Cross-Cultural Collaboration Through Persuasive Technology

For our approach and specific kind of intervention to the problem at the intersection of intercultural communication and digital technologies, we developed a protocol for employing the collaborative use of digital technologies – including webcam-enabled Marratech video conferencing among students, teachers, and researchers distributed across universities in two countries; five collaborative blogs and a project wiki for rhetorical analysis of controversial political texts; webforums for peer review of research on rhetorical texts of cultural significance; and Google documents for collaborative writing concerning the development of intercultural competencies. Our project locates intercultural competencies within collaborative activities made possible by implementation of these sorts of information and communication technologies, challenging users to examine political perspectives and cultural assumptions in order to produce positive change in social, cultural, and international relations.

2.2 Pedagogy and Research Protocol

While we build on other scholarly models of globally-distributed teamwork, our project isolates diverse configurations of participants (small teams of 3-4 students; 1-1 partner interaction; large class conversations) for collaborative work facilitated by our dedicated collaboration stations, blogs, student wiki, and live video conferences. Our methodology uses video-conferencing technologies to facilitate collaborative projects and self-determined work by globally-distributed student teams that accomplish cross-cultural learning about how best to communicate with diverse audiences through digital modes. In this way, we strive as much to meet deep learning objectives about intercultural competencies as we do to meet digital technology aims for best practices among globally distinct collaborators. Thus, while we seek to foster effective intercultural communication and use ICTs as a means to reach that goal, at the same time, we also recognize improved competency in ICTs to be an educational need. Our activities include the following:

- Globally-distributed work by small groups of students that involved collaborative analysis of different texts (online ads, websites, political speeches, and cultural artifacts) through the use of the mobile, collaborative stations and video conferencing. In-class video exchanges between student pairs during which time they actively engage in more individualized collaboration leading to a deliverable (a written text, an oral presentation) that is shared with the class as a whole at the end of the session.
- Outside of class one-on-one real-time interaction between student pairs from the different countries, using video MSNchat or Skye-hosted exchanges.
- Asynchronous exchanges through e-mail, collaborative blogs, and wikis.

Our virtual "Cross-Cultural Rhetoric Center" (http://www.stanford.edu/group/ccr) serves as an online nexus for our collaborative endeavors, houses the digital repository of pedagogical apparatus (project materials such as lesson plans, related readings, primary texts for analysis), links to our asynchronous collaborative platforms (the wiki and blogs), identifies project publications, and provides a common virtual meeting ground for institutions interested in joining in our cross-cultural exchange.

3   Results

We found that globally-distributed team work mediated by effective use of digital technologies can motivate and influence people to approach cross-cultural communication and cultural exchanges with greater sensitivity, understanding, and ethical awareness in order to bring about positive international and social relations. Our analysis of data collected as part of our assessment process (comprised of surveys, exit interviews, and focus groups) shows that technologically-mediated collaboration benefits participants in allowing them to develop their analytic skills and persuasive abilities in rhetoric and argumentation while building intercultural competencies and sensitivity to international contexts.

3.1   Quantitative Assessment of Research

Initial quantitative data from our fall exit survey show successful accomplishment of specific project learning outcomes with mean ratings well above the midpoint (3.0 on 6.0 Likert scale). The highest rating (mean = 5.4) is for the measure "sensitivity to and consideration for others," two key traits identified in the scholarly literature as essential for effective intercultural communication. We also learned that a rhetorical approach to cross-cultural texts led to increased sensitivity and cultural understanding; students achieved deep learning of intercultural competencies from collaborative rhetorical analysis of political texts (mean = 5.3), from analysis of writing (mean = 5.1) and from exchange of cultural identity (mean = 5.0).

In rating activities designed to facilitate intercultural competencies and cross-cultural collaboration (see Figure 1), our findings indicated that students learned most when working within a globally-distributed team across both countries mediated by effective use of information and communication technologies or ICTs (mean = 5.1).

Subsequent to this data collection, the study team redesigned the implementation of technology at both Örebro and Stanford to facilitate group collaboration in a

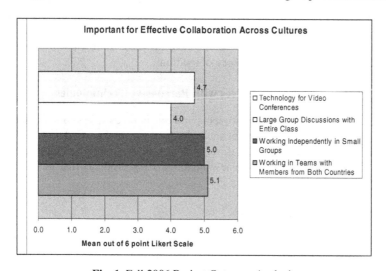

Fig. 1. Fall 2006 Project Outcome Analysis

dedicated learning space. In Winter 2007, we put our redesign into practice through the acquisition and effective implementation of dedicated collaboration stations at both Örebro and Stanford. This new, strategic use of technology enabled students to form strong interpersonal relationships that facilitated more effective group work.

3.2 Qualitative Assessment of Research

The qualitative data confirms these findings. One open-response from our data collection reads as follows: "I learned that by doing group work assignments [in globally-distributed teams or pairs], our ideas can really form within the cross-cultural context. We can really learn a great amount by sharing these ideas found within these small exchanges."

The exit narrative of Dennis Rydgren, a Swedish student, confirms these findings: "The idea to have a cross-cultural rhetoric education between Örebro and Stanford is something quite unique. We as students believed it to be a first step towards a global university and a new kind of education." In his closing evaluation, Dennis asserted the project provided "a foundation for global collaborations later on in life. The use of the Internet in education, and the doors it opens [...] gives the student 'global experience' not only through the social factor but also in a technical way." His words show development of intercultural competencies – sensitivity towards and understanding of others on a cultural level – as mediated by the technological practices of the project.

4 Significance and Implications

The project implementation and the data analysis both confirm the importance of strategic implementation of digital technologies as a persuasive tool for cross-cultural understanding and positive change with regard to intercultural competencies. We find the use of technologically-mediated collaboration to be an influential tool with regard to social relationships and improved cross-cultural understanding. Our research shows that three factors need to be met in the establishment of an effective protocol for digitally mediated cross-cultural collaboration and consequent intercultural understanding: *dedication of focus* to the task at hand; *simulated proximity* to the communicators; and close *transparency* of medium.

4.1 Observations for Best Practices with Persuasive Technologies

Our project discovered that when students and teachers learn best practices for using information and communication technologies, they gain knowledge not simply in modes for digital discourse but the development of tools to build relationships, cross-culturally situated knowledge, and new media writing products that in turn advance research and learning in the field.

4.2 Scalability and Sustainability

Now that the research protocol has been established, the project can scale up to include additional partners, across countries and institutions. In year 02 of our project, we plan to broaden our collaboration to include partners in Sweden (at Södertörn,

Uppsala, and Umeå) and internationally (University of British Columbia, Canada; University of Sydney, Australia; and University of Cape Town, South Africa).

This diversification across institutions is possible because, once the technology and protocol are in place, the project is highly sustainable given a dedicated project instructor and minimal infrastructure. The long-term sustainability of using computers to change human attitudes and behaviors in positive ways merits closer examination, and we have plans to follow our study participants as they graduate and move into professional careers that will place them in the global market place. As a future project, we seek to track the effective of the participation in an intercultural rhetoric collaboration for how it might have had lasting persuasive effects on their worldviews, approaches to cross-cultural differences, and strategies for intercultural communication.

The stakes are high for this project, for, as Larry Samovar, Richard Porter, and Edwin McDaniel argue in their seminal work, *Intercultural Communication,* "successful intercultural communication is a matter of highest importance if humankind and society are to survive" [9].

References

1. Lovitt, C.R., Goswami, D.: Exploring the Rhetoric of International Professional Communication, Baywood, NY (1999)
2. Barnlund, D.: Communication in a Global Village, Basic Concepts of Intercultural Communications, pp. 35–42. Intercultural Press (1998)
3. Scollen, R., Scollen, S.W.: Intercultural Communication. Blackwell, Oxford (1995)
4. Selfe, C., Hawisher, G.: Global Literacies and the World Wide Web. In: Selfe, C., Hawisher, G. (eds.) Passions, Pedagogies, and 21st Century Technologies, Utah State UP, Logan, 1999, Routledge, New York (2000)
5. Abbott, C.: ICT: Changing Education. Routledge/Falmer, London (2000)
6. Godwin-Jones, R.: Blogs & Wikis: Environments for On-line Collaboration. In: Language and Learning 7(2), pp. 12–16 (May 2003), Godwin-Jones, R.: Emerging Technologies: Skype and Podcasting: Disruptive Technologies for Language Learning. Language and Learning 9(3), pp. 9–12 (September 2005)
7. Bekkering, E., Shim, J.P.: i2i Trust in Videoconferencing. Communications of the ACM 49(7), 103–107 (2006)
8. Fruchter, R., Chen, M., Ando, C.: Geographically Distributed Teamwork Mediated by Virtual Auditorium. In: Rosenberg, D., Nishida, T., Fruchter, R. (eds.) Proc. of SID2003 2nd Social Intelligence Design Symposium, London, UK (2003)
9. Samovar, L.A., Richard, E.P., McDaniel, E.R.: Intercultural Communication: A Reader. Thomson Wadsworth (2005)

Group Reactions to Visual Feedback Tools

Joan Morris DiMicco[1] and Walter Bender[2]

[1] IBM T.J. Watson Research Center, 1 Rogers St., Cambridge, MA 02142 USA
[2] MIT Media Lab, 20 Ames St., Cambridge, MA 02139 USA
joan.dimicco@us.ibm.com, walter@media.mit.edu

Abstract. This paper presents findings on how individuals respond to receiving feedback on their participation levels during meetings. Comparing in-lab and natural group settings, repeated use, and differing information displays, we found that individuals vary on how useful and informative they found the feedback. Their ratings were most influenced by how the tool was first introduced to them and whether or not there was redundancy in the feedback.

Keywords: Behavior feedback, face-to-face interaction, computer-supported cooperative work.

1 Introduction

Organizations use groups for making decisions rather than individuals because, by pooling skills, intellectual abilities, and information sources, groups have the ability to make higher quality decisions than individuals working alone. However, group interactions are often complicated by social factors preventing them from realizing their potential [1]. To address this issue, our research has been focused on developing behavior feedback tools that assist groups in realizing their over-reliance on dominant viewpoints in a discussion [2, 3]. We believe that if a group becomes aware of extreme imbalances in its turn-taking and participation, it can assess and determine the best method for correcting its own processes. Towards testing this belief, we developed an application called Second Messenger that reveals information about the ongoing social dynamics within face-to-face groups through social visualizations of speaking patterns and frequencies.

While our central interest has been determining if feedback tools do in fact assist groups in changing their behavior [2], the reality is that if these tools are to be integrated into organizations and used to change real-world decision-making processes, it is critical that we also understand how individuals feel in response to the feedback tools being present. Specifically we want to know if individuals consciously use the feedback made available, if they believe the information provided is informative, if they find the tools useful for their tasks, and perhaps most importantly, how willing they are to incorporate them into their real-world group interactions.

To answer these questions, we ran two studies, one in the lab and one in the field, in order to understand user responses and how they varied across different situations. Our studies found consistent results across user groups and when the results are taken

Y. de Kort et al. (Eds.): PERSUASIVE 2007, LNCS 4744, pp. 132–143, 2007.
© Springer-Verlag Berlin Heidelberg 2007

as a whole, they provide insight into the factors that most influence perceptions of feedback technology.

This paper begins with a brief background on group decision-making research, an overview our system used to provide feedback to groups about their behavior, and a discussion of related work. Then we present the design and results of our two studies. Our results will show that under all conditions individuals were comfortable with the information shown to the group and found the tools to be more informative and useful, when their purpose was explained. What differed across the conditions was that groups exposed to multiple types of tools found the tools less informative on subsequent uses, and the most useful tool was the one that was provided after a meeting and showed the most detail, as compared with a simpler, during-meeting tool.

2 Background

The reason we suggest behavior feedback tools may assist face-to-face interactions is that group decision-making is fraught with complications. Social psychologists have demonstrated that when groups have decision-making discussions, it is highly likely that they will inadequately share information relevant to the decision [4, 5]. Instead, a group will likely spend its time discussing initial reactions to the decision, to the detriment of considering options suggested later in the discussion [1, 6-8]. And through the process of discussing the prevailing viewpoint, individuals in the group will likely become more strongly committed to their initial inclination [9, 10]. Each of these systematic flaws increases the likelihood that groups will make strong commitments to flawed decisions.

There are different ways of combating this problem, yet the prevailing conclusion is that if groups welcome the consideration of multiple viewpoints and minority opinions into their discussions, information sharing and decision-making will improve [4, 5, 10].

One metric for measuring individual contribution to a group collaboration is to measure the amount of time a person speaks during a discussion, because imbalances between individual contributions can signal that a group is overly relying on the opinions of the most vocal members. As discussed by Weisband, Schneider and Connolly [11], individuals use cues such as social status and physical appearance to form expectations about how much someone will contribute to a discussion, and these expectations actually provide people the opportunities to speak and influence the decision-making process. Studies have shown that individuals with higher social status, yet lower amounts of information to contribute, often speak more and have more influences on final outcomes, than those who speak less [12]. The implication of this finding is that because those who speak the most have more influence on group outcomes, they can draw the group towards their preferred decision outcome, to the detriment of considering other options [1]. While equal participation will not solve the challenges of group collaboration, when there are process flaws, correcting extreme inequality in individual contribution is one mechanism that may rebalance the amount of influence each individual has on the decision outcome.

3 Second Messenger

Second Messenger, our platform for providing feedback to groups, allows for visual displays of participation levels and turn-taking patterns to be shown either during face-to-face meetings or afterwards in the form of a visual replay. By highlighting extreme imbalances, Second Messenger is designed to give feedback to groups which will persuade them to change and improve their decision-making processes.

The system collects group speaking patterns by requiring each person using the system to wear a noise-canceling microphone that detects when he or she is speaking. The application aggregates time-stamped moments of individual speech to create a record of who spoke when in a meeting and uses this log to create visualizations, to be viewed either real-time or post-interaction.

In our first exploration [3], we presented participation information to groups in the form of a histogram, projected off to the side of a room during a 15-minute discussion, as shown in Figure 1. The groups in this experiment were given no explanation as to the purpose of the display and were instructed to use it as they wished. In response to this arrangement, survey responses from the 48 subjects indicate that individuals did not find the display distracting and that they did not find it very useful for the task or informative about the group. The average usefulness rating was 2.69 (std err 0.24) and the average rating for informative was 3.09 (std err 0.27), both on a scale of 1 to 7.

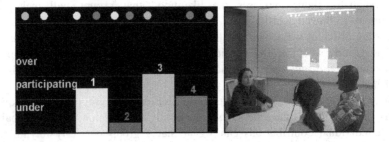

Fig. 1. Histogram display screenshot and shown projected onto wall

In our next iteration on this design, shown in Figure 2, Second Messenger represents each person as a circle, where the size of the circle reflects the relative participation level of the individual. The circles can be arranged with a mouse to reflect the physical arrangement of the face-to-face group members. In this way, there is little ambiguity as to who is represented by each circle. Additionally, the flexible arrangement allows the display to be shown on a tabletop monitor, as an alternative to a wall-projection. The screenshot in Figure 2 shows the relative participation levels of six individuals and the photograph in Figure 2 shows two members of a group using the display on a tabletop monitor.

An alternative display option, shown in Figure 3, is a timeline of who spoke at each moment in the meeting, which is designed to be viewed as a visual replay after a discussion. The circles down the left side represent the individuals and the horizontal lines extending from the circles have vertical blue bars at the moments when that individual spoke. To highlight moments of overlapping speech, translucent vertical red lines are drawn where more than one person spoke. The replay can be viewed with a two-minute or five-minute window, providing a detailed look of the meeting's turn-switching. By watching this display immediately after an interaction, at ten-times the speed of the original interaction (without audio), this display supports a user in reviewing who spoke when and who gained the floor at moments of overlapping speech. Figure 3 shows an entire 20-minute discussion amongst a group of six, which is the same conversation visualized in the screenshot in Figure 2.

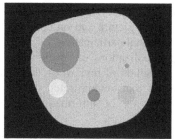

Fig. 2. Circle display screenshot and shown on tabletop display

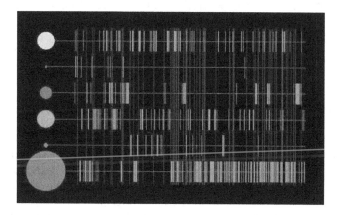

Fig. 3. Timeline display shown as a replay

4   Related Work

The type of detection and visualization of speech data done in Second Messenger has been done in earlier work by Kazman, Hung and Mantei [13] in a conference-calling application and also by Chen [14] in an application for remote classrooms. Both of these applications provide remote behavior awareness, with a focus was on assisting groups manage who holds the floor.

Providing social tools during face-to-face interactions for the purpose of improving group interaction is a growing research area within ubiquitous computing, as summarized by Iqbal [15]. Kulyk and Sturm [16, 17] experimented with simple visualizations of participation and eye gaze that took the form of circle displays and found preliminary evidence that these visualizations also led to more equitable participation. In terms of personal reactions to the displays, Sturm [17] found that groups were generally satisfied with their tools, felt they were useful, and would want to use them again. They gathered these qualitative reactions from a focus group and early experiments. In another example, Morris, et al. [18] presented personalized, dynamic histograms of speaker participation levels on a shared tabletop display and found that groups with such displays had greater participation equity. Mengis and Eppler [19] looked at the behavioral impact of more complex, information-rich visualizations and found that when groups were supported with visualizations, they would focus more on the construction of the big picture and on common ground in their decision making, and less on conflict and equal participation.

Our work [2] has found that providing visualizations of speaking patterns as a replay, immediately after an interaction as a method of review, produced significant group behavior changes, and for those groups that demonstrated poor information exchange, they exhibited more effective sharing of information in subsequent meetings.

As the evidence mounts that visualizations of social behavior can generate positive changes in face-to-face group behavior, we were motivated to explore in more depth the issues of acceptance and appreciation for these feedback tools. As tool designers, we want groups to welcome persuasive tools into their real-world settings, but if groups do not perceive the tools as helpful, informative, or useful, the tools will never leave the research laboratory. Therefore, we more systematically explored the issues that Sturm, et al. [17] looked at, by asking 76 users in a laboratory study and 12 users in regular group meetings how distracting, useful, and informative our tools were.

5   The Studies

As mentioned, our first study [3] indicated that users of Second Messenger were not distracted by the tool, but also did not find the information to be particularly useful or informative. To examine this issue further, we ran two more studies using our new interfaces, during which we asked more detailed questions. We wanted to know if users actually looked at the display during a meeting, how useful and informative they found a *replay* of information as compared to *real-time* information, how comfortable users were with the shared information, and if they were willing to have this type of display available in other meetings. These questions are listed below in Table 1, as we asked them in our survey.

The first study was run in the lab with 19 groups of four people each using different combinations of the Circle display and Timeline display. The second study was in the natural setting of real-world meetings, where two groups used our Circle display during their regular meeting. The next sections present these two studies.

Table 1. Survey questions asked of all subjects

Asked after real-time feedback:
– Did you look at the display during the task? (yes/no) – Did you find the display distracting? – How useful did you find the display for completing the task? – How informative did you find the display about the group's behavior?
Asked after replay feedback:
– How useful did you find the replay for reflecting on the previous task? – How informative did you find the replay about the group's behavior?
Asked at end of experiment:
– How comfortable were you with having this information shown to the group during the task? – How comfortable do you think the other group members were having this information shown? – Would you want to have this type of information available in other types of meetings you attend? (scale from 'never' to 'always')
All questions were asked on a 7-point scale from 'not at all' to 'very,' except where noted.

5.1 Laboratory Study

In our lab study, groups of four had two 15-minute discussions, during which they performed two 'hidden profile' tasks, as described by Wittenbaum and Stasser [20, 21]. The basic premise of these tasks is that groups must come to consensus on a decision for which not everyone is provided all of the facts. So the challenge is to share information appropriately to locate the best decision.

Groups were provided either the Circle display during their two discussions (Figure 2) or the Timeline display as a replay after the first discussion (Figure 3), or both displays, one for their real-time discussions and one for a replay. With this design, we were able to measure whether or not groups responded differently to these two displays, if their responses changed during a second usage of a real-time display, and if combining the tools was of benefit to users. Table 2 outlines these three conditions, which we refer to as Lab1, Lab2, and Lab3.

The basic task of the experiment was the same as in our original Histogram experiment [3], but a crucial change was made in the *presentation* of the tools. Before the experiment began, each group was given a full explanation of how the awareness tool (or tools) worked and were told the displays were there to assist in determining if there was an imbalance in the consideration of opinions. All groups were told that overlooking an opinion of someone could lead to inferior decisions. The purpose of this brief lesson in group dynamics was to assist groups in understanding how to use the tools' feedback. By altering the experimental protocol (from no explanation to full disclosure) *and* changing the visual display (from histogram to circles) means we cannot directly compare our findings from this study to our original experiment, but we felt that explaining to groups how the tools could be used would be of great benefit to the users. (Our other publication discussing this study [2] explains how the control groups, who did not see any displays, also received this instruction but did not alter their behavior.)

For the study, a total of 76 subjects were recruited from the university community and randomly assigned to 19 four-person groups to use the tools during their

Table 2. The three different conditions in the lab study

Condition	Displays	Description	Sample Size
Lab1		**Real-time groups**: real-time Circle display shown during two 15-minute discussions	28 people, 7 grps of 4
Lab2		**Real-time + Replay groups**: real-time Circle display shown during two 15-minute discussions, and after the *initial* discussion, replay display shown	16 people, 4 grps of 4
Lab3		**Replay groups**: after a 15-minute discussion, replay display shown before proceeding to next discussion	32 people, 8 grps of 4

discussion tasks. The average subject age was 26, and about three-fourths of the subjects were students and one-forth were members of the larger university community.

Results from the Laboratory Study. In response to the survey questions in Table 1, users reported whether or not they looked at the displays, if they were distracted, if they found them useful or informative, how comfortable they were with this information displayed, and if they would be willing to use these tools in other meetings.

Users reported looking at the displays, not being distracted, and being comfortable seeing the information. Subjects across all three conditions rated the feedback tools in similar ways along several parameters. Almost all subjects reported looking at the real-time display during their meeting (42 of the 44 real-time subjects). Subjects did not find the real-time display to be distracting: the average rating of distraction was 2.55 (1='not at all' and 7='very'). On the questions of how comfortable people were with the information displayed on the tool, all three conditions reported being comfortable with the information (average 5.66 out of 7) and believed others in the group to also be comfortable (average 5.45 out of 7). The averages for each of these questions, divided out into the three conditions, are detailed in Table 3.

Useful and informative. Figure 4 illustrates the ratings subjects gave for how 'useful for the task' and 'informative about the group' they found the displays. The data indicate that there were significant differences between the laboratory conditions ("useful" ANOVA, $F(2,73)=17.808$, $p<0.001$; "informative" ANOVA, $(F(2,73)=5.775$, $p<0.01)$. Specifically, the individuals who were shown the *replay* feedback (Lab3, highlighted with an asterisk in Figure 4) found feedback to be significantly *more useful and informative* than those subjects in Lab1 and Lab2 (post-hoc Tukey tests were all $p<0.005$).

We also found that those individuals who saw *both* the real-time and replay feedback (Lab2) did not consider the replay to be more useful or informative than the real-time display. In a t-test comparing conditions Lab2 and Lab3 and their ratings of the replay feedback, it was found that the individuals who *only* saw the replay found the replay to be significantly more useful and more informative ($t(46)=-2.800$, $p<0.01$; $t(46)=-2.900$, $p<0.01$). This appears to be a situation in which providing multiple, redundant sources of feedback diminished the benefit of the individual tools.

Differences between first and second use. In Lab1 and Lab2, groups had real-time feedback available during two discussions (the darkest bars in Figure 4 are the ratings from the second discussion). Within Lab1, there were no changes in how useful or

Table 3. Lab study results found to be consistent across conditions

Condition	Looked?	Distracting?		Comfortable?		Others comfortable?	
	Average	Average	Std Error	Average	Std Error	Average	Std Error
Lab1	93%	2.36	0.29	5.63	0.33	5.38	0.24
Lab2	100%	2.94	0.39	5.56	0.33	5.38	0.26
Lab3	n/a	n/a	n/a	5.74	0.23	5.58	0.19

Table 4. Field study results found to be consistent across conditions

Condition	Looked?	Comfortable?		Others comfortable?	
	Average	Average	Std Error	Average	Std Error
Group1	83%	5.33	0.76	5.17	0.31
Group2	100%	6.33	0.49	5.50	0.43

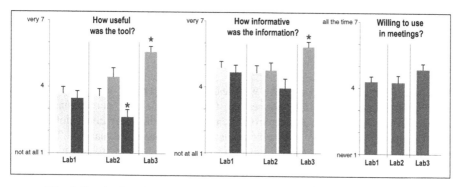

Fig. 4. Results from lab study. Error bars represent standard error of the mean.

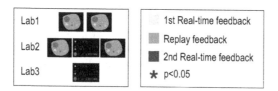

Fig. 5. Legends for interpreting Figure 4

informative the users found the real-time feedback, but in Lab2, where replay feedback was also provided, groups found the second instance of real-time feedback to be less useful than the replay feedback (paired t-test, $t(15)=-3.612$, $p<0.005$). They also reported looking at the real-time display less the second time than the first time (100% to 75% looked, paired t-test, $t(15)=2.236$, $p<0.05$).

This finding provides mounting evidence that a combination of real-time and replay feedback diminishes its usefulness on repeated use, but if the feedback is provided with no redundancy in information, there is no decrease in usefulness on a second usage.

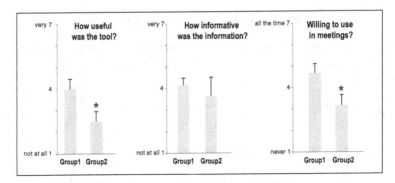

Fig. 6. Results from field study. Error bars represent standard error of the mean.

Willingness to use again. Our final result from the lab study is that users were somewhat willing to use the displays in meetings and there were no differences seen between the conditions. The average response across all conditions was 4.46 out of 7 and the average values from each condition are shown in the right-most graph in Figure 4.

5.2 Field Study

While the lab study described above was designed to determine how factors such as information presentation and number of usages influenced perceptions of the feedback tools, by the nature of controlled experiments, the study could not measure the influence of prior group history or realistic group meeting dynamics. Therefore, we additionally asked two real-world groups to use the real-time Circle display during one of their regular meetings.

The first group (Group1) was a computer science research group with six members. Their hour-long meeting began with a brief status-update period and then one student spent the rest of the meeting soliciting feedback from the group on his research project.

The second group (Group2) was a team of six professionals who teach courses on team leadership and meeting facilitation within our university. They used the tool during an hour meeting with a designated topic and discussion leader.

Both groups were given an explanation of how the tools worked and our theories as to how and why these tools may be beneficial to them, just as the lab groups were told. Additionally, these groups were told to incorporate the tools as they wished, either talking explicitly about them or not, as they felt it was appropriate.

Results from the Field Study. As in the lab study, these users filled out surveys to provide us their opinions on the feedback tools. Overall, their responses did not vary greatly from the laboratory groups.

Real-world users reported looking at the displays and being comfortable with the information shown. Eleven out of the twelve subjects in the field looked at the displays during their meetings. They also reported being comfortable with having the information shown to the group (5.83 out of 7.0) and thought others in the group were also comfortable (5.34 out of 7.0). We find these results encouraging because these groups were having discussions with real-world consequences and had established relationships with those in the room. The averages ratings broken out by condition are in Table 4.

Useful versus informative. In terms of how useful and informative the real-world groups found the information, the two groups rated the information equally informative as the laboratory groups did (giving an average rating of 3.92 out of 7.0). For how useful the displays were for the task at hand, the group of professional facilitators (Group2) found the displays to be less useful for their meeting than the research group (Group1) (t-test, $t(10)=-2.42$, $p<0.05$).

Differences in willingness to use again. The professional facilitators (Group2) were less interested in using the feedback tool again, as compared to the research group (Group1) (t-test, $t(10)=-2.36$, $p<0.05$). Compared with the laboratory study groups, Group2's rating averaged lower as well.

Along these two dimensions of usefulness and willingness to use, we theorize that the professional facilitators, while finding the displays to be informative, have less use for them in their daily meetings because they are already aware of their meeting dynamics due to their professional focus. Of all of our study participants, they may have found the tool to be redundant with their existing skills and therefore of less benefit.

6 Discussion

The universal findings across all groups, both in the lab and out in the field, were that individuals reported looking at the displays and being comfortable with the feedback being shared with the group. But depending on the condition, individuals differed in how useful and informative they found the feedback tools.

We found that detailed, post-meeting feedback was most well received, being rated as the most useful for the task, the most informative about the group, and as the tool groups were most willing to use again. We found that real-world groups did not differ substantially from our experimental groups, except in that experts in group facilitation found the information less useful and were less interested in having the tool in future meetings. When redundant information was shown, individuals lowered their ratings on how useful and informative the information was during a second meeting. But when the information was novel, either because it had not been presented before or it was not part of the group's natural skill set, groups found the tools to be useful for their meeting and were more willing to use it in future meetings. Compared with our previous experiment [3], where groups received no instruction about the purpose of the tools, these individuals found the tools to be more useful and informative across the spectrum. The average useful rating increased from 2.96 to 4.30 and the average informative rating increased from 3.08 to 5.03 (both on a scale of 1 to 7).

Our main conclusions from these studies are that users respond well to tools that provide them information that they otherwise wouldn't have access to, that they prefer details afterwards as compared to real-time summaries, and when the purpose of the tools is explained, they understand the applicability of the information to their tasks. While our expert facilitator group enthusiastically volunteered to try out Second Messenger during one of their meetings, they were the least enthusiastic about using it again. This indicates that the ideal user population for feedback tools such as Second Messenger may be those groups that have no prior experience in the domain of improving group processes.

7 Conclusion

Our purpose in building persuasive technology [22] is to create collaborative systems that make groups aware of discrepancies between their decision-making goals and their expressed behaviors. By making groups aware, the system can persuade groups to more thoroughly consider their decision approach and to alter it in productive ways. Our rational for this approach is that social psychologists suggest that one way a group can improve its interaction and consequently its productivity is by having a high-level understanding of its emotional and social interaction [1].

But to develop successful behavior feedback tools for face-to-face groups, it is crucial to design them such that individuals positively respond to them and wish to deploy them in their meetings.

Our goal with these two studies was to gauge how individuals felt about having feedback presented to them in different contexts and in different forms. Given our findings, our advice to designers of social feedback tools is to be less concerned about distracting or making individuals socially uncomfortable, but instead to focus on training individuals on the social purpose of the tool and on providing the most details possible about social behavior within the display, without presenting redundant information.

Acknowledgments. We thank the participants in our studies, particularly the real-world groups, for welcoming our software into their meetings. The Digital Life and information:organized research consortia of the MIT Media Lab provided the funding for this research.

References

1. Janis, I.L.: Groupthink: Psychological studies of policy decisions and fiascos. Houghton Mifflin, Boston (1982)
2. DiMicco, J., Hollenbach, K., Pandolfo, A., Bender, W.: The Impact of Increased Awareness while Face-to-Face. Human-Computer Interaction 22 (2007)
3. DiMicco, J.M., Pandolfo, A., Bender, W.: Influencing Group Participation with a Shared Display. In: CSCW '04, Chicago, IL, ACM, New York (2004)
4. Stasser, G., Titus, W.: Effects of Information Load and Percentage of Shared Information on the Dissemination of Unshared Information during Group Discussion. J. of Personality and Social Psychology 53, 81–93 (1987)
5. Stewart, D.D., Stasser, G.: The Sampling of Critical Unshared Information in Decision-Making Groups: The Role of an Informed Minority. European J. of Social Psychology 23, 95–113 (1998)
6. Whyte, G.: Decision failures: Why they occur and how to prevent them. Academy of Management Executive 5, 23–31 (1991)

7. Bray, R.M., Johnson, D., Chilstrom, J.T.J.: Social Influence by Group Members with Minority Opinions: A Comparison of Hollander and Moscovici. J. of Personality and Social Psychology 43 (1982)

8. Myers, D.G., Bishop, G.D.: The Enhancement of Dominant Attitudes in Group Discussion. J. of Personality and Social Psychology 20, 385–391 (1971)

9. Brown, R.: Group Polarization. In: Brown, R. (ed.) Social Psychology, pp. 200–248. Free Press, New York (1986)

10. Moscovici, S., Zavalloni, M.: The Group as a Polarizer of Attitudes. J. of Personality and Social Psychology 12, 125–135 (1969)

11. Weisband, S.P., Schneider, S.K., Connolly, T.: Computer-Mediated Communication and Social Information: Status Salience and Status Differences. The Academy of Management Journal 38, 1124–1151 (1995)

12. Bales, R.F.: Interaction process analysis: a method for the study of small groups. Addison-Wesley, Reading (1950)

13. Kazman, R., Hung, W., Mantei, M.: Dynamic Meeting Annotation and Indexing. In: 1995 Pacific Workshop on Distributed Multimedia Systems, Honolulu, HI, pp. 11–18 (1995)

14. Chen, M.: Visualizing the Pulse of a Classroom. In: International Conference on Multimedia (MM'03), Berkeley, CA, ACM, New York (2003)

15. Iqbal, R., Sturm, J., Terken, J., Kulyk, O., Wang, J.: User-Centred Design and Evaluation of Ubiquitous Services. In: ACM SIGDOC '05, Conventry, UK, pp. 138–145 (2005)

16. Kulyk, O., Wang, J., Terken, J.: Real-Time Feedback on Nonverbal Behaviour to Enhance Social Dynamics in Small Group Meetings. In: Renals, S., Bengio, S. (eds.) MLMI 2005. LNCS, vol. 3869, pp. 150–161. Springer, Heidelberg (2006)

17. Sturm, J., Iqbal, R., Kulyk, O., Wang, J., Terken, J.: Peripheral Feedback on Participation Level to Support Meetings and Lectures. In: Designing Pleasurable Products Interfaces (DPPI), Eindhoven Technical University Press (2005)

18. Morris, M.R., Morris, D., Winograd, T.: Individual Audio Channels with Single Display Groupware: Effects on Communication and Task Strategy. In: CSCW'04, Chicago, IL, pp. 242–251. ACM, New York (2004)

19. Mengis, J., Eppler, M.J.: Knowledge integration in face-to-face communication and the moderating effect of a collaborative visualization tool (2006), http://www.scientificcommons.org/14519968

20. Wittenbaum, G.M., Hollingshead, A.B., Botero, I.C.: From Cooperative to Motivated Information Sharing in Groups: Moving Beyond the Hidden Profile Paradigm. Communication Monographs 17 (2004)

21. Stasser, G., Stewart, D.: Discovery of Hidden Profiles by Decision-making Groups: Solving a problem versus making a Judgment. J. of Personality and Social Psychology 63, 426–434 (1992)

22. Fogg, B.J.: Persuasive Technology: Using Computers to Change What We Think and Do. Morgan Kaufmann Publishers, Boston (2003)

Can Brotherhood Be Sold Like Soap...Online?
An Online Social Marketing and Advocacy Pilot Study Synopsis

Brian Cugelman, Mike Thelwall, and Phil Dawes

University of Wolverhampton
Statistical Cybermetrics Research Group and Wolverhampton Business School

Abstract. Having engaged one billion users by early 2006, the Internet is the world's fastest-growing mass communications medium. As it permeates into countless lives across the planet, it offers social campaigners an opportunity to deploy interactive interventions that encourage populations to adopt healthy living, environmental protection and community development behaviours. Using a classic set of social campaigning criteria, this paper explores relationships between social campaign websites and behavioural change.

Keywords: social marketing, advocacy, internet, online, behaviour, campaign.

1 Introduction and Background

Over 50 years ago, the psychologist G. D. Wiebe asked the question 'Can brotherhood be sold like soap?' In his paper, 'Merchandising Commodities and Citizenship on Television'[1], Wiebe proposed that organizations which successfully 'sell' intangible social objects—such as goodwill, respect for the environment or community development—would be more successful if they sold their social objects the way marketers sell sports cars or mouth wash. To test this notion, Wiebe developed a set of five criteria (Table 1) and used them to evaluate how social campaigns compared to commercial marketing practices. After evaluating four social campaigns by his five criteria, Wiebe concluded that the more social campaigns resembled commercial marketing practices, the better their chance of success.

Beyond frequently quoting Wiebe's famous question, his criteria were deemed success factors for non-profit campaigns by the marketing authority Philip Kotler [2] who also compared them to marketing's 4Ps—product, price, place, promotion—in his 1971 article where he coined the term 'social marketing' [3]. Although Wiebe's criteria are over 50 years old, they still stand as success criteria for social campaigns; and with their conceptual relationship to the 4Ps—which are the primary behavioural exchange model used for social marketing (SM)—they provide a tested and relevant framework.

One meta-analysis that compared several web-based versus non-web-based health intervention studies showed that online programmes significantly increased participants' knowledge and health related behaviour [4]. A number of publications showcase counter campaigns that pit the 'good guys' against the 'bad guys' such as

Y. de Kort et al. (Eds.): PERSUASIVE 2007, LNCS 4744, pp. 144–147, 2007.

health campaigns against tobacco companies [5, 6] or drug use [7]. The most promising research addresses online persuasion. For example, a person's willingness to forward email is impacted by length, media attachments and positivity [8] while website loyalty is impacted by usability, trust and user satisfaction [9].

Table 1. Wiebe's (1951) criteria for campaign success

Wiebe's (1951) criteria	Online application
Force: The intensity of a person's motivation (both before and after experiencing campaign messages) towards a campaigns goal	A person's disposition towards a social issue is the same online or offline
Direction: Knowledge of how and where to respond to a campaign's message; or in other words, how to reach the social mechanism	The clarity of an email, hyperlink, site design or web advertisements that direct people to a website (social mechanism)
Distance: An individual's estimate of the time, energy and cost required to engage the social mechanism or achieve the behavioural goal	The amount of time, energy and hassle required to find a website and complete an online task
Social mechanism: The agency or place that enables people to translate motivations into actions	A website or online application where users can interact to complete behavioural goals
Adequacy: Ability and effectiveness of the social mechanism to help people act out the campaign's behavioural goal	The degree of credibility, and intuitiveness of a website's social mechanism

Using Wiebe's five criteria as a framework, this paper presents the findings from a pilot study intended to identify factors of online campaigns that influence users' behaviour.

2   Case Study and Methods

In 2005, the Global Call to Action against Poverty—an international anti-poverty campaign in over 100 countries—pressured world leaders to meet commitments on poverty, development, trade and debt; while advocating the United Nations' Millennium Development Goals. In 2006, an in-depth assessment of the campaign's 48 websites [10] was conducted on behalf of the campaign's secretariat, the NGO network Worldwide Alliance for Citizen Participation (CIVICUS).

Having been requested to evaluate the campaign's SM and advocacy capacity, Wiebe's criteria and behavioural change impact questions were built into the research tools. An online survey—in English, French and Spanish—ran from January to May 2006, obtaining 196 user responses from 23 of the 48 websites. For this pilot study, the independent variables (IV) came from questions inspired by Wiebe's criteria—or with clear conceptual linkages—and were grouped into his five criteria. The dependent variable (DV) was derived from the question, 'As a result of this website have you noticed a change in your willingness to take action?'

Correlation and linear regression were used to examine the associations between each of Wiebe's five criteria and the DV. All strong associations are highlighted; while many insignificant relations are not featured due to space limitations in this synopsis. There are a number of limitations. First, this pilot study uses data intended for a broad review with face-value questions. Second, the grouping of some questions by Wiebe's criteria could be challenged on the basis of ambiguous conceptual fits. Third, the study was conducted while the campaign was in a dormant state and respondents are likely to represent loyal users. Fourth, the three survey languages may have contributed a degree of bias. For these reasons, this study only claims to be an exploratory pilot study.

3 Findings and Conclusions

When examining the relationships between Wiebe's five criteria and the DV, standard demographics—such as sex, age, occupation, nationality or the way users accessed the Internet—showed no significant associations.

Table 2. The regression models for each criteria group

Criteria	Adj R^2	ANOVA±	Variables	B	SE B	β
Force	.194	F(3,154) =12.365	Motivated by site information	.427	.155	.214**
			Motivated by national issues	.445	.130	.254***
			Number of topical interests	.034	.016	.161*
Direction	.142	F(2,156) = 14.125	Finding information on the site	.198	.089	.205*
			Website's layout & design	.198	.078	.233*
Distance	.077	F(1,143) = 13.096	Time & energy demanded	.206	.057	.290****
Mechanis m	.208	F(2,155) = 21.587	Social networking options	.186	.065	.242**
			Activism options	.226	.066	.289***
Adequacy	.246	F(2,148) = 25.491	Helpful to studies or interests	.215	.065	.280***
			Content & information quality	.235	.068	.295***

*P<.05, **P<.01, ***P=.001, ****P<.0005, ± all ANOVA at P<.0005

While fitting the linear regression model (Table 2), each of Wiebe's criteria were evaluated separately; only distance behaved unexpectedly. The strongest **force** variables showed that target audiences who did the most, visited the site frequently and considered themselves campaign supporters. However, these variables were highly correlated with the other IV and were removed from the model. Celebrities drove many people to the campaign websites; however, website information was more associated with the DV. Users driven by national issues in their home country and who were interested in a broad number of social causes were the most active. The **direction** variables showed that better designed and more usable websites were more persuasive. Users were more active on sites with better rated layout, design and findability. The **social mechanism** variables showed that sites with the biggest impact on user's willingness to take action had more online advocacy mechanisms (such as e-petitions) and more opportunities for users to interact. The **adequacy** variables showed that the quality of the online social mechanism related to mobilization success. Users' rating of website credibility was removed from the model due to its very high correlation with the other IV. Content, information quality and a sites' helpfulness related to the IV. The **distance** variables showed that website users were willing to expend considerable time and energy to participate in the campaign. SM literature advocates that people are unlikely to act if behavioural objectives are too inconvenient, unpleasant or costly [11]. This difference, and whether or not users consider themselves supporters, may mark key delimiters between populations that are receptive to advocacy versus SM.

Though this analysis compared Wiebe's criteria to a user's willingness to take action, the survey also considered two other behavioural variables: first, the total number of reported actions taken and second, users' visit frequency. Combined with the DV these three behavioural variables had a Cronbach's Alpha of 0.62 which shows acceptable consistency among the survey's three separate behavioural measures. Online marketing literature provides a basis for explaining the association between visits and behaviour. Termed 'loyalty', online marketing consider visit frequency a precursor to two behavioural objective: opting-in to newsletters and buying products [9].

Wiebe's five criteria proved to be a useful broad framework for organizing a number of key online campaigning attributes. However, conceptual overlap and statistical pressure to arrange the variables in different ways supports the conclusion that each of Wiebe's five criteria are a good basic set of requirements for effective campaigns, but they cannot provide an overall framework the growing body of research related to online behavioural change.

References

1. Wiebe, G.D.: Merchandising Commodities and Citizenship on Television. Public Opinion Quarterly 15(4), 679 (1951)
2. Kotler, P., Roberto, E.: Social Marketing. The Free Press, New York (1989)
3. Kotler, P., Zaltman, G.: Social Marketing: An Approach to Planned Social Change. Journal of Marketing 35(3, 2) (1971)
4. Wantland, D., et al.: The effectiveness of web-based vs. non-web-based interventions: a meta-analysis of behavioural change outcomes. Journal of Medical Internet Research 6(4) (2004)
5. Ribisl, K.: The potential of the Internet as a medium to encourage and discourage youth tobacco use. Tobacco Control 12, 48–59 (2003)
6. Lin, C., Hullman, G.: Tobacco-prevention messages online: social marketing via the web. Health Communication 18(2), 177–193 (2005)
7. King, L.: Using the Internet to facilitate and support health behaviors. Social Marketing Quarterly 10(2), 72–78 (2004)
8. Lin, T., et al.: Why are some e-mails forwarded and others not? Internet Research 16(1), 81–93 (2006)
9. Flavian, C., Guinaliu, M., Gurrea, R.: The role played by perceived usability, satisfaction and consumer trust on website loyalty. Information and Management (2004)
10. Cugelman, B., Kumar, K.: GCAP Review of Campaign Websites. CIVICUS (2006)
11. McKenzie-Mohr, D.: Promoting a sustainable future: an introduction to community-based social marketing, National Round Table on the Environment and the Economy, Ottawa (1995)

Social Comparisons to Motivate Contributions to an Online Community

F. Maxwell Harper[1], Sherry Xin Li[2], Yan Chen[3], and Joseph A. Konstan[1]

CommunityLab[*]

[1] University of Minnesota, Minneapolis, MN 55455
{harper,konstan}@cs.umn.edu
[2] University of Texas at Dallas, Richardson, Texas 75083
sherry.xin.li@utdallas.edu
[3] University of Michigan, Ann Arbor, MI 48109
yanchen@umich.edu

Abstract. It is increasingly common for online communities to rely on members rather than editors to contribute and moderate content. To motivate members to perform these tasks, some sites display social comparisons, information designed to show members how they compare to others in the system. For example, Amazon, an online book store, shows a list of top reviewers. In this study, we investigate the effect of email newsletters that tell members of an online community that their contributions are above, below, or about average. We find that these comparisons focus members' energy on the system features we highlight, but do not increase overall interest in the site. We also find that men and women perceive the comparisons very differently.

Keywords: Social influence, social comparison, persuasion, online community.

1 Introduction

In December, 2006, Time Magazine awarded its annual Person of the Year award to "You" [8] in a nod to the changing nature of the Internet. No longer are Web sites exclusively created by editors and read by everyone else; increasingly, they allow content to be contributed by anyone who so wishes. Wikipedia, MySpace, and YouTube have become some of the top-visited sites on the Web[1], based entirely on content contributed by their members. As a case in point, the Web page displaying the Person of the Year article contains several buttons that make it easy for readers to recommend the article to others via Web sites such as Facebook.

What motivates people to edit encyclopedia entries at Wikipedia, write movie reviews at Rotten Tomatoes, or share Time Magazine articles at Facebook? On the surface, many of these types of contributions have little personal benefit – editing an article in Wikipedia may help other users, but takes one's own time. Therefore, people must be motivated by intrinsic factors – for example, a desire to achieve status within a community [2], or a desire to reciprocate the efforts of other users [13].

---

[*] CommunityLab is a collaborative project of the University of Minnesota, University of Michigan, and Carnegie Mellon University. http://www.communitylab.org

[1] As measured by Alexa Traffic Rankings (http://alexa.com)

Y. de Kort et al. (Eds.): PERSUASIVE 2007, LNCS 4744, pp. 148–159, 2007.

We may think of Web sites built on member contributions as public goods, subject to the problems of free-riding. We know from economics research that the environment in which decisions are made affects contributions [11]. Thus, designers of Web sites can hope to affect the volume of user contributions through design. They might take action to change the costs of the contribution by making contributions easier to make. For example, social networking sites such as LinkedIn provide tools for members to import their contact lists, to save them the effort of entering contact information manually. Other sites attempt to increase the benefit to contributors. For example, the technology news-oriented site Slashdot allows members to unlock extra features after they have provided high-quality contributions to the site.

Previous research on the voluntary provision of public goods has shown that information about social norms can affect contributions. For example, people recycled more materials when they were provided with information about how much other people had recycled [15]. Can a similar comparison make a Wikipedia member edit more articles or a Rotten Tomatoes member write more movie reviews?

1.1 Background: Social Influence and Comparison

To evaluate our abilities, actions, and opinions, we compare ourselves to others [16]. In some cases, we make these comparisons because we are presented with information about others' actions or information revealing hidden social norms. Social influence and comparison has been the subject of much study in the social sciences; we use this work to inform our research on comparisons in an online system.

It matters who we compare ourselves to. Festinger, in his classic work on social comparison [6], theorized that we compare ourselves to others who are better off for guidance, while we compare ourselves to others who are worse off to increase our self-esteem. Subsequent research, however, has found conflicting results regarding so-called upwards and downwards comparisons [16]. Wheeler and Miyake found that upward comparison decreased subjects' feelings of well-being, while downward comparison increased feelings of well-being [17]. However, Lockwood et al. found that upward comparisons can inspire people if success seems attainable [12], and Buunk et al. found that downward comparisons actually make individuals feel worse about themselves in some contexts [3]. Thus, we are left with little guidance about how comparisons made in an online system will make users feel – it is apparently highly dependant on the context and the individual.

We can be more hopeful that social comparisons can be used to motivate individuals to increase contributions to a public good. Several studies have shown that making social norms visible can increase pro-social behavior. Frey and Meier conducted a study in which subjects were given information on the percentage of people donating to a social fund. They found that showing a percentage reflecting greater participation led subjects to participate more themselves [7], but only for those subjects who had not already participated in the past. Croson and Shang found a similar result in testing social influence on donations to a public radio station. In this study, first-time donors who were told that another member had contributed $300 gave 29% more than first-time donors who were not given that information [5]. However, a meta-analysis of studies such as these shows that so-called feedback interventions often lead to negative effects on performance [10].

There is beginning to emerge research on the effect of social information in online systems. Cheng and Vassileva examined the effect of making reputation visible in an online system for sharing information about research papers. They found that while the display of reputation increased contributions, some users contributed low-quality content simply to achieve higher reputation [4]. Beenen et al. emailed members of a movie recommendation system with individual and group goals. They found that setting specific goals led members to rate more movies than setting non-specific goals [1]. They propose in discussion that performance goals may actually become less effective when they are not realistic for users to accomplish.

1.2 Research Questions

In this research, we use email to deliver a feedback intervention to make the norms of an online community of users salient. We extend prior work in several ways. First, we investigate the effect of leveraging social influence in an anonymous online system. Second, we investigate the effect of upwards, downwards, and no-difference comparisons. Our goal is to determine methods for eliciting additional contributions from these members. We investigate the following research questions:

RQ Activity. *How does social comparison in an online community affect members' propensity to visit and contribute?*

RQ Perception. *To what extent do members of an online community believe themselves to be motivated by social comparison?*

In subsequent sections, we describe a field study designed to answer these research questions. In this study, we find: (1) that messages containing comparison information focus members' energy to improve their relative standing, but do not increase overall interest in the community, and (2) that men and women believe themselves to be motivated by comparison information in very different ways.

2 Research Context

To evaluate the effects of comparative messages, we ran a field study in MovieLens, an online movie recommendation Web site (http://movielens.org) where members rate movies and receive personalized movie recommendations (see Fig. 1 for a screenshot). MovieLens uses a collaborative filtering algorithm [14] to predict how well members will like movies in its database. Because collaborative filtering works based on finding statistical correlations between users or items in the database, MovieLens relies on member-contributed ratings data. Newly-released movies and rarely-viewed movies are especially difficult to recommend due to a scarcity of ratings. 6.8% of the movies in MovieLens's database have fewer than 10 ratings, below the threshold required by the collaborative filtering algorithm to make predictions. Thus, one of the goals of this study is to find ways to encourage members to rate more of the movies they have seen.

Fig. 1. Screenshot of the MovieLens home page

At the time of this study, MovieLens did not contain exhortations to rate movies. Also, members had no way to see one another's ratings, activity, or opinions. When members joined the system, they were told that by rating more movies, they would receive more accurate recommendations. In addition to this information, a number at the top of each page reminded members of how many movies they had rated; this was hyperlinked to a page with statistics about those ratings.

So why do MovieLens members rate? A survey of MovieLens members showed that different members were motivated to rate movies in different ways: most rated to improve their recommendations, some rated for the fun of it, and others rated to help the system or for other reasons [9]. This survey also revealed that MovieLens members did not often think about one another. Few members claimed to rate movies to voice their opinion or to influence others.

2.1 Injecting Social Comparisons: Personalized Email Newsletters

To deliver our intervention, we designed two personalized email newsletters to send to MovieLens members. The experimental version contained a message about how many movies the recipient of the email had rated compared with other members in the system. The control version contained information about the member's ratings without comparison to other members.

Both the experimental and the control newsletter were similar in design. Each was formatted in html, although members with text-only email clients received a text-only version. Each contained a header with the MovieLens logo and some non-personalized statistics about the site. Below the header was a section with personalized information according to the subject's experimental group, as described below. Following this was a section containing a short news item about recent feature additions to MovieLens, and finally a section containing a reminder that this newsletter was sent as part of an experiment. Part of a sample email newsletter is shown in Fig. 2.

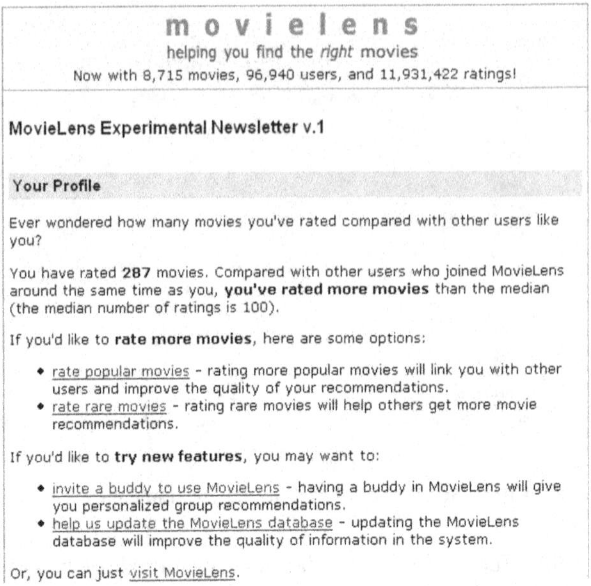

m o v i e l e n s
helping you find the *right* movies
Now with 8,715 movies, 96,940 users, and 11,931,422 ratings!

MovieLens Experimental Newsletter v.1

Your Profile

Ever wondered how many movies you've rated compared with other users like you?

You have rated **287** movies. Compared with other users who joined MovieLens around the same time as you, **you've rated more movies** than the median (the median number of ratings is 100).

If you'd like to **rate more movies**, here are some options:

- rate popular movies – rating more popular movies will link you with other users and improve the quality of your recommendations.
- rate rare movies – rating rare movies will help others get more movie recommendations.

If you'd like to **try new features**, you may want to:

- invite a buddy to use MovieLens – having a buddy in MovieLens will give you personalized group recommendations.
- help us update the MovieLens database – updating the MovieLens database will improve the quality of information in the system.

Or, you can just visit MovieLens.

Fig. 2. One version of the email newsletter, sent to above average members

To deliver the social comparison, the experimental newsletter contained the following text at the top of the message:

Ever wondered how many movies you've rated compared with other users like you? You have rated [num_ratings] *movies. Compared with other users who joined MovieLens around the same time as you, you've rated* [more, fewer, about as many] *movies than the median (the median number of ratings is* [median_ratings]*).*

In contrast, the control newsletter contained a personalized message about members' participation in MovieLens without any comparison to other members:

Here are some statistics about your ratings behavior for one popular movie genre. About [percent] *of the movies that you've rated are comedies. Your average rating in this genre is* [average_rating].

Values for items in brackets were personalized based on the member's usage history or experimental group assignment, as described in the methods section.

The newsletter followed this personalized message with five links: (1) rate popular movies, (2) rate rare movies, (3) invite a buddy to use MovieLens, (4) help us update the MovieLens database, and (5) just visit MovieLens. These links were clarified by neighboring text that explained the benefit of these actions. For example, the link "rate rare movies" was followed by the text "rating rare movies will help others get more movie recommendations".

Because our results rely on members understanding and acting on the email newsletter that we sent, we pre-tested the usability of the newsletter via 14 phone interviews with MovieLens members. We found that, in general, members were able to understand the contents. 10 of the 14 subjects understood the concept of a median, while the remaining 4 interpreted the word as "average". 11 out of 14 subjects, after being asked to look away from the newsletter, were able to recall whether the newsletter had said they were above, below, or about average.

3 Methods

To solicit volunteers for the study, we emailed 1,966 MovieLens members, chosen randomly from those who had logged in during the past year, who had rated at least 30 movies, and who had given us permission to send them email. This email contained a link to a MovieLens Web page with a consent form describing the study[2]. 629 members clicked on the email link, of whom 398 consented to participate in the study. The methods described in this paper are part of a larger study, unpublished, extending our work in [9]; we report on the results of 268 of these subjects and a subset of our experimental manipulations in this paper. The other 130 subjects were used to test an economic theory of inequality aversion.

We randomly assigned half of the 268 subjects to an experimental group and half to a control group. Subjects in the experimental group would receive an email newsletter with ratings comparison information, while subjects in the control group would receive a newsletter without comparisons, as described above. Since we were comparing members based on how many movies they had rated, we wished to ensure that new members to the system were not being (unfairly) compared with long-time members. Thus, we further divided subjects into three equal-sized groups based on their seniority in MovieLens (see Table 1). Within each of these seniority-based groups, we call the one-third of subjects with the most ratings "above average", the one-third with the fewest ratings "below average", and the final one-third "average". These labels correspond to whether the subject was told that he or she had rated more, fewer, or about the same number of movies as the median member in their age group.

Table 1. Number of subjects and average activity prior to the study by treatment. By definition, members with more seniority had belonged to the site longer on average. As expected, members with more seniority had rated and logged in more often on average.

Treatment	Seniority	N	Avg # Weeks Member	Avg # Logins	Avg # Ratings
Control	New	45	12.5	8.6	287.0
	Mid	45	50.3	42.8	431.0
	Old	44	214.6	153.9	747.5
Comparison	New	45	15.2	12.9	399.1
	Mid	45	63.5	63.2	502.4
	Old	44	233.0	225.8	898.5

---

[2] This study was approved by the Institutional Review Board at the University of Minnesota.

Members who consented to participate in this study were immediately redirected to an online survey. This survey was designed to collect subjects' perceptions of the benefits and costs of using MovieLens, using questions drawn from our earlier study [9], as well as to discover how they believed they compared with other members in the study in terms of ratings. Two weeks after sending the initial invitation to participate in the study, we personalized and sent the email newsletter manipulation. We logged when subjects clicked on links in the newsletter as well as their actions in MovieLens following the email. Finally, one month after sending the email newsletter, we emailed subjects one final time asking them to take another survey. This survey asked members how well they liked the newsletter, and which links they thought were valuable. Subjects in the experimental condition were reminded of the comparison they saw in the newsletter and were asked how it made them feel.

4 Results

Upon sending the email newsletter manipulation, subjects immediately began to visit MovieLens and rate movies. In the week following the manipulation, 49.3% (132/268) of subjects clicked one or more links in the email message, 60.4% (162/268) of subjects logged in, and 48.5% (130/268) of subjects rated one or more movies. The five links displayed in the email newsletter were not clicked or acted on with equal likelihood; see Table 2 for a summary.

Table 2. Response to the five suggested actions in the email newsletter across all experimental conditions, including the number of users who clicked each link in the newsletter, and the number of users who performed the suggested action in the week following the manipulation

Suggested Action	# Users to Click	# Users to Act
rate popular movies	54	120
rate rare movies	79	78
invite a buddy to use MovieLens	7	2
help us update the MovieLens database	23	22
just visit MovieLens	19	162

4.1 Effect of Social Comparisons on User Activity

Propensity to Click. Subjects who received the social comparison manipulation were no more or less likely to click on a link in the email newsletter. 48.5% (65/134) of subjects in the control condition clicked on one or more links, as compared with 50% (67/134) of subjects in the comparison condition (ChiSquare=0.06, df=1, p=0.80). Also, there was no significant variation between the comparison directions in terms of subjects' propensity to click (ChiSquare=0.91, df=3, p=0.82) – subjects told they had rated fewer movies than other users clicked the least (44.4%), while subjects told they had rated more movies than others clicked the most (53.3%).

However, there was some variation in the links that subjects chose to click, as summarized in Table 3. For example, members told they had rated about the same number of movies as other members were nearly twice as likely to click on the link *just visit MovieLens* as other members, although this effect is not statistically significant (ChiSquare=1.29, df=1, p=0.26). Subjects told they had rated more movies than other members were most likely to click the two links under the heading "try new features": *invite a buddy to use MovieLens* and *help us update the MovieLens database* (ChiSquare=7.26, df=1, p<0.01). And finally, subjects told they had rated fewer movies than other members were most likely to click *rate popular movies*, although the effect is not statistically significant (ChiSquare=2.39, df=1, p=0.12).

Table 3. Percentage of subjects clicking on each of the five links in the email newsletter by social comparison condition. Although there were no significant differences between overall click rates based on the direction of the comparison, there were differences in which links subjects chose to click.

Comparison	Click Target				
	Rate Pop.	Rate Rare	Invite Buddy	Maintain DB	Just Visit
No Comparison	16.4%	33.6%	0.7%	9.7%	6.0%
Rated Fewer	28.9%	15.6%	2.2%	6.7%	6.7%
Same	25.0%	34.1%	0.0%	0.0%	11.4%
Rated More	17.8%	26.7%	11.1%	15.6%	6.7%

Propensity to Act. Subjects receiving the social comparison manipulation rated significantly more movies the week after the email than subjects in the control group (means 13.15 vs. 6.66, F=4.70, p=0.03). As shown in Table 4, subjects receiving any of the three comparison directions averaged more movies rated than subjects in the control group receiving no comparison. Subjects that were told they had rated fewer movies than other members rated significantly more movies in the week following the manipulation than other subjects (means 19.1 vs. 8.0, F=7.68, p<0.01). This group was also the only one to rate more movies in the week following the manipulation than their lifetime per week average.

Table 4. Average activity in the week after the email newsletter, and the average difference between this activity and members' lifetime per week activity. Members told they had rated fewer movies than others saw the largest increase in ratings, while members told they had rated about the same number of movies as others saw the largest increase in login activity.

Comparison	Ratings	Ratings/Week Change	Logins	Logins/Week Change
No Comparison	6.66	-7.08	1.36	0.45
Rated Fewer	19.09	11.06	0.78	0.46
Same	8.20	-1.71	1.52	0.87
Rated More	12.04	-17.95	2.02	0.32

There was no significant difference in number of logins in the week following the manipulation between the control group (mean 1.36) and the experimental group (mean 1.44) (F=0.07, p=0.79). As shown in Table 4, subjects in all conditions averaged more logins in the week following the email newsletter than their lifetime per week login average. Subjects told they had rated fewer movies than other members logged in the fewest times (mean 0.8) in the week following the manipulation (F=3.43, p=0.07), although their rate of logging in increased at approximately the same rate as subjects in the control group.

4.2 User Perceptions of the Social Comparisons

78.7% of subjects (211/268) participated in the survey that we launched one month after the email newsletter, including 104/134 subjects in the control group and 107/134 subjects in the experimental group. 50 women and 152 men took the survey (9 participants declined to identify their gender).

When asked if they liked receiving the email newsletter, subjects averaged 2.2 on a 5 point Likert scale ranging from strongly agree (1) to strongly disagree (5). There was no difference in responding to this question between the control and experimental subjects or between subjects with different comparison directions.

Subjects were asked to agree or disagree that "I didn't care" about the comparison in the newsletter. Overall, 48.1% of subjects agreed; there were no significant differences between the experimental groups or the directions of comparison. However, men were less likely to agree than women (40.3% vs. 68.2%, ChiSquare=5.33, df=1, p=0.02).

Subjects were asked if they agreed that "I wanted to do something to help increase my score". Subjects told they had rated fewer movies than others were the most likely to agree (53.8%), followed by those told they had rated about the same number as others (48.5%), or more than others (28.9%).

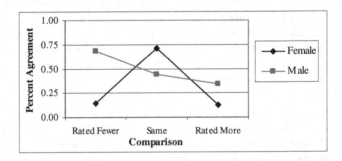

Fig. 3. Percent of subjects agreeing that "I wanted to do something to help increase my score" by comparison condition and gender. While gender is not a statistically significant predictor of response, comparison condition and the interaction between condition and gender are both significant.

There were differences between men and women in how much they agreed that they wanted to do something to increase their score. Women were most motivated to agree when they were told they were the same as others (71.4%), while men were most motivated to agree when they were told they had rated fewer movies than others (68.4%). In a logistic regression model to predict whether a subject wanted to do something to increase his or her score, both the experimental group (p=0.05) and the interaction between experimental group and gender (p=0.02) were significant. Gender was not significant (p=0.13), although there is a trend that men (43.1%) were more motivated to agree than women (28.9%). See Fig. 3 for a graph of the interaction between comparison condition and gender.

Those members who agreed that the newsletter made them want to do something to increase their score actually used the system more than those who disagreed. They had rated more movies in the week after the manipulation (means 19.9 vs. 8.8, F=4.30, p=0.04). They also logged in slightly more in the week after the manipulation (means 1.80 vs. 1.50), but that difference is not statistically significant (F=.27, p=.60).

5 Discussion

RQ Activity. *How does social comparison in an online community affect members' propensity to visit and contribute?* While subjects who received an email message with the comparison manipulation were no more likely to click on one of the links or log in to the system, they were more likely to rate movies. Thus, we find that a comparison makes no difference to a member's interest in using the system, but that it changes their focus within the system.

One important question this raises is whether or not shifting members' attention towards rating might cause them to do less in other areas of the system. We cannot answer this question definitively in our study, but we can give some preliminary data. Subjects receiving the comparison manipulation contributed fewer edits to the MovieLens database (editing 48 entries) compared to the control group (editing 118 movies). This is, however, not a statistically significant difference (F=2.37, p=0.12). Future work should look at whether the effects of social comparisons or other non-monetary incentives are inherently zero-sum, or if these features can instead boost overall levels of member activity.

We also found that subjects who were told they had rated fewer movies than others rated the most movies and changed their rating behavior the most in the week following the newsletter. One potential caveat to this result is that the marginal cost of providing ratings increases over time, as members find it increasingly difficult to find seen but unrated movies in the system [9]. However, we note that members who were told they had contributed fewer ratings didn't just rate popular movies. In fact, in the week following the manipulation, this group rated more rarely-rated movies[3] per member (1.27) than any other group (the other three groups averaged 1.11). This difference is not statistically significant (F=0.06, p=0.81), but it does underscore the fact that these members were contributing ratings of value to the system.

RQ Perception. *To what extent do members of an online community believe themselves to be motivated by social comparison?* We see from the behavioral data that subjects from all conditions were approximately equally likely to click on a newsletter link and visit MovieLens the week after the manipulation was made. Also, there was no difference across conditions in how well members claimed to like the newsletter. The interesting aspect of these data is that there was no apparent negative side-effect of telling below-average members how they compare. In fact, 44% of

---

[3] Rated fewer than 250 times. By comparison, the top 100 movies average about 28,000 ratings.

these subjects agreed that "I didn't care" about the comparison, while only 8% agreed that they felt envious about other members. However, we remain cautious recommending our particular design for use in real systems; in a telephone interview before the study, one subject professed to feeling slighted that the newsletter said he was below average.

Men and women appeared to have interesting and significant differences in how they perceived the comparison information. In general, men were more likely to say they wanted to take action, and less likely to agree that "I didn't care" about the comparison. Just as interesting, women appeared to be most motivated by a message that their contributions were average, a result that would not have been predicted by any theories we know of. In fact, conformity theory [2] would predict quite the opposite. We are unsure of the generality of this result, and we are hopeful that other researchers will investigate it further.

6 Conclusion

In this study, we used email newsletters to tell members of an online movie recommendation site how they compared with other members in terms of movie ratings. In so doing, we established a social norm in a community where such a norm had been absent. We found that this type of comparison is potentially a powerful way to redirect members' attention – while members who received a comparison message rated more movies than members in a control condition, they were no more likely to click on links in the email newsletter or visit the site.

Online communities wishing to promote contributions of a certain kind may wish to display information that leads members to evaluate their level of contribution. While many Web sites display information about superstar users (such as with Amazon's "Top Reviewers" list), it is also possible to compare users with their peers in the system. In this way, users may be motivated by the presence of more attainable goals [12]. However, since our results also provide support for the notion that upward comparisons are the most motivational, systems may wish to adopt a "carrot on a stick" approach to keep goals just out of reach.

Our study has limitations. We have only presented short-term data regarding the effect of social comparison. Additional work is needed to determine whether the continuing presence of such a feature can lead to long-term behavioral changes. Also, while we presented survey data that shows significant differences between men and women in terms of their perceptions of online social comparisons, further work is needed to translate this result into useful design principles.

In future work, we hope to continue to investigate the use of non-monetary incentives in online communities. We are especially interested in two common design features which facilitate social comparison: leaderboards and contribution-based status levels. We are also interested in developing and evaluating personalization algorithms that find especially compelling comparisons for display by leveraging the system's knowledge of users' relationships, interests, and behavior. We hope that this research will lead to the development of tools that will help online communities improve, focus, or diversify contributions from their members.

Acknowledgments. We would like to thank Bob Kraut and Sara Kiesler for their help developing survey questions, Shilad Sen for reviewing a draft of this paper, our CommunityLab colleagues for their support and helpful comments, and MovieLens members for making this research possible. This work is funded by the National Science Foundation, grant IIS 03-24851.

References

1. Beenen, G., Ling, K., Wang, X., Chang, K., Frankowski, D., Resnick, P., Kraut, R.: Using Social Psychology to Motivate Contributions to Online Communities. CSCW (2004)
2. Bernheim, D.: A Theory of Conformity. The Journal of Political Economy 102(5) (1994)
3. Buunk, B., Collins, R., Taylor, S., VanYperen, N., Dakof, G.: The Affective Consequences Of Social Comparison: Either Direction Has Its Ups And Downs. Journal of Personality and Social Psychology 59(6) (1990)
4. Cheng, R., Vassileva, J.: User Motivation and Persuasion Strategy for Peer-to-Peer Communities. HICSS (2005)
5. Croson, R., Shang, J.: Field Experiments in Charitable Contribution: The Impact of Social Influence on the Voluntary Provision of Public Goods. Knowledge@Wharton (2005)
6. Festinger, L.: A Theory of Social Comparison. Human Relations 7 (1954)
7. Frey, B., Meier, S.: Social Comparisons and Pro-social Behavior - Testing Conditional Cooperation in a Field Experiment. American Economic Review 94(5) (2004)
8. Grossman, L.: Time's Person of the Year: You. Time Magazine (December 25, 2006), http://www.webcitation.org/5Lh4GdH4l
9. Harper, F., Li, X., Chen, Y., Konstan, J.: An Economic Model of User Rating in an Online Recommender System. User Modeling (2005)
10. Kluger, A., Denisi, A.: The Effects Of Feedback Interventions On Performance: A Historical Review, A Meta-Analysis, And A Preliminary Feedback Intervention Theory. Psychological Bulletin 119(2) (1996)
11. Ledyard, J.: Public Goods: A Survey of Experimental Research. In: The Handbook of Experimental Economics, Princeton University Press, Princeton (1994)
12. Lockwood, P., Kunda, Z.: Superstars And Me: Predicting The Impact Of Role Models On The Self. Journal of Personality and Social Psychology 73(1) (1997)
13. Rabin, M.: Incorporating fairness into game theory and economics. The American Economic Review 83(5) (1993)
14. Resnick, P., Iacovou, N., Sushak, M., Bergstrom, P., Riedl, J.: Grouplens: An Open Architecture For Collaborative Filtering Of Netnews. CSCW (1994)
15. Schultz, P.: Changing Behavior With Normative Feedback Interventions: A Field Experiment on Curbside Recycling. Basic and Applied Social Psychology 21(1) (1999)
16. Suls, J., Martin, R., Wheeler, L.: Social Comparison: Why, With Whom, and With What Effect? Current Directions in Psychological Science 11(5) (2002)
17. Wheeler, L., Miyake, K.: Social Comparison In Everyday Life. Journal of Personality and Social Psychology 62(5) (1992)

Can Companies Initiate Positive Word of Mouth?
A Field Experiment Examining the Effects of Incentive Magnitude and Equity, and eReferral Mechanisms

Jan Ahrens and Michal Ann Strahilevitz

Golden Gate University San Francisco, USA
jbahrens2002@yahoo.com, marketingprofessor@gmail.com

Abstract. This research examines strategies for generating electronic referrals (eReferrals). Acquiring customers through Word of Mouth (WOM) appeals to companies because of the perceived transmitter credibility as well as low customer acquisition cost. Company-initiated eReferrals, a form of online WOM, offer marketers a way to influence customers through encouraging WOM. This research utilized a field experiment focusing on company-initiated eReferrals. Several independent variables were manipulated including incentive magnitudes for the referring party and the party being referred. The dependent variables were the number of referrals made and the number of referrals that led to sales. As expected, larger incentives increased referral rates. In addition, we found that offering the same magnitude incentive to both the referrer and referee led to a greater number of referrals. However when offer incentive magnitudes were not equitable, those with higher offers for the referrer performed better than those with a higher offer for the referee.

Keywords: Word of Mouth, WOM, Word-of-Mouth, Referrals, Electronic Referrals, eReferrals, Internet Marketing, Online Marketing, Customer Acquisition, B2C, Consumer Marketing, Viral Marketing.

1 Introduction

Before newspapers, radio, television and the Internet, there was personal communication, often called Word of Mouth (WOM). Compared to advertising created and communicated by the marketer, WOM through a friend or acquaintance is considered to carry more credibility [1, 2]. It also allows a message to spread without the expense of paid media space.

A subset of WOM communication is referrals. Referrals are best described as one consumer's promotion of a product or service. The referral can be targeted to just one other person (1:1) or to a group of people (1:Many). Referrals can take many forms in offline or online environments. In an offline environment, referrals are typically in person or through telephone conversations. In an online environment, consumers typically generate referrals from emails, instant messages, and comments posted in blogs or chat rooms. WOM significance is heightening from technology development such as product complexity [3] and consumer use of the Internet. Online venues such

Y. de Kort et al. (Eds.): PERSUASIVE 2007, LNCS 4744, pp. 160–163, 2007.
© Springer-Verlag Berlin Heidelberg 2007

as blogs and message boards allow consumers to spread WOM [4] on a large scale to personal acquaintances as well as to strangers. Company-prompted eReferrals can be encouraged by marketers using a variety of methods including a "tell-a-friend" option on the company webpage as well as offering consumers a place to post comments and product ratings.

However, many companies struggle to figure out which strategies will be most effective in eliciting eReferrals. Harnessing the power of the Internet in new forms, such as eReferrals, would benefit marketers immensely.

While WOM has received attention in the literature, no work to date has examined the effects of incentives and referral mechanisms on eReferrals. In this research we began with a series of in-depth interviews, with men and women who frequently shop online, to explore the motivations of electronic referrers as well as the perceptions of these motives by referees. In our field experiment, we compared different incentive magnitudes for referrers and referees. In addition, we also compared a variety of suggested mechanisms for making eReferrals. Specifically, we compared: 1) asking a customer to invite a friend using the company's website mechanism by providing the friend's email address (*invite*), 2) asking a customer to forward an email from the company to a friend (*forward*), and 3) asking a customer to post comments about the company to a 3rd party website (*post*). We measured both the magnitude of referral activity and the effect that the suggested mechanism had on results.

2 Research Methodology

The research project was comprised of three separate studies. The first two studies were in-depth interviews used to inform the design of the experiment. We interviewed customers of an online wedding photography site, Bella Pictures, as well as members of an online sports picking website, Pickspal, to conduct the interviews. These interviews aided in creating a more thorough understanding of eReferral activity including consumer perception of privacy issues, incentives and referral mechanisms.

The main study was a field experiment applied to members of Ebates, an online shopping mall that provides cash back for shopping through Ebates at popular online stores. Consumers selected for the study were members who had purchased through Ebates within the past twelve months and had not opted-out of email communication from the company. Participants were randomly assigned to the 27 experimental conditions in a between-subject, multi-factor design.

Participants were 149,000 Ebates members. An additional cell of more than 85,000 Ebates' members was set aside as a "no email" condition from which to track the incremental effects of our test. Two factors were varied to meet the objectives of the research study. The first tested the effect of incentive magnitude for the referrer and the referee. This allowed us to explore the importance of equity for offer incentives between the person doing the referring (referrer) and the person being referred (referee). It also allowed us to examine the role of the incentive magnitude of the referrer and referee independently. In each cell, an incentive was always offered to both the referrer and the referee. The incentive level was varied for the tests and included the incentive levels of $5, $10, $25 and $50. There were eight incentive combinations for the referrer/referee: $5/$5, $5/$10, $5/$25, $5/$50, $25/$25, $10/$5, $25/$5, and $50/$5.

The second factor used to meet the objective of the research study was the effect of the nature of the solicitation, or mechanism. Three mechanisms were used to suggest to referrers how they could contact potential referees. The first was considered a control email message that had previously been used by Ebates. It asked members to "*invite*" friends to try Ebates, and in its text included a webpage link to which the current member could give friends' email addresses to Ebates. Ebates then emails the prospective members inviting them to join. The second type was newly designed for this study, and asked the current member to "*forward*" the email to friends. In the email text there was a message to the current member and also a message to the prospective members. The intention of this test was to understand whether the ease of forwarding a message affected the response rate. The third type of mechanism was also newly designed for the study and asked the current member to "*post*" a message about Ebates on public websites. In the email message, the current member was given a recommended paragraph and a unique URL to "cut and paste" to a website. The member would then receive credit for any new members acquired. The intention of this test was to understand the effect of a person's outreach to a larger, and often unknown, group of people. The first two types, then, studied the effect of person-to-person (1:1) eReferrals. The third type studied the effect of person-to-group (1:Many).

3   Summaries of Results and Discussion

Two measurements for each cell and group were tracked: the number of referred members (prospects who registered but had not yet made a purchase) and the number of referred buyers (those new members who had purchased within the expiration period and qualified for the incentive). Only those members and their prospects who became buyers within the three week expiration period received the incentives.

In terms of incentive magnitudes, larger incentives overall yielded significantly better results than the control offer of $5/$5. (See Table 1.) In cells which the referrer was offered a higher incentive than the referee ($10/$5, $25/$5, $50/$5), the results yielded significantly more new referrals (members) and new buyers than the same larger incentives when offered to the referees ($5/$10, $5/$25, $5/$50). (See Table 1.) Implications of these results indicate that in an inequitable incentive scenario, results are better when the current member is offered more than the prospective member.

Offering an equivalent incentive to the referee yielded more new referrals and new buyers than offering a lower or higher incentive to the referee (e.g. $25/$25 versus $5/$25 and $25/$5). When the combination offer was increased for the referrer to $50/$5, the results were better than the $25/$25 equitable offer. However, when the combination offer was $5/$50, the $25/$25 equitable offer performed better. (See Table 1.)

Regarding the referral mechanism, both new suggested methods of *forward* and *post* resulted in significantly more referrals over the control *invite* methodology. (See Table 2.) For the forward mechanism, our in-depth interview results suggest that the 'ease of referring,' and increased privacy are likely to be what positively affected referral rates. In other words, consumers may respond better to the *forward* mechanism over the *invite* mechanism because it requires less work and does not require providing the friend's email address to the firm. Success from the *post* methodology was likely the result of the wider reach of the mechanism. Instead of *forwarding* or *inviting* one friend at a time, it was suggested that members *post* the information on a public website and reach an audience many multiples the size of their friend pool.

Table 1. Incentive Summary

Referrer $ Incentive	Referee $ Incentive	# Members Who Received Email	% New Members Referred	% New Buyers Referred
$5	$5	17,406	1.3	0.5
$5	$10	17,339	1.6	0.5
$5	$25	17,495	2.0	0.8
$5	$50	12,728	3.4	1.7
$25	$25	12,760	4.2	2.1
$10	$5	17,368	4.4	1.4
$25	$5	12,507	3.3	1.3
$50	$5	5,086	5.4	3.0
Total Control Cells ($5/$5)		17,406	1.3	0.5
Total Referrer Higher $ Cells		34,961	4.2	1.6
Total Referrer Lower $ Cells		47,562	2.2	0.9

Table 2. Mechanism Summary

	# Members Who Received Email	% New Members Referred	% New Buyers Referred
Invite – All Cells	37,601	2.4	1.0
Forward – All Cells	37,490	3.2	1.3
Post – All Cells	37,605	3.2	1.3

References

1. Arndt, J.: Role of product-related conversations in the diffusion of a new product. Journal of Marketing Research 4, 291–295 (1967)
2. Day, G.S.: Attitude change, media and word of mouth. Journal of Advertising Research 11, 31–40 (1971)
3. Godes, D., Mayzlin, D., Chen, Y., Das, S., Dellarocas, C., Pfeiffer, B.: The firm's management of social interactions. Marketing Letters 16, 415–428 (2005)
4. Mayzlin, D.: Promotional chat on the Internet. Marketing Science 25, 155–163 (2006)

Source Salience and the Persuasiveness of Peer Recommendations: The Mediating Role of Social Trust

Peter de Vries and Ad Pruyn

Twente University,
Marketing Communication and Consumer Psychology
7500 AE Enschede, The Netherlands
{p.w.devries,a.t.h.pruijn}@utwente.nl

Abstract. A lack of trust and face-to-face interaction prevents many people from purchasing online. Relevant research aimed at overcoming such problems is often based on the assumption that providing social information increases trust. These studies, however, have yielded inconsistent results, arguably because trust is usually treated as a unidimensional concept. This study targets the influence of social information on trust by taking account of the multidimensional nature of trust. Peer recommendations in product judgment tasks were hypothesized to affect consumers' product attitudes via social trust, rather than competence, if peer images are available and uncertainty associated with products is high. Results indeed support mediation by social trust, but only for experience products.

Keywords: E-commerce, peer recommendations, social trust, social presence.

1 Introduction

With so many companies venturing online, numerous aspects of the consumption process no longer require people to leave the confines of their homes. Many consumers are, nevertheless, hesitant to engage in online transactions. Of the various obstacles mentioned, the most prominent are privacy and security issues (28 – 31 %), lack of customer service (22 - 28 %), including the inability to reach someone in case of problems while shopping and after sales, and lack of interaction (9 – 15 %) with salespersons or friends [1]. These findings underscore the importance of two factors distinguishing online from offline purchasing. The first factor concerns the lack of face-to-face interaction; the second factor involves the higher uncertainty experienced online, which requires greater trust to reduce it [2].

Trust is generally considered to reduce uncertainty [3], and is, therefore, a crucial factor for people to engage in online transactions. It is often regarded as having multiple dimensions, some of which involve emotions and attributions to agents, whereas others are more calculative in nature. Lewis and Weigert [4], for example, distinguished between cognitive and emotion-based trust (cf. [5], [6]), with assessments of competence feeding the former, and integrity, goodwill and value congruence the latter. Similarly, Mayer, Davis and Schoorman [7] distinguished

Y. de Kort et al. (Eds.): PERSUASIVE 2007, LNCS 4744, pp. 164–175, 2007.
© Springer-Verlag Berlin Heidelberg 2007

between ability, integrity and benevolence (cf. [8], for an overview, see [9], [7]). In a face-to-face sales situation, consumers may base their trust on the salesperson's perceived benevolence, honesty or integrity as well as more calculative assessments, such as competence and ability. By contrast, trust of an online consumer in the selling party is less likely to involve such attributions [cf. 10], as specific interaction partners are not present – at least not physically. Consequently, trust in online contexts could be argued to be frailer and, perhaps, more unstable than interpersonal trust.

Not surprisingly, a frequently adopted approach has been to implement some kind of "social touch" in online interactions, particularly computer-mediated communication, under the assumption that social information is beneficial for trust to occur. As noted by Corritore, Wiedenbeck, and Kracher [11], however, studies on the effectiveness of photographs and biographical information in terms of online trust have so far yielded contradictory results. Riegelsberger [12], for instance, only found a positive effect of images on self-reported trust after a superficial exploration of an e-commerce vendor's website; once users proceeded beyond the initial exploration, this effect disappeared. Walker, Sproull, and Subramani [13], on the other hand, found a difference between questionnaires conducted with talking-face and text displays, in that participants interacting with a talking-face display spent more time, made fewer mistakes, and wrote more comments than those with text displays. Tourangeau, Couper, and Steiger [14], who focused on social presence in web and interactive voice response surveys, hardly found any such differences: manipulations of gender using male and female pictures merely resulted in small effects on reported gender attitudes and on some of the items used to measure socially desirable response. In addition, Riegelsberger [12] argued that the use of images may decrease usability as they may clutter the interface.

Few researchers have, however, taken account of the multidimensional nature of trust (but see [9]). Yet the availability of social information about a physically absent other in online interactions is most likely to appeal to the social dimensions of trust. In addition, studies on social presence and trust as a unidimensional concept are often based on the assumption that the mere experience of social presence is beneficial for trust to emerge (e.g. [9], [15], cf. [16], in the context of media richness). The valence of a trust judgment, however, is not likely to depend on the mere presence or absence of an image, but also on the attributions made to the salient person [17]; the experience of social presence can only be expected to aid trust formation when the portrayed person is actually perceived as trustworthy; moreover, it could also decrease trust.

1.1 Social Information in Online Contexts

Several theoretical perspectives exist that can be used to explain the effect of social cues on consumer cognition and behavior in situations in which the communication medium is limited in its ability to transfer social information.

Short et al. introduced the concept of social presence, defined as the "degree of salience of the other person in the interaction and the consequent salience of the interpersonal relationships" ([18], p. 65; for an overview of various definitions, see

[19]). Social presence can be applied to situations in which someone else is physically present, but also to interactions in which the presence of an other is merely implied or imagined (cf. [20]), as would be the case when a consumer visits an e-commerce website with images of persons or biographical notes. In a similar vein, Gefen and Straub [9] argued that pictures of people on websites can convey a sense of personal, sociable, and sensitive human contact, and thus increases the experience of social presence.

The Social Influence model of Deindividuation Effects (SIDE, e.g., see [21], [22]) uses social categorization processes to explain how individuals form impressions of others in computer-mediated communication. The Social Information Processing Theory (SIPT, e.g., see [23], [15]) argues that individuals not only adapt to cues such as conventional content features and linguistic strategies, but also to chronemic and typographic elements. The Hyperpersonal Perspective, which can be seen as an extension of SIPT, focuses more specifically on how online information is processed. Analogous to SIDE, this perspective holds that receivers engage in attributional processes in order to reduce uncertainty, and do so in an exaggerated manner, based on limited information. In other words, minimally available information about partners will lead to overattribution and exaggerated perceptions. When faced with a low-cue interactive online environment, people will use whatever social information they can find to form attributions and perceptions about the other online individuals they are interacting with. By thus constructing mental models, people and situations will start to make sense, a realization that reduces uncertainty.

E-commerce is generally considered to be an environment with high risk and uncertainty; increasing trust by means of social information therefore seems worthwhile. The influence of images of peer recommenders on consumer trust depends on the attributions people make towards the displayed person. Consumers may attribute such traits as trustworthiness, benevolence and integrity to the displayed person, depending on his or her characteristics, in which case they may be more willing to base their product attitude on his or her recommendation. Recommendations of someone who appears to be untrustworthy, however, will be far less effective in influencing product attitudes.

The effectiveness of peer recommendations is, furthermore, dependent on the type of product. Search products, for instance, are products whose quality can be determined before the actual purchase on the basis of its characteristics [24], and are typically associated with lower levels of uncertainty than experience products (or services), whose quality can only be ascertained after purchase [25]. Finally, credence category products can often not be evaluated even after consumption [26], likely evoking even more uncertainty in the consumer. The higher the perceived uncertainty, the more important trust will become as a means to reduce this uncertainty [3], [27]. Trust can, therefore, be expected to play a more important role in consumers' judgments of products and decisions in terms of product choice when the focal product belongs to the experience or credence category, rather than the search category. In turn, this would imply that the decision to follow a peer's recommendation is less likely to be based on his or her trustworthiness in case of search product than experience or even credence products.

1.2 The Current Research

An experiment was conducted to test whether the use of personal images influences the persuasiveness of a recommendation, and whether this effect is mediated by trust. Participants viewed a search, experience, or credence product, and subsequently received a peer recommendation. The peer's opinion was either favorable towards the focal products or unfavorable, and was either accompanied by a portrait image (i.e., an individuating cue) or not. Those who were exposed to the image either saw a very trustworthy peer, or someone who was not trustworthy.

H1: Individuating cues influence the effectiveness of peer recommendation; specifically, participants will be more likely to base their product attitudes on the recommendations of a trustworthy peer than of an untrustworthy peer;

H2: The influence of individuating cues on the effectiveness of peer recommendation is mediated by social trust rather than competence; specifically, when the peer is visualized by an image, this relationship is mediated by social trust, contrary to when no image is provided;

H3: The effects specified in previous hypotheses are expected to be more prominent for credence than for experience, and more for experience than for search products.

2 Method

2.1 Pilot Study

Twente-five images, both images of people judged to be high as well as low in trustworthiness, were taken from the A-Face image database [28]. This set of images was pilot-tested among sixty graduate and undergraduate students at the University of Twente. They were asked to rate the general trustworthiness (i.e., topic independent) of the displayed persons on a 7-point scale. Two images, one scoring high in trustworthiness and one low ($M = 4.98$, $SD = 1.13$ versus $M = 2.57$, $SD = 1.23$)[1], were selected as stimulus material for the Individuating Cue conditions.

2.2 Participants and Design

Fifty-seven participants at the University of Twente (age: $M = 21.86$, $SD = 2.05$; 29 females, 28 males) took part in this study, which had a 3 (Individuating Cue: no image versus low trustworthiness versus high trustworthiness) * 3 (Product Category: search versus experience versus credence) * 2 (Recommendation: favorable versus unfavorable) design. Individuating Cue was varied between-participants, and Product Category and Recommendation constituted within-participants variables.

2.3 Procedure

Participants, assigned to separate computers, learned that they would participate in a study concerning product impression formation. The products they were asked to

---

[1] In the A-Face database [28] these images corresponded with the following trustworthiness ratings on a 9-point scale: $M = 6.51$, $SD = 1.64$ and $M = 3.75$, $SD = 2.15$ respectively.

judge were typical exemplars of the three product categories; two similar digital cameras were used as search products, the experience category was represented by two similar last-minute travel arrangements to two different locations in Turkey (a popular destination among Dutch tourists), and the credence category consisted of two brands of vitamin pills. These were all existing products and care was taken to ensure that brand names were illegible, to prevent any interfering effect of brand preference.

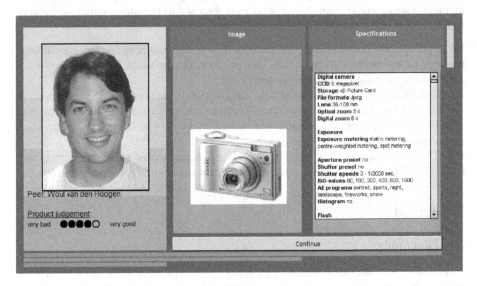

Fig. 1. Screen shot, showing an image and specifications of a digital camera (search category), a peer image (high trustworthiness Individuating Cue condition) and his recommendation (favorable)

These six different products were randomly presented onscreen, and had to be judged in terms of quality one by one. Participants could base their judgments on the available product images and specifications. In addition, each product was accompanied by a peer recommendation, which was manipulated to be either favorable, or unfavorable towards the focal product (see Figure 1). Thus, within each product category participants viewed one product accompanied by favorable, and one by unfavorable peer recommendation. The favorable and unfavorable recommendations consisted of a high (approximately four) and low (approximately one) number of dots respectively, on a total of five. No argumentation was made available as part of the recommendation, as the perceived quality of these arguments could influence participants' perception of competence of the peer, which could thwart the trustworthiness manipulation.

The source of this recommendation was identified with a name (identical for all participants), and, depending on the Individuating Cue condition, accompanied by an image. In one condition, the image portrayed a person who was rated as highly trustworthy in the pilot study, whereas in the other condition an untrustworthy person was displayed; in a third, control condition only a silhouette was shown.

After each product trial participants were asked to rate their attitude towards the product. After completion of all six trials, participants were asked to rate trust in the peer (on multiple dimensions), the experience of social presence, and the uncertainty they associated with each of the products.

3 Results

3.1 Uncertainty Ratings

The ratings of uncertainty associated with purchasing the products of each category showed a highly significant main effect of Product Category, $F (2, 108) = 15.07$; $p < .01$. Planned contrasts revealed significant differences between the search and experience products ($M = 4.75$; $SD = 1.27$ versus $M = 5.91$; $SD = 0.91$; $F (1, 54) = 32.53$; $p < .01$), but not between the search and credence products ($M = 4.86$; $SD = 1.62$. Therefore, whereas the search and experience products used in this experiment conform to the uncertainty assumption, the credence products do not.

3.2 Scale Construction

Competence. This measure was constructed by averaging items regarding the extent to which participants believed the portrayed peer to (a) know what is important to consumers, (b) be able to empathize with consumers, (c) possess sufficient knowledge to be able to give good product judgments, (d) be competent, (e) be capable of giving good product judgments, and (f) the extent to which participants felt they knew what to expect of the peer (Cronbach's Alpha = .88; cf. [7], [9]).

Social Trust. This measure was constructed by averaging items concerning attributions such as benevolence and honesty (cf. [7], [9]). Specifically, these items targeted (a) the peer's integrity, (b) his honesty, (c) the extent to which participants believed the peer to be willing to do his utmost to give good product advice, and (d) the extent to which was believed to have consumers' best interest at heart (Cronbach's Alpha = .85).

Social Presence. Social presence was measured with a 12-item scale, requiring participants to rate on semantic differentials e.g., how personal (versus impersonal), friendly (versus unfriendly), or natural (versus unnatural) they believed this way of providing product advice was [18] (Cronbach's Alpha = .91). An analysis of variance to which this measure was subsequently subjected did not reveal a significant effect of Individuating Cue, however.

3.3 The Effect of Peer Recommendations on Product Attitude

An overall analysis of variance did not reveal any direct evidence to suggest that providing individuating cues positively influences the degree to which product attitudes are affected by recommendations. Besides non-significant main effects of Recommendation, and Individuating Cue on product attitude, the required interaction between Recommendation and Individuating Cue did not reach significance either.

Table 1. Average ratings of product attitude (7–point scale), and standard deviations as a function of Product Category, Individuating Cue and Recommendation; higher scores indicate more favorable attitudes

| | | Recommendation | | | | |
| | | Favorable | | Unfavorable | | |
Product Category	Individuating Cue	M	SD	M	SD	N
Search	Control	5.05	0.97	4.26	1.24	19
	Trustworthy	5.11	0.99	4.58	1.30	19
	Untrustworthy	4.95	1.39	4.68	1.16	19
	Total	5.04	1.12	4.51	1.23	57
Experience	Control	4.89	1.33	4.95	1.31	19
	Trustworthy	4.95	1.22	4.11	1.29	19
	Untrustworthy	4.53	1.17	4.84	1.21	19
	Total	4.79	1.24	4.63	1.30	57
Credence	Control	4.32	1.42	3.63	1.26	19
	Trustworthy	3.79	1.18	4.53	1.39	19
	Untrustworthy	3.58	1.39	3.79	1.27	19
	Total	3.89	1.35	3.98	1.34	57

The three-way interaction of Recommendation, Individuating Cue, and Product Category, however, did reach significance, $F (4, 108) = 2.80; p < .03$.

To test whether the influence of product advice depends both on provision of individuating cues and product category, separate analyses were conducted for each of the product categories. Specifically, for each category, participants' attitude towards the focal product was subjected to an analysis of variance, in which Individuating Cue was entered as between-participants independent variable, and Recommendation (favorable versus unfavorable) as within-participants independent variables. Table 1 shows means and standard deviations.

Search Category. In the search product category, participants judgments of the product they were shown appeared to be significantly influenced by the favorability of peer's recommendation, $F (1, 54) = 7.13; p < .01$. Participants' judgments were higher after positive peer advice than after negative advice ($M = 5.04$; $SD = 1.12$ versus $M = 4.51$; $SD = 1.23$). No significant main effect of Individuating Cue, or a significant interaction of Individuating Cue and Recommendation was found, however. These findings illustrate that in the search condition, participants' opinion concerning the focal products were influenced by the valence of the peer's advice, regardless of whether the peer was visualized by an image of a trustworthy or untrustworthy person, or not.

Experience category. Analyses of participants' opinions regarding the experience products showed these not to be influenced by either Recommendation or Individuating Cue. However, these variables appeared to interact, but not at the required level of significance, $F (2, 54) = 2.96; p < .06$. Further analyses revealed a significant effect of Recommendation in the high trustworthiness Individuating Cue condition, $F(1, 54) = 5.70$; $p < .03$. No effects were found in the other two conditions (see Figure 2). These analyses show that the effectiveness of peer advice was highest when the peer was portrayed as a trustworthy person; when no image was provided, or an image of someone not regarded as trustworthy, the opinion voiced by the peer did not result in any effects on participants' attitude towards the focal product.

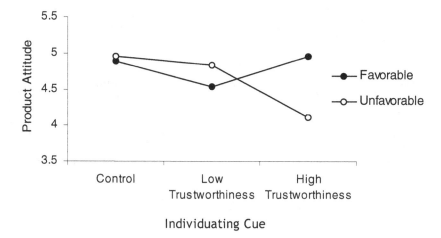

Fig. 2. Average product attitude as a function of Individuating Cue and Recommendation in the Experience Product Category

Credence category. In this category, products could not be shown to be judged significantly more positively after positive peer advice; no significant main effect of Individuating Cue was found either. However, Recommendation and Individuating Cue interacted significantly, $F(2, 54) = 3.76$; $p < .04$. Closer examination of interaction revealed two trend-level effects, a nearly significant difference between the favorable and unfavorable Recommendation condition within the high trustworthiness Individuating Cue condition , $F(1, 54) = 3.95$; $p = .05$, and a marginally significant effect within the control condition, in which no personal image was supplied, $F(1, 54) = 3.41$; $p = .07$. In the low trustworthiness condition, on the other hand, no significant difference between the Recommendation conditions was found. In sum, favorability of peer recommendations appeared to exert influence on participants' subsequent product attitude in the control and high trustworthiness conditions of Individuating Cue; however, whereas in the control condition a positive advice resulted in a more positive product attitude and vice versa, in the high trustworthiness condition this pattern was reversed, with positive peer advice causing lower rather than higher attitude ratings. Although it did not reach the required level of significance, this adverse finding will be elaborated on in the discussion.

3.4 Mediation Analyses

Mediation analyses were conducted in conformity with the procedure outlined by Baron and Kenny [29], to test whether the effect of personal images on the effectiveness of recommendations with regard to product attitudes is mediated by the social dimension of trust. Specifically, the magnitude of the difference between product attitudes after favorable versus unfavorable peer recommendations were hypothesized to be affected by Individuating Cue via the social rather than cognitive dimension of trust (i.e., competence). As Individuating Cue constituted a categorical rather than an ordinal variable, however, the control condition, in which no image was available to participants, was taken separately. The effect of the remaining two conditions, i.e., high and low trustworthiness images, could thus be examined using regular regression analyses.

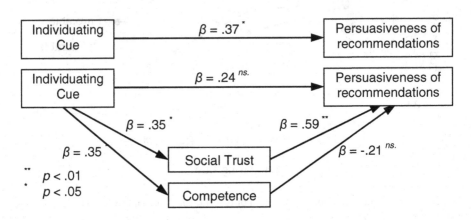

Fig. 3. Analysis of social trust and competence as mediators for the effect of Individuating Cue on the effectiveness of recommendations on product attitude (experience category)

First, the influence of social trust and competence on the difference in participants' product attitudes was assessed for the control condition only. No significant influences of social trust or competence were found in either of the product categories. Both competence and social trust could, therefore, not be shown to have had any influence on the effectiveness of Recommendation.

Next, the two experimental conditions of Individuating Cue were analyzed. The first step was to check whether these manipulations exerted any influence on social trust and competence. Social trust was shown to be significantly affected, $\beta = .35$; t $(36) = 2.19$, $p < .05$; a similar result was found for competence, $\beta = .35$; $t (36) = 2.22$, $p < .05$.

Subsequently, direct relationships between Individuating Cue and product attitudes were tested for each of the product categories. Within the search and credence categories no direct relations could be established, which effectively rules out mediation in these categories. In the experience category, on the other hand, a regression analysis revealed a significant direct effect of Individuating Cue on product attitudes, $\beta = .37$; $t (36) = 2.35$, $p < .03$. Adding social trust and competence as predictors in the regression analyses resulted in non-significant effects of Individuating Cue, and competence on attitudes. Social trust, on the other hand, was shown to have a significant effect, $\beta = .59$; $t (36) = 3.16$, $p < .01$ (see Figure 3).

In sum, the addition of particularly social trust to the regression model effectively lowered Individuating Cue regression coefficient from $\beta = .37$ to $\beta = .24$; the mediation hypothesis is, therefore, tenable. Providing images of trustworthy and untrustworthy persons, therefore, affects the effectiveness of recommendations, and this effect is explained by social trust, rather than competence, as a mediating variable. In addition, mediation of social trust occurs only in the experience product category.

4 Conclusions and Discussion

The overall analyses did not reveal direct evidence to suggest that providing individuating cues positively influences the degree to which product attitudes are affected by recommendations regardless of product category (Hypothesis 1), or that social trust mediated this relationship (Hypothesis 2). Nevertheless, the significant three-way interaction of Individuating Cue, Recommendation and Product Category indicates that the actual occurrence of the expected two-way interaction depends on the category to which the focal product belongs, which supports Hypothesis 3. Specifically, participants' attitude regarding the search products was influenced by the favorability of peer recommendations regardless of whether the peer was visualized by an image of a trustworthy or untrustworthy person or was not visualized at all. In case of experience category products, however, the effectiveness of peer recommendations was highest when the peer was portrayed as trustworthy; when no image was provided, or an image of someone who was not regarded as trustworthy, the opinion conveyed by the peer's recommendation did not result in any effects on participants' product attitude.

Oddly, in the credence category, favorable peer recommendations tended to decrease rather than increase attitude ratings. Another anomaly regarding this category is that the difficulty to assess credence product quality was not translated into higher uncertainty ratings. Nevertheless, vitamin pills have been argued to be typical examples of credence products [32]. We have no conclusive explanation for these rather counterintuitive findings. Perhaps participants thought it highly unlikely that a mere peer could be well enough informed to advise others about the credence products used in this study. After all, credence products and services are hard to judge in terms of quality, a fact that applies to everyone in equal measure, peer or participant. This would imply that credence category products and services are the least suitable for use in online product reviews.

Finally, the mediation analyses conducted here show the relationship between individuating information and the degree to which recommendations influenced product attitudes (i.e., recommendation effectiveness) to be mediated by social trust, but not by competence – at least, in the experience product category. In other words, providing personal images caused participants to assess the portrayed peer in terms of benevolence, honesty, and integrity, causing the peer's recommendations to gain in persuasiveness. Interestingly, this suggests that people may make attributions to a peer who is not perceived to be physically but only virtually present as a result of availability of a portrait. The fact that most people are likely to be aware that mere e-commerce sites are inanimate and thus cannot actually be honest or benevolent or hold intentions in the same way other people do, is by no means detrimental to this conclusion. In fact, this is in keeping with Dennett's [30] contention that people frequently adopt an intentional stance towards inanimate objects, because doing so allows for easier prediction and interpretation of displayed behavior. Additionally, Nass and Moon [31] found that people mindlessly apply well-learned social rules and expectations to computers, although they are aware that a computer is not a person and does not warrant attributions as such.

The study presented here focused on the role of social trust and its link with the concept of social presence, while taking into account consumers' perceptions of the portrayed person. Although the experience of social presence was not affected by the manipulations, we feel that the concept of social presence in combination with the social dimensions of trust deserves to be explored further. After all, the social presence measure remaining impervious to manipulations could reasonably be explained by its low validity in other contexts than for which it was devised, and the subtlety of the effects under scrutiny here, rather than consumers not being in any way responsive to social cues in e-commerce.

References

1. Ahuja, M., Gupta, B., Raman, P.: An empirical investigation of online consumer purchasing behaviour. Communications of the ACM 46, 145–151 (2003)
2. McKnight, D.H., Chervany, N.L.: What trust means in e-commerce customer relationships: An interdisciplinary conceptual typology. International Journal of Electronic Commerce 6, 35–59 (2002)
3. Luhmann, N.: Trust and power: Two works by Niklas Luhmann. John Wiley Sons, Chichester (1979)
4. Lewis, D., Weigert, A.: Trust as a social reality. Social Forces 63, 967–985 (1985)
5. McAllister, D.J.: Affect- and cognition-based trust as foundations for interpersonal cooperation in organizations. Academy of Management Journal 38, 24–59 (1995)
6. Johnson, D., Grayson, K.: Cognitive and affective trust in service relationships. Journal of Business Research 58, 500–507 (2005)
7. Mayer, R.C., Davis, J.H., Schoorman, F.D.: An integrative model of organizational trust. Academy of Management Review 20, 709–734 (1995)
8. Yamagishi, T., Yamagishi, M.: Trust and commitment in the United States and Japan. Motivation and Emotion 18, 130–166 (1994)
9. Gefen, D., Straub, D.W.: Consumer trust in B2C e-commerce and the importance of social presence: experiments in e-products and e-services. Omega 32, 407–424 (2004)
10. Siegrist, M., Cvetkovich, G.T., Gutscher, H.: Shared values, social trust, and the perception of geographic cancer clusters. Risk Analysis 21, 1047–1053 (2001)
11. Corritore, C.L., Kracher, B., Wiedenbeck, S.: Online trust: concepts, evolving themes, a model. International Journal of Human-Computer Studies 58, 737–758 (2003)
12. Riegelsberger, J.: Trust in Mediated Interactions. Doctoral thesis, University of London, United Kingdom (2005)
13. Walker, J., Sproull, L., Subramani, R.: Using a human face in an interface. In: Proceedings of the Conference on Human Factors in Computing Systems, pp. 85–99 (1994)

14. Tourangeau, R., Couper, M.P., Steiger, D.M.: Humanizing self-administered surveys: Experiments on social presence in web and IVR surveys. Computers in Human Behavior 19, 1–24 (2003)
15. Rocco, E.: Trust breaks down in electronic contexts but can be repaired by some initial face-to-face contact. In: CHI 1998 Proceedings, pp. 496–502 (1998)
16. Bos, N., Olson, J., Gergle, D., Olson, G., Wright, Z.: Effects of four computer-mediated communications channels on trust development. In: CHI 2002 Proceedings, vol. 4, pp. 135–140 (2002)
17. Chen, S., Chaiken, S.: The heuristic-systematic model in its broader context. In: Chaiken, S., Trope, Y. (eds.) Dual-process theories in social psychology, pp. 73–96. The Guilford Press, New York (1999)
18. Short, J., Williams, E., Christie, B.: The social psychology of telecommunications. Wiley, London (1976)
19. Biocca, F., Harms, C., Burgoon, J.K.: Toward a more robust theory and measure of social presence: Review and suggested criteria. Presence 12, 456–480 (2003)
20. Latané, B.: The psychology of social impact. American Psychologist 36, 343–356 (1981)
21. Spears, R., Lea, M.: Panacea or panopticon? The hidden power in computer-mediated communication. Communication Research 21, 427–459 (1994)
22. Postmes, T., Spears, R., Lea, M.: Breaching or building social boundaries? SIDE-effects of computer-mediated communication. Communication Research 25, 689–715 (1998)
23. Walther, J.B.: Interpersonal effects in computer-mediated communication: a relational perspective. Communication Research 19, 52–90 (1992)
24. Nelson, P.: Advertising as information. Journal of Political Economy 82, 729–754 (1973)
25. Klein, L.R.: Evaluating the potential of interactive media through a new lens: Search versus experience goods. Journal of Business Research 41, 195–203 (1998)
26. Darby, M.R., Karni, E.: Free competition and the optimal amount of fraud. Journal of Law and Economics 16, 67–86 (1973)
27. Giddens, A.: The consequences of modernity. Stanford University Press, Stanford, CA (1990)
28. McKimmie, B.M., Chalmers, K.: Academic Facial Attributes Catalogue [internet database]. School of Psychology, University of Queensland (2002), http://www.psy.uq.edu.au/a-face
29. Baron, R.M., Kenny, D.A.: The moderator-mediator variable distinction in social psychological research: Conceptual, strategic, and statistical considerations. Journal of Personality and Social Psychology 51, 1173–1182 (1986)
30. Dennett, D.C.: The intentional stance. The MIT press, Cambridge, MA (1987)
31. Nass, C., Moon, Y.: Machines and mindlessness: Social responses to computers. Journal of Social Issues 56, 81–103 (2000)
32. Girard, T., Korgaonkar, P., Silverblatt, R.: Relationship of type of product, shopping orientations, and demographics with preference for shopping on the internet. Journal of Business and Psychology 18, 101–120 (2003)

An Examination of the Influence of Involvement Level of Web Site Users on the Perceived Credibility of Web Sites

Susan Ferebee

2971 W. Agena Drive, Tucson, AZ 85742
ferebees@gmail.com

Abstract. This study examined how Web site user involvement affects perceived credibility of Web sites. The study determined the relationship between two variables: enduring involvement and situational involvement and the study measured the effect of these two independent variables and the interaction effects on the perceived credibility of Web sites. A supplemental analysis assessed whether the four groups produced by the factorial design varied with regard to the Web site element categories noticed during credibility evaluation. The research found that the interaction effect between enduring involvement and situational involvement significantly influenced perceived credibility. Additionally, the user's focus shifted to a more central focus when situational involvement was introduced and different Web site elements were noticed.

Keywords: Credibility, Involvement, Web Design, Computer-Mediated Communication.

1 Introduction

Credibility influences a communicator's ability to persuade and is the most important contributing factor to persuasion (Hovland & Weiss, 1951). Organizations trying to persuade consumers in the online environment are unclear as to how to communicate credibility on a Web site. Fogg, Soohoo, et al (2002) showed that the elements Web users identify as credibility markers on a Web site are not the items they notice or use when they evaluate credibility of a Web site. Further research was needed to reveal accurate credibility markers for Web sites and it became important to determine what Web site elements users do notice when evaluating credibility.

Involvement level influences what people notice (Bransford, Brown & Cocking, 1999; Caine & Caine, 2000; Cho, 1999; Fogg, 2003; Petty & Cacioppo, 1979; Wathan & Burkell, 2002) and might be a relevant factor in how people assess credibility. Involvement is the result of "a person's perceived relevance of a subject, based on inherent needs, values, and interests" (Zaichkowsky, 1985, p. 342).

The problem is that research has not provided empirical data showing the relationship between involvement level and perceived credibility (Fogg, Soohoo, et al., 2002). If involvement level influences the Web site elements noticed during credibility assessment (Fogg, 2003), this could significantly affect Web site design strategies and improve Web developers' ability to create persuasive sites. The study discussed in this paper was an expansion study of Fogg, Soohoo, et al. (2002) to examine the influence of Web user

Y. de Kort et al. (Eds.): PERSUASIVE 2007, LNCS 4744, pp. 176–186, 2007.

involvement level on what Web site elements were noticed and on how those elements noticed affected perceived credibility of the Web site. Prior to this study inadequate guidelines existed to aid Web designers in effectively communicating credibility. This study suggests improved guidelines based on the study results.

The theoretical basis of this study parallels Fogg, Soohoo, et al. (2002) with regard to credibility but extends the credibility discussion to include both source and message credibility and discusses how the online environment might alter credibility perception. The concept of computer and electronic information credibility proposed by Fogg and Tseng (1999), suggests that factors other than source become relevant. Self (1996), Dutta-Bergman (2004), and Collins (2004) suggest that message credibility is separate from source credibility. Rieh (2002) finds that individuals evaluating credibility online are more influenced by source credits at the institutional level than at the creator level. The emerging credibility construct that can be applied to electronic information is one in which source and message characteristics interact to influence the overall credibility perception. In addition, characteristics of the receiver, the delivery medium, and the context of the message will influence both source and message credibility (Wathan & Burkell, 2002).

Additional concepts relevant to this study include involvement (enduring situational, and response), focus (central and peripheral), and computer mediated communication. The theoretical basis of this study with relation to involvement relies on the work of Celsi and Olson (1988) who define involvement as a state of mind called "felt involvement" (p. 211) which occurs through the combined influence of situational involvement (SI) and enduring involvement (EI) types (Houston & Rothschild, 1978). According to Celsi and Olson, "felt involvement" is a function of both situational sources of personal relevance (SSPR) and enduring or intrinsic sources of personal relevance (ISPR), and is the "overall subjective feelings of personal relevance" (p. 211). Once the mental state of "felt involvement", (p. 211) is reached through the interactive affect of SSPR and ISPR, that mental state then influences both response involvement (cognitive processes) and behaviors

This study examined the response involvement cognitive process of focus. The type of focus (either central or peripheral) that a person uses in credibility evaluation might be a factor in determining the elements noticed during that evaluation. Petty and Cacioppo (1979) propose that high-involvement encourages a central route to cognitive processing, leading to a more detailed examination of facts. Low-involvement leads to a reliance on peripheral cues for evaluation. Table 1 provides a summary and explanation of the involvement types referred to in this study.

Fogg (2003) proposes the Prominence-Interpretation theory to explain the difference noted in what people say indicates credibility on Web sites, and what they, in fact, notice when making the assessment (Fogg, Marshall, et al., 2001; Fogg, Soohoo, et al., 2002). The theory proposes that when individuals assess Web credibility, two things must occur. First, the Web site user must notice something. Once the user notices a Web site element, he or she interprets or judges that element. If an element is never noticed, it will not affect the credibility assessment, even though the user might consider that factor important. Fogg identifies involvement level of the users as a factor that will influence what is noticed.

Table 1. Involvement Type Summary

	Definition	Example
Enduring Involvement (EI)	**Involvement that is persistent and relates to intrinsic values (Houston & Rothschild, 1978).**	**A person is involved in Christian-based groups because of strong Christian upbringing and education.**
Situational Involvement (SI)	**Involvement that is short-lived and is induced when a circumstance generates concern from an individual with regard to how he or she will behave in the situation (Houston & Rothschild, 1978).**	**This same person awakes in a burning apartment building and other individuals are trapped in that building also.**
Involvement State of Mind	**Mental state created by causal antecedents of enduring and situational influences (Celsi & Olson, 1988)**	**The same individual's involvement state of mind is the combined influence of Christian values and a life-threatening situation in which others' lives are also at risk.**
Response Involvement	**The complexity of the cognitive processes generated by involvement (Houston & Rothschild, 1978).**	**The individual experiences cognitive processes of attention, focus, comprehension, and inference triggered by the enduring and situational involvement.**

The importance of involvement level on persuasion suggests the need to look at how involvement level might influence perceived credibility in the online environment. This study examined the influence of user involvement level on the type of focus the user applied, on the Web site elements noticed, and on the perceived credibility of the Web site.

2 Methodology

A 2 X 2 (Enduring Involvement X Situational Involvement) design identified any potential interactions that exist between EI level and SI level. There were four possible effects of interest: 1) a significant main effect of EI, 2) a significant main effect of SI, 3) a significant interaction between EI and SI, and 4) a null effect (Trochim, 1999). The study identified two levels of EI and two levels of SI as illustrated in Table 2. The potential interactions are identified by the following abbreviations, which are used going forward in this paper: LEI – low enduring involvement with no situational involvement, HEI – high enduring involvement with no situational involvement, LEIS – low enduring involvement with situational involvement, and HEIS – high enduring involvement with situational involvement.

Table 2. 2 X 2 (Enduring Involvement X Situational Involvement) Design (Trochim, 1999)

	Low Enduring Involvement (LEI)	High Enduring Involvement (HEI)
No Situational Involvement (no decision task) (Non-Treatment Group)	LEI	HEI
Situational Involvement (decision task) (Treatment Group) SI	LEIS	HEIS

The subjects for the experiment were 190 participants selected from graduates of University of Phoenix, employees at America on Line, Intuit, Lucent Technologies, and the Ebay and Google user groups. The target population for this study was Internet users that range in age from 18 to 70.

2.1 Experiment

The study used a convenience sample of 190 participants selected from graduates of University of Phoenix, employees at America on Line, Intuit, Lucent Technologies, and the Ebay and Google user groups Participants were randomly assigned to a treatment or non-treatment group. Participants in both groups were given a link to the Charles Schwab Web site. Participants in the non-treatment group were instructed to view the Web site and to evaluate the site based on how credible he or she felt the site was. Participants in the treatment group were asked to answer specific questions based on information they found on the Web site. This task was designed to introduce situational involvement with the Web site. After answering these questions, the participants were then asked to evaluate the credibility of the Web site. Participants were also asked to write comments about the credibility of the Web site that they examined or used.

2.2 Methodology

This study measured EI in the topic of financial planning using Mittal's (1995) semantic differential involvement scales. In addition, the study measured the response involvement, focus ((Celsi and Olson, 1988) using the number of peripheral cues (design look, context, or receiver opinion) versus central cues (source or message) used in the credibility evaluation. Situational involvement was manipulated by randomly assigning participants to a treatment group that performed a task using the Charles Schwab finance Web site.

This study measured each participant's perception of the source credibility of the Charles Schwab Web site using Web credibility scales developed by Collins (2004).

Age, gender, and education level have been shown to influence perceived credibility (Johnson & Kaye, 1998). These demographic data were captured as part of the survey instrument.

To measure the influence of involvement level on the perceived credibility of Web sites, it was necessary to account for any other effects that might influence perceived credibility. Predisposition to trust (Collins, 2004) was measured as a covariate using four of the McKnight, Choudhury, and Kacman (2002) disposition to trust scales. One survey question was added to measure the participant's previous success in investment.

Table 3. Web Site Element Categories and Subcategories

Source	Message	Medium	Context	Receiver
Identity	Information Focus	Organization	Advertising	Past Experience with Site
Name Recognition	Information Accuracy	Information Design	Affiliations	General Suspicion
Reputation	Information Bias	Design Look	Sponsorship	General Like/Dislike
Motivation of Source	Information Usefulness	Readability		Performance on Test
	Information Clarity	Site Functionality		
	Corrections/ Mistakes	Perceived Security		
	Writing Tone	Technical Capability		
	Privacy			
	Customer Service			

2.3 Categorizing Comments

Data preparation involved coding of the comments written by participants. The same coding categories for comments were used as those developed for the Fogg, Soohoo, et al. (2002) study. In addition, the comment categories were grouped into Wathan and Burkell's (2002) five characteristics that influence credibility perception. For this study, two other coding categories were added, based on the review of literature. Perceived security (Jarvenpaa et al., 1999) and technical capability (Schweiger, 2000) were categories placed under the Medium group. Table 3 shows the individual categories and groupings.

3 Results

Table 4 indicates that enduring involvement on its own did not produce a significant result in the Web site elements noticed. In other words, if an individual had a high level of involvement in the topic of financial planning,, that individual did not notice significantly different Web sites than an individual with little or no interest in the topic. Situational involvement, when introduced, did produce a significant difference in the Web site elements noticed. The interaction effect between enduring and situational involvement on the Web site elements noticed during credibility evaluation was also significant.

Table 4. Chi-square Test for Differences in Web Site Elements Noticed by Involvement Level

Variable	Chi-Sq	Critical Value	DF	P value
Difference in Web site elements noticed based on EI	1.924	7.82	3	0.588
Difference in Web site elements noticed based on SI	15.647	7.82	3	0.001
Differences in Web site elements noticed based on EIxSI	18.775	16.92	9	0.027

Table 5 shows the significant effect of situational involvement on focus type. When situational involvement with the Web site was introduced by asking the user to use the site to search for specific information, the user showed a significant shift to a more central focus, regardless for the user's enduring involvement level in the topic of financial planning.

Table 5. Chi-square Test for Differences in Focus Type by Involvement Level

Variable	Chi-Sq	Critical Value	DF	P value
Difference in focus type based on EI	0.798	5.99	2	0.671
Difference in focus type based on SI	28.473	5.99	2	<0.0005

Table 6 summarizes the two-way ANOVA tests for perceived credibility by the main effect of EI and SI and the interaction effect of EI and SI. Individually, neither EI nor SI had a significant influence on the perceived credibility of the Web site. However, the interaction effect between EI and SI did produce a significant difference in how the Web site's credibility was perceived. When the covariates of predisposition to trust and past experience in investing were removed, the interaction effect remained significant.

Table 6. Summary of Two-way ANOVA tests for Perceived Credibility

Source	Adj Sum of Squares	df	Adj Mean Square	F-ratio	p-value
EI	2.2469	1	2.2469	2.44	0.121
SI	0.0662	1	0.0662	0.07	0.739
EIxSI	4.4359	1	4.4359	4.81	0.030
EI (covariate removed)	0.0112	1	0.0112	0.01	0.905
SI (covariate removed)	0.2948	1	0.2948	0.37	0.545
EIxSI (covariate removed)	3.0512	1	3.0512	3.87	0.051

4 Discussion

The study results suggest there is a significant difference in the Web site elements noticed as influenced by the interaction effect of situational involvement and enduring involvement (see Figure 1). Situational involvement generates more notice of the message category while non-situational involvement generates more notice of the medium category. A high enduring involvement level appears to increase notice of items in both the message and source categories for non-situational involvement participants. For participants with situational involvement, a high enduring involvement level appears to reduce the focus on the medium category. Enduring involvement level appears to influence the receiver category.

An interesting finding was that HEI users with no situational involvement mediate their credibility judgment with their experience and opinion. The findings that LEI users rely on credibility markers in the medium category align with the findings in Fogg, Soohoo, et al. (2002).

For this study, a central focus was defined as a focus on message and source. Interestingly, for all combinations of EI and SI and for differing levels of EI, the percentage of focus on source is consistent, supporting Dutta-Bergman's (2004) suggestion that judgment of source credibility continues throughout the viewing of the

Web site content and that message content influences how source is judged. Based on this current study, it might be inferred that for low involvement users, the medium category influences how source is judged.

It is the focus on message that changes with different involvement levels. Both with LEI and HEI, when SI is introduced, the focus on message almost doubles. And, as focus on message increases, it is the focus on the medium that decreases, while focus on the source remains relatively the same.

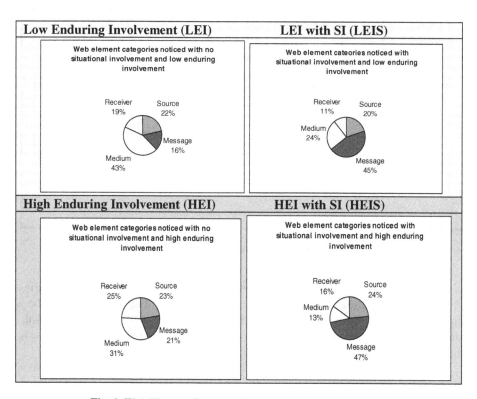

Fig. 1. Web Element Categories Noticed by Involvement Level

The combined influence of enduring and situational involvement has a significant and perhaps apparent effect on perceived credibility of Web sites. As Figure 2 illustrates, when situational involvement is introduced to participants with high enduring involvement, a central focus develops and perceived credibility of the Web site increases. In comparison, when situational involvement is introduced to participants with low enduring involvement, although a central focus develops, the perceived credibility of the Web site decreases.

The results of the study support that involvement level influences three factors: !) user focus type, 2) Web site elements noticed, and 3) perceived credibility. The way that involvement level influences these factors was interesting and somewhat unexpected. There were no main effects of enduring or situational involvement on

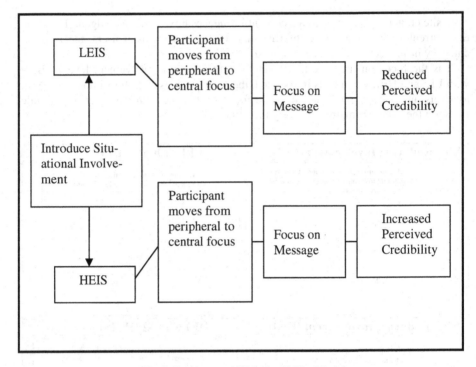

Fig. 2. Involvement-Web Credibility Model

perceived credibility, but there was a significant interaction effect. While enduring involvement, on its own, did not influence perceived credibility, it appears to be a predictor of perceived credibility when situational involvement is introduced. Situational involvement appears to be the primary driver of a change in focus type, and in the different Web site elements noticed because of that focus change.

Future research should focus on how involvement level is affecting the interpretation of credibility markers by looking at the cognitive processes of attention, comprehension, and inference (Houston & Rothschild, 1978). There is evidence in the literature to support that LEI Web users do not link messages to personal needs or interests (Hawkins and Hoch, 1992) and this might explain differences in interpretation of markers between LEI and HEI users. This possibility needs to be explored through empirical research.

References

1. Bransford, J.D., Brown, A.L., Cocking, R.R. (eds.): How people learn: Brain, mind, experience and school. National Academy Press, Washington, DC (1999)
2. Caine, R.N., Caine, G.: Brain/mind learning (2003), (Retrieved February 2, 2003) from,http://cainelearning.com/brain
3. Celsi, R., Olson, J.: The role of involvement in attention and comprehension processes. Journal of Consumer Research 15(2), 210–224 (1988)

4. Cho, C.H.: How advertising works on the WWW: Modified elaboration likelihood model. Journal of Current Issues and Research in Advertising 21(1), 33–50 (1999)
5. Collins, J.: Measuring credibility assessment targets in web-based information Unpublished doctoral dissertation. Nova Southeastern University, Florida (2004)
6. Dutta-Bergman, M.J.: The impact of completeness and web use motivation on the credibility of e-health information. Journal of Communication 54, 253–269 (2004)
7. Fogg, B.J.: Prominence-interpretation theory: Explaining how people assess credibility online. In: CHI 2003 Extended Abstracts on Human Factors in Computing Systems, pp. 722–723. ACM Press, New York (2003)
8. Fogg, B.J., Marshall, J., Laraki, O., Osipovich, A., Varma, C., Fang, N., Paul, J., Rangnekar, A., Shon, J., Swani, P., Treinen, M.: What makes a web site credible? A report on a large quantitative study. In: Proceedings of ACM CHI 2001 Conference on Human Factors in Computing Systems, pp. 61–68. ACM Press, New York (2001)
9. Fogg, B.J., Soohoo, C., Danielson, D., Marable, L., Stanford, J., Tauber, E.R.: How do people evaluate a web site's credibility: Results from a large study. Consumer WebWatch Research. (2003), http:// www.consumerwebwatch.org/news/report3_credibilityresearch/ stanfordPTL_abstract.htm
10. Fogg, B.J., Tseng, H.: The elements of computer credibility. In: Proceedings of the SIGCHI Conference on Human Factors in Computing Systems: The CHI is the Limit, pp. 80–87 (1999)
11. Hawkins, S.A., Hoch, S.J.: Low-involvement learning: Memory without evaluation. Journal of Consumer Research 19, 212–225 (1992)
12. Houston, M.J., Rothschild, M.L.: Conceptual and methodological perspectives on involvement. In: Jain, S.C. (ed.) Research frontiers in marketing: Dialogues and directions, pp. 184–187. American Marketing Association, Chicago (1978)
13. Hovland, C.I., Weiss, W.: The influence of source credibility on communication effectiveness. Public Opinion Quarterly 4(15), 635 (1951)
14. Jarvenpaa, S., Tractinsky, N., Saarinen, L.: Consumer trust in an internet store: A cross-cultural validation. Journal of Computer-Mediated Communication, 5 (2) (1999)
15. Johnson, T.J., Kaye, B.K.: Cruising is believing? Comparing internet and traditional sources on media credibility measures. Journalism and Mass Communication Quarterly 75, 325–340 (1998)
16. McKnight, H.D., Choudhury, V., Kacmar, C.: Developing and validating trust measures for e-commerce: An integrative typology. Information Systems Research 13(3), 334–359 (2002)
17. Mittal, B.: A comparative analysis of four scales of consumer involvement. Psychology and Marketing 12(7), 663–682 (1995)
18. Petty, R.E., Cacioppo, J.T.: Issue involvement can increase or decrease persuasion by enhancing message relevant cognitive responses. Journal of Personality and Social Psychology 37, 1915–1926 (1979)
19. Rieh, S.Y.: Judgement of information quality and cognitive authority in the Web. Journal of the American Society for Information Sciences and Technology 53(2), 145–161 (2002)
20. Schweiger, W.: Media credibility - experience or image?: A survey on the credibility of the World Wide Web in Germany in comparison to other media. European Journal of Communication 15(1), 37–59 (2000)
21. Self, C.C.: Credibility. In: Salwen, M.B., Stacks, D.W. (eds.) An integrated approach to communication theory and research, pp. 421–441. Lawrence Erlbaum, Mahwah, NJ (1996)
22. Sternthal, B., Phillips, L., Dholakia, R.: The persuasive effect of source credibility: A situational analysis. Public Opinion Quarterly 42 (fall), 285–314 (1978)

23. Trochim, W.: The research methods knowledge base. Cornell Custom Publishing, Cornell University, Ithaca (1999)
24. Wathan, C.N., Burkell, J.: Believe it or not: Factors influencing credibility on the web. Journal of the American Society for Information Science and Technology 53(2), 134–144 (2002)
25. Zaichkowsky, J.L.: Measuring the involvement construct. Journal of Consumer Research 12, 341–352 (1985)

Embedded Persuasive Strategies to Obtain Visitors' Data: Comparing Reward and Reciprocity in an Amateur, Knowledge-Based Website

Luciano Gamberini, Giovanni Petrucci, Andrea Spoto, and Anna Spagnolli

HTLab, Dept. of General Psychology, University of Padova, via Venezia 8,
35131 Padova, Italy
{luciano.gamberini,anna.spagnolli}@unipd.it,
{giovanni.petrucci,andreaspoto}@gmail.com

Abstract. This study compares the relative effectiveness of two different persuasive strategies embedded in the rationale of a website. The visitor is asked for his/her contact information either prior to or after having access to the guidelines for managing multimedia files offered by the site. Asking for personal data prior to access represents a reward strategy for obtaining such data. In contrast, asking for personal data after access represents a reciprocity strategy. In addition, the mediating effect of website features displaying "social proof" (such as visits counter) is explored. The analysis of the amount and type of contact information provided shows that a persuasive strategy based on reciprocity is more effective than one based on reward. Also, the presence of social proof features seems counterproductive when using a reciprocity strategy, while it seems to improve the visitors' compliance with the request when using a reward strategy. The results are discussed in terms of adequacy of the persuasive strategy to the specific website genre.

Keywords: reciprocity, reward, persuasion, personal information, social proof, websites.

1   Introduction

Persuasion consists of the process through which the attitudes and behaviors of an agent are intentionally conveyed in a certain direction by another agent without coercion. Finding an effective way to achieve persuasion and identifying the conditions upon which it occurs are classic endeavors in social psychology, and represent a way to expose one of the main mechanisms through which social power and control are exerted. The goal is to cause the actor take a certain physical action such as buying a product or a symbolic action such as expressing an opinion by implicitly or explicitly constructing such an action as accessible and desirable.

As mediated communication and the Internet have started to become common in everyday life, the study of this kind of manipulation has shifted from human interaction to human-computer interaction by including machines in the category of persuasive agents. The concept of affordances, based on making some invitations to

Y. de Kort et al. (Eds.): PERSUASIVE 2007, LNCS 4744, pp. 187–198, 2007.

action more apparent and explicit in order to orient the users' operations [1] already implies in essence the idea of making the machine persuasive. Any user scans the environment for cues, in order to understand in which scenario s/he's entering and what actions are feasible there [2, 3]. By offering access to some actions and resources, the landscape of what is possible and desirable can be intentionally manipulated. The ways in which a technology becomes a persuasive agent even in the absence of any explicit persuasive content are addressed by a field of research denominated "captology" [4], which underlines that by incorporating the right cues in the machine, both at a "micro" (some elements embedded in the artifact) and at a "macro" level (the artifact as a whole), one can covertly orient the user in a certain direction, without any explicit persuasive intent.

Because voluntary transfer of personal information [5, p. 218] is controversial, it is a conduct into which people need to be persuaded. On the one hand, giving personal information may be perceived as natural in commercial transactions, regardless of the media through which they occur; on the other hand, people are alerted that providing personal data can be risky [6]. The fact that the data collection takes place on-line may increase cautiousness, because the Internet appears ephemeral, anonymous, and, for non experts, tricky [7]. Reports demonstrate that people are generally more concerned about their privacy being threatened by the Internet than by other media or technologies. The controversial value of giving up personal information through websites is shown by [5], a study that presents participants with screenshots of thirty retail, medical and financial websites and asks them to express their agreement with various kinds of behaviors related to personal information transfer. Respondents agree that there are severe risks in revealing information to websites (identity theft, receiving unsolicited advertising, theft of credit card,...) but at the same time are willing to reveal this kind of information to websites of well-known brands and of medical and health companies. A website is positioned by the visitors within or outside the repertoire of the trustable ones due to their reliance on cues disseminated all over the website as well as on its brand [8]. One of the embedded ways in which the website can make a certain action appear as possible, legitimate or worthwhile is by framing this action within an acceptable kind of transaction. Websites may persuade visitors into leaving their personal data if this action becomes reasonable to them.

A common way to convince someone to take a certain action is to provide him/her with a reward. A reward strategy of persuasion implies that a person gives something in order to receive something valuable in return, both in economic and in symbolic terms. This resonates with theories according to which people are motivated opportunistically to find the maximum gain from a situation, and will then be likely to perform a certain action if it is advantageous. On the other hand, providing a reward automatically frames that exchange as one in which each participant just wants to gain something and action has no intrinsic motivation. This is probably why some research has found negative effects of rewards, at least on immediate compliance with the specific request that is connected to the reward. [8] showed that rewards increase personal concerns for privacy issues, [9] found that rewards work with personal identifiable information and low reputation firms, not with demographic information and high reputation firms. [10] raised the issue of promotion reactance, and explained in these terms the preference found for effort-congruent rewards, namely rewards that are congruent with the kind of effort devoted to achieve them.

An alternative strategy is represented by reciprocation. Reciprocation, or reciprocity, implies that a person provides something valuable to her interlocutor after having received something valuable from that interlocutor. In other words, while a reward strategy requires that something be given in order to obtain a valuable resource, with reciprocity the valuable good is obtained in advance and unconditionally. This is why reciprocity has been used to reduce inter-group competitive behavior and enhance cooperation [11 in 12] between groups in conflict. Reciprocity also works in marketing, where unilateral concessions from the seller, such as special offers or discounts, are likely to be followed by purchases [13 in 12; 14]. [15] made a survey within employees of a U.S. health care provider, to study the relationship between IS providers and IS users. He treated reciprocity as the existence of correspondent behaviors (but not similar behaviors) between the two departments and found support for the idea that users' actions towards the IS department reciprocate those actions taken by the IS department; the quality of the users' response to the IS department reflects their assessment of the IS department's action towards them. [16] studied the extent to which reciprocity applies when the counterpart is a computer. In their experiment reciprocity was operationalized as the production of an action (the user helping the computer) after a similar action produced by the other party (the computer helping the user). They found that framing the exchange within a social dynamic of reciprocity increased the helpful conduct on the users' part.

The aim of the present study is to compare reward and reciprocity as persuasive strategies for collecting information in an amateur, knowledge-based website. In addition, we wanted to study some components that are frequently added to knowledge-oriented websites and make them seem inhabited, such as visits' counter, a list of people connected, or the number of people present on the website. These "liveliness" signals can provide some forms of social proof by showing other people's relation with the website [17] and can then affect the compliance with the request, moderating the effect of the persuasive strategies implemented. To our knowledge, these specific website features have not previously been investigated for their persuasive effect [18, 19].

2 Research

2.1 Material

A new website was built for the study in order to allow us to embed the persuasive features of interest, and to control the log files of the visits. Since the expertise of a website or IT provider is believed to foster its credibility and trustworthiness, and is influenced by its look and focus [18, 19], we built a knowledge-based website, which provided specific guidelines for transcoding and recoding multimedia files (non standard Video-CD or XVCD, and DVD video). The guidelines were written by one of the authors, and the appearance of the website, quite simple in its graphics and with an essential selection of colors, resembled others of similar topic (Figure 1). The guidelines were written in Italian, whereas most similar Internet guides are in English.

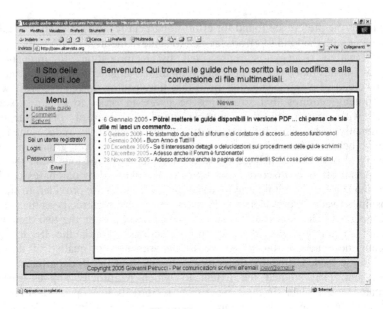

Fig. 1. Home page

In addition to the guidelines, the website featured a forum, a news section, a registration mask, and the owner's contact information (name, surname, e-mail). Most importantly, it contained a survey section with a *questionnaire* and a *form*. Taking this survey represented the behavior with respect to which we measured the relative effectiveness of the different persuasive strategies. Because the visitor bumped into the request to participate in the survey as s/he tried to link to the guidelines, the giving/taking rationale between accessing the guidelines and providing personal information was emphasized. Depending on the persuasive strategy embedded in the website, access to the guidelines was provided upon or prior to the submission of the survey. Specifically, in the "reward" strategy, the guidelines were not accessible until the form was submitted. In contrast, in the "reciprocity" strategy, the guidelines were immediately accessible. The survey was justified by the owner's study project (as was actually the case), so that filling it in was a way to help him. The questionnaire asked for the visitor's opinion about the website graphics and usability, and the visitor's connection modality and expertise (see Appendix). The private information form followed the last item of the questionnaire in the same page and included six types of information to be provided in dedicated fields: (1) name, (2) surname, (3) e-mail, (4) country, (5) province, and (6) city. Filling out the survey was motivated by the owner's need to contact the visitor again for the evaluation of the final version of the website. The questionnaire and form were submitted together in one step by pressing a "submit" button.

The website could also include some features showing its 'liveliness', as explained in section 1: a visitors' counter, a registration mask, a registered visitors counter, the number of people present on the website at each moment and a preview of the last message posted in the forum section (Figure 2).

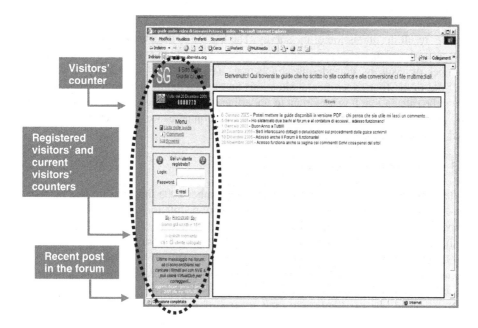

Fig. 2. The "liveliness" accessories on the left side of the page

In order to ensure a wide compatibility with different computers' configurations and Internet connections, and a stability in the appearance of the website regardless of the browsers, only PHP and HTML were used. The server-side nature of PHP relieves the visitor's browser from the need for plug-ins installation.

2.2 Design

The study manipulated two variables: persuasive strategy (reward versus reciprocity) and "liveliness" features (present versus absent). Four different versions of the website were then created: reward with liveliness, reward without liveliness, reciprocity with liveliness, and reciprocity without liveliness.

Thanks to our study apparatus, the effectiveness of the persuasive strategies and liveliness features could be based on the recording of the users' behaviors, not on self-reports. The kind of action that was monitored as a dependent variable was the compliance with the request to participate in the survey. The following measures were collected:

a) the number of questionnaires returned. The score was 1 if the visitor filled in the questionnaire, 0 if s/he did not.
b) the provision of the contact information. The score was 1 if the visitor filled in at least one field, 0 if s/he did not fill in any information field.
c) the amount of contact information provided. The measure ranged from 1 to 6 for each respondent according to the amount of information provided (e-mail, name, surname, nation, city, province).

We also kept track of both the number of visits resulting and the number of visits that did not result in submission of the survey. The log file in the server recorded the session ID, visitor's domain, IP, page, and login. This information was used to calculate the number of visits by considering connection, navigation and disconnection from the website in the four experimental situations and by excluding the administrators' visits from the calculation. It is important to underline that this is not a measure of the amount of visitors, but of visits. The log files and the questionnaires were collected on the server and were accessed with an administrator password.

2.3 Participants and Procedure

After some tests with expert users, on 20th December 2005 the web site was launched on-line. The potential visitors to this website were people to whom the website could appear as a valuable resource, such as people interested in reading the guidelines in Italian. The recruiting strategy consisted of posting messages containing a brief description of the guidelines and the link to the website on knowledge-based Italian communities on multimedia encoding. Messages were posted in compliance with the specific etiquette of each community.

Each visit was randomly assigned to one of the four experimental conditions thanks to a generator of random numbers embedded in the server. When the visitor tried to link to the guidelines, s/he was presented with the request for taking the survey, which was mandatory in order to access the guidelines in the reward group. Because of the cookies left on the visitor's machine, any subsequent visit from the same computer was assigned to the same condition until the survey was completed and submitted. When a user did complete the survey, it then disappeared from the website to prevent the same person from taking several surveys during multiple visits. The data collection took place from 20th December 2005 to 27th February 2006.

3 Results

The goal of the study was to measure the effectiveness of different persuasive strategies implemented in the website. Both strategies were successful if visitors complied with the owner's request to take the survey, which was explicitly associated with access to the guidelines. More specifically, the behavior that indexed the effectiveness of the persuasive strategies was the completion of the form with the contact information, not the participation in the survey altogether. This has both theoretical and methodological reasons. Regarding the first, providing contact information created more of a dilemma since it required users to give up privacy. In addition, because this information was meant to be used for further contacts and collaboration, providing it demonstrated a (nominal) availability to commit to collaboration in the long run. Regarding the methodological reasons, filling in the questionnaire did not have intermediate options; visitors either filled the questionnaire in completely or ignored it. Therefore, it could not provide nuanced measures of effectives. Most importantly, while it was possible to determine how many visitors did not complete the contact information part, it was not possible to determine how many visitors did not return the questionnaire. The 429 visits paid to the website during the period in which data were collected did not represent the number of visitors we had. That is because the same person could have paid more than one visit (in case they had to interrupt their first visit, or wanted to have one more look at the guidelines to check for updates), or - even if we deleted from the dataset repeated visits from the same computer (IP) - the same person could have accessed the site from different computers. Returning the usability questionnaire was then not the dependent variable but a criterion to create the sample; effectiveness was measured by the amount of contact information provided out of the surveys taken. In this way, we obtained in this way a sample of 80 surveys, 67 of which included the provision of contact information.

The sheer number of visits ending with the provision of contact information out of all the visits ending with a response is higher in the reward condition (31 out of 37) than in the reciprocity condition (31 out of 43). However, if we measure the amount of contact information provided, which could range from 0 to 6, and calculate mean and standard deviation, we obtain the values in Table 1.

Table 1. Means and standard deviations of contact information for each condition

Conditions	Personal Data	
	M	**SD**
Reward without liveliness	2.64	2.46
Reward with liveliness	3.72	2.85
Reciprocity without liveliness	5.43	1.31
Reciprocity with liveliness	4.43	2.03

A T –test shows that the amount of contact information provided is significantly higher in the reciprocity condition ($t=3.884$, $df=78$, $p<.01$). Instead, the presence of liveliness elements, instead, does not affect significantly the amount of contact information provided. An ANOVA performed on the mean of contact information provided by each respondent showed an interaction effect between the two independent variables ($F_{1,76}=4.206$, $p<0.5$): even though the amount of contact information provided by respondents remains higher with a persuasion strategy based on reciprocity, liveliness features diminish this amount in the reciprocity conditions (from 5.43 to 4.43), and increase it in the reward conditions (from 2.64 to 3.72).

Which kind of contact information is more often returned? Figure 3 shows that, regardless of the "fear of spam," the e-mail address is the most frequent information provided. In addition, we can mention that even in the 9 cases in which only one or two pieces of contact information was provided, most of them (8 cases) included the e-mail address.

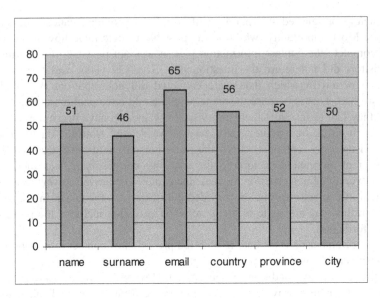

Fig. 3. The amount of respondents providing each of the six kinds of contact information included in the form

4 Discussion and Conclusion

The main aim of the paper was to compare the effectiveness of two persuasive strategies embedded in the structure of the interaction with a website. Interaction consisted mainly in accessing some guidelines, and this was associated with taking a survey according to a reward or a reciprocation rationale. The results show that reward produces a larger number of forms than reciprocation, but not a higher amount of contact information. This seems to suggest that whereas a reward seems to motivate the participation, the quality of this participation is not as good as the one obtained with a reciprocation strategy. The better success of "reciprocity" seems to show the inadequacy of an opportunistic strategy if a good form of collaboration is sought in the respondents.

The overall result is in line with other studies showing that the reward strategy may be counterproductive under some circumstances. The kind of personal data provided more often complied better with the motivation for the request, namely the need for further contact, showing at least an acknowledgment of that motivation. The reason for this in our own study is probably due to the kind of website created and the fact that some persuasive strategies fitted it better. The web site had an amateur appearance, the identity of the owner and his needs were made transparent, and the site was introduced within specialized Internet fora. The visitors may have framed the situation as an exchange of resources and obeyed a rule for gift exchange and peer cooperation [20]. They acted according to what seems reasonable and appropriate even though it may be more costly. For this reason it could be interesting in a critique of this study to compare it with website of a different nature in which peer cooperation is not evoked as a framework. The nature of the website may also explain the interaction effect found since the website focused on technical information about multimedia files. People in the reward condition, who needed to believe that the website content was valuable in order to have a motivation to go though the survey before accessing the guidelines, may have relied on the liveliness elements as a social proof of this value. People in the reciprocity condition did not need this social proof and may not have viewed the liveliness feature as a measure of the quality of the website. Instead, that feature may have lessened the importance of a personal reciprocity contract between them and the website owner.

Further studies on the nature of the reciprocity situation could be done by manipulating the quality of the website material and the kind of interlocutor. In fact, reciprocation starts with an unconditioned move from one party, but is absolutely not a form of spontaneous and improvised interaction. There are appropriate ways to reciprocate and sometimes the exchange is not successfully framed within the norm of reciprocity [21]. Further studies could examine what makes reciprocation work. For instance, since reciprocation is based in the adequacy of the transaction, reciprocity may not lead into the visitors leaving information or leaving good information if s/he is discontent with the kind of resources provided to them. Similarly, whether the user leaves information may depend on whether the website owner also discloses his/her own contact information. In our study there was a strong parallelism since the private information required was almost the same as that provided by the website owner (name, surname, e-mail address), which according to [22] could have facilitated the visitors' self-disclosures. [23] restricts the meaning of reciprocity to the returning of similar goods or acts, calling the case of exchange of different goods "complimentarity." It would then also be interesting to investigate whether similarity is needed or if reciprocity works insofar as moves or goods exchanged are reciprocally adequate according to social norms. Finally, we created the "liveliness" features category by including several different elements that could be investigated separately to determine what they actually meant to the visitor. For instance, is the visitor counter per se perceived as a social proof of popularity or is there a threshold, maybe varying with the website genre? Also, the "liveliness" features did not relate directly with the behavior required of the user (filling in the questionnaire) but with the website as a whole. It would be interesting to investigate their effect in case social proofs were provided about the visitors' compliance with taking the survey.

In conclusion, our results suggest that some persuasive strategies embedded in the website are more able than other in convincing people to provide information, including more sensitive, private information such as surname and e-mail. Setting up the right social scenario makes the provision of contact information a legitimate behavior, avoiding both opportunism and cautiousness.

Acknowledgements. The authors would like to thank the anonymous reviewers for their valuable suggestions.

References

1. Norman, D.A.: The Psychology of Everyday Things. Basic Books, New York (1988)
2. Spagnolli, A., Varotto, D., Mantovani, G.: An Ethnographic, Action-Based Approach to Human Experience in Virtual Environments. International Journal of Human-Computer Studies 59(6), 797–822 (2003)

3. Bourdieu, P.: Outline of a Theory of Practice. Cambridge University Press, Cambridge (1977)
4. Fogg, B.J.: Persuasive Technology: Using Computers to Change What We Think and Do. Morgan Kaufmann, San Francisco (2003)
5. Baumer, D.L., Earp, J.B., Evers, P.S.: Tit for That in Cyberspace: Consumer and Website Responses to Anarchy in the Market for Personal Information. North Carolina Journal of Law and Technology 4(2), 217–274 (2003), http://www.jolt.unc.edu/vol4I2/pdf/v4I2-baumer.pdf
6. Cavusoglu, H., Mishra, B., Raghunathan, S.: The Effect of Internet Security Breach Announcements on Market Value: Capital Market Reactions for Breached Firms and Internet Security Developers. International Journal of Electronic Commerce 9(1), 69 (2004)
7. Hoffman, D.L., Novak, T.P., Peralta, M.: Building Con Trust On-Line. Communications of the ACM 42(4), 80–85 (1999)
8. Andrade, E., Kaltcheva, V., Weitz, B.: Self-Disclosure on the Web: The Impact of Privacy Policy, Reward and Brand Reputation. Advances in Consumer Research 29, 350–353 (2002)
9. Teo, H.H., Wan, W., Li, L.: Volunteering Personal Information on the Internet: Effects of Reputation, Privacy Initiatives, and Reward on Online Consumer Behavior. In: Teo, H.H. (ed.) Proceedings of the 37th Hawaii International Conference on System Sciences (2004), Retrieved on April 5, 2006, http://csdl2.computer.org/comp/proceedings/hicss/2004/2056/07/205670181c.pdf
10. Kivetz, R.: Promotion Reactance: The Role of Effort-Reward Congruity. Journal of Consumer Research 31, 725–736 (2005)
11. Lindskold, S.: Trust Development, the GRIT Proposal and the Effects of Conciliatory Acts on Conflict and Cooperation. Psychological Bulletin 85, 772–793 (1978)
12. Smith, E.R., Mackie, D.M.: Social Psychology. Taylor and Francis, London (2000)
13. Cialdini, R.B., Vincent, J.E., Lewis, S.K., Catalan, J., Wheeler, D., Darby, B.L.: Reciprocal Concessions Procedure for Inducing Compliance: The Door in the Face Technique. Journal of Personality and Social Psychology 31, 206–215 (1975)
14. Sherry, J.F.: Gift Giving in Anthropological Perspective. The Journal of Consumer Research 10(2), 157–168 (1983)
15. Carr, C.L.: Reciprocity: The Golden Rule of IS-User Service Relationship Quality and Cooperation. Communications of the ACM 49(6), 77–83 (2006)
16. Fogg, B., Nass, C.: How Users Reciprocate To Computers: An Experiment That Demonstrates Behavior Change. In: CHI '97 Extended Abstracts on Human Factors in Computing Systems: Looking To the Future, Atlanta, Georgia, March 22 – 27, pp. 331–332. ACM Press, New York (1997)
17. Cialdini, R.: Influence: Science and Practice. Harper Collins, New York (1993)
18. Fogg, B.J., Marshall, J., Kameda, T., Solomon, J., Rangnekar, A., Boyd, J., Brown, B.: Web Credibility Research: A Method for Online Experiments and Early Study Results. In: Proceedings of CHI'01, Extended Abstracts on Human Factors in Computing, pp. 295–296 (2001)
19. Fogg, B.J.: Credibility and Computing Technology. Communications of the ACM 42(5), 39–44 (1999)
20. Hemetsberger, A.: Fostering Cooperation on the Internet: Social Exchange Processes in Innovative Virtual Consumer Communities. In: Broniarczyk, S.M., Nakamoto, K. (eds.) Advances in Consumer Research, 29th edn., pp. 354–356 (2002)
21. Nemeth, C.: Bargaining and Reciprocity. Psychological Bulletin 75(5), 297–308 (1970)

22. Moon, Y.: Intimate Exchanges: Using Computers to Elicit Self-Disclosure from Consumers. Journal of Consumer Research 26, 323–339 (2000)
23. Gouldner, A.W.: The Norm of Reciprocity: A Preliminary Statement. American Sociological Review 25, 161–178 (1960)

Appendix: The Questionnaire

1. I link di questo sito ti sono sembrati facilmente distinguibili dal resto del testo? [*Did the links in this website appear to you as easily distinguishable from the rest of the text?*] ¨ Sì [*Yes*] No [*No*]
2. Sono più pratici i link di colore blu o dello stesso colore del testo? [*Which links are more practical, the blue ones or those of the same color as the text?*]
    ¨ Blu [*Blue*] ¨ Stesso colore del testo [*same color as the text*]
3. Le dimensioni di questo testo ti sembrano adeguate per una pubblicazione ufficiale (come ad esempio la graduatoria di un esame)? [*Does the size of this text suit that of an official publication, such as the ranking in an examination?*]
    ¨ Troppo piccole [*Too small*]
    ¨ Adeguate [*Adequate*]
    ¨ Troppo grandi [*Too big*]
4. Che browser stai usando in questo momento? [*Which browser are you using right now?*]
    ¨ Internet explorer
    ¨ Mozilla
    ¨ Opera
    ¨ Altro_____ [*Other*]
5. Come sei venuto a conoscenza di questo sito? [*How did you know about this website?*]
    ¨ Consiglio di un amico (es forum) [*A friend's suggestion, e.g. forum*]
    ¨ Motore di ricerca [*Search engine*]
    ¨ Altro_____ [*Other*]
6. Da dove sei collegato ad Internet in questo momento? [*From where are you currently connected to the Internet?*]
    ¨ Casa [*Home*]
    ¨ Lavoro [*Work*]
    ¨ Altro_____ [*Other*]
7. Di che tipo di connessione disponi? [*Which connection are you using?*]
Indica il tipo di connessione [*Please indicate the type of connection*]
    ¨ Dial-up analogica 56 kbps [*56 kbps analogical dial up*]
    ¨ ISDN 64 o 128 kbps [*64 or 128 kbps ISDN*]
    ¨ ADSL non so che velocità [*ADSL, I do not know which speed*]
    ¨ ADSL 256 kbps
    ¨ ADSL 640 kbps
    ¨ ADSL 1.2 Mbps
    ¨ Cable (maggiore di 1.2 Mbps) [*more than 1.2 Mbps*]
    ¨ Non so [*I don't know*]
    ¨ Altro_____ [*Other*]

8. Quante ore trascorri su Internet? (navigazione web) [*How many hours do you spend on the Internet (Internet navigation)?*]
    ¨ Indica quanto tempo navighi [*Indicate how long you navigate*]
    ¨ 1-2 ore al mese [*1-2 hours a month*]
    ¨ 1-2 ore alla settimana [*1-2 hours a week*]
    ¨ 1 ora al giorno [*1 hour a day*]
    ¨ Più di un'ora al giorno [*more than 1 hour a day*]
9. Quanto sei esperto di Internet? [*How much Internet expertise do you have?*]
Indica cosa conosci del Web [*Indicate what you know of the web*]
¨ Navigo abbastanza, più la pratica che la teoria [*I navigate quite a bit, more practice than theory*]
    ¨ Ho studiato calcolatori e reti, più la teoria che la pratica [*I studied computers and networks, more theory than practice*]
    ¨ Quasi professionale, sia la pratica che la teoria per concetti [*Almost professional, both practice and theory by concepts*]
    ¨ Professionale, sia la pratica che la teoria e la programmazione [*Professional, practice, theory and programming*]

I dati raccolti verranno trattati secondo le vigenti disposizioni in materia di Privacy dei Dati Personali: verranno gestiti personalmente da >name< e non saranno ceduti a terze parti a nessun titolo; non verranno utilizzati per nessuno scopo all'infuori della presente ricerca. I suddetti dati non verranno usati in alcun modo per generare posta non richiesta ("spam"): le eventuali comunicazioni saranno relative alla ricerca presente e ad eventuali seguiti. Per eventuali rettifiche o cancellazioni dei dati contattare direttamente >name<. [*The data collected will be treated according to the current regulations on personal information privacy: the data will be handled personally by >name<, and won't be given to third parties for any reason. The data will not be used for any other goal than the present research. The abovementioned information will by no means be used to generate unsolicited e-mail ("spam"). Any possible communications will be relative to the current research and its continuation. For corrections or deletion of personal information, please contact >name< directly.*]

The form collecting the contact information (name, surname, e-mail, country, province, city) follows.

The Behavior Chain for Online Participation: How Successful Web Services Structure Persuasion

B.J. Fogg and Dean Eckles

Persuasive Technology Lab
Center for the Study of Language and Information
Stanford University
{bjfogg,eckles}@stanford.edu

Abstract. The success of many online services today depends on the company's ability to persuade users to take specific actions, such as registering or inviting friends. We examined over 50 popular Web services of this kind to understand the influence processes and strategies used. We found that successful online services share a pattern of target behaviors that can be viewed as part of an overall framework. We call this framework the "Behavior Chain for Online Participation." This paper briefly presents the general idea of a *behavior chain* and applies it to understanding persuasion patterns found online. We then illustrate the Behavior Chain for Online Participation by applying it to the Web service LinkedIn and other popular services. Future research may identify behavior chains in other domains and develop new research methods for validating behavior chains.

Keywords: Persuasive technology, participatory media, online communities, behavior change, captology, influence, persuasion, World Wide Web.

1 Introduction

Whether working as a social actor, a tool, or a medium, interactive technologies can change people's attitudes and behaviors using influence strategies established by the social sciences [9, 10]. Persuasive technology is ubiquitous on the Web, and many Web services are successful in bringing about behavior change. This paper examines a pattern of behavior change found across many successful Web services.

1.1 Successful Patterns on the Web

Current Web services exhibit considerable variety in how they structure user involvement; however, patterns can be identified among many successful Web services [6]. This is to be expected for two reasons. First, many Web services have similar behavioral goals for their users (e.g. registration for the service, getting others to join). Second, services that develop good tactics for achieving those behavioral goals succeed while others fail and many new Web services are then patterned after services that are succeeding.

Previous academic work and industry practice has identified some small-scale patterns as best practices in the real world and online (e.g., five star ratings) for

Y. de Kort et al. (Eds.): PERSUASIVE 2007, LNCS 4744, pp. 199–209, 2007.

achieving particular behavioral goals [12, 21]. This paper aims to identify patterns in the sequence of target behaviors of Web services and the means by which those goals are achieved.

1.2 Behavior Chains

Influence strategies can examined individually, but the rich reality of persuasion is sequential: multiple strategies are often used in succession, with each strategy helping the persuader meet intermediate behavioral and attitudinal goals from which new strategies can be applied [8, 11, 5, 22, 23].[1] We call such a pattern of behavioral goals a *behavior chain*. A behavior chain can be represented in a flow chart that consists of *Phases* each made up of one or more goals we call *Target Behaviors*. In the course of this paper we aim to establish one behavior chain as a common and successful pattern on the Web – and as a framework for researching and designing for persuasion in many Web services.

To be sure, the sequencing of target behaviors is not new. Our investigations into the pattern of online behaviors helped us see similar patterns in the offline world, which included persuasive domains such as sales, religious conversion, and dating. In these and other situations, the target behaviors happen in sequence or in sequential clusters. Our paper will focus exclusively on the patterns of persuasion in the online world.

1.3 Participatory Media and User-Created Content

In an increasing number of popular Web services, key behavioral goals for the service depend on users creating content, inviting others to use the service, and otherwise directly contributing to the value of the service. All users are not expected to contribute in the same way, but users are exposed to a variety of influence strategies that lead them to create value for themselves and others, including the act of paying attention to the user-generated content.

Influencing users to create and contribute compelling content and evangelize the service to their contacts are challenging behavioral goals. These goals differ from other long-established purposes for commercial web services (e.g. getting users to make a purchase or spend time consuming traditionally produced content). In many cases, achieving these new goals with some initial users can provide valuable means for achieving the latter with subsequent users. For example, user-contributed reviews on Amazon can encourage satisfying purchases by others [20]. Likewise, attention data and ratings allow YouTube to give top billing to the video content users are likely to consume and then, in turn, refer to their friends [25].

Many online experiences today give users a substantial role in content-creation, user-recruitment, and community building. However, no framework has yet been proposed to show the temporal, contingent, and persuasive aspects of these target behaviors online. Describing one such framework is the goal of this paper.

---

[1] "Sequential requests" have been widely studied, but this most work focuses on a small number of short sequences. The most widely known and studied of these are the Foot-in-the-Door and Door-in-the-Face strategies [5]. For applications to persuasive technology, see [13, 14].

2   The Behavior Chain for Online Participation

We identified the behavior chain reported on in this paper through case studies of over 50 Web services. We examined how these services influence users – from motivating them to visit the site to inspiring them to create the very content that makes the service valuable to others [4]. As the patterns of persuasion became apparent, we iteratively developed flowcharts to describe the sequences we recognized repeatedly. We call this pattern the Behavior Chain for Online Participation – henceforth, the Behavior Chain. Figure 1 is a diagram that represents the Behavior Chain.

The Behavior Chain consists of three Phases, each with at least two Target Behaviors. As users move along the Behavior Chain, the Target Behaviors generally become more demanding. User behavior in the final Phase contributes to the service's appeal to new users. The next section explains this framework in more detail through an extended case study and additional examples.

3   Paths Along the Behavior Chain

When people use successful Web services today, they almost always follow a path through the Behavior Chain.

There are multiple paths through the three Phases of the Behavior Chain, some of which are more common than others. To illustrate how a service influences users to move along the Behavior Chain, this section of our paper primarily considers a single service, LinkedIn, through the lens of the Behavior Chain. Along the way we identify other Web services that use similar techniques to achieve the same Target Behaviors and highlight alternative methods applied to each part of the Behavior Chain.

LinkedIn. LinkedIn is a Web service for professionals seeking to sustain, leverage, and expand their professional networks for career advancement, filling open employment positions or contracts, gaining knowledge from domain experts, and maintaining professional relationships [19]. It fits into the social network genre of Web services. Each LinkedIn user creates a profile detailing educational and professional background and interest in being contacted. Each user also designates other existing users as their connections or invites non-users to fulfill this role.

3.1   Phase 1 – Discovery

In the first Phase of the Behavior Chain, users become aware of the Web service; this is the *Discovery* Phase. This Phase includes two Target Behaviors – that potential users learn about the service in a way that supports further Target Behaviors on the chain and that potential users visit the Web site. In Phase 1 the most common order is that users first *Learn about service* and then *Visit the site*. However, the reverse is also prevalent. After describing each Target Behavior in Phase 1, we give examples of both orders.

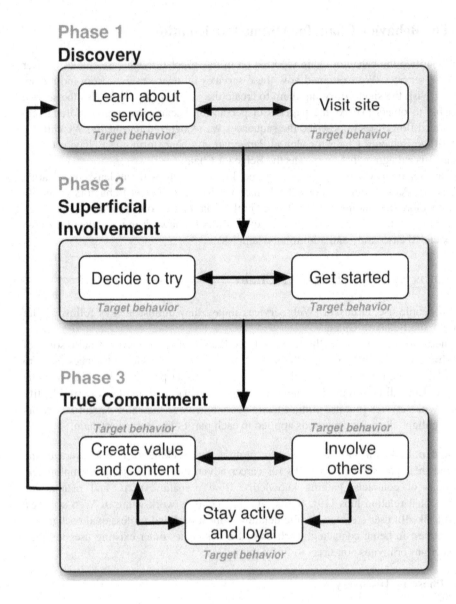

Fig. 1. The Behavior Chain for Online Participation. The Behavior Chain is found across many successful Web services. It consists of three Phases, each with multiple Target Behaviors. When users reach the *True Commitment* Target Behaviors – specifically *Create value and content* and *Involve others* – they contribute to the service's ability to influence new users to follow the behavior chain. (We acknowledge help from Mike Krieger and Jyotika Prasad in creating the early versions of this diagram).

Learn About Service. Most Web site operators seek ways to motivate people to learn about their service. Users can learn about a service from many sources – e.g. email from friends, word-of-mouth, in traditional media, or embedded on another Web site. How and what users hear about a service is key to their decision to move further down the Behavior Chain. For example, a trusted friend's email saying, "This site is a cool!" will likely offer more motivation than an unknown blogger linking to a Web site. Strategies for creating awareness about Web services introduce a close connection with the Phase 3, because established users and their creations can attract others to join them in using a Web service, leading to the looping back or "viral" element that Web site operators seek.

Visit Site. In most cases, Web site operators use a variety of methods to motivate people to visit their site. Many are directly tied to how users hear about the service. For example, a user who has posted pictures of a new baby on a Web site can likely motivate relatives to visit the site for the first time. In other examples, a social filtering service, such as Digg.com, can influence people to go to a site for the first time, based the credibility of the community's aggregated recommendation. A user's first visit to a site creates opportunities to educate and influence, preparing the path for moving new users further down the Behavior Chain.

Flickr.com serves as a helpful example of the persuasion dynamics in Phase 1. When a user of the photo-sharing Web service Flickr invites a friend to use the service, Flickr leverages the inviting user's credibility to educate the recipient about Flickr and influence them to visit. The invitation arrives as an email with the friend's name, not 'Flickr', as the sender. The Flickr system helps people perform Target Behavior *Learn about service* even before visiting the site. Specifically, the default email message to new people includes information about Flickr; furthermore, part of the message is not editable by the sender, but no distinction is made between these sections for the recipient. Informed about Flickr and that it "takes less than a minute" to sign up, the recipient can be motivated to *Visit site*, a key Target Behavior in Phase 1.

The Target Behaviors can happen in reverse sequence in Phase 1. For the other order – *Learn about service* after *Visit site* – let us turn to LinkedIn. As in the Flickr example, the start of Phase 1 for a potential user relies on value created from existing users who are in Phase 3 of the Behavior Chain.

LinkedIn creates a basic public profile for all users and optimizes the profiles for search engines. The public profile shows only the user's name and industry, but it also includes links to join LinkedIn and establish the existing user as a connection.

Potential users who search the Web for the name of someone, such as a business colleague, may get search results that point them to a LinkedIn profile for that person. As a result, without any previous knowledge of LinkedIn, a potential user can go to a LinkedIn page. Note that the Target Behavior *Visit site* comes before *Learn about service*. In this case, the Phase 1 sequence of LinkedIn is the reverse of Flickr.

Yet Linkedin functions much like Flickr in motivating users to go from Phase 1 to Phase 2. In both cases, the site functionality is limited until users get involved with the service. In the LinkedIn example, the potential user sees a colleague's basic profile online, which creates a positive association with the service. However, the potential user cannot see the colleague's full profile until after registration. Knowing that additional information about a colleague is available can be a compelling incentive to take action. As a result, with the positive association and motivation in place, the potential user is likely to transition from Phase 1 *Discovery* to Phase 2 *Superficial Involvement*.

3.2   Phase 2 – Superficial Involvement

In Phase 2 of the Behavior Chain, Web services influence users to *Decide to try* and to *Get started* with the service (e.g. by creating an account, starting to consume content). Both of these Target Behaviors are aspects of *Superficial Involvement*.

A unifying feature of the Target Behaviors in Phase 2 is that they consist of one-time actions. In other words, compliance is the goal in Phase 2 rather than seeking a long-term behavior change. Despite the short-term nature of these Target Behaviors, the methods used to influence users has implications for Phase 3, where long-term behavior change is the goal. For example, if a Web service gains compliance in Phase 2 in ways that damage trust, then the user may be less likely to Transition to Phase 3. Successful Web services must gain compliance in Phase 2 while preparing the path for *True Commitment* in Phase 3.

Decide to Try. One Target Behavior in *Superficial Involvement* is *Decide to try*. This means that users decide that they will use this service to meet some needs or fulfill some desires of theirs. In some cases, drawn by such things as new baby photos, users may not recognize they are preparing mentally to invest themselves in a new online experience. Indeed, the psychological mechanism behind *Decide to try* is a worthy area for future experimental research.

Get Started. Another Target Behavior in this Phase is *Get started*. For many Web services, this includes signing up for the service by creating a free account. Registration is often necessary to make possible subsequent behaviors, such as creating content tied to an identity. Furthermore, registration opens new channels of communication (e.g. email updates) and makes new persuasive techniques possible (e.g. tailoring over months of use). But there is often a trade-off here: a very short account creation process can make it more likely users will sign up, because less effort is required from users. However, gathering additional user information early in the Behavior Chain may benefit the Web service more. How to best balance these competing needs – making registration simple versus gathering user information early – is a rich area for future research.

LinkedIn uses at least three techniques to influence users to get started. On its home page, LinkedIn highlights the ease of joining by stating: "Create your profile and make 5 connections in 5 minutes." Perhaps more interesting is how they use their existing users to influence new visitors to the home page. LinkedIn emphasizes that "People you know are already LinkedIn" and encourages users to find (by name) someone they know who is a member. After a user chooses to get started, LinkedIn opts to gather more information than many sites, but once the process is complete, users already have connections with other users.

Again, there is no single order for the Target Behaviors in Phase 2. Different services – and even the same service – structure these steps in various ways. Sometimes users may decide to try the service only after getting started (e.g. registering on the site). Sometimes sites encourage users to get started with the service before having to make a commitment to it. This latter option is most common with Web service that focus largely on consumption; that is, many successful Web services allow people to view content on the site without registering first (e.g. YouTube, Flickr, eBay, MySpace). Other types of sites also allow people to use the service before registering: uploading photos to share (as on Bubbleshare), editing a page (as on Wikipedia), or personalizing the service (as on Google Personalized Home Page). This approach can delay user decision-making about whether to seriously commit to using the service until after users have more first-hand experience. This in turn leads to Phase 3 – *True Commitment*.

3.3   Phase 3 – True Commitment

In the previous Phase, users become involved in the service but generally without making a large or permanent investment in using the site. Deeper investment comes in the *True Commitment* Phase (c.f. [24]): users contribute value, involve others in the service, and continue to be active and loyal users. These three Target Behaviors are often closely linked, as a single user action can create value, involve others, and ensure a return visit soon.

Unlike in previous phases, the Target Behaviors of *True Commitment* go beyond one-time compliance; that is, this phase is characterized by longer-term Target Behaviors that involve creating habits in users. For example, a user commenting on a video just once, while potentially valuable, is not the primary goal in Phase 3. Instead, in this Phase, Web services aim at creating habits, e.g., persuading users to frequently comment in response to videos. Influence strategies that achieve compliance at the cost of credibility (e.g. the Door-in-the-Face strategy) are more likely to fail in Phase 3 [c.f. 3].

The Target Behaviors of Phase 3 contribute to a service's success in introducing and moving other users through the chain. For this reason, Figure 1 includes a path from Phase 3 to Phase 1.

Create Value and Content. User behavior can make the service more valuable to others. This happens when users explicitly create valuable content that others will consume (e.g. a video or a book review). But users can also incidentally contribute to the automated construction of others' experiences with the service (e.g., with attention and purchase data). Some contributions fall between these two points: when, for example, users give rating to videos on Amazon or NetFlix, though they may recognize that others will consume this in some way (e.g., through an average rating or tailored recommendations), their motivation for this behavior may not involve others' experience (e.g., a user may want to improve the system's personal movie recommendations). That is, user motivation to rate content is to help themselves, not others. Of course, the incentives for different contribution will vary [7, 15], even within the same service. Examples follow:

LinkedIn uses several strategies in influencing users to create value for the service – whether it is completing a profile, recommending a contractor, or creating a job posting.

LinkedIn encourages users to complete their personal profiles by tracking their progress on prominently displayed progress bar and noting how much a specific action would increase "profile completeness".

LinkedIn uses reciprocity to motivate recommending a service provider, such as a lawyer, to contacts: along with a list of recommendations from a user's network, LinkedIn notes that "your network has recommended [X] services, but you haven't recommended any. It only takes a minute to return the favor."

LinkedIn and other services also use quick, positive feedback to encourage content creation. This can be as simple as a thank-you immediately following a submission. But often other users' responses serve as feedback. By promoting the newest content, many services (including Yahoo! Answers, Flickr, YouTube, and LinkedIn) make immediate feedback from others very likely. This technique connects two Target Behaviors in this Phase: *Create value and content* leads to *Involve others*. In other words, the original content creation motivates comments and replies from other users, thereby involving them and providing a reward for the original contribution.

Stay Active and Loyal. Web services benefit when their users repeatedly choose to always use one Web service instead of competing alternatives. Web services often implement strategies to encourage repeated visits to their site.

LinkedIn updates their users by email about changes in their networks (e.g. career updates by friends, an increase in the size of their networks). These emails encourage users to return to LinkedIn, and the emails often recommend taking action in a related way (e.g. updating one's own profile, adding new contacts). Key information is not included in the email; that is, only by clicking on a link in the email and visiting LinkedIn will allow the users to find out the details. To encourage more visits than update emails, a user's LinkedIn home page always includes the most recent updates about their network – a positive reinforcement for frequent visits.

Involve Others. Increasing the number of users, especially committed users, of a Web service is a common goal. Many Web services enlist their current users towards this Target Behavior by persuading them to involve others to use the service. This can happen in one of several ways. For example, on social network sites, users invite others to be their friends. But in other sites or in a different context on the same site, users involve others in a much more content-centric way, such as clicking a link to share a video with a friend.

Because having a number of contacts is a prerequisite for many uses of the service, many social network sites use reduction [9] extensively to encourage establishing and expanding one's network. LinkedIn and several others services support bulk imports from online and desktop email software.

This Target Behavior goes beyond encouraging non-users to sign up. For example, on Facebook, a social network service, many user actions help keep others involved in the service. As part of its encouragement to create a complete profile, LinkedIn influences users to get recommendations about their past work; users thereby invite non-users to register to recommend them or involve existing users in the service again.

4   Implications for Designers

The Behavior Chain has two key implications for designers of Web services. It can motivate decisions about how to structure target behaviors and which influence strategies to apply to for each target behavior.

Follow Existing Patterns. To create a successful Web service, designers should pay attention to the persuasion patterns identified in this paper. Like established best practices on a smaller scale, the Behavior Chain captures the state-of-the-art on successful Web services. That is, how the framework orders and links the Phases and Target Behaviors is based on patterns among successful Web sites, so in following this pattern one is employing a chain that is most likely to lead to success. Choosing to pursue a different path – breaking new ground – is admirable and might work, but this approach is risky.

Match Goals and Strategies. Some of the behavioral goals in the Behavior Chain are one-time behaviors – compliance is the goal – while others are best served by creating long-term habits. Likewise some influence strategies are more appropriate for gaining compliance than creating habits, and vice versa. By identifying the type of behavior change and the influence strategies suited to that type, designers can make informed choices about which influence strategies to implement.

5   Directions for Future Research

This work in outlining the Behavior Chain also suggests directions for the future study of persuasion and the development of new research methods.

Other Behavior Chains. This paper uses the concept of a behavior chain largely to a single end – understanding how Web services sequence intermediate goals and influence strategies to achieve difficult behavior change. But this concept can be pressed into service elsewhere. Smoking cessation, online commerce, and perhaps even courtship for marriage could be described with behavior chains. Future research could identify successful behavior chains in an array of other domains, including health, gaming, and grassroots political action. These behavior chains can be mapped and compared to each other to understand the structure of persuasion over time at a deeper level.

Research Methods. We developed and validated this behavior chain through numerous case studies, but new, general methods are needed for more rigorous evaluation. The current work leaves many research questions open, and identifying behavior chains elsewhere on the Web may be more difficult. We anticipate the development of new methods for evaluating successful patterns of behavior change online.

Acknowledgments. We would like to thank our students from the 2006 Stanford course on persuasive technology for creating many of the case studies from which the Behavior Chain was developed. We would also like to thank Mike Krieger and Jyotika Prasad for creating early versions of the Behavior Chain diagram.

References

1. Bagozzi, R.P., Dholakia, U.M., Mookerjee, A.: Individual and group bases of social influence in online environments. Media Psychology 8, 95–126 (2006)
2. Birnbaum, M.H.: Human research and data collection via the Internet. Annual Review of Psychology 55, 803–832 (2004)
3. Buller, D.B., Burgoon, J.K.: Interpersonal Deception Theory. Communication Theory 6(3), 203–242 (1996)
4. Captology.tv. http://captology.tv
5. Cialdini, R.B., Goldstein, N.J.: Social Influence: Compliance and Conformity. Annual Review of Psychology 55(1), 591 (2004)
6. Danaher, B.G., McKay, H.G., Seeley, J.R.: The information architecture of behavior change websites. Journal of Medical Internet Research 7(2) (2005)
7. Dholakia, U.M., Bagozzi, R.P., Pearo, L.K.: A social influence model of consumer participation in network- and small-group-based virtual communities. International Journal of Research in Marketing 21(3), 241–263 (2004)
8. Dillard, J.: The current status of research on sequential-request compliance techniques. Personality and Social Psychology Bulletin 17, 282–288 (1991)
9. Fogg, B.J.: Persuasive Technology: Using Computers to Change What We Think and Do. Morgan Kaufmann, San Francisco (2003)
10. Fogg, B.J., Nass, C.: How users reciprocate to computers: an experiment that demonstrates behavior change. In: CHI '97 Extended Abstracts on Human Factors in Computing Systems: Looking To the Future, Atlanta, Georgia, March 22 - 27, 1997, pp. 331–332. ACM Press, New York, NY (1997)
11. Guadagno, R.E., Asher, T., Demaine, L., Cialdini, R.B.: When saying yes leads to saying no: Preference for consistency and the reverse foot-in-the-door effect. Personality and Social Psychology Bulletin 27, 859–867 (2001)
12. Guadagno, R., Cialdini, R.: Online persuasion and compliance: Social influence on the Internet and beyond. In: Amichai-Hamburger, Y. (ed.) The social net: Human behavior in cyberspace, pp. 91–113. Oxford University Press, New York (2005)
13. Guéguen, N.: Foot-in-the-door technique and computer-mediated communication. Computers in Human Behavior 18(1), 11–15 (2002)
14. Gueguen, N., Jacob, C.: Fund-Raising on the Web: The Effect of an Electronic Foot-in-the-Door on Donation. CyberPsychology & Behavior 4(6), 705 (2001)
15. Hars, A., Ou, S.: Working for free? - Motivations for participating in open source projects. International Journal of Electronic Commerce 6(2), 25–39 (2001)
16. Kapoor, N., Konstan, J.A., Terveen, L.G.: How peer photos influence member participation in online communities. In: CHI '05 Extended Abstracts on Human Factors in Computing Systems, Portland, OR, USA, April 02 - 07, 2005, pp. 1525–1528. ACM Press, New York (2005)
17. Kelman, H.C.: Compliance, Identification, and Internalization: Three Processes of Attitude Change. Journal of Conflict Resolution, Studies on Attitudes and Communication 2(1), 51–60 (1958)

18. Khaled, R., Barr, P., Noble, J., Biddle, R.: Investigating Social Software as Persuasive Technology. In: Proc. of Persuasive 2006, pp. 104–107 (2006)
19. LinkedIn., http://www.linkedin.com
20. Schafer, J.B., Konstan, J.A., Riedl, J.: E-commerce recommendation applications. Data Mining and Knowledge Discovery 5(1/2), 115–153 (2001)
21. Skitka, L.J., Sargis, E.G.: The Internet as Psychological Laboratory. Annual Review of Psychology 57(1), 529 (2006)
22. Spears, R., Postmes, T., Lea, M., Wolbert, A.: When are net effects gross products? The power of influence and influence of power in computer-mediated communication. Journal of Social Issues 58, 91–107 (2002)
23. Spector, B.I.: Negotiation as a Psychological Process. The Journal of Conflict Resolution, Negotiation 21(4), 607–618 (1977)
24. Thompson, L.F., Meriac, J.P., Cope, J.G.: Motivating online performance: The influences of goal setting and Internet self-efficacy. Social Science Computer Review 20, 149–160 (2002)
25. YouTube. http://youtube.com

Exploring Persuasive Potential of Embodied Conversational Agents Utilizing *Synthetic* Embodied Conversational Agents

John Shearer, Patrick Olivier, Marco De Boni, and Robert Hurling

Culture Lab – Newcastle, Grand Assembly Rooms, King's Walk, Newcastle University,
Newcastle upon Tyne, NE 1 7RU, UK
`john.shearer@ncl.ac.uk, p.l.olivier@ncl.ac.uk`
Unilever Corporate Research, Unilever Colworth Sharnbrook, Bedford, MK44 1LQ, UK
`marco.de-boni@unilever.com, bob.hurling@unilever.com`

Abstract. This study presents *synthetic embodied conversational agents*, and how they can be used to explore the persuasive potential of *real* embodied conversational agents. Utilizing a novel Wizard-of-Oz style approach and a direct measure of behavior change we explore whether 'ideal' embodied conversational agents have a similar persuasive impact as real people, and demonstrate the importance of visually perceiving for embodied conversational agents to be persuasive.

Keywords: persuasion, embodied conversational agents, virtual characters.

1 Introduction

The behavior of present-day embodied conversational agents (ECAs) is limited compared to real humans, especially with respect to non-verbal behavior. Previous research indicates that ECAs have social influence [1], with computer interfaces (such as ECAs) treated as social actors [2]. A *synthetic* ECA appears to be a real (computer generated) ECA, but in fact is simply video and audio transmission of a real human transformed giving the appearance of an ECA –the behavior is that of a real human, resolving the behavioral limitations of present-day ECAs. We consider 'persuasion' to mean the change of interactant B's behavior caused by interactant A. Significant previous work exists on persuasion and social influence [1, 3, 4] using self-reports of attitudes/beliefs, but little work has measured behavior change directly, which is the focus of this study. Present-day ECAs have demonstrated social influence [1, 2, 5].

2 Implementation of Synthetic Embodied Conversational Agent

It is not presently possible to evaluate the persuasive effect of ECAs with behavioral quality approaching that of real humans, due to them having only limited behavioral fidelity. Synthetic ECAs bypass the behavioral quality limitation of present ECAs. Synthetic ECAs use a real human (a wizard) for the behavioral functionality

Y. de Kort et al. (Eds.): PERSUASIVE 2007, LNCS 4744, pp. 210–213, 2007.

implemented either by driving a real ECA from motion capture and speech recognition of the wizard, or by transforming video and audio of the wizard. We use the video/audio transformation approach using only commodity hardware.

Present day ECAs appear to be computer generated. This is not due the lack of technology, but merely that it is not presently used in these agents. Photo-realistic ECAs have a natural advantage in terms of persuasive potential, but a photo-realistic synthetic ECA driven by a real person would be indistinguishable from a real human and would therefore be inappropriate for this study. The synthetic ECA must appear to be computer generated to support the belief that it is a real ECA. Furthermore, it was important to verify that people believed the synthetic ECA to be a real ECA, not a synthesized one, so as a precursor to the study on persuasion we ran a study using eye-tracking and questionnaires to determine differences in perception of the synthetic ECA and beliefs about it. The results (yet to be published) conclude that subjects believed the synthetic ECA to be a real ECA.

Audio was transformed using commercial voice transformation software MorphVox [6] and was synchronized with the video which was transformed by 'cartoonising' each frame using a custom real-time algorithm based on cartoonising filter in the GIMP[7], implementing in EyesWeb [8]. Previous work cartoonising video streams has been for augmented reality[9] and for creating differing video styles[10].

Fig. 1. Synthetic Embodied Conversational Agent

3   Persuasive Effect of Synthetic Embodied Conversational Agents

Persuasive effect was measured directly by giving each subject the opportunity to donate money (from zero to £10 in 50p increments) from their payment to a single specific charity after interacting with the synthetic ECA presenting information on that charity. Measuring behavior change for *each* subject is impossible. Asking subjects to donate before hand or asking how much they *would* donate would inevitably influence the later donation. But, behavior change can be measured over a group of subjects. Subjects were randomly assigned to one of four conditions:

1. *human* – subjects saw real video and audio of wizard; wizard saw and heard the subject – control condition.
2. *synthetic ECA* **with** *video* – subjects saw transformed video and audio of the wizard; wizard saw and heard the subject – ECA with vision condition.
3. *synthetic ECA* **without** *video* – subjects saw transformed video and audio of the wizard; wizard only heard the subject – ECA without vision condition.
4. *audio only* – subjects only heard real audio of the wizard; wizard could only hear the subject – telephone style condition.

The human wizard was a female in all conditions, appeared the same throughout the study and believed she was engaged only in a video chat. Both male and female wizards would allow measuring gender impact, but the focus was not on gender differences, and it requires more subjects. A variety of previous studies [3, 4] have investigated gender effects and our conclusions cannot be validly applied to males wizards. Each experiment was self-guided with no interaction with the experimenter.

We predicted that subjects would donate most under the human condition, with reduced donations under the other three conditions, also that the synthetic ECA *with* video condition would have more donated than *without* video – reflecting the believed importance of seeing the other interactant. Pre-interaction and post-interaction questionnaires were included for completeness and verification, but did not include measures directly relevant to the study – merely concerning the nature of the interaction; the subjects' beliefs as to the computer-generated or human nature of the character; and a personality test (Myer's Briggs).

4 Results

Statistical analysis showed non-normal distribution of donations making both ANOVA and t-Tests invalid, so a non-parametric Kruskal-Wallis test was performed. The test statistic (Chi squared) was 7.754, equating to a probability of 0.051. Strictly this should be <0.05 to go on to further comparisons of the means – but 0.051 is near enough. A Wilcoxon test was run to compare non-normally distributed means, finding the probability for the difference between synthetic ECA *with* and *without* video to be p=0.003. A Bonferroni correction was applied due to multiple paired comparisons giving a significance criteria as 0.05/6 = 0.0083.

Table 1. Amount donated to charity vs condition – 76 subjects (44 female; 32 male)

		Mean	N	Std. Dev.
	synthetic ECA **with** video	£3.50	21	£3.17
condition	audio only	£2.94	18	£3.67
	Human condition	£2.47	19	£3.58
	synthetic ECA *without* video	£1.36	18	£1.62
	Total	**£2.61**	**76**	**£3.17**

No significant difference was found between any other pairs of conditions, so we cannot support the hypothesis that a synthetic ECA is less persuasive than a real human, and the large variances preclude concluding that they are equally persuasive. Additionally, no significant genders differences were found, though previous studies [3, 4] suggests there may be significant gender differences. With the limited subject numbers these may have been missed

In summary we can conclude that there is a reasonably robust significant difference between the female synthetic ECA *with* and *without* video, and therefore that female ECAs with vision have a greater persuasive potential than female ECAs without vision.

5 Discussion

Results indicate similarity between how persuasive female *synthetic* ECAs are as compared to humans, but we cannot draw hard conclusions about that similarity. Results show that it is important for female synthetic ECAs to be able see their interactants. As subjects were unaware that the synthetic ECA was not a real ECA, we conclude that seeing their interactants is important for persuasion in *real* ECAs.

Results are limited the interactions within a webcam interface context and may not generalize to more realistic environments and do not apply to agents that are more pro-actively persuasive. The quantization of monies given to subjects and exact denominations may have affected the amounts donated. The large variances require a larger numbers of subjects for more conclusive results.

It might be expected that with audio only condition would have the lowest donation, but this wasn't the case. A variety of theories could be presented as to why the audio condition had a similar persuasive effect as the conditions with video transmission in both directions. Perhaps, when unable to see an agent the subjects no longer expects appropriate non-verbal behavior, putting the whole interaction under different assumptions. In contrast, in the synthetic ECA *without* video condition we could perhaps presume that subjects expect non-verbal behavior in response to their own non-verbal behavior, but it cannot be provided.

Overall, we conclude that it is important for female ECAs to be able to see their interactants to effect behavior change. This demonstrates the utility of future work using simple vision methods (and other modalities) to inform the behavior of ECAs.

References

1. Bailenson, J.N., Yee, N.: Digital Chameleons. Psychological Science (2005)
2. Reeves, B., Nass, C.I.: The media equation: how people treat computers, television, and new media like real people and places. Cambridge University Press, New York (1996)
3. Baylor, A.L.: Interface Agents as Social Models: The Impact of Appearance on Females' Attitude Toward Engineering. In: CHI, ACM Press, Montreal, Canada (2006)
4. Blascovich, J.: A theoretical model of social influence for increasing the utility of collaborative virtual environments. In: Collaborative virtual environments, pp. 25–30. ACM Press, Bonn, Germany (2002)
5. Fogg, B.J.: Persuasive Computers: Perspectives and Research Directions. CHI 98 , 225–232 (1998)
6. Screaming Bee: MorphVox. Screaming Bee LLC (2006)
7. Kimball, S., Mattis, P.: GNU Image Manipulation Program (2006)
8. Camurri, A., Coletta, P., Massari, A., Mazzarino, B., Peri, M., Ricchetti, M., Ricci, A., Volpe, G.: Toward real-time multimodal processing: EyesWeb 4.0. AISB 2004 Convention: Motion, Emotion and Cognition, Leeds, UK (2004)
9. Fischer, J., Bartz, D.: Real-time Cartoon-like Stylization of AR Video Streams on the GPU. In: Wilhelm Schickard Institute for Computer Science, University of Tübingen (2005)
10. Wang, J., Xu, Y., Shum, H.-Y., Cohen, M.F.: Video Tooning. In: SIGGRAPH, 23th edn., pp. 574–583. ACM, Los Angeles, CA, USA

The Importance of Interface Agent Visual Presence: Voice Alone Is Less Effective in Impacting Young Women's Attitudes Toward Engineering

Rinat B. Rosenberg-Kima[1], Amy L. Baylor[1], E. Ashby Plant[2], and Celeste E. Doerr[2]

[1] Center for Research of Innovative Technologies for Learning
(RITL), Florida State University
Innovation Park, 2000 Levy Avenue, Bldg. A, Suite 320
Tallahassee, FL 32310-2735
[2] Department of Psychology, Florida State University
Tallahassee, FL 32306
{rr05,abaylor}@fsu.edu, {plant,doerr}@psy.fsu.edu

Abstract. Anchored in social agency theory, recent research has emphasized the importance of anthropomorphic interface agents' voice to impact learning-related outcomes. Nevertheless, literature on human social models suggests that the appearance of an interface agent may have important implications for its ability to influence attitudes and self-efficacy. Therefore, we hypothesized that visual presence of the interface agent would result in more positive attitudes toward engineering and greater self-efficacy than the presence of a human voice alone. In accordance to our hypothesis, results revealed that participants who interacted with the visible agents reported significantly greater utility for engineering, greater self-efficacy, and greater interest in engineering related fields than those who interacted with a human voice. Thus, the current work indicates the importance of anthropomorphic agent's visibility in changing attitudes and beliefs.

Keywords: Anthropomorphic interface agents, persuasion, attitude change, computer-based social modeling.

1 Introduction

In this experimental study, we investigated the role of animated anthropomorphic interface agent visual presence in influencing female students' beliefs and attitudes toward engineering.

Even though women have achieved increasing inclusion and success in professions that were formerly occupied primarily by men, they remain under-represented in the field of engineering [1]. Women's under-representation in engineering may result in part from female students' negative beliefs regarding engineering and their ability to succeed at it [2].

Literature on social models suggests that a persuasive agent's appearance would have important implications for its ability to influence attitudes and self-efficacy [e.g., 3, 4], implying the importance of the model's visual presence. Therefore, we

Y. de Kort et al. (Eds.): PERSUASIVE 2007, LNCS 4744, pp. 214–222, 2007.

expected that visual presence of an interface agent in the current study would result in more positive attitudes toward engineering and greater self-efficacy than the presence of a human voice without a visible agent.

1.1 Animated Interface Agents as Social Models

According to Bandura [3], much of our learning derives from vicarious experience. Social modeling of behaviors enables us to learn new behaviors, strengthens or diminishes previously learned behaviors, and reminds us to perform behaviors about which we had forgotten. Social models can also influence people's attitudes [4]. In particular, observing a social model who is similar to oneself perform a behavior provides people with information relevant to their likely self-efficacy for similar behaviors [5].

Thus, one way to change young women's attitudes toward engineering can be to provide them with a female engineer model. Even though a human model may provide a higher level of interactivity and response, providing students with young, female social models in math and the hard sciences may be problematic because it would contribute to the already burdensome workloads faced by women in nontraditional fields [6]. Moreover, different students may benefit from different types of models (e.g., models that differ in ethnicity, age, gender, etc.). Therefore, it would be useful to find alternative mechanisms for providing a model that is both easily accessible for a large population of students and that can be personalized depending on the individual needs of the students.

Interface agents, as anthropomorphic "simulated humans" can potentially serve as simulated social models to impact beliefs and attitudes. Recent empirical evidence indicates that interface agents can positively influence users' interest and motivation [e.g., 7, 8-10]. Interface agents can also influence self-efficacy [11], which is the belief that one is competent to meet the demands of a situation.

Extensive research has demonstrated that people tend to apply human social rules to computer technologies [e.g., 12, 13-15]. In a series of studies, Nass and his colleagues demonstrated how individuals consistently applied social rules and expectations to computers [13]. Initially, Nass et al [14] demonstrated how people responded to the computer personality the same way they would have responded to similar human personality. In particular, they found that the participants correctly identified the computer's personality type (dominant vs. submissive) and preferred and were more satisfied by interacting with a computer that matched their own personality. Additionally, they demonstrated that individuals apply gender stereotypes to computers [16], ethnically identify with computer agents, and exhibit social behaviors toward computers [13]. Furthermore, Sproull et al [17] found that people respond differently to a talking-face display compared to text-only display. They attributed some personality attributes to the faces differently than to the text display, reported higher levels of arousal, and presented themselves in a more positive light when interacting with the talking-face display.

Young women are particularly influenced by the communication and relational aspect of agents and may be more influenced by them than males [7, 8]. Baylor et al [11] found that pedagogical agent social models were effective in improving young women's attitudes and beliefs about engineering-related fields. Furthermore, the agent models that were most similar to the young women tended to be the most effective for influencing the women's self-efficacy and stereotypes. Therefore, interface agents, as simulated social models, may be particularly helpful in affecting young women's attitudes and self-efficacy with respect to engineering.

1.2 The Impact of Animated Interface Agent's Voice

According to social agency theory [18], social cues in a multimedia message (e.g. on-screen agent with human voice [19]) lead learners to approach computerized learning contexts as interpersonal, conversational contexts. Once learners interpret their multimedia experience as social, the rules of human-to-human communication [15] apply, thus the social partner encourages the learner to make sense of what the computer is saying by engaging in deep cognitive processing [18, 19]. Hence, different features of the communicator such as voice and appearance may affect the cognitive processes in different ways.

In accordance with social agency theory, several studies have found evidence for the importance of the speaker's voice. Learners who received a narrated animation about lighting formation performed better on a learning transfer test when the interface agent had a standard accent compared to foreign accent, and when the agent's voice was human rather than machine synthesized [18]. Likewise, Atkinson et al [19] found that learners who studied a set of worked-out examples involving proportional reasoning performed better on near and far learning transfer tests and rated the agent more positively when the animated agent had a human voice compared to machine synthesized voice. Those findings are consistent with the predictions of social agency theory and cognitive load theory.

While there is well documented research showing the effect of an animated agent compared to no agent at all [e.g., 9] or compared to text only [e.g., 10, 17, 20], it is not clear whether the voice is the most important feature of the animated agent. In particular, it is not clear whether an animated agent will result in higher levels of learning and greater change of attitudes than simply hearing the communicative message (i.e., voice-only) within the same computer-based environment. With respect to learning outcomes, Atkinson [20] found that participants who were exposed to the agent in combination with narrated instructions achieved higher scores on both near and far transfer tests than did participants who were exposed to voice only. Those results suggest that the dual mode of presentation enhances learning outcomes in a multimedia learning environment [20, 21]. In contrast, Moreno et al [10] found that the visual presence of the agent was no more effective than a voice-only condition, suggesting that students' participation and communication modality (auditory rather than visual) may be the only factors that account for the deep understanding of an agent-based computer lesson [10].

While results regarding agent presence on learning and performance are mixed, to our knowledge, there is no research that has investigated the effect of agent presence on persuasion, in particular for influencing attitudes.

1.3 Purpose of Study

The purpose of the current study was to investigate the effect of animated agents, compared to voice-only, on young women's beliefs about engineering-related fields.

In particular, we were interested in young women's attitudes about whether engineering is useful and engaging, their interest in taking engineering-related classes, and their self-efficacy for engineering-related fields.

2 Method

Of interest in the current work was whether the animated agents were more effective for influencing young women's attitudes and self-efficacy than simply responding to the voice-only persuasive communication within the computer-based environment. Therefore we replicated the identical procedure from Baylor et al, [11] but exposed participants to voice only conditions (varied by gender). Participants came from the same general population as the original sample, which consisted of female undergraduate students enrolled in an introductory educational technology course at a Southeastern public university. Here we present the findings comparing the Baylor et al [11] findings with the 2 additional voice-only conditions. As an initial step, we wanted to test whether the most effective agents from the previous work (the young, cool, attractive agents) were more effective than the voice-only appended control conditions. Thus, the current work compares the young, cool, attractive male and female agent conditions (see Figure 1) from Baylor et al [11] with the appended voice-only male and female conditions.[1]

2.1 Participants

Participants included 89 female undergraduate students enrolled in an introductory technology course who consented to participate (age M = 19.7, SD = 2.98). Of the participants, 68 were Caucasian, 5 were African-American, 3 were Asian/Asian American, 1 was Native American, 6 were Hispanic/Latino, 3 were biracial, and 3 were multiracial.

2.2 Research Design and Independent Variables

The study employed a 2 (gender: male vs. female) x 2 (agent visibility: not visible/voice-only vs. visible) between subjects factorial design. Participants were exposed to one of the four conditions.

The agents were designed to be young (~25 years), cool (operationalized by clothing and hairstyle), and attractive (operationalized by facial features) and varied by gender. The agents were empirically validated to confirm that the target population perceived them as young, cool, and attractive [11]. The agents (see Figure 1) were created in Poser©. One male and one female human voice were recorded using the same script and similar inflection and tone. These sound files were used for both the visible agent conditions and the voice-only conditions, all within the same computer-based environment.

---

[1] In an initial analysis of the other agents it was determined that the old, uncool, unattractive agents were more effective than voice-only, but the effects were weak and of marginal statistical significance.

Fig. 1. Male and female visible agents

For the agent conditions, the audio files were synchronized with the agents using Mimic2Pro© to create lip-synching and emotional expressions. Several deictic gestures (e.g., pointing, head nod) were also included. These gestures were identical for all agents. A fully integrated environment was created using Flash MX Professional©.

2.3 Dependent Variables

Because mathematics and the hard sciences (e.g., chemistry, physics) are familiar academic subjects to female undergraduates and are strongly related to the field of engineering, we measured participants' attitudes and beliefs regarding these two engineering-related fields. The four dependent variables were utility, engagement, self-efficacy, and interest.

The dependent variables were all measured using a 7-point, Likert-type scale. Items for these scales were duplicated, so that half of the items in each scale referred to math and half referred to the hard sciences. Eight items (i.e., four for math and four for science) assessed participants' beliefs about the utility of engineering ($\alpha = .84$; e.g., "I would have many career opportunities if I was a hard sciences"). Six items assessed the degree to which participants found engineering engaging ($\alpha = .83$; e.g., "The subject of math is boring"). Ten items assessed participants' self-efficacy in engineering related fields ($\alpha = .89$; e.g., "I am confident that I could do well in math classes"). Finally, eight items assessed the participants' interest in taking engineering related classes ($\alpha = .88$; e.g., "I will take a hard sciences course as an elective").

2.4 Research Environment

The assigned agent (set in a coffee shop location) introduced itself and provided a twenty-minute narrative about four female engineers, followed by five benefits of engineering careers. This script was validated as effective in Baylor & Plant [9]. Periodically, the participants interacted with the agent to continue the presentation. In the voice-only condition the agent was not visible, but the interaction and the environment were the same.

2.5 Procedure

The experiment was conducted in a regularly-scheduled classroom lab session where students accessed the online module through a web-browser (see Figure 2 for screen-shot). The students were presented with one of the four conditions (voice-only male, voice-only female, female agent, male agent). Participants in the voice only samples and the agent samples were randomly assigned to either a male or female condition. Following completion, participants answered the online post-survey questions.

Fig. 2. Sample screenshot with visible agent

3 Results

To determine the effects of agent appearance, a series of 2 (female vs. male) x 2 (voice only vs. agent) between-groups ANOVAs were performed on each of the key dependent variables (see Table 1).

3.1 Impact on the Beliefs About the Utility for Engineering

The analysis for utility revealed a significant main effect for agent visibility, $F(1,89) = 15.77$, $p < .001$. Participants who interacted with the visible agents were significantly more likely to believe that there is high utility for engineering than those who interacted with voice-only, d = .89, a large effect. There was no significant difference between the female (agent or voice-only) and male (agent or voice-only) messages.

3.2 Impact on Self-Efficacy

The analysis of self-efficacy in engineering-related fields also revealed a significant main effect for agent visibility, $F(1,89) = 11.81$, $p < .001$. Participants who interacted with the visible agents were significantly more likely to report high self-efficacy in engineering-related fields than those who interacted with voice-only, d = .72, a large-moderate effect. There was no significant difference between the female (agent or voice-only) and male (agent or voice-only) messages.

3.3 Impact on Interest in Engineering-Related Fields

The analysis of interest in engineering-related fields revealed again a significant main effect for agent visibility, $F(1,89) = 5.32$, $p < .05$. Participants who interacted with the visible agents were significantly more likely to report high interest in engineering-related fields than those who interacted with voice-only, d = .52, a moderate effect. There was no significant difference between the female (agent or voice-only) and male (agent or voice-only) messages.

3.4 Impact on Engagement in Engineering-Related Fields

Participants who interacted with the visible agents were more likely to report high engagement in engineering-related fields than those who interacted with voice-only, but the effect was only marginal, $F(1,89)=2.67$, $p = .106$. There was no significant difference between the female (agent or voice-only) and male (agent or voice-only) messages.

Table 1. Scores for each dependant variable

Measure	Visible Agent (N=47)		Voice-Only (N=49)	
	M	SD	M	SD
Utility	4.79	1.06	3.69	1.37
Self-efficacy	3.97	1.16	3.07	1.35
Interest	3.10	1.36	2.39	1.35
Engagement	4.01	1.45	3.54	1.45

4 Discussion

The current study examined the effect of animated agents, compared to voice-only, on young women's beliefs about engineering-related fields. In particular, we were interested in young women's attitudes about whether engineering is useful and engaging, their interest in taking engineering related classes, and their self-efficacy for engineering-related fields.

Drawing from the literature on social models suggesting that an agent's appearance has important implications to influence attitudes and self-efficacy [e.g., 3, 4], we hypothesized that the visual presence of an interface agent would result in more positive attitudes toward engineering and greater self-efficacy than the presence of a human voice without a visible agent.

In accordance with our hypothesis, we found that participants who interacted with the visible agents were significantly more likely to believe that there is high utility for engineering, were significantly more likely to report high self-efficacy in engineering-related fields, were significantly more likely to report high interest in engineering-related fields, and were more likely to report high engagement in engineering-related fields (only marginal effect) than those who interacted with a human voice.

A possible limitation to this study is the lack of a pre-test control for the students' attitudes towards engineering. Pre-existing differences between the groups could be claimed to be an alternative explanation to the results. Nevertheless, a pre-test in this case would have exposed the participants to the content and purpose of the persuasive message, thereby negating the purpose of the study (e.g., through expectancy or demand effects). Alternatively, by randomly assigning participants to experimental conditions, we were able to examine differences between the experimental groups without cueing participants to the content of the persuasive message.

The results provide support for the importance of the visual presence of an animated agent in attempting to change young women's attitudes toward engineering-related fields [10]. These findings suggest that the visual presence of a computer-based "social model," is significantly more persuasive than just hearing voice alone. It should be noted that our sample included only female participants; further research should investigate the role of agent's presence on male participants.

The current work adds to the growing empirical evidence showing that interface agents can positively impact attitudes and beliefs. In particular, the current work demonstrates the importance of agent visibility for persuasion. While voice alone may be sufficient for learning-related outcomes [10, 18-20], a visible agent together with the voice may be significantly more effective for attitude change. In future research we plan to further investigate this topic by comparing a visible agent with a computer-generated voice to a human voice with no visual agent as well as examining the effects of the persuasive message in the long term by observing the retention rates of female engineering students.

Acknowledgments. This work was supported by the National Science Foundation, Grant HRD-0429647.

References

1. Goodman, I.F., et al.: Final report of the women's experiences in college engineering project. Goodman Research Group, Inc. Cambridge, MA (2002)
2. Shashaani, L.: Gender differences in computer attitudes and use among college students. Journal of Educational Computing Research 16, 37–51 (1997)

3. Bandura, A.: Self-efficacy: The exercise of control. W.H. Freeman and Company, New York (1997)
4. Goethals, G.R., Nelson, R.E.: Similarity in the influence process: The belief-value distinction. Journal of Personality and Social Psychology 25(1), 117–122 (1973)
5. Bandura, A., Schunk, D.H.: Cultivating competence, self-efficacy, and intrinsic interest through proximal self-motivation. Journal of Personality and Social Psychology 41(3), 586–598 (1981)
6. Hersh, M.: The changing position of women in engineering worldwide. IEEE Transactions on Engineering Management 47(3), 345–359 (2000)
7. Baylor, A.L.: Expanding preservice teachers' metacognitive awareness of instructional planning through pedagogical agents. Educational Technology, Research & Development 50, 5–22 (2002)
8. Baylor, A.L.: The Impact of Pedagogical Agent Image on Affective Outcomes. In: International Conference on Intelligent User Interfaces, San Diego, CA (2005)
9. Baylor, A.L., Plant, E.A.(eds.): Pedagogical agents as social models for engineering: The influence of appearance on female choice. In: Looi, C.K., et al. (eds.) Artificial intelligence in education: Supporting Learning through intelligent and socially informed technology, vol. 125, pp. 65–72. IOS Press, Amsterdam (2005)
10. Moreno, R., et al.: The case for social agency in computer-based teaching: Do students learn more deeply when they interact with animated pedagogical agents? Cognition and Instruction 19(2), 177–213 (2001)
11. Baylor, A.L., et al.: Pedagogical Agents as Social Models for Female Students: The Effects of Agent Appearance on Women's Attitudes and Beliefs. in Manuscript under review (2007)
12. Nass, C., Lee, K.N.: Does computer-synthesized speech manifest personality? Experimental tests of recognition, similarity-attraction, and consistency-attraction. Journal of Experimental Psychology-Applied 7(3), 171–181 (2001)
13. Nass, C., Moon, Y.: Machines and mindlessness: Social responses to computers. Journal of Social Issues 56(1), 81–103 (2000)
14. Nass, C., et al.: Can Computer Personalities Be Human Personalities. International Journal of Human-Computer Studies 43(2), 223–239 (1995)
15. Reeves, B., Nass, C.: The media equation. Cambridge University Press, New York (1996)
16. Nass, C., Moon, Y., Green, N.: Are machines gender neutral? Gender-stereotypic responses to computers with voices. Journal of Applied Social Psychology 27(10), 864–876 (1997)
17. Sproull, L., et al.: When the interface is a face. Human-Computer Interaction 11(2), 97–124 (1996)
18. Mayer, R.E., Sobko, K., Mautone, P.D.: Social cues in multimedia learning: Role of speaker's voice. Journal of Educational Psychology 95(2), 419–425 (2003)
19. Atkinson, R.K., Mayer, R.E., Merrill, M.M.: Fostering social agency in multimedia learning: Examining the impact of an animated agent's voice. Contemporary Educational Psychology 30(1), 117–139 (2005)
20. Atkinson, R.K.: Optimizing learning from examples using animated pedagogical agents. Journal of Educational Psychology 94(2), 416–427 (2002)
21. Mayer, R.E.: Multimedia learning: Are we asking the right questions? Educational Psychologist 32(1), 1–19 (1997)

Embodied Agents on a Website:
Modelling an Attitudinal Route of Influence

Pablo Lambert- Diesbach[1] and David F. Midgley[2]

[1] Associate Professor, Group Sup-de-Co
17000 La Rochelle
(Research Fellow, ESSEC Asian Center)[1]
`diesbachp@esc-larochelle.fr, diesbach@essec.fr`
[2] Professor, INSEAD
Bd de Constance, 77305 Fontainebleau
`david.midgley@insead.fr`

Abstract. Embodied virtual agents (called hereafter EVAs) are animated, virtual objects, which move, talk, and look like human beings. We propose a possible route which may help better understand how observed effects of an agent on an interface user occur. We relate the concept of embodied agent to literatures in marketing and psychology, which justify the introduction of the concept of attitude. A route of influence and a model are elaborated, proposing effects of agents presence and congruency, on attitudes, and behavioural and intentional dimension of the website power of retention, or "stickiness". The model is tested, results are discussed, research contributions and limits are commented.

Keywords: Embodied agents, interaction, attitudes, brand relationship.

1 Introduction

Embodied virtual agents are more and more used in different contexts such as teaching, socialization, chats, and brand websites. We have already observed many of their effects, but a theoretical reflection is still necessary. We propose to modelize such effects and to relate them to traditional constructs in psychology and marketing.

2 Theoretical Framework

Definition of an Embodied Virtual Agent

A virtual agent is an *autonomous* creature, following Blumberg's (e.g. [1]) understanding of the word. It moves in such environment, performing different tasks,

---

[1] Pablo Diesbach is a research fellow at ESSEC Asian Center in Singapore. Partial support by the Singapore Economic Development Board is gratefully acknowledged. Partial support by the Singapore Economic Development Board, funding by FRANCE TELECOM R&D Center, and the collaboration of MYDAVI.COM in supplying the tested virtual agents, are gratefully acknowledged.

Y. de Kort et al. (Eds.): PERSUASIVE 2007, LNCS 4744, pp. 223–230, 2007.

with more or less intelligence, or autonomy. It can be made visible and is hence called embodied virtual agent (EVA). Definitions may be found in the literature ([2], p.3; [3], p. 554; [4], p.488). An EVA can be considered not only as a virtual piece, which actually constitute an element of design of an interface, but also as a human or human-like counterpart. Its characteristics of embodiment or incarnation, is therefore crucial. Cassel & al. ([5,6,7,8]) focus on that type of agents, as does most of the research related to persuasion processes in a man-agent interface context [3,9,10,11,12,13].

Cassel (ibid) and Donath [14,15] highlight the crucial importance of the agent's design characteristics. Design means here the "physical appearance"[2]. An agent may be characterized by its physical design, by its verbal and non-verbal language [16,3,14,8,17,18,19,20], by its voice, size, body, clothing (including clothes, accessories), i.e. everything that might generate affective and symbolical reactions [21,22], and last by its functionalities. An embodied agent is therefore both a design element of an electronic interface such as (e.g.) a website; but it is also an animated object that we treat like a human or a social being. As such, literatures dealing with humans reactions to elements of design (e.g. in Psychology and in Advertising), and with human reactions to humans or images of humans, might help. Such literatures also propose a construct of "attitude", useful in our intent to propose a model here.

Explaining the Effects of Agents in Term of Persuasion

Observed Effects, Persuasion, Behaviour

When exposed to an electronic interface and/or an embodied agent, an individual reacts as if exposed to an interaction with another social being [23,24,25,26,27], and more if the interface seems "natural", credible [1,26]. A number of works observe "approach behaviours" by individuals exposed to an EVA [4,6,7,28, 29].

A Need for Human or Humanlike Interactions

Human beings in general look for social contacts in very distinct interaction situations, such as shopping [30,31,32,33], information search [34,35,36,37], games and leisure [38,39,40]. Holbrook [41,42,43] conceptualizes a typology of "consumption benefits", applicable in an internet context [44,45], which integrates that need. Such findings might explain why "naturalness" seems so important for the user in a man-robot or man-machine interaction [1,46,47,48,49]. The role of affect in interacting with the interface, and its perceived benefits, become crucial [50,51, 52,45]. There could be some innate "need for interaction", which the EVA might meet. EVAs are therefore also a component of interface human and social dimension and hence possible drivers of positive or negative behaviours and intentions of behaviours as in other service encounters [53,54,55,56,57,58].

---

[2] We therefore do not understand "design" as is understood by computing engineers, for whom "design" means the functionalities of a software, or the set of actions it may perform.

3   Proposal for Modelling the Effects of Virtual Agents

Questioning the Dominant Approach: Roles of Attitudes and Congruency

Most of the quoted articles studying the effects of an EVA have not integrated, in our opinion, a real theoretical reflection on why such effects may be generated. They lack a real modelling effort. In a number of cases for example, scholars quote some other scholars who refer to the need for "naturalness", that is, the need for a natural-like, credible EVA, and give it the status of a framework. We fully share the opinion that an agent should be credible and natural-like. But still this does not help modelling. As such, a substantial part of the research on the subject could be considered as somehow a-theoretical. Hence the concept of attitude toward an agent or a site, and of hierarchy of attitudinal effects (HAE). An EVA may also have effects, not only through its presence but also through its design: hence the concept of agent-website congruency.

The Concepts of Attitude, Proposal of an Attitudinal Hierarchy of Effects

A first approach could be considering the concept of Attitude, and integrating it into a sequence of step-by-step or "hierarchy", of effects. Attitude may be defined as a durable disposition, to answer in a constant way to some situation, stimuli, aspects, characteristics, of an object, a person, an environment, etc. The referred "object" may also be a brand, a product or service, an outlet [59,60,61,62,63,64]. Attitudes have been integrated into a succession of effects generated by the stimulating object, called a "hierarchy of effects" (e.g. [64,65,66]. The concepts of attitude and of hierarchy of attitudinal effects (HAE) have been extended to the internet context [67,68,69][3]. Muller (2004) and Diesbach [12] propose to integrate the succession of effects from the website on the attitude toward the site, then on the attitude toward the brand with comprehensive operationalizations. Diesbach adds to it the concept of "attitude toward the embodied virtual agent", considering that an EVA may be considered as a virtual salesperson of service personnel. The concept of Attitude towards the salesperson [34,35,36], whether the "agent" is real or virtual, makes sense. We therefore propose a HAE which integrates constructs of attitudes related to man-man interaction in a marketing context (Atde towards salesperson), and of attitudes related to a man-agent and man-machine interaction (A_{eva} and A_{ws}). Last, we posit a specific order: it is assumed that the formation of an attitude towards the EVA (A_{eva}) may precede the formation of the attitude towards the website (A_{ws}) and finally the attitude toward the brand (A_b). Other orders as well as double direction effects among such attitudes, might be posited, but we made the present choice, as a first step in investigating the possible HAE in man-machine and man-agent interaction.

The Concept of Agent-Website Congruency

Research in Environmental psychology has first focused on the role of design elements such as music, noise, odor, colors, etc., on affective reactions in a first step,

---

[3] We nevertheless criticize Karson & Fischer because the measurement of the construct of attitude (here "attitude toward the site") lacks validity, as its operationalization is too poor to really measure such attitude, hence a problem of construct validity.

and on intentional and actual behavioral reactions called approach-avoidance reactions, in a second step. Such framework has been applied with questionable results, in a marketing context-particularly music or colors in an advertising context. Then it was posited that such ambiance or design elements had effects not only through the affective reactions, but also through the *congruency* of such cues. Congruency refers to how much an element of design fits, corresponds to the global object/support to which it is attached. Research in advertising and consumer behavior, does use the concept of congruency between an element of design and a more global object or support. In advertising for example, the congruency between an ambience music and the commercial environment, is studied (Rieunier 2000; Diesbach 2002), or with the advertising message in which it is used, offline or online ([70], Galan 2003). Scott (1994) study the symbolic dimension of advertising images and on the role of its congruency with the ads or environment in which it is used. Last, Kroeber-Riel (1979, 1984) shows that the congruency of a human image, with the advertised products and brand values, have effects on consumers' attitudinal and intentional reactions (he doesn't name the construct).

We define EVA-website congruency as the degree to which the EVA corresponds to its website. Agent's presence and congruence are expected to generate positive effects. Our hypothesis posit a positive effect of agent presence on the three attitudes, navigation duration, and intention to return and to recommend. They also posit a positive moderating effect of agent congruency, on those effects of the presence.

4 Test of the Model and Results

An experiment was conducted in the FRANCE TELECOM R & D laboratory, in the Man-Machine Interface Division in 2004. An external agency randomly recruited 392 subjects, to perform a data-collection-oriented navigation on two informational brand websites (Primolea (Olive oil) and Traser (Diving watches)). A total of 344 valid questionnaires and 155 purified log files (only for Traser site) are collected. Hypothesis, extracted from a larger model, are numbered from H5 to H18. Numbers are unchanged so to keep consistency with future publications on the original model:

Results and Discussion

The hierarchy of effects is validated, with some limits. The first step of the hierarchy of effects (H5: effects of congruency on A_{EVA}) is not validated. Effects among attitudes are validated (H6, H7, H8: $\beta st=+0.21$ to 0.62). Effects of attitudes on intention to revisit and to recommend are validated (H14, H16, H18: $\beta st=+0.45$ to 0.80). Nevertheless, effects of attitudes on the behavioural components (H13, H15, H17) are not validated. Most effects, when significant, are *quite homogeneous,* without being exactly equal, across the two tested sites (Chow tests). That is, the type of site itself seems to have little effect on the validation of such route of influence.

Contributions and Limits of the Research

We have recorded some of the important results in the literature on man-agent interaction, and have highlighted that most researches conducted on EVAs do not propose a comprehensive enough theoretical framework. This research proposes a model which may explain a part of the observed effects. It posits a hierarchy of attitudinal effects (HAE), and effects of such HAE on behavioural and intentional criterion variables, which form a construct of stickiness. Hypothesis are tested. The attitudinal route is partly confirmed, but some effects are not significant: our model is then insufficiently specified. Another, alternative or complementary approach, could deepen in our integrating the research in Environmental psychology, and study an affective route.

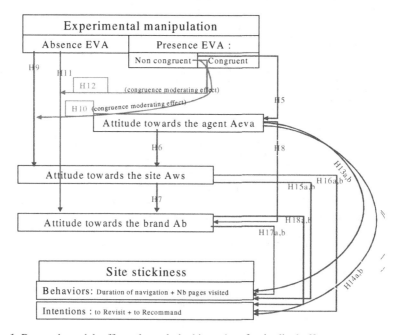

Fig. 1. Research model, effects through the hierarchy of attitudinal effects

Last, one limit is inherent to any experiment: we have controlled a number of variables such as the real navigation on the site and exposition to the agent, gender, age, but in spite of a large sample the generalizability of our findings is limited by the fact that we cannot know if other non-controlled variables have had an effect, such as (without being exhaustive): expertise online, innovativeness, attitude towards internet in general, etc. This last point also opens a number of research avenues.

References

1. Mitchell, B.B.: Old tricks, new dogs: Ethology and interactive creatures, PhD dissertation. MIT-MEDIALAB, p. 146 (1996)
2. Cassell, J., Bickmore, T.: External Manifestations of Trustworthiness in the Interface. Communications of the ACM 43(12), 50–56 (2000)
3. Burgoon, J., Bonito, J.A., Bengtsson, B., Cederberg, C., Lundeberg, M., Allspach, L.: Interactivity in human-computer interaction, a study of credibility, understanding and influence. Computers in Human Behavior 16, 553–574 (2000)

4. Cooke, A., Sujan, H., Sujan, M., Weitz, B.: Marketing the unfamiliar: The role of context and item-specific information in electronic-agent recommendations. Journal of Marketing Research 39, 488–497 (2002)

5. Cassell, J., Bickmore, T., Campbell, L., Vilhjálmsson, H., Yan, H.: Human conversation as a system framework: designing embodied conversational agents. In: Cassell, et al. (eds.) Embodied Conversational Agents, pp. 29–63. MIT Press, Cambridge (2000a)

6. Cassell, J., Bickmore, T., Campbell, L., Vilhjálmsson, H., Yan, H.: More than just a pretty face: Conversational protocols and the affordances of embodiment, Working paper, MIT, Gesture and Narrative Language Group (2000b)

7. Cassell, J., Ananny, M., Basu, A., Bickmore, T., Chong, P., Mellis, D., Ryokai, K., Smith, J., Vilhjálmsson, H., Yan, H.: Shared reality: Physical collaboration with a virtual peer, Working paper, MIT, Gesture and Narrative Language Group (2000c)

8. Cassell, J.: Embodied Conversational Agents: representation and intelligence in user interface. AI Magazine 22(3), 67–83 (2001)

9. Bickmore, T.: Social Dialogue is Serious Business. In: Proceedings of CHI 2002 Workshop on socially adept technologies, p. 5 (2002)

10. Timothy, B.: Relational agents, Effective change through human-computer relationships, Phd Dissertation, MID, Medialab, p. 284 (2003)

11. Diesbach, P.B., Jeandrain, A.C.: Online immersion and emotional reactions online: proposal of an integrative model. Advances in Consumer Research, Seoul, 20 (2004)

12. Diesbach, P.B.: Embodied virtual agents and brand website stickiness, PhD Thesis, ESSEC-IAE of Aix-en-Provence, p. 686 (2006)

13. Rolland, S., Wallet-Wodka, D.: Electronic agents on the internet : A way to satisfy the consumer? DMSP, Working paper 320, p. 19 (June 2003)

14. Donath, J.: Mediated faces, in Cognitive Technology: Instruments of Mind. In: Beynon, Nehaniv, Dautenhahn (eds.) Proceedings, CI 2001, Warwick, p. 18 (2001a)

15. Donath, J.: Being real: Questions of Tele-Identity, in The Robot in the Garden: Telerobotics & Telepistemology in the age of the Internet, pp. 296–311. MIT Press, Ken Goldberg (2001b)

16. Judith, B., Thomas, B., Michel, P.: Nonverbal behaviors, persuasion, and credibility. Human Communication Research 17(1), 140–169 (1990)

17. Paul, E., Wallace, F.V.: The repertoire of nonverbal behavior: Categories, origins, usage and coding. Semiotica 1, 49–98 (1969)

18. Paul, E., Wallace, F., Maureen, O.: Smiles when lying. In: Ekman & Rosenberg, ch. 9, pp. 201–215 (1997)

19. Ekman, P., Rosenberg, E.: What the face reveals, Basic and applied studies of spontaneous expression using the Facial Action Coding System, p. 495. Oxford University (1997)

20. Ekman, P.: What we have learned by measuring facial behavior? In: Ekman & Rosenberg, pp. 469–485 (1997)

21. Elisabeth, H.: Comprehending symbolic consumption: Three theoretical issues. In: Holbrook, Hirschman (eds.) Symposium on Symbolic Consumption, NYU, pp. 4–6 (1980)

22. Rebecca, H.: Apparel as communication. In: Holbrook, Hirschman (eds.) Symposium on Symbolic Consumption, pp. 7–15 (1980)

23. Bartneck, C.: Affective expressions of machines, ISBN 90-444-0027-4, p. 44 (2000)

24. Bartneck, C.: Affective expressions of machines. Human factors in Computing systems, pp. 189–190 (2001)

25. Nass, C., Lombard, M., Henriksen, L., Steuer, J.: Anthropocentrism and computers. Behaviour and Information Technology 14(4), 229–238 (1995)

26. Nass, C., Reeves, B.: The Media Equation, SLI. Cambridge University Press, Cambridge (1996)
27. Nass, C., Moon, Y.: Machines and mindlessness: Social responses to computers. Journal of Social Issues 56(1), 81–103 (2000)
28. Koda, T., Maes, P.: Agents with faces: The effect of personification. In: Proceedings of the 5th International Workshop on Robot and Human Communication (RO-MAN 96) (1996)
29. Economou, D., Mitchell, W., Boyle, T.: Pedagogical virtual actor technology development based on real world applications and user needs, Working paper, p. 11, AAAI (2003)
30. Bloch, P., Masha, R.: Shopping without purchase: An investigation of consumer browsing behavior. Advances in Consumer Research 10, 389–393 (1983)
31. Peter, B., Daniel, S., Nancy, R.: Consumer search: an extended framework. Journal of Consumer Research 13, 119–126 (1986)
32. Andrew, F., Ven, S.: The depersonalization of retailing: its impact on the « lonely » consumer. Journal of Retailing 67 (1991)
33. Underhill, P., Schuster, S.: Why we buy? The Science of Shopping, p. 280 (1999)
34. Babin, B., Boles, J., Darden, W.: Salesperson stereotypes, consumer emotions, and their impact on information processing. Journal of the Academy of Marketing Science 23(2), 94–105 (1995)
35. Babin, L., Babin, B., Boles, J.: The effects of consumer perceptions of the salesperson, product, and dealer on purchase intentions. Journal of Retailing and Consumer Services 6, 91–97 (1999)
36. Barry, B., William, D., Mitch, G.: Work and/or fun: measuring hedonic and utilitarian shopping value. Journal of Consumer Research (1994)
37. Boulaire, C., Balloffet, P.: Freins et motivations à l'utilisation d'Internet: une exploration par le biais de métaphores, Recherches et Applications en Marketing, pp. 21–39 (January 1999)
38. Bourgeon, D., Filser, M.: Les apports du modèle expérientiel à l'analyse du comportement dans le domaine culturel. Recherches et Applications en Marketing 4, 5–26 (1995)
39. Hirschman, E.: Consumers and their animal companions. Journal of Consumer Research 24, 616–632 (1994)
40. Holbrook, M., Hirschman, E.: The experiential aspects of consumption: Consumer fantasies, feelings and fun. Journal of Consumer Research 9, 132–140 (1982)
41. Holbrook, M.: Emotion in the consumption experience: Toward a new model of the human consumer. In: The Role of Affect in Consumer Behavior, Peterson, Hoyer, Wilson, pp. 17–52 (1986)
42. Holbrook, M.: The nature of customer value: An axiology of services in the consumption experience. In: Service Quality: New directions in theory and practice, Sage pp. 21–71 (1994)
43. Morris, H.: Introduction to consumer values. In: Holbrook (ed.) Consumer value: A framework for analysis and research, London: Routledge, pp. 1–18 (1999)
44. Helmé-Guizon, A.: Le comportement du consommateur sur un site marchand est-il fondamentalement différent de son comportement en magasin? RAM 16(3), 25–37 (2001)
45. Mathwick, C., Malhotra, N., Rigdon, E.: Experiential value: Conceptualisation, measurement and application in the catalog and Internet environment. Journal of Retailing 77, 39–56 (2001)
46. Klein, J., Moon, Y., Picard, R.: This computer responds to user frustration: Theory, design and results. Interacting with Computers 14, 119–140 (2002)
47. Moon, Y., Nass, C.: How "real" are computer personalities? Psychological responses to personality types in human-computer interaction. Communication Research 23, 651–674 (1996)

48. Rosalind, P.: Affective computing, p. 292. MIT Press, Cambridge (1998)
49. Picard, R., Klein, J.: Computers that recognize and respond to user emotion: Theoritical and practical implications, Medialab Tech Report n.538; Interacting with Computers (2001)
50. Csikszentmihalyi, M., Lefèvre, J.: Optimal experience in work and leisure. Journal of Personality and Social Psychology 56, 815–822 (1989)
51. Csikszentmihalyi, M.: Flow, the psychology of optimal experience, Ed. Harper & Row (1990)
52. Csikszentmihalyi, M.: The costs and benefits of consuming. Journal of Consumer Research 27, 267–272 (2000)
53. Baker, J., Cameron, M.: The effects of the service environment on affect and consumer perception of waiting time: An integrative review and research propositions. Journal of the Academy of the Marketing Science 24(4), 338–349 (1996)
54. Julie, B., Michael, L., Dhruv, G.: An experimental approach to making retail store environmental decisions. Journal of Retailing 68(4), 445–461 (1992)
55. Julie, B., Parasuraman, P., Dhruv, G.A.: The influence of store environment on quality inferences and store image. Journal of Academy of Marketing Science 22(4), 328–339 (1994)
56. Diesbach, P.B, Galan, J.P, Chandon, J.L.: Impact de la présence d'un agent virtuel incarné sur le pouvoir de rétention du site web : une analyse comportementale par les fichiers log, In: Filser, M. (ed)11th Research conference of Burgundy in Marketing, p. 17 (October 2006)
57. Diesbach, P.B., Galan, J.P.: L'agent virtuel incarné dans la distribution en ligne: cadre théorique et revue de littérature. In: 6th Conference on E-marketing, U. Nantes, p. 24 (September 2006)
58. Zeithaml, V., Bitner, M.: Services Marketing, Integrating customer focus across the firm, p. 668. McGraw Hill, New York (2003)
59. Bagozzi, R., Gopinath, M., Nyer, P.: The role of emotions in marketing. Journal of the Academy of Marketing Science 27, 184–206 (1999)
60. Batra, R.: The Role of Affect in Consumer Behavior. In: Peterson, Hoyer, Wilson, (eds.) pp. 17–52 (1986)
61. George, B., Michael, B.: Advertising and promotion: An integrated marketing communications perspective. McGraw Hill, New York (1998)
62. Derbaix, C.: The impact of affective reactions on attitudes toward the advertisement and the brand. Journal of Marketing Research 32(4), 470–479 (1995)
63. Derbaix, C., Pham, M.: Pour un développement des mesures de l'affectif en marketing : synthèse des pré-requis. Recherches et Applications en Marketing 4, 71–87 (1989)
64. MacKenzie, S., Lutz, R., Belch, G.: The role of attitude toward the ad as a mediator of advertising effectiveness. Journal of Marketing Research 23, 130–143 (1986)
65. Fishbein, M., Ajzen, I.: Belief, attitude, intention and behavior. Addison-Wesley, Reading (1975)
66. Ray, M., Sawyer, A., Rothschild, M., Heeler, R., Strong, E., Reed, J.: Marketing communication and the hierarchy of effects. In: New models for mass communication research, vol. 2, Sage (1973)
67. Stevenson, J., Bruner II, G., Kumar, A.: Webpage background and viewers attitude. Journal of Advertising Research , 29–34 (2000)
68. Bruner, G.C., Kumar, A.: Web commercials and advertising hierarchy-of-effects. Journal of Advertising Research 40(1/2), 35–42 (2000)
69. Chen, Q., Wells, W.: Attitude toward the site, Journal of Advertising Research, 27–37 (1999)
70. Karine, G.: Influence de la musique sur les réponses des consommateurs à la publicitél, PhD Thesis, University Rennes 1, p. 665 (1998)

Is it Me or Is it what I say?
Source Image and Persuasion

Hien Nguyen and Judith Masthoff

Computing Science Department, University of Aberdeen
{hnguyen,jmasthoff}@csd.abdn.ac.uk

Abstract. In a persuasive communication, not only the message but also the source of the message can influence the persuasibility of the audience. This paper investigates whether displaying a static image of the source can affect the perceived credibility of a message that aims to promote regular exercise. We find a clear influence of the source's appearance on the source's credibility and that this effect is topic dependent. We also explore how the perceived source's credibility for a particular topic correlates with the perceived credibility of a message on that topic.

1 Introduction

Persuasive communication is "any message that is intended to shape, reinforce or change the responses of another or others." [1]. In other words, in a persuasive communication, a source tries to influence a receiver's attitudes or behaviours through the use of messages. Each of these three components (the source, the receiver, and the messages) affects the effectiveness of persuasion in different ways. Over the years, the three most recognised characteristics of the source that influence their persuasiveness are *perceived credibility*, *likeability* and *similarity* [2,3]. These are not commodities that the source possesses, but they are the perception of the receiver about the source. *Appearance cues* of the source (e.g. a white lab coat can make one a doctor or a scientist, while untidy dressing can make one less trustworthy) have been shown to affect his/her perceived credibility [4]. There is also some evidence that *physical attractiveness* can positively influence persuasion: for instance, it has been shown that attractive communicators had more success in getting students to sign a petition [5].

This raises the question of whether showing the source of information visually can influence the perceived credibility of the information. This problem has been looked at by a number of researchers and mixed results have been found. Two studies at Boston University showed that people were more willing to cooperate with a human-like character when that character had been made more attractive [6]. However, attractiveness alone was not sufficient to predict cooperation: subjects cooperated less with a more attractive, but dog-like character. Adding a formal photograph of an author has been shown to improve the trustworthiness, believability, perceived expertise and competence of a web article (compared to an informal or no photograph) [7]. However, adding an image of a person did not increase the perceived trustworthiness of a recommendation

Y. de Kort et al. (Eds.): PERSUASIVE 2007, LNCS 4744, pp. 231–242, 2007.

system [8]. It has been suggested that a photo can boost trust in e-commerce websites, but can also damage it [9].

The reason of these inconsistent results may well be that the source's perceived credibility is topic dependent. When delivering information about a topic, a speaker might have high credibility in certain aspects but low credibility in others. For instance, a doctor might be more credible than an athlete while talking about the benefits of exercise on health. In contrast, an athlete might have an edge over a doctor while talking about fitness programs. Meanwhile, someone who is similar to the user might be the most persuasive character should the user need social support.

A source's credibility may also depend on characteristics of the receiver: a series of studies by Baylor has shown a positive influence of the similarity of human-like agents to subjects (in terms of e.g. gender and ethnicity) on credibility of a teacher agent and motivation for learning (e.g. [10]). She found that people have preferences about whom they would like to interact with.

In this paper, we investigate whether displaying the source of information can influence the credibility of a message that aims to promote regular exercise. In particular, we investigate whether this effect depends on the perceived credibility of the source on the topic of the message.

2 Experiment 1: Validation, Credibility and Preference for Source

The aim of this experiment is two-fold. Firstly, we want to establish the perceived age, gender, profession, attractiveness, trustworthiness, and expertness (on two topics) for various potential source images. We hope to find a subset of images with good inter-subject agreement on all these criteria. These images can then be used in future experiments. The second aim of the experiment is to investigate the correlation between these criteria (and characteristics of the participants) and the preference people have for whom they want to learn from about each of the two topics.

2.1 Experimental Design

Fifty-one participants took part in the experiment (see Table 1 for the distribution of age and gender). Participants were staff and graduate students of the university, but came from all areas and professions.

Table 1. The distribution of participants' age and gender

	Gender		Age			
	Female	Male	18-20	21-24	25-29	>= 30
Number of subjects	32	19	5	17	9	20

Participants were presented with 16 head and shoulder images of doctors and sport instructors / athletes (see Table 2 and 3). All images were taken from Microsoft Clipart (using search keywords like doctor and sport) and varied in age, gender, and profession (as identified based on the tags used in Clipart for each image). The presentation order of the images was randomized for each participant to control for order effects.

Table 2. Eight of the images shown to the participants (all of doctors) and results

1	Doctor 17		Doctor 16; Other 1	2
	Attractive 2.9 (0.7)		Attractive 3.0 (0.9)	
	Trustworthy 3.9 (0.8)		Trustworthy 4.1 (0.7)	
	H Exp 4.1(0.6) #H 1 E Exp 3.0 (0.9) #E 1		H Exp 3.8 (1.1) #H 7 E Exp 3.0 (0.8) #E 1	

3	Doctor 15; Other 1; Sport Instructor 1;	Doctor 14; Other 3	4
	Attractive 3.4 (0.6)	Attractive 2.4 (0.6)	
	Trustworthy 4.1 (0.8)	Trustworthy 3.2 (0.9)	
	H Exp 4.1 (0.6) #H 1 E Exp 3.5 (0.5) #E 1	H Exp 3.5 (1.3) #H 1 E Exp 2.5 (1.1) #E 0	

5	Doctor 16; Sport Instructor 1	Doctor 15; Other 1 Sport Instructor 1;	6
	Attractive 2.7 (0.6)	Attractive 2.7 (0.8)	
	Trustworthy 4.6 (0.5)	Trustworthy 3.7 (0.7)	
	H Exp 4.0 (0.8) #H 1 E Exp 3.4 (0.7) #E 1	H Exp 3.9 (0.7) #H 2 E Exp 3.5 (0.6) #E 3	

7	Doctor 16; Sport Instructor 1	Doctor 11; Other 6	8
	Attractive 3.3 (0.7)	Attractive 2.5 (0.7)	
	Trustworthy 4.5 (0.5)	Trustworthy 3.8 (1.0)	
	H Exp 4.1 (0.8) #H 8 E Exp 3.5 (0.6) #E 2	H Exp 4.0 (0.9) #H 1 E Exp 3.4 (0.6) #E 0	

[*] H Exp, E Exp: Expertness on the health benefits of exercise, fitness programs respectively; #H, #E: number of subjects who picked this image as their favourite to learn from about the health benefits of exercise and fitness programs respectively; for most results mean (stdev) are given.

Participants were divided into four groups (to limit the time needed to perform the experiment and to avoid interaction effects between the questions). We asked each group to judge one or more characteristics of the person given in each image, namely:

- (Group A: 17 participants) *gender* (male or female), *most likely profession* (choosing from: doctor, sport instructor, other), and *age* (< 25, 25-30, 30-40, 40-45, or > 45)
- (Group B: 13 participants) *attractiveness*

- (Group C: 11 participants) *trustworthiness*
- (Group D: 10 participants) *expertness* with respect to (1) the health benefits of exercise, and (2) fitness programs.

A person's attractiveness, trustworthiness, and expertness were measured using 15 five-point Semantic Differential scale items developed by Ohanian [11] (see Appendix A for exact wordings).

Next, all participants were presented with a webpage showing all 16 images (the order of the images was also randomized for each participant and each image was scaled down so that all images fitted on one screen in a 4x4 table). They could hover

Table 3. Eight of the images (all of sports people except image 11) and results

9	Doctor 1; Other 5; Sport instructor 11;		10	Sport instructor 11; Other 6	
	Attractive 3.8 (0.8)			Attractive 2.8 (0.9)	
	Trustworthy 3.2 (1.1)			Trustworthy 3.0 (0.9)	
	H Exp 3.7 (0.6) E Exp 3.9 (0.5)	#H 5 #E 14		H Exp 3.6 (1.0) E Exp 4.0 (0.7)	#H 6 #E 9
11	Doctor 17		12	Doctor 1; Other 5; Sport instructor 11;	
	Attractive 3.0 (0.8)			Attractive 3.6 (0.6)	
	Trustworthy 4.1 (0.7)			Trustworthy 3.9 (0.9)	
	H Exp 3.9 (0.6) E Exp 3.5 (0.7)	#H 1 #E 0		H Exp 3.8 (0.7) E Exp 4.1 (0.5)	#H 5 #E 12
13	Doctor 1; Other 5 Sport instructor 11;		14	Doctor 2; Other 13 Sport instructor 2;	
	Attractive 2.8 (0.9)			Attractive 2.4 (0.5)	
	Trustworthy 4.3 (0.5)			Trustworthy 3.3 (1.2)	
	H Exp 3.3 (0.9) E Exp 3.7 (0.9)	#H 1 #E 2		H Exp 3.0 (0.9) E Exp 3.1 (1.1)	#H 3 #E 2
15	Other 7; Sport instructor 10;		16	Doctor 1; Other 13 Sport instructor 3;	
	Attractive 2.6 (0.9)			Attractive 2.5 (0.9)	
	Trustworthy 4.3 (0.6)			Trustworthy 3.8 (0.9)	
	H Exp 3.5 (0.8) E Exp 3.6 (0.8)	#H 7 #E 3		H Exp 3.2 (1.2) E Exp 3.2 (1.2)	#H 1 #E 1

* See Table 2 for legend.

on each thumbnail to see the full size version. They were asked to choose whom they would like to learn from about each topic (i.e. health benefits of exercise and fitness programs), and the rationale for their decision.

2.2 Results and Discussion

Tables 2 and 3 show the results of the experiment, excluding results on gender and age to increase readability. With the odd exception, gender was completely agreed upon. There was more variation in the perception of age, but participants still tended to agree on a person looking older or younger (and for most images, there was a clear majority for one age category). The perception of profession was in accordance with expectation in fourteen out of sixteen images (in the sense that the majority of subjects agreed the image looked like a doctor or sports instructor respectively). The perceived profession of images 14 and 16 was not according to expectation, so these images are not suitable for further experiments.

The low standard deviations show that participants tended to agree on attractiveness, trustworthiness and expertness. Interestingly, all images were judged to show trustworthy people (with a lowest average of 3.0 for image 10, which is clearly above a neutral 2.5). Also, none of the images where judged to show really unattractive people (the lowest average was 2.4 which is close to neutral).

Independent sample t-tests indicated that profession influences perceived expertness. Doctors are perceived as more expert with respect to the health benefits of exercise than sport instructors (average 3.92, stdev 0.21 vs. average 3.59, stdev 0.18, $p<0.05$), while sport instructors are perceived as more expert with respect to fitness programs than doctors (average 3.86, stdev 0.22 vs. average 3.26, stdev 0.34, $p<0.05$). However, interestingly, almost all doctors (with the exception of image 4 who had a neutral score of 2.5) are perceived as having expertise in fitness programs, and all sport instructors are perceived as having expertise in the health benefits of exercise. Quite probably, sport instructors are assumed to be interested in exercise not just for the sake of exercise, but also because they care about the health aspects.

Our results also showed that there is a clear preference about whom people want to learn from about fitness programs. Forty subjects chose a sport instructor while nine subjects chose a doctor to learn from about fitness programs (two subjects who chose image 14 were not counted). However, the same does not hold for the topic of health benefits of exercise. Twenty-four subjects chose a sport instructor and twenty-three subjects chose a doctor to learn from about the health benefits of exercise (three subjects who chose image 14 and one subject who chose image 16 were not counted).

We found a correlation between expertness, as well as attractiveness, and the preference of the source for fitness programs (Pearson coefficient = 0.738 and 0.666 respectively, $p<0.01$), but not for health benefits. This means participants preferred to learn about fitness programs from an attractive looking expert in that area. The images for each topic that were selected most often also had the highest credibility (defined as the combination of attractiveness, trustworthiness and expertness). Despite this, no correlation was found between credibility, nor trustworthiness, and the preference of the source for either topic. Our qualitative analysis also confirmed this result. A healthy (but not overly fit) appearance, friendliness (both can be considered elements of attractiveness), and expertise were mentioned the most among reasons for choosing the preferred source. A list of all criteria mentioned by subjects is given in Table 4.

Table 4. Criteria used by subjects to choose whom to learn from

Health benefits of exercise		Fitness programs	
Criteria	No of subjects mentioned	Criteria	No of subjects mentioned
Fit (but not overly fit)	16	Fit (but not overly fit)	16
Friendly	10	Expert	16
Expert	9	Friendly	6
Nice	8	Fun	3
Near my age	3	Serious and committed	2
Unfit	3	Same gender	2
Approachable	3	Near my age	1
Same gender	2	Nice	1
Fun	2	Non judgmental	1
Non judgmental	2	Mature	1
Serious and committed	2	Approachable	1
Mature	1	Unfit	1
Credible	1		
Relaxed	1		

There was no correlation between the participants' gender and the gender of the selected image for both topics (using Pearson Chi-square). We also did not note an effect of the participants' age. So, for the given topics, similarity in the strict sense of age and gender between the source and the participant seems to have little effect (though some participants did regard this as important, see criteria mentioned above). However, similarity is a much broader concept than just age and gender (see e.g. research in the SIDE paradigm, [12]).

3   Experiment 2: Credibility of Source and Message

3.1   Experimental Design

In this experiment, we explore whether the social appearance of the source in the form of a static image influences the perceived credibility of the message. Following our discussion in Section 1, we proposed the following hypothesis:

H1: The perceived credibility of a message on a topic is positively related to the perceived credibility of the source on that topic (as resulting from the source's social appearance).

Fifty-nine participants took part in the experiment. Participants were staff and graduate students of different departments across the university (including secretarial staff).

All participants were shown two messages: a first about the health benefits of exercise and a second about fitness programs. We composed the messages based on the information available on www.mayoclinic.com and www.nutristrategy.com. Participants were asked to read the two given messages carefully. After reading each message, they judged its credibility by rating 15 items on a seven-point Likert scale. The items were developed and validated by Hong [13] for assessing the credibility of health-related websites. They assess four commonly recognised dimensions of credibility: goodwill, expertise/trustworthiness, depth, and fairness (see Appendix B for exact wordings). The items were ordered such that no two items from the same dimension appeared sequentially.

Participants were randomly divided into three groups (see Table 6 for demographics of the groups). The messages for Highly Credible Image and the Lowly Credible Image groups prominently showed a source image. The messages for No Image group lacked any image of the source. For the Highly Credible Image group, the images chosen were the most credible source images for the topics (as determined in Experiment 1): image 7 for the message about the health benefits of exercise and image 12 for the message about fitness programs. For the Lowly Credible Image group, the images chosen were the least credible source images for the topics (as determined in Experiment 1): image 4 for the first message and image 8 for the second message. All images used are shown in Table 5.

Table 5. Characteristics of the images used in the experiment as determined in Experiment 1

		7	12	4	8
Attractiveness		3.28	3.63	2.38	2.52
Trustworthiness		4.52	3.85	3.22	3.83
Expertness	H*	4.05	3.82	3.47	3.96
	E*	3.53	4.13	2.53	3.38

* H: Health benefits of exercise; E: Fitness program

Participants also indicated the extent to which they already knew the information presented to them, their knowledge on the topic before the experiment. The exact wordings and results are shown in Table 6. Please note that the first four questions were asked at the start of the experiment, and the last two at the end. There were no significant differences between the groups on any of these questions.

3.2 Results and Discussion

Table 7 shows the results of the experiment. We averaged the results on each dimension to get an overall score of credibility. Our hypothesis posited that the presence of an image of a highly credible source increases the perceived credibility of the message and that of a lowly credible source decreases the perceived credibility. So, we expected the message credibility to be highest for the Highly Credible Image group, lowest for the Lowly Credible Image group, and in between for the No Image group.

Table 6. Participants' backgrounds

		Highly Credible Image		Lowly Credible Image		No Image	
Gender		M	F	M	F	M	F
		6	13	4	15	8	13
I am currently doing some form of exercise		Yes	No	Yes	No	Yes	No
		9	10	14	5	15	6
I am more educated about my health than most people*		4.95 (1.03)		5.11 (1.37)		5.14 (1.31)	
I have full knowledge of the benefits (consequences) of regular exercise (or the lack of it)*.		5.47 (1.31)		5.32 (1.38)		5.43 (1.36)	
I already knew all the information presented**	Health	2.63 (1.16)		2.79 (0.71)		3.29 (1.27)	
	Exercise	2.37 (1.07)		2.47 (0.61)		2.86 (1.20)	

* 1 = strongly disagree 7 = strongly agree
** 1 = everything 7 = nothing

As shown in Table 7, the average results for the health benefits of exercise follow these predictions perfectly, both for every individual dimension and for overall credibility. However, this is only partly shown to be statistically significant. Though a one-way ANOVA indicated that there is indeed a difference on credibility among the three groups as predicted (F=3.26, p<0.05), only the contrast between the Highly Credible Image group and the Lowly Credible Image group was significant (Tukey, p<0.05).

The average results for fitness programs are clearly less in accordance with our hypothesis. The average results for the Highly Credible Image group are still higher than the average results for the Lowly Credible Image group for every dimension and for overall credibility. However, the average results for No Image group are clearly not following the hypothesis: the overall credibility and trust/expertise are very similar to those of the Highly Credible Image group and depth is even higher. No statistical differences were found. Maybe participants did not pay as much attention to the second message and its associated questions as they had to the first one. Messages were quite long (576 words for the first one, and 919 words for the second one), and maybe participants were tired and less motivated when they started on the second message. The increased length of the second message may also have had an impact. We also note that unfortunately the groups were not equal in the sense that the majority of participants in the Lowly Credible Image and No Image groups are currently exercising, which was not the case for the Highly Credible Image group. We do not think this will have affected the results for the health benefits of exercise, considering the groups were equally aware of the health benefits of exercising. However, it may well have had an impact on the results for fitness programs. A follow-up experiment will be needed to investigate these issues further.

It should be noted that the images we used for the Lowly Credible Image group still had a reasonable credibility. It would have been easy to use images with lower credibility, increasing the difference between the Highly and Lowly Credible Image groups (and the Lowly Credible Image and No Image groups). However, we wanted to make this experiment as realistic as possible, using images a designer might have used.

The task given in the experiment was based on self-reporting of the various credibility dimensions after reading the messages, which may have reduced the need for participants to carefully assess them. We would like to increase participants' engagement by giving them a more direct task, e.g. deciding which particular exercise they are going to do themselves.

As shown in Table 6, participants already knew most of the information presented. This may have created a reverse effect in which the credibility of the message influenced the credibility of the source as suggested in social psychology [4], rather than the other way around. The fact that participants already knew most of the information may also have resulted in them having no difficulty in processing the information. Therefore, they may have been less influenced by peripheral cues such as the message source [14]. This is inline with research in the domain of e-commerce [9] which also suggested that the effects of specific interface elements (e.g. photos) on trust may be mediated by other site variables.

Table 7. Average score and standard deviation of each group (HC=Highly Credible Image, LC=Lowly Credible Image, NI=No Image)

	Fairness	Depth	Goodwill	Trust/Expertise	Credibility
Health benefits					
HC	4.61 (1.09)	3.79 (1.26)	5.60 (1.00)	4.46 (0.95)	4.62 (0.84)
LC	4.01 (1.35)	2.88 (1.01)	4.90 (1.02)	3.83 (1.19)	3.90 (0.84)
NI	4.07 (1.25)	3.63 (1.32)	5.18 (0.95)	4.32 (0.92)	4.30 (0.90)
Fitness programs					
HC	4.80 (1.37)	3.51 (1.18)	4.65 (0.44)	4.51 (0.73)	4.37 (0.74)
LC	4.67 (1.16)	3.11 (1.22)	4.42 (0.35)	4.09 (1.04)	4.07 (0.73)
NI	4.63 (1.07)	3.76 (1.38)	4.40 (0.44)	4.51 (0.98)	4.32 (0.76)

In summary, we found some evidence for the topic of the health benefits of exercise that the credibility of a source image influences the credibility of the message. However, the results of the experiment were not as supporting of our hypothesis as they could have been, and clearly follow-up research in this area is needed.

4 General Discussion

In this paper, we investigated whether people have a preference about whom they would like to learn from about a certain topic and whether an appearance of the source in the form of a static head and shoulder image can influence the perceived credibility of the message.

To avoid any overgeneralization of our conclusions, we will first discuss the limitations of the study. Firstly, the majority of our participants are female, and over 30 years old. Hence, any findings in this paper should only be generalized to other demographics with care. Secondly, findings in this paper are restricted to the subject of promoting the health benefits of exercise and how to choose the most suitable fitness program.

Our experiments suggested that the source's appearance can influence his/her perceived credibility. This effect is topic dependent. For each topic, people do have a preference for whom they would like to learn from. This is very important in the process of designing onscreen characters as choosing the most liked character might create a better initial relationship between the system and the user. Furthermore, adding an image of a highly credible source with respect to the topic discussed in the message can have a positive effect on the message's perceived credibility. Finally, our experiments suggested a number of criteria for choosing the appropriate image for the topic of promoting health benefits of exercise and fitness programs.

In the future, we would like to investigate this issue further by extending our experiments in various ways. Firstly, we plan to develop our own credibility scale that is more suitable for our chosen topics based on our findings in Experiment 1. This could result in a more precise measure of credibility with respect to our chosen topics. Secondly, we would like to redesign the experiment in a more direct, task-based design which does not rely purely on self-report. Furthermore, we plan to explore the effect of social presence of the source in different form (e.g. animated characters, voice).

The use of social presence of the source is not restricted to its visual appearance alongside the message. It can be utilized in other ways to win trust and credibility from users. For instance, studies in psychology have shown the positive effects of social norms and indirect communication on persuasion [3,4]. By using a team of onscreen characters, we can simulate the effect of social norms by having each character repeat the same information in different ways. We can also simulate the effect of indirect communication by having the characters converse with each other while the user pays attention to the dialogue. We have started to explore these ideas, and some preliminary results can be found in [15].

References

1. Miller, G.R.: On being persuaded: Some basic distinctions. In: Roloff, M.E., Miller, G.R. (eds.) Persuasion: New directions in theory and research, pp. 11–28. Berverly Hills, CA: Sage (1980)
2. O'Keefe, J.D.: Persuasion: theory and research. Newbury Park, CA: Sage (1990)
3. Stiff, J.B.: Persuasive Communication. The Guildford Press, New York (1994)
4. Aronson, E.: The social animal. Worth (2004)
5. Chaiken, S.: Communicator Physical Attractiveness and Persuasion. Journal of Personality and Social Psychology 37, 1387–1397 (1979)
6. Parise, S., Kiesler, S., Sproull, L., Waters, K.: Cooperating with life-like interface agents. Computers in Human Behavior 15(2), 123–142 (1999)

7. Fogg, B.J., Marshall, J., Kameda, T., Solomon, J., Rangnekar, A., Boyd, J., Brown, B.: Web Credibility Research: A Method for Online Experiments and Early Study Results. In: CHI 2001, pp. 295–296 (2001)
8. deVries, P.: Social presence as a conduit to the social dimensions of online trust. In: Persuasive Technology Conference, pp. 55–59 (2006)
9. Riegelsberger, J., Sasse, M.A., McCarthy, J.D.: Shiny happy people building trust? Photos on e-commerce websites and consumer trust. In: Proceedings of CHI 2003, pp. 121–128 (2003)
10. Baylor, A.L., Rosenberg-Kima, R.B., Plant, E.A.: Interface Agents as Social Models: The Impact of Appearance on Females' Attitude Toward Engineering. CHI 2006 Montreal, Canada (2006)
11. Ohanian, R.: Construction and validation of a scale to measure celebrity endorsers' perceived expertise, trustworthiness, and attractiveness. Journal of Advertising 19(3), 39–52 (1990)
12. Spears, R., Postmes, T., Lea, M., Wolbert, A.: When are net effects gross products? The power of influence and the influence of power in computer-mediated communication. Journal of Social Issues 58, 91–107 (2002)
13. Hong, T.: Contributing factors to the use of health-related websites. Journal of Health Communication 11, 149–165 (2006)
14. Petty, R., Cacioppo, J.: The elaboration likelihood model of persuasion. Advances in Experimental Social Psychology 19, 123–205 (1986)
15. Nguyen, H., Masthoff, J., Edwards, P.: Persuasive effects of embodied conversational agent teams. In: Proceedings of the 12th International Conference on Human-Computer Interaction, Beijing, China (in press, 2007)

Appendix A

A person's attractiveness, trustworthiness and expertise scale developed by Ohanian [11].

	5	4	3	2	1	
Attractiveness						
Attractive	__	__	__	__	__	Unattractive
Classy	__	__	__	__	__	Not classy
Beautiful/Handsome	__	__	__	__	__	Ugly
Elegant	__	__	__	__	__	Plain
Sexy	__	__	__	__	__	Not sexy
Trustworthiness						
Dependable	__	__	__	__	__	Undependable
Honest	__	__	__	__	__	Dishonest
Reliable	__	__	__	__	__	Unreliable
Sincere	__	__	__	__	__	Insincere
Trustworthy	__	__	__	__	__	Untrustworthy
Expertise						
Expert	__	__	__	__	__	Not an expert
Experienced	__	__	__	__	__	Inexperienced
Knowledgeable	__	__	__	__	__	Unknowledgeable
Qualified	__	__	__	__	__	Unqualified
Skilled	__	__	__	__	__	Unskilled

Appendix B

Health-related websites' credibility scales developed by Hong [13]

Factor	strongly agree				strongly disagree		
	1	2	3	4	5	6	7
Fairness							
This page provides information that is neutral	–	–	–	–	–	–	–
This page provides information that is **not** balanced	–	–	–	–	–	–	–
This page is biased in the information it provides	–	–	–	–	–	–	–
This page is slanted in the information it provides	–	–	–	–	–	–	–
This page is even-handed in presenting information	–	–	–	–	–	–	–
Depth							
This page does **not** provide in-depth information	–	–	–	–	–	–	–
This page is **not** comprehensive	–	–	–	–	–	–	–
This page offers everything you need to know on the topic	–	–	–	–	–	–	–
Goodwill							
This page has my interests at heart	–	–	–	–	–	–	–
This page is uncaring about its visitors	–	–	–	–	–	–	–
This page is **not** concerned about its visitors	–	–	–	–	–	–	–
Trust/Expertise							
This page appears to have experts on the topic discussed	–	–	–	–	–	–	–
This page is ethical	–	–	–	–	–	–	–
This page appears to be a leader in its area of specialty	–	–	–	–	–	–	–
This page is **not** trustworthy	–	–	–	–	–	–	–

Digital Television as Persuasive Technology

Duane Varan and Steve Bellman

Interactive Television Research Institute
Murdoch University
Murdoch, Western Australia 6150
varan@itri.tv, bellman@itri.tv

Abstract. The advent of digital television technologies will rapidly expand viewer interaction with computer-mediated television. This paper reports on research demonstrating how new computer-mediated TV advertising models, including iTV microsites and telescopic ads, are superior to their linear counterparts. The authors argue that, in part, such superiority may result from the degree to which interactivity heightens mental engagement (facilitating a shift from peripheral to central message processing) and empowers viewer choice, thereby positively predisposing viewers to the persuasive content they encounter. The authors warn of potential negative fallout, however, where viewer expectations are not met. Although there might be potential 'distraction' effects associated with processing both video and interactive layered content, testing among college students demonstrated no adverse effects associated with such concurrent message processing. The opportunities associated with further research in this new arena of captology are explored.

1 Introduction

A wide confluence of factors including both channel and platform multiplication, audience fragmentation and the evolution of new audience metrics are ushering in a period of significant market disruption for the television industry. The advent of digital technologies, including digital video recorders (DVRs), internet protocol television (IPTV), interactive television (iTV), portable video (across iPods, mobile phones and a range of other portable devices), video-on-demand (VOD), high definition (HD) and digital television (DTV) are rapidly accelerating the industry's changing dynamic. As countries around the world increasingly mandate analog shut-off dates, facilitating a switch-over to digital television (for the US this date is set for 2009), public access to such digital platforms will expand dramatically. Although many dimensions of these new digital platforms capitalize on the traditional strengths of linear TV, the ability of such systems to facilitate user interaction and choice positions television's new frontier as perhaps another unique front among evolving persuasive technologies.

This paper draws on research supervised by the authors to explore how framing television's new frontier as a 'persuasive technology' may help better visualize new opportunities associated with the medium. The authors are currently engaged in a large research project exploring this theme further which has, as its sponsors, many of

Y. de Kort et al. (Eds.): PERSUASIVE 2007, LNCS 4744, pp. 243–252, 2007.

the world's leading advertising brands and media networks including the ABC, Coca-Cola, Comcast, DirecTV, ESPN, General Motors, Kelloggs, Kraft, McDonalds, Masterfoods/Mars, Microsoft, NBC, Nike, Procter & Gamble, Turner Broadcasting, TV Guide, Verizon, Visa, and Warner Bros. among others. Although the findings associated with this research are currently bound by non-disclosure obligations (part of an 18-month embargo), it is still possible to explore some of the research by drawing on post-graduate student research and other research conducted by the authors which is currently past the industry embargo period. This paper provides an overview of some of this research to date and concludes with an exploration as to how television's new frontier might be positioned as a unique persuasive technology. Just as captology can explore how computing affords advantages over human communication persuasion, so too can it explore how digital interactive television platforms facilitate advantages over traditional linear television persuasion.

2 New Persuasive TV Models

Although the advent of new digital technologies has generated considerable fear among those associated with the television industry, leading some to predict the demise of the 30 second commercial altogether [1], others have turned their attention to exploring new advertising models enabled by television's new digital character. The ID!As forum, facilitated by the Digital Media & Advertising Strategy Group (DiMAS), and Carat's Media Exchange both provide examples of collective industry initiatives designed to cultivate such models. DiMAS' Ad Lab has taken this further by bringing together advertisers, content providers and technology enablers to produce interactive simulations of many of these new ad models. Increasingly, moreover, digital platforms worldwide are deploying new advertising models capitalizing on the interactive characteristics of such digital platforms.

In the UK, for example, the Sky digital satellite platform has pioneered interactive TV ad models (iTV microsites) enabling viewers to press a red button on their remote control during a 30 second commercial to access additional advertising content, including sample requests, product information, interactive branded games and more. For the most part, such systems facilitate viewer interaction using either data carousels (which continually circulate the enhanced data layer) or hidden virtual channels (which viewers are switched to when they interact with the iTV application). More recently, Tivo introduced 'telescopic' advertising models whereby additional video content is pre-loaded into viewers digital recorders so as to be accessed (similar to a virtual channel) later (during ad breaks, for example) on demand. By late 2006, most US cable and satellite platforms, including Comcast, Cox, DirecTV, the Dish Network and Time Warner, had introduced a range of such new interactive TV ad models.

Unfortunately, however, research associated with these new interactive ad models remains largely proprietary and industry-based. Although several case studies of successful iTV applications have been published (e.g. [2], [3], [4]), few have compared the effectiveness of these applications against controls (i.e. linear TV). Where such control has been attempted, the environment has been unrealistic, relying on computer screens in a desk-top environment rather than TV in a living room context [5], or in-home studies using 'two screens' (people interacting with their computer while watching TV rather than on interactive layers superimposed over the TV) designed to emulate iTV [6], [7].

To test the effectiveness of such new ad models, vis-à-vis traditional linear TV, we have conducted a series of experiments accommodating human subjects in mock-living rooms where they view our television treatments in an environment designed to more closely emulate the in-home experience. In this environment, we have tested a range of new ad models drawing on the key features of those iTV models most commonly deployed thus far. Our research has consistently found such models to be superior to their linear counterparts.

For example, in a study exploring interactive microsites (as pioneered by Sky in the UK) whereby viewers have the opportunity to access additional ad content on TV in the form of web-like pages, Bellman, Pribudi and Varan [8] found that ad recall associated with interaction with a single iTV ad was not only greater than a single linear ad exposure, but was on par with three repeat linear exposures – long considered the industry convention for minimum exposure [9]. Likewise, a study we conducted [10] exploring the effects associated with telescopic ads (additional video long-form advertising accessed on-demand during a 30-second ad) found that not only were such telescopic ads superior to their traditional 30-second counterpart in terms of attitudes towards the ad, brand and purchase intention (even controlling for self-selection effects), but they were also superior to the long-form ads themselves. In other words, the telescopic ads deliver superior effects that cannot be explained on the basis of the additional content exposure alone.

Accordingly, there is a need to explore the superior effects associated with television's new digital frontier to better understand not only *whether* they are more effective (as asserted here), but more importantly, if so… *why*? Here, perhaps, a new strand of the captology discourse may lend insight.

3 Cognitive Engagement

Mental engagement with program content is often a central objective associated with television viewing. Those who produce programs and those who advertise make implicit assumptions regarding the extent to which viewers 'attend' to their television content. With television viewing becoming part of an increasingly diverse and complex media landscape, TV viewing is progressively becoming more polychronic, with viewers engaged in concurrent tasks while they watch, including internet surfing, reading and talking. Given this context, does interactivity improve mental engagement with program and advertising content?

One might assume that a central characteristic of interactivity is that, by its very nature, it increases viewer engagement. Every time a viewer presses a button on a remote control, she is engaging with the content in an active mental state. One potential benefit associated with iTV, therefore, is a capacity to increase viewer involvement as a result of the interaction facilitated between viewers and their remote controls.

To test this proposition, Yeo [11] developed interactive TV ads for both high involvement (Acer Computers) and low involvement (Oreo cookies) products. Subjects were divided into two cells: a control cell which saw linear non-interactive executions of the two ads and a treatment cell exposed to the two interactive ads. The interactivity in the ads was identical in style to that dominant in the UK at the time; that is, a viewer pressed a red button on their remote control during the ad in response to a call-to-action banner, which then took the viewer to a television microsite (walled garden) with web-style content associated with the product. The Acer ad provided product information whereas the Oreo ad allowed viewers to create the Oreo cookie best suited to their taste.

The central focus of the research was on *cognitive elaboration*; the degree to which viewers think about the ads and relate them to their lives. Greenwald and Leavitt [12] maintain that such elaboration constitutes the highest of four levels of ad message involvement (preattention, focal attention, comprehension and elaboration). Such elaboration is measured by having subjects list all thoughts related to the content of the ad and having researchers independently code such thoughts for the type (central vs. peripheral) and intent (positive, negative, curiosity and neutral) of thoughts as well as for the presence of elaborations [13].

For both the high and low involvement ads, the impact was dramatic. Interactivity had resulted in a significant increase in cognitive elaboration ($p < .0001$) – in fact, such elaboration had almost doubled! There was also strong evidence of a shift from peripheral to central message processing. There was clear support, therefore, for the assumption that iTV increases the degree to which those interacting engage with the content.

Surprisingly, however, such elaboration did not necessarily translate into higher ad impact. Although there was a higher degree of elaboration as a result of interacting, the advertising effects differed between the two ads. With the Oreo interactive ad, the increased elaboration did translate into a significant increase in the favorability of attitudes towards the ad, brand and purchase intentions. But in the Acer ad, there was no significant impact. We have observed similar trends in data associated with campaigns deployed over interactive television platforms: in some cases, the results are spectacular – in others quite disappointing. Indeed, interactivity appears to amplify media effects. How can this be explained?

The qualitative component (unreported) of this research suggested that in the case of the Oreo ad, viewers got more than they expected. They went into the interactive microsite with low expectations and were pleasantly surprised. This translated into a new-found passion for the brand. In the case of the Acer interactive ad, however, viewers went in expecting detailed information about the product range, only to be disappointed by the limited range of information available. Viewer expectation, therefore, may potentially be a key moderator of the interactive television viewing experience.

Beyond the issues associated with such expectation delivery, however, the increase in elaboration itself may partially explain the effect. Studies in psychology have long demonstrated that merely thinking about a subject polarizes attitudes [14]. Other studies have also demonstrated that strong elaboration can result in counter-arguing, making viewers increasingly critical of the content they are exposed to [15]. Although our study was largely exploratory in nature, it suggests that iTV content will tend to polarise audience satisfaction – raising the stakes, so to speak, as a result of its higher viewer engagement. Interactive TV content, therefore, potentially delivers greater impact as a result of heightened engagement, but this also comes with a high degree of risk, delivering strong returns when resonates content effectively with viewer expectations, but potentially damaging the viewing experience when these expectations are violated.

As a result of these findings, we propose that the shift from peripheral to central message processing could well be a characteristic associated with the sensory dimension of computer-mediated television [16]. Our research suggests that, when compared to linear TV, interactive TV amplifies and polarizes existing attitudes. This makes it all the more important to engage in audience research in advance of content deployment as there is higher potential fallout associated with failure to meet consumer expectations. It also demonstrates, however, how such platforms afford potentially superior environments for persuasive content where viewer expectations are either met or, ideally, surpassed.

4 The Power of Choice

Our cognitive engagement study left us questioning the expectations with which viewers initially encounter iTV ad content and led us to speculate that the element of viewer choice might positively predispose viewers to the content they encountered. Although such choice created a potentially positive bias initially, we assumed, there appeared to be dire consequences where expectations were violated given the viewer's greater investment of self (potential ego-effects).

Specifically, we assumed that choice potentially generates dissonance. As a result of such dissonance, a range of dissonance-reduction behaviors might then influence attitude formation. In turn, dissonance-induced subjects may seek to internally justify their decisions. Accordingly, we hypothesized that viewers experiencing dissonance would more actively search for cues to reinforce that their decision was right. This, we believed, would increase with higher levels of dissonance reflecting a higher need, on the part of the viewer, to justify (internally) that their decision was correct.

To test this possibility, Tanjic [17] conducted an experiment manipulating levels of cognitive dissonance associated with viewing choice. Viewers were randomly allocated into three cells: a control cell with no interactive content; a treatment cell experiencing 'low-level' dissonance; and a treatment cell experiencing 'high-level' dissonance. The two treatment cells were exposed to a television program with a novel twist whereby for the last ad in the ad break, the viewer was presented with an on-screen choice between three different product categories. In other words, viewers were forced to choose the ad they wanted to see. In some cases, this choice was easy (low-level dissonance) because the choice involved a compelling category paired against two non-compelling product categories. For others, however, the choice was made more difficult (high-level dissonance) because all three product categories had equal appeal. In this way, the study could triangulate between the effects of both interactive versus non-interactive advertising and high versus low-level dissonance. It is important to note that Tanjic's experiment, like most other such studies [e.g., 18], did not control for the presence of such dissonance at an individual level. Rather, she pre-tested ads for their levels of appeal and involvement and used these measures for the manipulation of dissonance. Accordingly, a range of theoretical constructs might also account for the study results. Nonetheless the study helped us to explore the broader issue of the potential effects associated with viewer choice.

Interestingly, there was no difference between the non-interactive (control) and low-level dissonance conditions. However, the high-level dissonance treatment resulted in a significant increase in attitude towards the ad, brand and purchase intention (all measures comparing high-level dissonance with either low-level dissonance or no choice relative to these indices had p values less than .01), validating the assumptions upon which the study was based. In other words, the interactive TV platform facilitated a positive bias to the ad content for viewers experiencing high levels of dissonance. Interactive TV, under these circumstances, was demonstrated to deliver a more positive ad viewing environment – an important consideration for advertisers given the largely defensive nature of TV ad viewing.

This might suggest that another dimension associated with understanding how linear and interactive TV platforms differ might focus on the potentially positive characteristics of meaningful choice, which may positively bias viewers to the persuasive messages they then encounter. Clearly, the dimensions associated with choice transcend those explored here. Hopefully, however, the study helps highlight the need to better understand how computer-mediated television may differ from its linear counterpart, suggesting a need for further research in this area.

5 Distraction

It is important, however, that our exploration of television's new frontier not limit itself to potential positive effects alone. In many ways, such interactive platforms may be inferior to their linear counterparts. One potential area where such inferiority may be apparent is in potential distraction effects associated with competing cognitive load as viewers attempt to process both linear video content and interactive enhancements.

As noted earlier, however, viewers are increasingly engaged in a wide range of concurrent tasks while viewing traditional television. Recent research at Ball State University has highlighted the degree to which viewers are talking on the phone, surfing the internet, reading magazines, talking with others and engaging in a wide range of other tasks as they watch television [19]. The additional layers of interaction embedded in new television program content, however, may further introduce distraction effects resulting in lower, rather than higher persuasive effects.

A number of our studies to date have attempted to isolate the potential effects associated with divided cognitive load so as to better understand audience message processing. While this is often a key issue, potentially challenging viewer engagement, younger audiences appear to have a high propensity to process multiple sources. In one study, conducted by Bollig [20], we tested an ad model deployed by MTV in the UK whereby game content ('pong') was superimposed over an entire ad pod to encourage viewers to stay on the channel during the ad break. We manipulated speed of play and ad message content to test for potential 'distraction' effects across diverse viewing contexts.

Although the MTV 'game over ad break' model was successful in the UK in reducing channel zapping when it deployed in 2002, it was ultimately taken off air due to advertiser concern with potential loss of ad impact due to divided ad message processing. Instead, it was transformed so as to be superimposed over program content (pausing the game during ad breaks). Surprisingly, questions associated with ad impact in the 2002 version (game over ad break) were never tested empirically by either the advertisers or MTV. The new model was always treated as a trade-off: lower ad avoidance (by holding the viewer over the ad break) but at the cost of potentially lower ad impact (resulting from the distraction of the game). This assumption of reduced message processing capacity is consistent with one school of thought regarding distraction and ad impact (beginning with Haaland & Venkatesan [21]).

An alternative perspective, first explored by Festinger & Macoby [22], however, maintains that people's capacity to counter-argue is diminished through distraction effects, lowering their defenses to persuasive message content (thus maximizing impact). Under this assumption, certain ads appearing during the MTV game over ad model should have been more, rather than less, persuasive. Zimbardo, et al [23] tested a proposition remarkably similar to the MTV game over ad model years before interactive TV systems enabled the deployment of such a model. In their study, the Zimbardo research team provided subjects with a number summation task during ad breaks. Consistent with Festinger & Macoby, they found that persuasive impact was enhanced by this distracting task. Clearly, if the superiority of such models work due to this assumption, there might be a need for codes of practice or government regulation to curtail potentially adverse and/or unethical persuasive communication that relies on such cognitive overload for its effects.

To our surprise, our study found that despite the target population (college students) engaging with the game content enthusiastically, their capacity to process the 'background' ad was not distracted, resulting in ad impact statistically on par with control measures of traditional 30-second ads. This was not moderated by either speed of play or counter-arguing. In other words, there was neither evidence of a negative capacity to process ad-message content, nor was there support for superior effects due to diminished counter-arguing. This suggests that advertiser concern regarding the potential detrimental impact associated with ad message processing may have been unfounded. Far from representing a trade off, the model may have produced higher ad pod exposure without coming at the cost younger audiences, in particular, have a strong capacity to multi-task when consuming television content. It is important to note that as the study was conducted using university students only, the capacity of older audiences to attend to such parallel content remains untested.

Hence, although interactive of reduced impact. We believe this highlights the extent to which television technologies may present viewers with increasing demands for their cognitive load, our evidence suggests that viewers (at least young viewers) are able to manage this increased load effectively.

6 Key Directions for Future Research

The television industry is in the midst of a dramatic period of market change. Its transition to a digital future suggests that computer-mediated persuasion will become a growing area of research. Tragically, despite the rapid deployment of new ad models capitalizing on the new technology, academic research on the subject remains sparse. With few exceptions, the academic sector has largely failed to engage with television's shifting landscape. Academic publications seem to either be framed within a viewing context that seems more characteristic of the 80s than television's new frontiers or result in research which reduces the future to the internet alone, failing to appreciate the complex manner in which people are weaving digital technologies into their regular media diet.

Clearly, captology has much to contribute to the evolving discourse. This paper has summarized the results from our earlier research demonstrating that such models are superior to their linear TV counterparts. The more important question, however, is *why* are such interactive TV models superior? What theoretical frameworks best explain such superior effects? How might we explore the new television's capacity to persuade, whether as tool, medium or social actor?

Here, we hope to contribute to this dialog by suggesting potential moderating effects associated with heightened mental engagement (with interactivity facilitating a shift from peripheral to central message processing) and potential positive biases associated with choice. We have also found that despite fears that viewers are unable to process both video and interactive content, the evidence suggests that at least young viewers are able to concurrently process such content.

We hope that our research, though specific to television's evolving landscape, might also contribute to the wider captology discourse, highlighting new directions to further explore how computer-mediated communication facilitates new persuasive opportunities. One might assume that heightened cognitive engagement and positive choice bias might be inherent characteristics associated with computer-mediated communication. Research designed to explore such questions across other digital environments might help shed further light on this possibility.

For researchers, this is an exciting time. As the television industry grapples to define its new business, we have a unique opportunity to influence the evolution of ad models which may shape the contours of the industry for years to come. Certainly, one would hope that such engagement by the academic fraternity might results in business models which are more ethical in character and which respond better to the needs of viewers.

References

1. Jaffee, J.: Life After the 30-Second Spot: Energize Your Brand with a Bold Mix of Alternatives to Traditional Advertising. John Wiley and Sons, New Jersey (2005)
2. Leena, E.: Digital Television for All: User Preferences and Designers' Views on What Would Suit the User. In: Carbonell, N., Stephanidis, C. (eds.) Universal Access. Theoretical Perspectives, Practice, and Experience. LNCS, vol. 2615, Springer, Heidelberg (2003)

3. Nicholas, D., Huntington, P., Williams, P., Gunter, B.: Perceptions of the Authority of Health Information. Case Study: Digital Interactive Television and the Internet. Health Information and Libraries Journal 20(4), 215–224 (2003)
4. Harvey, B.: Better Television Audience Measurement through the Research Integration of Set-Top Box Data. Phase Two. In: WAM - Worldwide Audience Measurement 2004 - Television, Conference Proceedings. Amsterdam/New York: ESOMAR/ARF (2004)
5. Bezjian-Avery, A., Calder, B., Iacobucci, D.: New Media Interactive Advertising vs. Traditional Advertising. Journal of Advertising Research 38, 23–32 (1998)
6. Ekman, Inger, Lankoski, P.: Integrating a Game With a Story-Lessons From Interactive Television Concept Design. Computers & Graphics 28, 167–177 (2004)
7. Ernst, David, Mueller-Lust, R.: The Beauty of Enhanced TV: How Interactive TV Creates Audience Involvement in the Miss America Pageant. In: WAM - Worldwide Audience Measurement 2004 - Television, Conference Proceedings. Amsterdam/New York: ESOMAR/ARF (2004)
8. Bellman, S., Pribudi, G., Varan, D.: The Impact of Adding Interactivity to Television Advertising on Elaboration, Recall and Persuasion. In: Proceedings of the 2004 Annual Conference of the Australian and New Zealand Marketing Academy, Wellington (November 30, 2004)
9. Krugman, Herbert, E.: Why Three Exposures May Be Enough. Journal of Advertising Research 12, 11–14 (1972)
10. Reading, N., Bellman, S., Varan, D., Winzar, H.: Effectiveness of Telescopic Ads Delivered via Personal Video Recorders. Journal of Advertising Research 46(2), 217–227 (2006)
11. Yeo, F.: Persuasion through Interaction: An Exploration into the Effects of Interactive Television Advertising on Consumer Persuasion. Unpublished honours thesis: Murdoch University (2001)
12. Greenwald, A.G., Leavitt, C.: Audience Involvement in Advertising: Four levels. Journal of Consumer Research 11(1), 581–592 (1984)
13. Buchholz, L.M., Smith, E.R.: The Role of Consumer Involvement in Determining Cognitive Response to Broadcasting Advertising. Journal of Advertising 20(1), 4–17 (1991)
14. Tesser, A.: Self-Generated Attitude Change. In: Berkowitz, L. (ed.) Advances in Experimental Social Psychology, vol. 11, pp. 289–338. Academic Press, San Diego, CA (1978)
15. Burnkrant, R.E., Unnava, H.R.: Effects of Self-Referencing on Persuasion. Journal of Consumer Research 22(1), 17 (1995)
16. Fogg, B.J.: Persuasive Technology: Using Computers to Change What We Think and Do. Morgan Kaufmann Publishers, Amsterdam (2003)
17. Tanjic, S.: Viewer Choice and the Mediation of the Advertising Experience. Unpublished honours thesis: Murdoch University (2001)
18. Harmon-Jones, E.: Cognitive Dissonance and Experienced Negative Affect: Evidence that Dissonance Increased Experienced Negative Affect Even in the Absence of Aversive Consequences. Personality and Social Psychology Bulletin 26, 1490–1501 (2000)
19. Spaeth, J.: Mind the Measurement Gap: Measured and Unm-s-r-d Media Occasions. In: Proceedings of the 1st Annual ARF Audience Research Symposium, Advertising Research Foundation, New York (2006)
20. Bollig, A.: The Persuasive Effects of iTV Games: An Exploration into the Effects of Interactive Television Games on Television Advertising. Unpublished honours thesis: Murdoch University (2004)

21. Haaland, G.A., Venkatesan, M.: Resistance to Persuasive Communications: An Examination of the Distraction Hypothesis. Journal of Personality and Social Psychology 9(2), 167–170 (1968)
22. Festinger, L., Maccoby, M.: On Resistance to Persuasive Communications. Journal of Abnormal and Social Psychology 68(4), 359–366 (1964)
23. Zimbardo, P.M., Synder, M., Thomas, M., Gold, A.: Modifying the Impact of Persuasive Communications with External Distraction. Journal of Personality and Social Psychology 16(4), 669–680 (1970)

The Use of Mobile Phones to Support Children's Literacy Learning

Glenda Revelle, Emily Reardon, Makeda Mays Green,
Jeanette Betancourt, and Jennifer Kotler

Sesame Workshop
One Lincoln Plaza
New York, NY 10023
(glenda.revelle@sesameworkshop.org)

Abstract. The goal of this study was to develop a mobile-phone based intervention that would encourage parents to engage their children in daily literacy-learning activities. The intervention content included text messages for parents, audio messages for parents and children, and Sesame Street letter videos for children. Messaging to parents suggested real-world activities that they could use to engage their children in learning letters. Pre- and post-interviews indicated a significant increase in the frequency with which parents reported engaging their children in literacy activities after participating in this study. In addition, 75% of lower-income participants and 50% of middle-income participants reported that they believed watching the Sesame Street letter videos helped their children learn letters. More than 75% of participants reported believing that a mobile phone used in this way can be an effective learning tool, since mobile-phone delivery made it extremely easy to incorporate literacy activities into their daily routines.

Keywords: Mobile, Phone, Education, Learning, Literacy, Parents, Children, Sesame Street, Video, Audio, Text.

1 Introduction

This paper reports the design and implementation of an intervention using Sesame Street content intended to encourage parents to engage their preschool children in literacy learning. Research has consistently shown that children who do not already have an adequate start in literacy development by the time they reach school rarely learn to read on schedule [1], and continue to have difficulty throughout elementary school, as almost 90 percent of children identified as poor readers at the end of first grade are still identified as poor readers at the end of fourth grade [2]. Thus, early intervention during the preschool years is critical for children who are at risk with regard to learning to read.

Research has also shown that children from lower income families are at significantly greater risk with regard to reading than children from middle or higher income families [3]. Neuman & Celano [4] compared access to print in low-income neighborhoods and

Y. de Kort et al. (Eds.): PERSUASIVE 2007, LNCS 4744, pp. 253–258, 2007.

middle-income neighborhoods. They found strong inequities between the two communities in the likelihood that children would find books, see signs, labels, logos and encounter spaces that were conducive to reading. Furthermore, in low income families parents speak less to their children and use less complex sentences when contrasted with more affluent families [5].

While there are inequities in access to print and other language rich environments, there are fewer income inequities in access to media. Media can be excellent resources for teaching literacy because they have an eager audience. Children spend more time engaged with media than with any other leisure or academic activity and are media "multi-taskers" spending time with "new" (i.e. computers, internet, handheld devices) media while simultaneously using "old" (television, audio) media platforms [6]. Low-income and minority children spend an even greater amount of time with media (specifically television) than their middle-class, non-minority counterparts [6,7].

Educational media & technology have been found to promote literacy learning in both formal (e.g. school) and informal (i.e. home) environments when effective teaching techniques (e.g. phonemic awareness, phonics, fluency, vocabulary, and text comprehension) are applied [8,9,10]. Sesame Street content in particular has been shown to increase children's literacy skills on a variety of measures including phonemic awareness, knowledge of the alphabet and reading conventions, and motivation to read and write [11,12,13,14].

The intervention reported here was designed to deliver Sesame Street educational materials focused on learning letters via mobile phone to parents and preschool children from lower and middle income families. This intervention applied the elements of Fogg's "functional triad" model [15] of persuasive technologies in the context of using mobile phones to encourage and persuade parents to engage their young children in activities that are known to lead to growth in literacy skills. The functional triad framework suggests that people view or respond to persuasive technologies in three ways: as a tool that increases capabilities, as a social actor that creates relationships, and as a medium that provides experience. As a tool, the portability of the mobile phones made it easy for parents to access the target content anywhere and any time throughout the day. Text messages and subsequent audio messages led participants through a process, and videos served as motivating factors that helped children to learn letters. As a social actor, provision of messages from Sesame Street's Maria and Elmo modeled a target attitude by expressing an excitement about literacy. Moreover, Maria's messages provided social support via suggestions of real-world activities for parents to engage in with their children, and both Maria's and Elmo's messages established relationships with the participants through consistent contact and social delivery of information. As a medium, the audio and video messages sent to participants not only delivered information, but also served as a motivator for engaging in target behaviors. Collectively, these functions suggest the tremendous potential of the functional triad for mobile applications designed for parents and children.

2 Participants

Participants in this study were eighty parents/caregivers and their three to four-year-old children who lived in Los Angeles, Oakland or Fresno, CA. Approximately half of of the families were living at or below the poverty line and half were living above the poverty line.

Participants were given a video-capable phone and service upgrade. They committed to engaging in literacy activities with their children 3-4 times per week for 8 weeks. All parents participated in a training session before the 8-week intervention began, which included a review of what they should expect during the study, on overview highlighting the role of the parent as a child's first and most important teacher, and a review of how to use the phone for the study.

3 The Intervention

The intervention consisted of text messages, audio messages for parents, audio messages for children, and video for children. Text messages were sent to participants' mobile phones on Mondays, Wednesdays, Fridays and Saturdays at 7 a.m. for the eight-week duration of the study, prompting parents to access audio messages and videos for one letter per day. Audio messages and letter videos were made available in alphabetical order, with four letters introduced in each of the first two weeks and three letters per week thereafter, so that participants would have access to all 26 letters of the alphabet within the eight-week duration of the study.

Each day that a text message was sent, the parent was first prompted to access an audio message from Sesame Street's Maria regarding the letter of the day, suggesting real-world literacy activities for parent and child to do together as they went about their daily routines. For example, Maria might suggest that while the parent and child were in the supermarket they look for fruits and vegetables that begin with the letter C, and that the parent point out the name of the item in text on signs in the store.

Next, the parent was prompted to click on an "Elmo link" for that day's letter and hand the phone to the child. Clicking on the Elmo link initiated an audio message for the child from Sesame Street's Elmo. Elmo talked to the child about the letter of the day and some words beginning with the letter, and then introduced a video clip from Sesame Street related to that letter (for example, the video "C is for Cookie" was shown when the letter of the day was C).

If participants accessed the system three to four times per week with their children (which almost all of them did), then by the end of the eight-week study period parents received 26 literacy activity suggestions from Maria, one for each letter of the alphabet, and children saw a Sesame Street video clip for each letter of the alphabet. In addition, after the Sesame Street video clips for each week were introduced they remained available in a "letter library" that was available for the remainder of the study period so that children could re-access them at any time.

4 Results and Discussion

Preliminary analysis of usage data, tracking exactly what time of day each access to parent messages and child videos occurred, indicates that both parent materials and child-directed materials were more likely to be accessed during the week than on week-ends. The biggest usage "spike" for both parents and children on weekdays was within the first hour after the text messages were sent (at 7 am local time for the participants), and usage continued to remain fairly high until 10 am. Usage then declined through the middle of the day, and rose again between 5 pm and 9 pm. Weekend usage in general was lower than weekday usage, with the morning spike in children's usage lasting a little later, from about 7 am until noon. In general, participants accessed materials that were released near the beginning of the eight-week study more frequently than those released toward the end of the study, and also (each week of the study) accessed materials released earlier in the week more than those released later in the week. Over the full course of the eight-weeks, parent literacy tips were accessed far less frequently than the Sesame Street videos were accessed.

Evaluative research on this project was conducted by WestEd, in collaboration with Sesame Workshop and PBS, and has been reported separately [16]. Highlights from that report include:

- Participants in both income groups were more likely to initiate real-world *letter recognition* activities with their children after participating in this study, and lower-income participants were more likely to initiate real-world *letter sound* activities as well.
- Almost all participants reported that their children found the mobile phone controls easy to use and could play or replay videos on their own without parental assistance
- 75% of lower-income parents and 50% of middle-income parents reported that the alphabet video clips helped their children learn letters.
- Interestingly, parents reported that their children's knowledge of the Alphabet Song increased during this study. Since the song was not included in the intervention content, parents attributed this change to their children's increased general letter knowledge.
- More than 75% of participants in both income groups believed *to a good extent* or *to a great extent* that a mobile phone used in this way can be an effective learning tool.

In summary, this study demonstrates that if multimedia literacy content is delivered to parents via mobile phone, they will access it and both parents and children will use it. By parents' report, using such materials influenced their own behaviors (prompting them to engage their children in more activities designed to increase their literacy skills) and influenced their children's awareness of and knowledge regarding letters. Parents in this study reported that they wanted to be involved in their children's early literacy development, and viewed the mobile delivery model as an effective way to support their efforts and their children's development.

These findings indicate that this mobile technology-based literacy intervention served as a highly effective use of persuasive technology. Participants reported enormous enthusiasm about the accessibility of the mobile device and content, which enabled them to access the information while at home, in the car, waiting in line or in another location. Moreover, parents in this study indicated that the ready access provided by mobile delivery made it extremely easy for them to fit literacy activities into their normal daily routines with their children. The technology-based persuasive messages inspired participants to engage in behaviors that would lead to increased literacy skills in their children. Given the extremely busy lives of today's families, mobile delivery of educational media shows enormous promise for encouraging increased parental involvement in their children's learning.

Encompassing all of the elements of Fogg's functional triad, the success of this intervention demonstrates an application of technology that is functional, usable and persuasive. The mobile-phone based experience increased participants' capabilities, provided engaging and meaningful experiences, and created social relationships with the Sesame Street characters that enabled both enjoyment and learning. Parents who participated in this study noted that the most important aspect of Maria's literacy tips was the way in which they served as reminders to make their children's early literacy development a priority [16, p. 55]. Such reports speak to the value of the mobile phone as an effective learning tool as well as to the persuasiveness of content delivered via this technology. Although more work is needed to develop programs that will deliver such content to the low income families who need it most at a price they can afford, the current study serves as a starting point indicating much promise in the possibility of utilizing mobile phones to persuade parents of the benefits of engaging their young children in literacy activities and to motivate children to want to learn.

Acknowledgments. This work was funded by the U. S. Department of Education through the PBS Ready To Learn program. The opinions and interpretations expressed herein are the views of the authors and do not necessarily reflect the official position of the funding agencies. The authors would like to thank our colleagues at PBS, GoTV Networks, Orange You Glad, Sprint and WestEd for their collaboration as partners on this project.

References

1. Snow, C.E., Burns, M.S., Griffin, P. (eds.): Preventing reading difficulties in young children. National Academy Press, Washington, D.C (1998)
2. Francis, D., Shaywitz, S., Stuebing, K., Shaywitz, B., Fletcher, J.: Developmental lag versus deficit models of reading disability: A longitudinal, individual growth curves analysis. Journal of Educational Psychology 88, 3–17 (1996)
3. Institute of Education Sciences, National Center for Education Statistics, US Department of Education: National Assessment of Educational Progress (NAEP) (2005)
4. Neuman, S., Celano, D.D.: Access to print in low-income and middle-income communities. Reading Research Quarterly 36, 8–26 (2001)
5. Hart, B., Risley, T.: Meaningful differences in the everyday experience of young American children. Paul H. Brookes, Baltimore, MD (1995)
6. Kaiser Family Foundation: Generation M: Media in the lives of 8-18 year olds. Menlo Park, CA (2005)

7. Bickham, D., Vandewater, E., Huston, A., Lee, J., Caplovitz, A., Wright, J.: Predictors of Children's Media Use: An Examination of three ethnic groups. Media Psychology 5, 107–137 (2003)
8. Mitchell, M., Fox, B.: The effects of computer software for developing phonological awareness in low-progress readers. Reading Research and Instruction 40, 315–332 (2001)
9. Waxman, H., Lin, M., Michko, G.: A meta-analysis of the effectiveness of teaching and learning with technology on student outcomes. Northwest Central Regional Educational Laboratory (2003)
10. Linebarger, D., Kosanic, A., Greenwood, C., Doku, N.: Effects of viewing the television program "Between the Lions" on the emergent literacy skills of young children. Journal of Educational Psychology 96, 297–308 (2004)
11. Wright, J., Huston, A., Scantlin, R., Kotler, J.: The early window project: Sesame Street prepares children for school. In: Fisch, S., Truglio, R. (eds.) "G" is for "Growing"; Thirty years of research on Sesame Street, pp. 97–114. Lawrence Erlbaum Associates, Mahwah, NJ (2001)
12. Ball, S., Bogatz, G.: The first year of Sesame Street: An evaluation. Educational Testing Service, Princeton, NJ (1970)
13. Fisch, S.: Children's learning from educational television: Sesame Street and beyond. Lawrence Erlbaum Associates, Mahway, NJ (2004)
14. Rice, M., Huston, A., Truglio, R., Wright, J.: Words from Sesame Street: Learning vocabulary while viewing. Developmental Psychology 26, 421–428 (1990)
15. Fogg, B.J.: Persuasive Technology: Using Computers to Change What We Think and Do. Morgan Kauffman Publishers, San Francisco, CA (2003)
16. Horowitz, J., Sosenko, L., Hoffman, J., Ziobrowski, J., Tafoya, A., Haagenson, A., Hahn, S.: Evaluation of the PBS Ready to Learn Cell Phone Study: Learning Letters with Elmo. Final Report to the U. S. Department of Education (September 2006)

Toward a Systematic Understanding of Suggestion Tactics in Persuasive Technologies

Adrienne Andrew, Gaetano Borriello, and James Fogarty

Department of Computer Science and Engineering,
University of Washington, Seattle, WA USA
{aha,gaetano,jfogarty}@cs.washington.edu

Abstract. The unique capabilities of mobile, context-aware, networked devices make them an interesting platform for applying suggestion in persuasive technologies. Because these devices are nearly always with their owners, can sense relevant information about the context of their use, and nearly always have network access, they enable the principle of *kairos*, providing the right information at the best time. Relatively little work has examined providing opportunistic, right-time, right-place suggestions or notifications that encourage people to change their behavior. This paper first discusses some of the challenges facing designers incorporating suggestions into their persuasive technologies. We then review a set of relevant persuasive technologies, focusing primarily on technologies in the health domain. We then identify a design space that represents tactics for building persuasive technologies, particularly suggestion technologies. We then explore how this design space of suggestion tactics can be used to evaluate, compare, and inform the design of new persuasive technologies.

Keywords: Mobile information systems, persuasive technologies, behavior modification.

1 Introduction

One billion adults worldwide are overweight, and 300 million of these are clinically obese [9]. These numbers demonstrate a global epidemic—one whose victims suffer from heart disease, stroke, hypertension and diabetes. Many of these diseases are provoked or aggravated by lifestyle choices related to diet and exercise. It has also been argued that technology has played a role in allowing many adults to maintain a sedentary lifestyle. As researchers, we feel it is important to develop technologies that encourage a healthy lifestyle. Persuasive technologies can play an important role in encouraging healthy behaviors.

Fogg identifies seven strategies for persuasive technology tools: reduction, tunneling, tailoring, suggestion, self-monitoring, surveillance, and conditioning [3]. When we reviewed existing persuasive technologies related to encouraging a healthy lifestyle, we found that some of these strategies were incorporated more often than others. In particular, we believe that suggestion technologies, which provide an intervention at an opportune moment for maximum effectiveness, are relatively

Y. de Kort et al. (Eds.): PERSUASIVE 2007, LNCS 4744, pp. 259–270, 2007.
© Springer-Verlag Berlin Heidelberg 2007

under-explored in existing persuasive systems. Existing examples of suggestion tend to be peripheral, with the technology occasionally using suggestions but primarily employing a strategy like self-monitoring, reduction or tailoring.

We are drawn to better understand this relatively under-explored aspect of persuasive technology by the fact that mobile, context-aware, networked systems are increasingly enabling the principle of *kairos*, presenting the right message at a time when it can be most effective. Context-aware devices can detect an appropriate context in which to pursue a persuasive intervention, and increasing device capabilities provide increasingly flexible means of pursuing that intervention. In addition, research on the nature of interruptions and when interrupting notifications will best be heeded offer to improve the effectiveness of suggestion technologies [2]. Ideally, these technologies can be combined to create effective suggestion technologies that provide appropriate information at the right time, in the right way.

As noted by Fogg, it is important for the community surrounding persuasive technologies to examine both strategies and tactics. Fogg elaborated the various strategies, but there is a need to further refine the possible *tactics* – how the strategies are realized – that will be most effective. The number of potential tactics is infinite, and the tactics available will change over time as available technologies change. However, the choice of tactic to use for a particular product will be important to the success of the product, and we should certainly be able to start enumerating what challenges and benefits have been associated with different tactics.

In this paper, we first explore some of the challenges we believe researchers and designers face when applying suggestion in persuasive technologies. We then present an analysis of the design space for tactics to implement suggestion, specifically focusing on mobile, context-aware, networked systems. This analysis of the design space is based on an exploration of persuasive technologies in the domain of healthy living. We then examine suggestion-based interfaces in the context of this design space. As a tool for researchers and designers, our analysis provides a set of dimensions to consider when designing, comparing, and evaluating persuasive technologies. We can also use this understanding of the design space to identify potential approaches that may have been overlooked.

2   Related Work

Fogg [3] describes seven types of *persuasive technology tools,* each of which employs a different *strategy* (or *principle*) to change attitudes or behaviors. He discusses their underlying principles and provides examples of each. We are interested in further exploring what in this framework is referred to as a *suggestion technology*—tools that employ the suggestion strategy. Fogg mentions that a persuasive technology product usually incorporates multiple tools, each informed by a different strategy; we believe that many of these strategies overlap, and later we discuss how other strategies are closely related to suggestion strategies.

Khaled et al [4] have investigated the role that culture may play in the effectiveness of persuasive technologies. They note that the distinction between individualist and collectivist cultures are the most significant, and in their analysis, believe that most of the persuasive tools Fogg presents are more likely to be effective in an individualist culture. The United States is a primarily individualistic culture. The only type of persuasive tool that Khaled et al believe may be more effective in a collectivist culture is that of suggestion. The reason for this belief that the power of suggestion may be more effective in a collectivist culture is that collectivists are "already used to acting upon the suggestions of others, this may mean that they will be more willing to accept suggestions made by persuasive technologies, especially if the persuasive technologies are perceived as in-group members", while "individualists tend to look to their own values and priorities to help them decide upon courses of action to take." As we discuss later, this may contribute to the lack of focus on suggestion technologies in general.

Mazzota et al [5] are researching the role of emotion and logic in argumentation strategies for persuasive dialogues, specifically in the domain of eating well. Their preliminary research shows that the most persuasive dialogs employ positive rather than negative arguments, that it is very uncommon for people to employ a purely logical argumentation strategy, and that most arguments appealed to emotional rather than logical elements. In their evaluation, emotional dialogs employing positive arguments were most persuasive, and adapting the message to the recipient's characteristics was also found to be important.

Bickmore et al [1] have researched the role of emotional and relational skills in a tool to support a health behavior change intervention for physical activity adoption. Their tool incorporated anthropomorphic avatars, which enabled them to explore the use of both verbal and nonverbal behaviors in the interface. The experiment was a 30-day trial consisting of three groups of subjects, in "relational", "non-relational", and "control" groups. They found that there wasn't a significant difference between the amount of physical activity performed by subjects in the "relational" versus "non-relational" groups; however, the subjects interacting with the relational agent reported a significantly greater desire to continue working with the relational agent.

Finally, we describe persuasive technologies for improving personal health. These are technologies that we included in our analysis; as there is not enough room to enumerate and describe all of them, we will use a few examples throughout the paper.

Nawyn et al. [6] has incorporated some of these ideas into a system to help people become more aware of and modify a very specific behavior—television watching. ViTo is an enhanced remote control for a media center that tracks a person's television watching goals. Once the daily goal has been reached, ViTo notifies the watcher and suggests alternative activities to pursue. Thus, they suggest replacing an "undesirable behavior" (watching TV) with a "more desirable behavior" (reading, listening to music, etc), and thus breaking the habitual cycle.

MPTrain [7] is an augmented music system for runners that integrates a heart rate monitor with an MP3 player. The runner specifies their target heart rate for different intervals during the run. Sensors monitor the runner's heart rate and pace throughout the run. Towards the end of a song, the system determines if the runner's heart rate is faster or slower than they wanted to achieve, and chooses the next song to be one with an appropriate number of beats per minute—either a slower or faster tempo as appropriate.

Nike+iPod [8] uses an iPod that communicates wirelessly with a sensor in the runner's shoe to help the runner keep track of their current pace and distance. With this information, the runner can adjust his workout as appropriate. The runner can also play a predetermined playlist to help guide the pace of the workout. After the workout, the runner connects the iPod to his computer, where the last workout's information is aggregated with past workout data. The user can track goals, challenge friends, and see how one run compare with others.

3 Importance and Challenge of Suggestion Technologies

First, we review seven of the persuasion strategies described by Fogg [3], and summarize them in Table 1. A suggestion technology says the right thing at the right time to be most effective at changing one's behavior. If someone has a goal of walking more steps in a day, an appropriate time to remind someone of this goal is when they are standing waiting for the elevator, or perhaps when they are driving and can be reminded to park further away from their destination before they reach the destination. Sometimes, the appropriate suggestion is retrospective—if someone is reviewing their progress for a day, a suggestion might be to take more walking breaks rather than sitting at their desk.

We define a suggestion technology as one that incorporates active notifications that contain information that allows someone to do something they might not otherwise have done. We would not consider a simple pedometer to be a suggestion technology, since it passively provides information. If it beeped every so often to remind the wearer to walk more, then it could be considered a suggestion technology.

The potential use of suggestion technologies spans a wide range of applications. One can imagine a suggestion technology to support elder care, reminding forgetful seniors when to take medicine, encouraging daily fitness routines, and helping to keep in touch with friends and family. Another application is health and fitness, where context-aware suggestion technologies can help individuals "stuck" in their routine identify where they may change, *in situ*, by making suggestions at the moment when he can best act on it. In this way, the suggestion technology can help them reframe the way they see the world and incorporate new behavioral strategies into their lives. Personal finance, energy conservation, and driving are examples of domains that may benefit from an effective context-aware, mobile suggestion technology.

Table 1. Review of Persuasive Strategies

Persuasive Strategy	Short Description
Reduction	Making a complex task simpler
Tunneling	Guided persuasion; giving control over to an expert
Tailoring	Customization; providing more relevant information to individuals
Suggestion	Intervene at the right time with a compelling suggestion
Self-monitoring	Automatically tracking desired behavior
Surveillance	Observing one's behavior publicly
Conditioning	Reinforcing target behavior

Few persuasive technologies take advantage of suggestions as the primary strategy for persuading. There are a number of reasons for this—first, that context-aware mobile systems are fairly new, and the technology is still being explored and its limits are still being tested. An effective suggestion strategy using a context-aware mobile system will require the system to be robust and predictable. It is also possible that culture certainly plays a role in the limited incorporation of suggestions into persuasive technologies. As discussed in [4], users in cultures that focus on the progress of individuals over the progress of the community, as is the case in the United States, will be less likely to follow a given suggestion. Therefore researchers in the United States may have a bias against building suggestion technologies. Informal conversations with designers of persuasive technologies for health are consistent with these challenges.

3.1 Overlapping Persuasive Strategies

Fogg's strategies for persuasive technologies are fairly well-defined, but there exist overlaps between the strategies. Here, we discuss strategies similar to the suggestion strategy.

Tunneling versus suggestion. Tunneling can be viewed as being at the extreme end of the spectrum of possible suggestion technologies. Tools that employ a tunneling strategy attempt to initially remove the subject's autonomy around a certain behavior, and dictate what that person should do. One common example is a personal trainer, to whom the subject has decided to listen to—more or less unconditionally—in order to reach a fitness goal. Rather than being required to learn about different ways to attain her goal, she gives herself over to the trainer, and does what she's told. This is pure suggestion—being told what to do and when. It is possible that the only difference between tunneling and suggestion is that the subject has given up autonomy and committed to following the suggestions from someone else.

Self-monitoring versus suggestion. Self-monitoring tools make it easier for someone to monitor their behavior. A suggestion system is likely to be monitoring what a user is doing, and making suggestions based on those inferences. If a suggestion incorporates some measure of a targeted behavior in the message, such as "if you walk to your next destination you'll reach your step goal for today", that's helping the person monitor their behavior.

Reduction versus suggestion. Reduction tools simplify a specified task by taking away complexity or reducing barriers. When a suggestion tool enables decision making on-the-fly, it begins to look more like a reduction strategy. Collecting information and making it easier to visualize the elements of a decision reduces the cognitive load on the user. For example, rather than navigating to web sites to find current traffic conditions, the persuasive system can proactively collect relevant data and suggest the path to be taken automatically.

Overall, the use of suggestions in a persuasive technology appears to be an underutilized approach that may be very valuable. We want to explore this issue. In the next section, we will outline how we will go about doing so. Our goal is to develop a set of guidelines to realize suggestion-oriented tactics in persuasive systems and thereby help future designers to more easily construct robust and useful systems.

4 Dimensions of the Suggestion Tactic Design Space

As a step toward systematically understanding suggestion tactics, we have identified dimensions that define the design space. To do this, we chose some persuasive technologies, most with the goal of improving health behaviors. Although we are primarily interested in suggestion technologies, we ensured that we chose a balance of technologies that were specifically designed to incorporate a suggestion strategy, and others that did not. We reviewed these technologies, and identified a list of dimensions that differentiated them. We then performed a review of the persuasive technology literature to identify other dimensions that we deemed important, even if there was no evidence of differentiation among the technologies on these dimensions.

The dimensions that describe the design space loosely break out into two categories: technological and content. The technological category is the *how* or the medium of the system: how the context sensing is done and how a message or information is communicated to the person. The content category is the *what* of the system: what content is presented to the person, such as general versus specific feedback, incorporating affect into the message, and applying logical versus emotional appeals to the person. Table 2 shows an overview of the design space, and we discuss each dimension in more detail below.

Once we identified the list of dimensions that describe the design space of suggestion tactics, we identified the placement of each technology in that multi-dimensional space. We did this by defining a *tactic profile*, which simply describes each dimension value for a given technology and defines where the placement of the technology in the design space. We then analyzed the tactic profiles of each technology to find any consistencies, inconsistencies or patterns. We also explored some example designs, comparisons, and evaluations, some of which we discuss later.

4.1 Technological Dimensions

Display or feedback mechanism. The notification mechanism for a suggestion will be embedded in one of three locations. First, it can be *embedded* in the appliance or technology that is being used, such as ViTo, where the feedback is presented in the remote control. This has the property of being special to the device, and constrained to displaying information primarily about that appliance only. The other two locations are generic displays that can potentially provide information or notification from multiple sources. Second is a *personal device*, such as a cell phone, PDA, or watch with a display. Third is an *environmental display*, such as an interactive wall, or a large wall display. Additionally, some technologies include more than one display or feedback mechanism, such as another, more capable interface that allows more detailed information to be displayed. One example is the Nike+iPod. During a run, the iPod Nano provides only the most relevant information, such as pace, time run, and distance run. However, after the run, the data is aggregated and runners have access to a website that lets them track their workouts and goals over the past few weeks or months.

Notification modality. This dimension describes which sensory inputs are used to present the suggestion to the subject. For our analysis, we break this into *visual*, *audible*,

Table 2. Overview of selected technologies

Technological Dimensions	Subtleness			Display			Notification Modality — Visual			Notification Modality — Audible			Context Source			Time-liness		Interac-tivity	
	Subtle	Obvious	Requires Acknowledgement	Embedded	Personal	Environmental	Text	Graphical	Animated	Spoken Text	Auditory Alert/Sounds/music	Tactile	Environmental	Personal	Manual Input	Just-in-time	Retrospective	Interactive/Dialog	Passive
MPTrain		X			X						X			X		X			X
Nike+iPod		X			X		X	X		X	X			X		X	X		X
ViTo	X		X	X			X				X		X			X		X	

Content Dimensions	Speci-ficity		Affect			Adaptive Affect	Argumen-tation Strategy		Overt-ness		Explicit-ness		Social Components		Public	
	General	Specific	Neutral	Positive	Negative	Uses Adaptive Affect	Logical	Emotional	Overt	Vague	Informative	Provocative	Personal	Team	Anonymous	Non-anonymous
MPTrain	X		X	X			X	X	X		X		X			X
Nike+iPod	X	X					X		X		X	X	X	X		X
ViTo		X	X				X	X				X	X			

tangible/tactile; we then further specify the categories. The visual category is further distinguished by text, graphics, or animations, and the audible category consists of spoken words and tones or chimes.

Sensor or Context Source. This dimension describes how the subject's relevant context is detected. We identified three context sources: *environmental, personal,* or *manual input.* These values are not exclusive and may be combined in one technology. Environmental sensor or context detection is embedded in the environment, including appliances. They are able to detect things like "someone turned on the TV", "someone is using the faucet", or when combined with a personal context source, who just turned on the TV or used the faucet. Personal context detection is when the sensors are in relation to the individual, and activity and context are detected for that person only. There may be some interaction with environmental sensors (such as a Wi-Fi access point to compute location, where the person carries a personal device that detects the access points located in the environment), but the sensing is person-centric. Context that is manually input is explicitly provided by someone who is in a position to observe and specify it to the system. This may be the case when it's difficult to automatically detect a context of interest, such as what food someone is eating.

Timeliness. This dimension describes whether a suggestion is provided *just-in-time* or *retrospectively.* Suggestion technologies are about making suggestions at the most effective point in time. If a technology that enables one to reflect on data about their behavior throughout the day, that period of reflection may be an opportune moment to suggest future behavior changes. An example of a retrospective condition is that you have gathered all this activity data for the day (or some period of time), and are reviewing it. The suggestion technology points out instances in time when you could have done something differently. This particular item links to both a self-monitoring strategy (via the review of behavior & identifying how/when to change it) and a conditioning strategy, where the timing can be used to provide positive feedback when a desired behavior is exhibited. One tool might incorporate both—immediate feedback when appropriate as well as suggestions when reviewing data.

Interactivity. This dimension refers to whether messages are simply presented, such as a message appearing on a display and then disappearing, or if they require some sort of acknowledgement or input. In the case where a designer prefers the technology to be minimally intrusive, a message won't require explicit acknowledgement from the subject. However, a designer may prefer to make technology require some action on behalf of the subject to make him more aware of his behavior. This interaction may simply be clicking a button saying "I choose to not follow this suggestion right now", or launching into a dialogue with the system which is trying to capture more information about the subject's current situation.

Subtleness of notification. This refers to the technological subtleness of the message-notification system, rather than the content subtlety. This technological subtlety is a continuous variable, with one end of the scale being a very subtle message, perhaps a peripheral light that flashes different colors or patterns to communicate something, and the other end of the scale being a very noticeable message that the subject is less likely to miss noticing or misinterpret. One example is the eWatch from CMU, which uses sensors to determine levels of interruptibility of the wearer, and tailors notifications appropriately.

4.2   Content Dimensions

Message specificity. This dimension indicates whether the messages tend to be relevant yet vague, or very specific. This is best explained with an example. An example of a vague yet relevant message is "good job", displayed when a person meets their activity goal for the day. An example of a specific message is "You've met your goal every day for the past 6 days—excellent!" The importance of this dimension is that messages that are too specific may be less appealing to users over time, but messages that are too vague could be misinterpreted.

Affect. Message content can be designed to minimize affect, or adopt a positive or negative affect. As we've discussed earlier, positive affect is more likely to engage the users.

Adaptive affect. This dimension indicates whether the tool incorporates adaptive affect into the messages. Technologies that incorporate this dimension were un-represented in our analysis, although research indicates that adapting affect in response to the recipient's state results in a more trustworthy system, and enhances the relationship between the recipient and the system. However, affect is still difficult to accurately detect.

Argumentation strategy. This dimension indicates whether the tool employs a logical or an emotional argumentation strategy for persuading. An example of a logical argumentation is to simply report on one's behavior (current step count is 2800, daily goal is 8500). An emotional argumentation strategy appeals to the recipient's emotional desire for reaching a goal. Rather than focusing simply on the logic ("you won't reach your goal if you don't walk more"), messages can appeal to the emotion of reaching a goal ("remember, this goal will help you get more fit so you'll look great on the beach in a month!").

Overtness. This dimension describes the overtness of a suggestion or message. An example of an overt message is "Parking further away allowed you to add 2800 steps to your daily goal—good job!", while a vague message might be "Good job—Keep working towards your goal!".

Explicitness. This dimension indicates whether a tool is informative or provocative in the suggestion. A simple example of an informative message is a pedometer which displays current and goal step counts. The suggestion is implied, rather than explicit. An example of modified pedometer that uses provocative messages may suggest going for a short walk, to ensure you meet your goal today.

Social components. This dimension describes the level of social integration the tool supports. Suggestions can be *personal*, where the information is provided only to the wearer, and no one else can see; *team-oriented*, where your information is shared within a known group or social network; or *public*. For public suggestions, the information may or may not be *anonymous*. In the case of not-anonymous, everyone can see your information, and knows that it comes from you. Anonymous public content refers to a situation where summary, anonymous overviews of the information are provided to everyone, but specifics about one person's performance are unclear. With this type of information, one can determine how personal data compares to the group as a whole.

5 Discussion

We were motivated to pursue this work because we thought it would be a useful tool for researchers and designers to design, compare, and evaluate suggestion tactics employing context aware mobile technologies, as well as identify areas of potential promise. In this section, we will describe some observations we had about the design space of these tactics and describe how this conception of the design space may be used to design, compare, and evaluate.

5.1 Comparing Two Technologies

This tool can be useful in comparing two technologies, particularly when used in conjunction with Fogg's guidelines. For an example comparison, we look at two technologies designed to support achieving running goals: the Nike+iPod and MPTrain.

The overarching goals of the two technologies are similar. However, they approach them differently. Nike+iPod provides current data throughout a run, and therefore requires the runner to be aware of their goal for that run and choose to adjust their pace using the feedback on the display to achieve that goal. MPTrain requires the runner to specify the workout in terms of intensity as measured by heart rate. It does not explicitly provide either the runner's current heart rate or target heart rate, but attempts to persuade the runner to change his running pace by playing music that has appropriately more or fewer beats per minute.

The Nike+iPod combines two commercial products for extra benefit. The MPTrain is a research project focusing primarily on whether an adaptive playlist can make it easier and more pleasurable for someone to reach their running goal. They both have the overarching goal of wanting to help people meet their running goals. However, the MPTrain project could dovetail nicely with the existing Nike+iPod.

There are two primary purposes one might have to compare the two technologies. The first is motivated by competition—if the MPTrain people are likely to try to build a product to compete with Nike+iPod. The other is motivated by collaboration, or working towards incorporating the MPTrain technology with Nike+iPod.

In either case, the comparison is mostly about how effective MPTrain is, and if it could be a substantial enough addition to a Nike+iPod system to support either a beneficial collaboration, or to recognize serious competition. Our comparison using this tool should be along the lines of how well the two technologies complement each other.

For this example, a quick comparison of the profiles indicates that the two technologies are likely compatible, and may be a good match. Both technologies are embedded into a personal device, but the Nike+iPod has a secondary display that provides another persuasive component to the overall project. The Nike+iPod provides multiple modalities of notification, while the only modality for MPTrain is the music. The other major difference we see is a difference in the specificity of the message. The Nike+iPod clearly displays the current pace, time and distance run, while the MPTrain simply plays music with a different number of beats per minute. The runner would likely need to be fairly sophisticated to determine what the change in music is revealing about the current run. Finally, the MPTrain also may contain an affective component, as different music can clearly invoke varying affect. Playing music with a high number of beats per minute could invoke a more positive affect than music with a low number of beats per minute.

5.2 Evaluating a New Persuasive Technology

The benefit of this tool for evaluating new persuasive technologies is primarily by providing a framework for which an evaluation occurs. One could imagine a situation where a new persuasive technology is built, or we could even use an existing persuasive technology. In any case, we want to understand how well the tool is working, and make it as effective as possible. If the profile of the existing technology indicates that it is neutral in affect, then we can attempt to incorporate positive affect into the device, and re-evaluate. Perhaps reviewing the tactic design space, along with the discussion about tradeoffs for each dimension and the profile, will help to identify where common problems might occur and potentially suggest improvements.

5.3 Identifying Fruitful Opportunities

As this design space becomes more populated both with persuasive technologies implementing these tactics and new technologies that enable these tactics, it will become easier to identify areas in the design space that are providing fruitful opportunities. From our initial populating of the design space, we discovered fairly few technologies that strongly incorporate adaptive affect, positive affect, or an emotional argumentation strategy. Adaptive affect is still a difficult technical problem, but positive affect and emotional argumentation strategies are two tactics that should be able to be incorporated fairly effectively.

5.4 Informing the Design of a New Persuasive Technology

This tool could be used to help inform the design of new persuasive technologies. One way to do this is to use the listed components as purely generative. There might be some constraints to a new project, such as what sensor platforms and displays one has available for use. Or, one might choose parameters for the new product based on the desired effect for each component. We believe that once this design space is more specified and we have spent more time placing existing technologies within the space, information about tradeoffs for each component choice will become more substantial.

6 Future Work

One important area of future work is exploring, expanding on, and documenting tradeoffs to consider when choosing a design point for each dimension of the tactic design space. We have begun this by collating related work, which informed the choice of some dimensions. Further work would include reviewing a more extensive collection of persuasive technologies and analyzing the tradeoffs each one experienced.

We also will further specify dimensions of the design space. One example is to incorporate specific approaches for integrating affect into a persuasive technology. Some of the dimensions we noted did not have enough examples of work in the form of actual systems to fully populate the dimension. We will need to rely on related research that is focused on exploring one part of a potential system, rather than an existing, complete system.

Finally, we intend to use this tool to inform our own work in the area of designing, building, and evaluating new persuasive technologies. As we go through this process, we believe this tool will be invaluable for helping to position our work in relation to other work, inform our design rationale, and provide a clearer path for evaluation.

Acknowledgments. Thank you to Yaw Anokwa, Karl Koscher and Jonathan Lester and for reviewing drafts and supporting related projects that informed this work.

References

1. Bickmore, T., Picard, R.: Establishing and Maintaining Long-Term Human Computer Relationships. ACM Transactions on Human-Computer Interaction 12(2), 293–327 (2005)
2. Fogarty, J., Hudson, S.E., Atkeson, C.G., Avrahami, D., Forlizzi, J., Kiesler, S., Lee, J.C., Yang, J.: Predicting human interruptibility with sensors. ACM Trans. Comput.-Hum. Interact. 12(1), 119–146 (2005)
3. Fogg, B.J.: Persuasive Technology: Using Computers to Change What We Think and Do. Morgan Kaufmann Publishers, San Francisco (2003)

4. Khaled, R., Barr, P., Noble, J., Biddle, R., Fischer, R.: Our Place or Mine?: Exploration into Collectivism-Focused Persuasive Technology Design. In: IJsselsteijn, W., de Kort, Y., Midden, C., Eggen, B., van den Hoven, E. (eds.) PERSUASIVE 2006. LNCS, vol. 3962, Springer, Heidelberg (2006)
5. Mazzotta, I., de Rosis, F.: Artifices for persuading to improve eating habits. In: AAAI Spring Symposium on "Argumentation for consumers of health care", Stanford (March 2006)
6. Nawyn, J., Intille, S., Larson, K.: Embedding Behavior Modification Strategies into a Consumer Electronic Device: A Case Study. In: 8th International Conference on Ubiquitous Computing, Orange County, USA (September 2006)
7. Oliver, N., Flores-Mangas, F.: MPTrain: a mobile, music and physiology-based personal trainer. In: MobileHCI '06. Proceedings of the 8th Conference on Human-Computer interaction with Mobile Devices and Services, Helsinki, Finland, September 12 - 15, vol. 159, pp. 21–28. ACM Press, New York, NY (2006)
8. Nike+iPod, http://www.nikeplus.com
9. World Health Organization, "Obesity and Overweight," Chronic Disease Information Sheet, http://www.who.int/dietphysicalactivity/publications/facts/obesity/en/index.html

Modelling a Receiver's Position to Persuasive Arguments

Hien Nguyen, Judith Masthoff, and Peter Edwards

University of Aberdeen
{hnguyen,jmasthoff,pedwards}@csd.abdn.ac.uk

Social psychology shows that the effect of a persuasive argument depends on characteristics of the person to be persuaded, including the person's involvement with the topic and the discrepancy between the person's current position on the topic and the argument's position. Via a series of experiments, this paper provides insight into how the receiver's position can be modelled computationally, as a function of the strength, feature importance, and position of arguments in a set.

1 Introduction

Persuasive communication is "any message that is intended to shape, reinforce or change the responses of another or others." [1]. Research in persuasive technology has focused extensively on generating persuasive messages [2,3,4,5] and increasing the credibility of the message's source [6], but substantially less work has been devoted to the receivers of the message. Although extremely strong, carefully selected and arranged messages from a highly trustworthy source will certainly improve the efficacy of a persuasive transaction, social psychologists have also acknowledged the importance of the receivers in the process. Over the years, the two most recognised characteristics of the receivers that influence their persuasibility are *message discrepancy* and *receiver involvement*.

1.1 Message Discrepancy and Persuasion

One goal of persuasion is to move the message receivers from their existing *position* towards a topic (i.e. how strongly supportive or against that topic they are) to a new position. In such scenarios, the position advocated in the persuasive messages is likely to differ from the receivers' existing position. This difference is referred to as *message discrepancy*.

On any given topic, there are likely to be a variety of points of views. This is especially true for controversial topics such as abortion or nuclear power. For such topics, a spectrum of positions needs to be constructed to represent the differing positions people might hold. Two theories in social psychology address this issue. First, Social Judgement Theory [7] divides the spectrum of positions into two parts: (1) *the latitude of acceptance* which includes positions that the receivers find acceptable, (2) *the latitude of rejection* which includes positions that the receivers find unacceptable. A message, when being judged, will fall into one of these two latitudes. For instance, somebody who is moderately against abortion, may still find the position

Y. de Kort et al. (Eds.): PERSUASIVE 2007, LNCS 4744, pp. 271–282, 2007.

acceptable that abortion should be allowed in case of rape. In contrast, for a pro-life campaigner, such a position is likely to fall into the latitude of rejection. These judgemental latitudes vary from person to person, and can be calculated by using an *Ordered Alternative Questionnaire* [8]. The theory proposes that attitude change increases with message discrepancy as long as the message falls within the latitude of acceptance, but it decreases if the discrepancy is so large that the message falls in the latitude of rejection.

Information Processing theory [9,10], on the other hand, proposes that attitude change is proportional to message discrepancy and is always in the direction advocated by the message.

Both theories have been supported by a considerable number of studies. They both agree that message discrepancy enhances the message's persuasiveness. However, extremely discrepant messages (those that fall in the receivers' latitude of rejection) may be discounted, counter-argued against, or perceived to be more psychologically discrepant than they objectively are (the *contrast effect*). Any of these outcomes could impair the messages' persuasiveness.

However, neither of these theories takes into account the effects of the content of the messages (e.g. their strength), and the receiver's involvement with the topic. Extremely strong messages, though falling in the latitude of rejection, may still be persuasive, especially to receivers who are not highly involved with the topic.

1.2 Message Strength and Persuasion

The strength of an argument is the extent to which the receiver finds it convincing. Psychology and argumentation theory have investigated a number of factors that influence the strength of an argument, such as rational versus emotional appeals [11,12,13], types of evidence (e.g. vivid examples vs. consensus statistical data), types of conclusions (e.g. clear vs. ambiguous), one-sided versus two-sided arguments [14], the order of arguments presented [4, 8], and the personalization of information in arguments [15,16]. Argumentation theory has also developed guidelines to construct convincing arguments [2,3,15,17], considering all these factors. These guidelines have been used in a number of systems to generate persuasive texts in different domains [5,18,19]. In this paper, we acknowledge that an argument's strength affects its convincingness. However, we consider the strength of an argument as an abstract concept (i.e. we will use strength in our models but will not model it).

1.3 Receiver Involvement and Persuasion

Social psychologists divide involvement into three types [20]:

- *Value-relevant* involvement reflects a set of core values or beliefs that defines a person's self-concept, hence forms the latitude of acceptance and rejection discussed above. The receivers' latitude of rejection becomes wider as they are more highly involved with a topic (e.g. devout Catholics may have a wider latitude of rejection for abortion). This implies that highly involved people are more reluctant to change than neutral people.

- *Outcome-relevant* involvement reflects what outcomes are important to the receivers (e.g. parents whose children are about to go to college may have more involvement with proposals to increase tuition fees). This type of involvement motivates receivers to carefully scrutinize the content of persuasive messages [21] [22]. Hence, it will enhance persuasive effects of strong messages and limit the effectiveness of weak messages. Attitude change if occurred will be strong and permanent.
- *Impression-relevant* involvement reflects concerns about the impressions they make on others (e.g. a teenager may worry about the opinion of his peer group). This has been found to inhibit attitude change, but this effect is weak in general.

2 Strategies for Modelling a Receiver's Position

This section outlines a number of computational strategies for modelling a receiver's position inspired by various theories in Social Psychology such as the Fishbein Model [23], Social Judgement theory [7], Cognitive Dissonance Theory [24], and Information Processing Theory [9,10]. In the following, we will use for argument i

- P_i for the position of the argument, i.e. the extent to which it supports the topic. P_i is scalar, with zero representing a neutral position, positive numbers representing positions in favour of the topic, and negative numbers positions against the topic.
- S_i for the strength of the argument, i.e. how strong it defends its claim(s), for instance by using convincing supporting evidence.
- I_i for the feature importance of the argument, i.e. how important the feature of the topic discussed in the argument is to the receiver. In other words, feature importance represents the receiver's outcome-relevant involvement.

2.1 Strategies Treating Arguments as a Set

The following strategies do not take the order of arguments into account, nor individual differences between receivers.

1. *Average of position (A).* This strategy has been inspired by Social Judgement Theory which states that people only think about the *position* of the arguments. Hence, the position RP of a receiver about a topic is the average of the positions of the arguments about that topic the receiver has heard:

   $RP = $ Average i: P_i

2. *Average of position and strength (AS).*

   $RP = \sum P_i * S_i / \sum S_{max}$, where S_{max} is the maximum strength an argument can take

3. *Average of position and feature importance (AI).*

   $RP = \sum P_i * I_i / \sum I_{max}$, where I_{max} is the maximum strength an argument can take

4. *Average of position, feature importance and strength (ASI).*

$$RP = \sum P_i*S_i*I_i / \sum S_{max}*I_{max}$$

5. **Most extreme (M)**. This strategy proposes that people will be influenced by the most extreme argument. This is inspired by Cognitive Dissonance Theory [24] which states that people have the tendency to drift to the extreme position.

$$RP = \text{Max } i: P_{i,} \qquad \text{for } i \text{ such that } \neg\exists j: P_i = -P_j$$

6. **MS**. $RP = \text{Max } i: P_i*(S_i/S_{max})$ for i such that $\neg\exists j: P_i*S_i = -P_j*S_j$

7. **MI**. $RP = \text{Max } i: P_i * (I_i/I_{max})$ for i such that $\neg\exists j: P_i*I_i = -P_j*I_j$

8. **MSI**. $RP = \text{Max } i: P_i*(S_i * I_i/S_{max} * I_{max})$ for i such that $\neg\exists j: P_i*S_i*I_i = -P_j*S_j*I_j$

2.2 Strategies Treating Arguments as a Sequence

Both Social Judgement Theory and Information Processing Theory predict that the position of the receiver influences their reaction to an argument. Hence, it matters in which order arguments are given. According to Information Processing Theory, the receiver's position RP_{n+1} at moment $n+1$ is

$$RP_n + \alpha(P_{n+1} - RP_n), \text{ with } 0 \le \alpha \le 1$$

According to Social Judgement Theory, the receiver's position at moment $n+1$ is

$$RP_n + \alpha(P_{n+1} - RP_n), \text{ if } P_{n+1} \text{ is within the latitude of acceptance given } RP_n$$
$$RP_n, \qquad\qquad \text{ if } P_{n+1} \text{ is outside the latitude of acceptance given } RP_n$$

Neither of these theories uses S_i or I_i. Incorporating these will make the formulas more complex. To complicate matters further, the *perceived* strength of an argument may well depend on the position of the receiver[1]. These issues go beyond the scope of this paper. To simplify matters, we will give the receiver a starting position of neutral (=0) in Experiments 2 and 3 below, and use sets of arguments rather than sequences.

2.3 Dependence on Receiver Characteristics

So far, we have ignored the possibility of differences between receivers. People are likely to differ in the ease with which they can be persuaded. The easiest way to model this would be to make α (in Section 2.2) receiver dependant (and add such an α to the models in section 2.1). Clearly, I_i will also need to be receiver dependant. For instance, the importance of the environment (as a feature discussed about the topic nuclear power) is likely to differ per person. This is in line with receiver involvement discussed in Section 1.2. The question arises whether P_i and S_i also need to be receiver dependant. It may well be that people differ in what they regard as a strong argument (in terms of evidence given), or what they regard the position of an argument to be. To investigate this, we conducted Experiment 1 described below.

---

[1] Similar to the assimilation effects described in [26].

3 Experiment 1: Consistency of Strength and Position

3.1 Experimental Design

The aim of this experiment was to investigate the extent to which people perceive the position and strength of an argument similarly.

First, subjects were briefed about the meaning of the position and strength of an argument. As the experiment aims to measure subjects' *objective* judgement, we raised their awareness of possible assimilation and contrast effects by asking them to read a paragraph discussing the two effects right before they started the experiment. This method has been used in psychology and has proven to be an effective means to reduce such effects [25]. Next, subjects were asked to rate ten different arguments, randomly selected from a set of 56. Using Likert scales, subjects rated each argument's position from -4 (extremely against) to +4 (extremely supportive) and its strength from 1 (extremely weak) to 7 (extremely strong).

Fifty-seven subjects participated in the experiment (40 male, 17 female; 20 aged between 18-24, 18 aged 25-29, 19 aged ≥30). All were staff and students of the University of Aberdeen. At the start of the experiment, subjects rated their opinion on nuclear power. Fifty subjects were close to neutral (between -2 and +2). Six subjects rated less than 10 arguments, while seven subjects rated more than 10 arguments.

We used 56 arguments about nuclear power collected from a variety of sources such as the BBC, Greenpeace, Daily Mail, and Government statements. Table 1 presents examples of the arguments used. Arguments varied in strength and position.

Table 1. Examples of the arguments used in Experiment 1

2	Nuclear power is too dangerous, too dirty and too expensive to be the answer to addressing climate change. The lowest estimate of building new reactors is £5.85-£8.37 billion, and they could not be built in time to head off global warming. So would it be worthwhile building ten more costly, hazardous plants which present terrorist targets in terms of offsetting greenhouse gases? No, because ten new plants would offset only 4-5 per cent of future estimated CO_2 emissions. In contrast, renewable energy is available now, can be built quickly, is economical, safe and doesn't leave us with piles of nuclear waste we simply cannot deal with.
12	Nuclear power is unpopular. A recent poll found that only 8% of people would prefer nuclear to renewable sources of energy if the costs were the same.
17	It is not a question of either nuclear or renewables, but that all alternatives to fossil fuels must be exploited to the full.
45	Nuclear power has had 30 years of subsidies, billions of pounds poured into it and it still only produces 7% of the world's energy.
68	Nuclear reactors are the epitome of a centralised, inherently inefficient distribution system, generating reasonably reliable base-load electricity from a small number of huge power stations. By their very scale, any new generation of reactors will compel dependence on that distribution system for the next 50 years, at exactly the time when we should be banking heavily on decentralised energy systems, maximising synergy between renewables, microgeneration, combined heat and power, local area networks and so on.

3.1.1 Results and Discussion

Figures 1 shows the results of the experiment in box plots[2] for position (a similar one for strength is not included due to space considerations). As each subject rated different arguments, we cannot easily calculate inter-rater consistency. However, two subjects rated the same 43 arguments. Their intra-rater agreement was high for position, but weak for strength (intra-class correlation coefficients of .910 for position and .295 for strength, $p<001$[3]). The box plots also show more consistency for position than for strength.

Some arguments are rated more consistently than others, as can be seen from the variation of box sizes in the figures. With regards to position, standard deviations varied between .70 for argument 2 and 2.47 to 2.76 for arguments 68 and 45 (see Table 1 for texts). Looking closer at the data, the most variation seems to arise when an argument contains elements that can be seen as against nuclear power as well as elements that can be seen as in favour. For instance, argument 68 says that nuclear power generates "reasonably reliable base-load electricity", but complains about its centralization. This can be explained by the concept of receiver involvement discussed in section 1.3 and incorporated in our models as I_i: subjects may vary in the importance they attribute to reliability of energy versus de-centralization. The variance for argument 45 is mainly due to two outliers, but this may still be influenced by the fact that "produces 7% of the world's energy" can be seen as a positive fact (rather than a negative one as intended by the author). Users do not always pay attention when reading arguments, and a word like "only" can be missed.

With regards to strength, standard deviations varied between .84 for argument 6 and 2.4 for 17. Based on subjects' comments, there was a lot of variation in the ways subjects decided on strength. Some subjects mentioned the credibility of the source (e.g. if evidence mentions a report, who has written that report), some did not trust

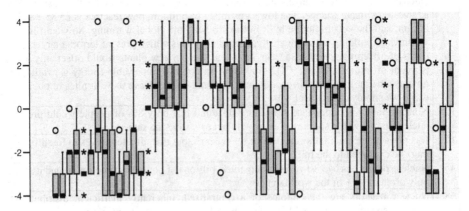

Fig. 1. Box plots of subjects' ratings of *position* for the 56 arguments (one per argument)

---

[2] Box plots show the distribution of a set of data by using the median, quartiles, and the extremes of the data set. The box shows the middle 50% of the data; the longer the box, the greater the spread of the data. The circles and stars indicate outliers.

[3] Cronbach's alphas are .952 for position and .616 for strength. Pearson correlations are .911 for position and .445 for strength.

percentage data while others saw it as evidence (like in argument 12), some subjects might have regarded an argument stronger if it is two-sided (like argument 17).

To conclude, this experiment shows that argument position is quite user independent, except that in composite arguments it may be influenced by user involvement. In contrast, strength is clearly user dependent. More work is needed to determine how to model individual user differences in the judgment of strength.

4 Experiment 2: Judgment of Single Arguments

4.1 Experimental Design

This experiment investigates whether and how subjects use position and strength when deciding on a receiver's position. Subjects were given four, randomly ordered, scenarios in which a fictional person[4] was presented with an argument about nuclear power. They were told the person was neutral before hearing the argument, had not heard it before, and that the features mentioned were important to the person. They were asked to predict this person's opinion on a scale from -4 to +4 after having heard the argument, and to explain their prediction.

The arguments used came from Experiment 1 (see Table 2), and were selected to have a good inter-rater consistency on position and strength[5]. Arguments varied in strength and were either lowly or highly discrepant from the neutral position. Thirteen subjects participated in the experiment (8 male, 5 female, aged between 24 and 55). All participants were Computing students and staff.

Table 2. Arguments used in Experiment 2, with position and strength found in Experiment 1

Case	Argument	Exp1 Mean (StDev)	
		Position	Strength
WeakL	Proper investment in renewables together with energy conservation and efficiency measures would eliminate the need to rely on nuclear power to meet Britain's greenhouse gas commitments.	-2.25 (1.16)	3.63 (1.69)
StrongH	Nuclear power is bad for your health. One particle of plutonium can cause fatal lung-cancer. The UK civil nuclear industry has a stockpile of 102 tonnes of plutonium with no plans for what to do with it.	-3.22 (1.09)	4.44 (1.74)
StrongL	A recent report comparing nuclear and decentralised energy scenarios found that the nuclear scenario is dirtier, more dangerous, less secure and over £1bn more expensive than a decentralised scenario.	-2.88 (0.64)	5.75 (0.89)
WeakH	Nuclear power is too dangerous, too dirty and too expensive.	-3.38 (1.06)	2.25 (0.89)

---

[4] We used four common male names (Adam, Peter, John and David) to minimize any bias participants might have about the effect of gender on perceiving arguments.

[5] Two subjects were excluded before using the results from Experiment 1, as they were outliers on almost all arguments they rated.

4.2 Results and Discussion

WeakL had a mean of -0.5 (stdev 1.53), StrongH -1.9 (1.75), StrongL -2.4 (1.20), WeakH -1.3 (1.39). There was a significant difference between WeakL and StrongH ($p<.05$), showing that a strong, highly discrepant argument has more persuasive effect than a weak, less discrepant argument. There was a significant difference between WeakL and StrongL ($p<.005$), showing that a strong argument has more effect than a weak argument, given that the two argument are roughly equally lowly discrepant. There was a significant difference between StrongL and WeakH ($p<.05$), showing that a strong, but less discrepant argument has more effect than a weak, but more discrepant argument. We also found a significant difference between strong and weak arguments (t-test, $p<.005$), but no significant difference was found between highly and less discrepant arguments ($p=0.7$).

We also explored which factors subjects considered to make their decisions. The two factors mentioned the most were the strength of argument (e.g. "weak argument, too subjective") and its relevance to the receiver (e.g. "speaks to all his interests"). Some subjects considered strength more important than relevance while others considered the opposite.

Pearson's r correlation coefficient was used to measure pairwise correlation between subjects. We found significant correlations between S1 & S13 (1.00), S2 & S11 (.990), and S7 & S12 (1.00). We found a weaker correlation among two sub groups of users: Group1 (S1, S4, S6, S13) (average $r = .731$) and Group 2 (S2, S3, S7, S11, S12) (average $r = .815$). We also calculated the intra-class correlation coefficient. A significant result ($p<0.05$) was found for all subjects (ICC: 0.194; Cronbach alpha: 0.803), Group 1 (ICC: 0.23; Cronbach alpha: 0.75) and 2 (ICC: 0.56; Cronbach alpha: 0.91). So to a certain extent, people perceive the impact of an argument similarly, though differences seem to exist. Further investigation is needed to explore which characteristics make people perceive an argument in the same way.

We compared the results of this experiment with the predictions by the models presented in Section 2. Note that only one argument was presented to the fictional persons (rather than the more complicated situation of a set of arguments used in Section 2). Also, this one argument was said to have high feature importance (removing any difference feature importance could make between the models). This results in many of the models of Section 2 giving the same prediction. For instance, taking the average or the maximum of one argument's position gives the same result. Therefore, we only need to investigate the predictions of A and AS (in this case A=AI=M=MI, and AS=ASI=MS=MSI). Table 3 shows the receiver position (RP) predicted by A and AS for the four scenarios. Model A predicts RP to equal the position. Model AS predicts RP to equal the position times strength divided by 7 (the maximum strength possible). We calculated predicted mean and StDev by using the data from Experiment 1 (using the data per subject rather than the average data). Comparing the RP predicted by the models with those predicted by our subjects clearly shows that the AS model corresponds better to the human prediction, so modeling strength improves predictions.

In conclusion, both our qualitative and quantitative analysis showed that while people definitely consider argument strength when perceiving arguments, we could not conclude whether argument's position is taken into account. When confronted

Table 3. Receiver positions as given by subjects in Experiment 2 and predictions of the models

Case	RP from Exp 2 Mean (StDev)	Prediction of RP by the models	
		A	AS
WeakL	-0.5 (1.53)	-2.25 (1.16)	-1.07 (0.79)
StrongH	-1.9 (1.75)	-3.22 (1.09)	-2.35 (1.11)
StrongL	-2.4 (1.20)	-2.88 (0.64)	-2.39 (0.72)
WeakH	-1.3 (1.39)	-3.38 (1.06)	-1.11 (0.60)

with one argument, the prediction of the models including argument strength clearly outperformed the prediction of the models ignoring argument strength.

5 Experiment 3: Judgment of Multiple Arguments

5.1 Experimental Design

The experiment aims to answer the following research questions (1) Do subject take into account the strength and the feature importance of arguments in a set? If so, which factor is more important? (2) Do subjects follow a clear strategy?

First, subjects were briefed about the meaning of the position, strength and feature importance of an argument. They were told that the position of an argument ranges from -4 (extremely against) to +4 (extremely supportive), the strength ranges from 1 (extremely weak) to 7 (extremely strong), and the feature importance ranges from 0 (not important at all) to 6 (extremely important). The first two scales were kept the same as in Experiment 1. We used 0 to 6 for feature importance, because we assumed that arguments about irrelevant aspects of the topic should be discarded.

Next, subjects were given the position, strength and feature importance of three abstract arguments (A,B,C) as perceived by a fictional person Adam. They were told that Adam was neutral about the topic to start with and had not heard the arguments before. Subjects were asked to predict Adam's position on the topic of the arguments after he heard these arguments, using a continuous scale between -4 and +4.

Table 4. Combinations of P,S,I used and predictions of receiver's position by the strategies

		Values			Predictions							
		P	S	I	A	AS	AI	ASI	M	MS	MI	MSI
Case 1	A	+3	4	0	+0.3	+0.3	-1.3	-1.0	-4.0	-2.9	-4.0	-2.9
	B	+2	7	0								
	C	-4	5	6								
Case 2	A	-3	7	0	-0.7	-1.2	+0.6	0.0	-2.0	-3.0	+3.0	-1.3
	B	-2	7	4								
	C	+3	3	6								
Case 3	A	-3	2	6	-0.7	+0.2	-0.8	0.0	-2.0	+3.0	-3.0	+1.5
	B	-2	5	3								
	C	+3	7	3								

Subjects were randomly assigned to one out of three conditions (see Table 4). Combinations were chosen in such a way that applying the strategies outlined in Section 2.1 would produce distinctive results (also shown in Table 3). To test our hypotheses (i.e. irrelevant arguments should be discarded), the first scenario contains two irrelevant arguments, the second one contains one irrelevant argument and the final one which is the most complex example contained no irrelevant argument.

Thirty two subjects (22 males, 9 females, 1 unidentified, aged from 24 to 61) participated in the experiment. They are staff and students of the University of Aberdeen. Two subjects clearly misunderstood the question, hence their results were discarded. Subjects were randomly assigned to one of the three cases.

5.2   Results and Discussion

Figure 2 shows a box plot and descriptive statistics for the results.

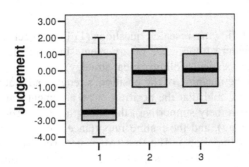

	Mean	StDev
Case 1	-1.69	2.21
Case 2	+0.06	1.42
Case 3	+0.05	1.44

Fig. 2. Box plots of subjects' prediction of position for the three cases

We explored whether subjects took strength and relevance into account by looking at the rationales given for their judgements (27 subjects provided these). Twenty-four subjects clearly said that they considered feature importance and twenty-three considered strength. Only one subject clearly stated that only strong arguments should be considered, though it should be noted that this argument had a feature importance of 0. So, it is safe to conclude that when judging the position advocated by a number of messages people do consider both the strength and outcome-relevance of each message. This result is also consistent with findings in Experiment 2.

Surprisingly, only nine out of twenty subjects who had to consider arguments that are not important said that arguments that have feature importance of 0 should be ignored regardless of their strength (e.g. A is irrelevant, A has little or no effect, A can be discounted, etc). Meanwhile, three subjects stated that strong, but irrelevant arguments have more effect on Adam's opinion than relevant but weaker arguments and two subjects think strong irrelevant arguments have little effects. Five subjects think strength and feature importance should be combined equally to form the arguments effectiveness. In the third case, two subjects thought that strength is more important than feature importance while one subject thought other wise, and four subjects thought that they should be combined equally. So, it is clear that people do take both strength and relevance into account when judging the position of the arguments. However, the weight of each element seems to differ among subjects.

The average positions in the latter two cases are very close to what the ASI strategy produced (0.06 vs. 0.0 and 0.05 vs. 0.0). However, this does not say much as the standard deviation in both cases is large (1.42 and 1.43). Seventeen subjects matched the ASI (6), AS (6), and M (5) strategy. Among them, fourteen subjects commented that they actually considered both strength and feature importance, while two did not give any comment. So while it is clear that people consider both strength and feature importance, they did not apply our strategies strongly.

6 Conclusions

An accurate prediction of a receiver's position after hearing one or more arguments may help a persuasive system to select the next argument to present (e.g. by choosing one within the latitude of acceptance). However, it is not easy to make such predictions as many factors play a role. In this paper, we have considered some of these factors, in particular argument strength, position and feature importance, and gained a better understanding of their relative roles.

Our experiments show that when judging the position of arguments, people consider both strength and feature importance; some consider one factor more important than others. While feature importance is clearly different from person to person, people perceive argument position, strength and its impact on their existing position rather consistently. People did not seem to follow clearly any of our suggested strategies.

The experiments in this paper are indirect in nature as subjects were asked to predict the position of a fictional person. We would like to perform more direct experiments; however, these would require a topic for which we know which arguments subjects have already heard (pointing towards use of an artificial domain).

The research presented in this paper is an important first step towards a computational model. We intend to extend it in various directions, investigating a.o.: the effect of a receiver's initial position on the impact of subsequent arguments paying particular attention to the order of arguments; how to model receiver characteristics that influence the perceived strength of arguments; and how to decide on the latitude of acceptance based on receiver characteristics and position.

References

1. Miller, G.R.: On being persuaded: Some basic distinctions. In: Roloff, M.E., Miller, G.R. (eds.) Persuasion: New directions in theory and research, pp. 11–28. Sage, Berverly Hills, CA (1980)
2. Marcu, D.: The conceptual and linguistic facets of persuasive arguments. In: ECAI Workshop - Gaps and Bridges: New Directions in Planning and Natural Language Generation (1996)
3. Mayberry, K.J., Golden, R.E.: For argument's sake: a guide to writing effective arguments. College Publisher, Harper Collins (1996)
4. Reed, C.A., Long, D.: Content ordering in the generation of persuasive discourse. In: IJCAI97. Proceedings of the 15th International Joint Conference on Artificial Intelligence, pp. 1022–1027. Morgan Kaufmann, Nagoya, Japan (1997)

5. Carenini, G., Moore, J.: Generating and Evaluating Evaluative Arguments. Artificial Intelligence 170(11), 925–952 (2006)
6. Fogg, B.J.: Persuasive technology: using computers to change what we think and do. Morgan Kaufmann, San Francisco (2003)
7. Sherif, M., Sherif, C.M.: Attitudes as the individual's own categories: The social judgment-involvement approach to attitude and attitude change. In: Sherif, C.W, Sherif, M. (eds.) Attitude, ego-involvement, and change, pp. 105–139 (1967)
8. O'Keefe, J.D.: Persuasion: theory and research. Sage, Newbury Park, CA (1990)
9. Wyer, R.S.: The quantitative prediction of belief and opinion change: A further test of subjective probability model. J. of Personality and Social Psychology 16, 559–570 (1970)
10. Hunter, J.E., Danes, J.E., Cohen, S.H.: Mathematical models of attitude change: Change in single attitudes and cognitive structure. Academic Press, New York (1984)
11. de Rosis, F., Grasso, F.: Affective natural language generation. In: IWAI 1999. International Workshop on Affective Interactions, pp. 204–218 (1999)
12. de Rosis, F., Mazzotta, I., Miceli, M., Poggi, I.: Persuasion artifices to promote wellbeing. In: Proceedings of the first International conference on Persuasive Technology, pp. 84–95 (2006)
13. Cavalluzzi, A., Carofiglio, V., de Rosis, F.: Affective Advice Giving Dialogs. Tutorial and Research Workshop on "Affective Dialogue Systems" (2004)
14. Aronson, E.: The social animal, Worth (2004)
15. Miller, M. D., Levine T. R.: Persuasion. An Integrated Approach to Communication Theory and Research. Salwen, M.B., Stack, D.W., Mahwah, New Jersey, 261-276 (1996)
16. Cialdini, R.: Influence: science and practice. Scott, Foresman (1988)
17. Corbett, E.P.J., Connors, R.J.: Classical Rhetoric for the Modern Student. Oxford University Press, Oxford (1999)
18. Guerini, M.: Persuasion Models for Multimodal Message Generation, PhD thesis (2006)
19. Reiter, E., Robertson, R., Osman, L.: Lessons from a failure: generating tailored smoking cessation letters. Artificial Intelligence 144, 41–58 (2003)
20. Johnson, B.T., Eagly, A.H.: Effects of involvement on persuasion: A meta-analysis. Psychological Bulletin 106, 290–314 (1989)
21. Petty, R., Cacioppo, J.: The elaboration likelihood model of persuasion. Advances in Experimental Social Psychology 19, 123–205 (1986)
22. Chaiken, S.: The Heuristic Model of Persuasion. In: Zanna, M.P., Olson, J.M., Herman, C.P. (eds.) Social Influence: The Ontario symposium, vol. 5, pp. 3–39. Erlbaum, Hillsdale, NJ (1987)
23. Fishbein, M., Ajzen, I.: Belief, attitude, intention, and behavior. Addison-Wesley, Reading, MA (1975)
24. Aronson, E.: The theory of cognitive dissonance: A current perspective. In: Berkowitz, L. (ed.) Advances in Experimental Social Psychology, vol. 4 (1969)
25. Sarup, G., Suchner, R.W., Gaylord, G.: Contrast Effects and Attitude Change: A Test of the Two-Stage Hypothesis of Social Judgement Theory. Social Psychology Quarterly 54(4), 364–372 (1991)
26. Masthoff, J., Gatt, A.: In pursuit of satisfaction and the prevention of embarrassment: Affective state in Group Recommender Systems. User Modeling and User Adapted Interaction (2006)
27. Moore, J.D.: Participating in explanatory dialogues: interpreting and responding to questions in context. MIT Press, Cambridge (1995)

Persuasive Recommendation: Serial Position Effects in Knowledge-Based Recommender Systems

A. Felfernig[1], G. Friedrich[1], B. Gula[2], M. Hitz[3], T. Kruggel[1], G. Leitner[3], R. Melcher[3], D. Riepan[1], S. Strauss[2], E. Teppan[1], and O. Vitouch[2]

[1] Computer Science and Manufacturing
[2] Cognitive Psychology
[3] Interactive Systems
Klagenfurt University, Universitaetsstrasse 65-67, A-9020 Klagenfurt, Austria
{alexander.felfernig,gerhard.friedrich,bartosz.gula,
thomas.kruggel,rudolf.melcher,gerhard.leitner,daniela.riepan,
sabine.strauss,erich.teppan,oliver.vitouch}@uni-klu.ac.at

Abstract. Recommender technologies are crucial for the effective support of customers in online sales situations. The state-of-the-art research in recommender systems is not aware of existing theories in the areas of cognitive and decision psychology and thus lacks of deeper understanding of online buying situations. In this paper we present results from user studies related to serial position effects in human memory in the context of knowledge-based recommender applications. We discuss serial position effects on the recall of product descriptions as well as on the probability of product selection. Serial position effects such as primacy and recency are major building blocks of persuasive, next generation knowledge-based recommender systems.

Keywords: persuasive technologies, recommender systems, knowledge-based recommendation, human memory, interactive selling.

1 Introduction

Recommender systems are among the most successful applications of Artificial Intelligence technologies. The major purpose of recommender systems is to improve the accessibility of complex and large product assortments for online customers. There are basically three different types of recommendation approaches. One of the most frequently used one is *Collaborative Filtering* [16, 29]. It implements the idea of word-of-mouth promotion where a buying decision is predominantly influenced by the opinions of friends and benchmarking reports. For instance, if two customers have bought similar books in the past and have rated those books in a similar way, positively rated books bought by only one of them, are recommended to the other customer. *Content-based Filtering* [26] is an information filtering approach that exploits item features a user has liked in the past to recommend new items. In contrast to collaborative approaches, content-based filtering cannot provide serendipitous recommendations. It recommends all items based on purchase information available from the current user. Both approaches are based on long-term user profiles and do

Y. de Kort et al. (Eds.): PERSUASIVE 2007, LNCS 4744, pp. 283–294, 2007.

not exploit deep knowledge about the product domain. Thus, they are excellent techniques supporting recommendation processes for simple products such as movies, compact discs or books. Compared to users purchasing simple products, those purchasing complex products such as financial services or digital cameras are much more in the need of information and in the need of intelligent interaction mechanisms supporting the selection of appropriate items. *Knowledge-based approaches* [6,9] make use of an explicit representation of product, marketing and sales knowledge. Such deep knowledge allows (a) the recommendation of items which fulfil certain quality requirements, (b) the explanation of recommended items, and (c) the support of users in situations where no solution can be found. In contrast to word-of-mouth promotion implemented by collaborative filtering, knowledge-based recommendation implements explicit sales dialogs which support users in the item selection process. In this paper we focus on knowledge-based recommender technologies that determine recommendations on the basis of explicit sales dialogs where users are confronted with questions related to their wishes and needs (preference elicitation phase – e.g., the tent recommender in Fig. 1). Elicited preferences are in turn used for calculating recommendations for the current user. After the completion of a sales dialog, a product comparison page is presented to the user which contains a set of alternative items (see Fig. 1). The simplified tent recommender depicted in Fig. 1 has been used as the basic stimulus/framework for user studies which are presented in the following sections.

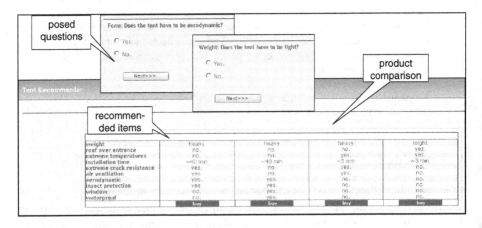

Fig. 1. Example Recommender Application

Knowledge-based recommender technologies have been successfully applied in different commercial environments, for example the recommendation of financial services [9] or restaurants [6]. A major reason for the successful deployment of those technologies is that users do not only receive recommendations but additionally are provided with a corresponding set of explanations as to why a certain item fits to the wishes and needs of a user. Features such as explanations significantly improve the trust of users regarding recommendations [9]. However, the development of recommender applications is still rather focused on an existing set of technical features. The effects of applying different theories about human memory in online buying situations have not been analyzed up to now. In this paper we present results of two empirical studies which investigate *serial position effects* [24] of human memory in the context of recommendation sessions. Primacy and recency as a specific form of serial position effects describe the phenomenon that information units at the beginning and at the end of lists are more likely to be remembered than those in the middle [10, 17]. Such effects may potentially occur in every situation where information is presented in list format. In knowledge-based recommenders, there are mainly three such listings: first, sequential product attribute questions in the dialog phase. Second, the order of product attributes on the product comparison page, and finally the order of products on the product comparison page.

In the relevant literature it has been argued that recommenders always persuade when recommending [14, 20, 35]. This interpretation is based on the fact that recommenders successfully support the effective identification of items which otherwise would not have been found by the customer and consequently not been purchased. We follow the definition of persuasion given in [10] where persuasion is defined as *the attempt of changing people's attitudes or behaviours or both*. Our overall hypothesis is that serial position effects can be successfully exploited for changing people's attitudes in the context of online buying situations. In contrast to [14, 20, 35] our approach actively exploits psychological theories for attaining persuasion effects. For this purpose, knowledge-based recommenders can constitute an ideal platform for installing persuasion technology. The deep understanding of persuasion mechanisms offers the possibility of exploitation and control. COHAVE[1] is an interdisciplinary research project at Klagenfurt University with the goal of building a general framework for exploiting persuasive mechanisms in knowledge-based recommendation. In this project, psychological theories from the areas of memory phenomena and decision theory are investigated, implemented and evaluated.

The remainder of the paper is organized as follows: in Section 2 an overview of related work is given and research questions are presented which are investigated in the follow-up sections. Section 3 and Section 4 present results of two studies investigating serial position effects in the domain of tents and digital cameras. The paper is concluded with Section 5 where an outlook on future work is given.

2 Persuasive Effects in Preference Construction

Position effects in human memory are one of the oldest phenomena investigated in experimental psychology [8, 19, 21, 24, 34]. Serial position effects are basic memory phenomena first discussed in 1878 [24]. The effect has originally been found in short-term memory tasks. It describes a specific order in the recall of a list of items, such as meaningless syllables [8], numbers [24] or names of common objects [19] which people had to learn by heart beforehand. In this context, recall accuracy of items from a list shows two patterns: a) items from the beginning of the list (primacy) and b) the items from the end of the list (recency) are better remembered than items from the middle of the list [13, 24]. Mostly, primacy and recency effects have been explained

---

[1] COHAVE is the acronym for Consumer Behavior and Decision Modeling for Recommender Systems funded by the Austrian Research Fund (FFG-810996)., see cohave.ifit.uni-klu.ac.at

as effects of the dual store account model of human memory [1], but there is also evidence for a serial position effect related to long-term episodic memory [23].

Order effects in persuasion and 'the motivation to think' have been discussed for example in [27]. It could be shown that under chunked conditions, participants who were highly motivated to think were more susceptible to primacy and recency effects than those low in motivation to think. There are numbers of studies dealing with both short- and long-term episodic memory tasks. The outcome of studies of long-term serial position effects [2, 17, 28, 30] using serial order reconstruction tasks show clear recency effects. [23] shows a corresponding effect in semantic memory tasks using verse hymns as stimuli, resulting in the first unequivocal demonstration of serial position effects in semantic memory. In contrast to most other work mentioned above we use meaningful product-features (questions) as stimuli which are used as information units in knowledge-based recommender systems. Information in knowledge-based recommender systems is usually presented in the form of ordered lists of questions, product attributes, and recommended products. Unlike meaningless material, this kind of information requires a higher level of semantic processing. The studies presented in this paper deal with primacy and recency effects in a semantic memory task and focus on the dialog and the product selection phase.

Research on consumer buying decision making argues that preferences are rather constructed spontaneously [3, 5, 25] than being stable. Following this interpretation, studies have recently shown several psychological phenomena that affect these short-term processes of preference construction. Through feature-based priming for instance, the background of an e-commerce site can guide the attention of customers towards specific product attributes [22]. The attention can also be influenced by the inclusion or exclusion of attributes in the dialog of a recommender system [15]. Both mechanisms contribute to the construction of consumer preferences and to the consideration of product attributes that otherwise may have been omitted. Taking into account these mechanisms can create a new possibility for product suppliers on e-commerce sites to emphasize on those product attributes with which they can outperform their competitors.

The major goal of this paper is to investigate to which extent serial position effects occur in the context of knowledge-based recommenders. Once serial position effects have been proven to work for such dialog systems, mechanisms for exploiting these effects can be implemented in knowledge-based recommender applications. The primacy and recency effect would thus influence the design of recommendation dialogs in terms of question ordering as well as the ordering of the product features. We assume that a supplier who tries to 'positively convince' (persuade) a customer of the quality of certain products should present the best attributes of her products at the beginning and at the end of product descriptions or result pages of a recommender-application. We examined our assumptions in two studies. Study 1 addressed the general question whether serial position effects occur for the recall of product attributes in the dialog phase of a recommender. In Study 2 we investigated whether serial position effects from the dialog phase directly influence product selection. In this context, we focused on answering the following research questions:

- o Q1: Do serial position effects exist for sentences and product feature descriptions?
- o Q2: Do serial position effects occur across different product domains?
- o Q3: Do serial position effects influence the importance of attributes in a purchase situation?
- o Q4: Do serial position effects in the dialog of a recommender influence product choices of customers?
- o Q5: Are product choices influenced by the order of attributes or products on a product comparison page of a recommender?

3 Serial Position Effects in the Recall of Product Descriptions

The goal of the study 1 was to investigate serial position effects in the recall of product descriptions related to tents and digital cameras. In this study, 14 product attributes of tents as well as of digital cameras were collected. For each product attribute a corresponding explanatory sentence has been formulated (e.g., 'with a waterproof tent you can camp on rainy days' or 'the lowest capacity of memory cards for digital cameras is 16 megabytes'). Such explanatory sentences have been integrated in a MS PowerPoint presentation with one sentence per slide. Each slide has been presented for 15 seconds. First, participants had to read each explanatory sentence. Subsequently the participants had to recall as many attributes from the list as possible (after viewing the whole slideshow). Immediately after the recall task, participants were asked to rate the importance of each attribute they remembered would have in a real purchase decision as well as to estimate the overall familiarity of an average consumer with an attribute on a 5-point Likert scale.

In order to design orthogonal attribute orders, an a priori expert rating for the expected overall familiarity of customers with product attributes has been performed. Based on this rating, two different attribute sequences (lists) have been implemented for each product domain by categorizing the attributes as familiar salient and unfamiliar salient. In the familiar salient-list the most familiar attributes were positioned in the beginning and end of the lists while the less familiar attributes were put in the middle. In the unfamiliar salient-list the less familiar attributes were presented in the beginning and end of the lists. The experiment was conducted with four different groups of subjects. In each group participants were confronted with one list version for digital cameras and one list version for tents (see Table 1).

Table 1. Groups and Attribute Sequences

group	attribute sequence 1	attribute sequence 2
1	digi_familiar_salient	tents_ familiar_salient
2	tents_unfamiliar_salient	digi_ unfamiliar_salient
3	digi_ unfamiliar_salient	tents_ familiar_salient
4	tents_ unfamiliar_salient	digi_ familiar_salient

$N = 72$ students of the Klagenfurt University (36.1 % female) with a mean age of 23.3 years ($SD = 5.1$) were tested in group sessions. Out of the 14 product attributes subjects recalled 8.2 attributes of tents ($SD = 4.0$) and 8.0 attributes of digital cameras ($SD = 3.38$). This difference is not significant.

Results for tents. For the analysis, attributes were combined into pairs according to their position within each list. The results of a computed two-factorial ANOVA show that the position of an attribute pair has a clear effect on the frequency of recall ($F(6, 70) = 5.75$, $p < .001$, $\eta^2 = .08$, see Fig. 2). The list-version had no influence on the frequency of recall ($p = .34$). Descriptively, the slightly incremented recall for middle attribute pairs (3-5) in the unfamiliar salient list reflects the fact, that in this list more familiar attributes were presented in the middle.

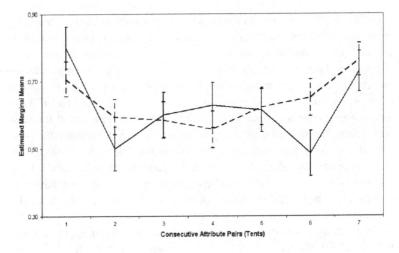

Fig. 2. Relative frequencies of recall for consecutive attribute pairs of tents (1-7). The continuous line corresponds to the results for the unfamiliar salient- and the dashed line to the familiar salient-list. The bars represent the standard errors in all figures.

The probability of recalling attributes from the first pair was .8 and the last pair .72. Combined over both lists we first tested the difference in recall between the first item pair and each of the remaining six pairs, and second, between the last pair and all the other pairs. The investigation of these specific contrasts results in a clear pattern: the probability to recall either the first (primacy) or last (recency) pair was significantly higher than the probability to recall any of the attribute pairs in the middle of the lists (five F-tests, all $p < .01$). At the same time the recall performance for the first and last pairs did not differ significantly. Combining the attributes in the middle into one group shows an even more pronounced position effect ($F(2, 70) = 13.28$, $p < .001$, $\eta^2 = .16$). The self reported knowledge about tents was coded into a dichotomous variable using a median split and has been included in the analysis. Subjects reporting higher knowledge were tending to recall more attributes. However, at least for tents serial position effects occurred independently of the self-reported product domain knowledge.

Results for digital cameras. We found a significant interaction between attribute position and attribute familiarity ($F(6, 70) = 6.05$, $p < .001$). Both serial position effects (primacy and recency) can only be found in the familiar salient-list which contained the more familiar attributes at the beginning and at the end (see Fig. 3). The pattern of results for specific contrasts is less clear than for tents: first and last attribute pairs were recalled significantly more often than the three pairs in the middle of the list but the differences to the second and last but one pair were not significant. Because there are no guidelines on how many items are to be involved in primacy and recency effects, the choice of pairs is arbitrary. Especially, for the pattern of results shown in Fig. 3, it seems more plausible to assume that all four attributes presented at the beginning of the list contributed to a primacy effect. For the unfamiliar salient-list it is noticeable that if no position effects occurred and only attribute familiarity influenced recall performance, the expected line in Fig. 3 should be inversely u-shaped. In this list, the most familiar attributes which were in the middle of the list, would be recalled more often than the less familiar attributes at the beginning and end of the list, which is not the case. A possible explanation would be that primacy and recency actually occurred in the unfamiliar salient-list and resulted in an improved recall performance on unfamiliar attributes.

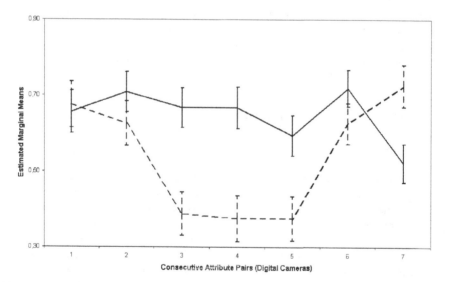

Fig. 3. Relative frequencies of recall for consecutive attribute pairs of digital cameras (1-7). The continuous line corresponds to the results for the unfamiliar salient- and the dashed line to the familiar salient-list.

Summarizing, serial position effects do exist for descriptions of product features presented subsequently (*Q1*). However, the effect was not as domain-independent as assumed manifesting itself less clearly in the domain of digital cameras (*Q2*). Also, the self reported domain knowledge did not suppress the effect. More knowledgeable participants also remembered attribute descriptions from the beginning and end of the lists more often then attributes in the middle.

Participants rated resolution and zoom of digital cameras to be the most important attributes in a real purchase situation and waterproofness and insect protection as the most important attributes of tents. In order to assess whether the position of attributes influenced the importance ratings (Q3), a two-factorial ANOVA for list-version and position was computed with three positions (beginning: first pair, middle: all five pairs in the middle and end: last pair). The importance ratings for digital cameras showed an interaction between list-version and position ($F(2, 56) = 21.26, p < .001$). The pattern does not seem to resemble an influence of serial position effects on importance ratings because more familiar attributes at the beginning and end were rated significantly more important than the attributes in the middle for the familiar salient-list and vice versa for the unfamiliar salient-list. This result shows that familiar attributes are rated as important. However, importance ratings of single attributes did differ according to our expectation depending on their position. For example additional lenses were rated significantly more important in the unfamiliar salient-list where this attribute was presented first than in the familiar salient-list where it was in the middle ($t(34) = -1.71; p = .04$). Importance ratings for attributes of tents varied depending on their position in the list. Attribute pairs at the beginning were rated more important than those in the middle ($F(1, 76) = 13.92; p < .001; \eta^2 = .16$) and also attribute pairs at the end were rated more important than those in the middle ($F(1, 76) = 4.85; p = .03; \eta^2 = .06$). The effect is larger for primacy than recency. This result implies that at least for tents the sequential order of product descriptions influences importance ratings and thus may influence actual product purchases. Among others, this question is pursued in the following study performed with an actual recommender (tent recommender application).

4   The Influence of Serial Position Effects on Product Choice

In order to test whether positions of product attributes in the dialog and product comparison page influence product choice we have constructed six versions of a tent recommender with 10 attributes. In a two-factorial ANOVA we first varied three different attribute orders in the dialog (random order, fixed order 1 and fixed order 2) and combined it with two different orders of attributes on the product comparison page. In both orders of attributes in product comparison the first four attributes listed were the same as the first and last two in the corresponding dialog (see Table 2).

To be able to compare product choices over all six versions we presented to each participant the same set of four tents on the comparison page. The four tents were defined by using the attribute importance ratings from study 1 (see Section 3). The multi-attribute utility value was about the same for each tent. Two of the tents were defined as 'target products', because they outperformed all others when judged on the first and last two attributes from the corresponding dialog only. If serial position effects from the dialog influence the perceived importance of attributes (as shown in study 1), participants should choose the target product more often when interacting with the recommender with fixed order 1 in the dialog compared to any other order. The order of products on the product comparison page was random for each participant. The task of the participants was first to choose the tent they would buy most likely in a real purchase situation and second, to rank all four tents' attractiveness. Participants were recruited from students of the Klagenfurt University. The possibility of winning 1 x €100 and 2 x €50 has been offered. Participants were randomly assigned to one of the six versions of a tent recommender. Finally, 650 valid sessions could be extracted from the log files. Mean age of participants was 25.3 years (SD = 6.48), 63 % of them were female. The median time to complete the dialog was ~2.5 minutes and it took ~1.8 minutes to choose and rate products.

Table 2. Dialog and Product Comparison Orderings

Comparison Ordering 1	Dialog Ordering 1	Dialog Ordering 2	Comparison Ordering 2	
1	1	6	6	1 -waterproof
10	2	7	5	2 -insect protection
2	3	8	7	3 -air ventilation
9	4	9	4	4 -installation time
3	5	10	8	5 -roof of entrance
8	6	1	3	6 -weight
4	7	2	9	7 -extreme temperatures
7	8	3	2	8 -extreme crack resistance
5	9	4	10	9 -aerodynamic
6	10	5	1	10 -window

Results. Across all six recommender versions target product 1 was preferred more than any of the three other products χ^2(3, N = 650) = 636.54; p < .001). It is noticeable that tent 1 outperformed all other tents in the set on two attributes rated as the most important ones. However, at the same time it showed worse quality on six attributes compared to one of the other tents. Taken together with the fact that products were generated with similar multi-attribute utility based on 'real' importance ratings (derived from study 1) this result suggests that participants based their choice only on a few important attributes rather than using all available information to decide. Support of this interpretation may be found in articles suggesting heuristic decision models like the lexicographic strategy or elimination by aspects [32, 33].

A two-factorial ANOVA with kind of dialog (three levels: random dialog, dialog 1 and dialog 2) and kind of product comparison (two levels: comparison 1 and comparison 2) was computed to determine effects on the relative frequency of booking the target product. Opposed to our expectations (*Q4* in Section 2), the frequency of booking the target product was not affected by the order of attributes in the dialog (F(2, 643) = .44; p = .65) but by the order of attributes on the product comparison page (F(1, 643) = 9.76; p = .002). 74 % of subjects interacting with product comparison 1 chose the target product but only 62 % of subjects interacting with product comparison 2 (see Fig. 4). The choice of the target product was not biased by subjective domain knowledge.

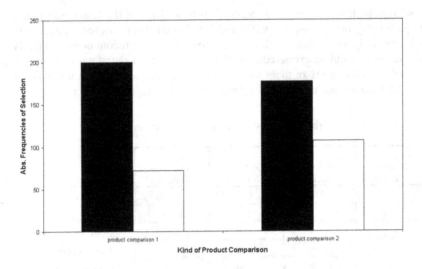

Fig. 4. Frequencies of product choice: tent 1 (black) vs. all other tents: (white)

To determine the relative impact of (a) *kind of product,* (b) *its position on the comparison page,* (c) *the question order in the recommender dialog,* and (d) *the attribute order in the product comparison page* on the choice behaviour of participants, a four-way frequency analysis was computed. The hierarchical log linear model describing the data best consists of two two-way interactions (position x product and attribute order x product) with likelihood ratio $\chi^2(76, N = 650) = 67.67; p = .74$. Especially the *attribute order* x *kind of product* interaction shows that depending on the kind of attribute order each tent was chosen more or less often than expected (see *Q5* in Section 2). While the target product was chosen more often than expected in product comparison 1 all other products were chosen more often than expected in product comparison 2. The second interaction (*product position* x *kind of product*) results from the fact that the target product was chosen more often than expected when it was presented as the first or last of all four tents, while there was an inverse trend for all other products. This implies that the order of products on product comparison pages has an influence on product choice. Summarizing, the order of attributes has an impact on product choice. Results of study 1 imply that attribute order in the dialog has an impact on the perceived attribute importance. Contrary to this result, no such impact of the dialog on product choices could be found in study 2 (a further clarification is needed in this context).

5   Conclusions and Future Work

The studies presented in this paper show that in the line of feature-based priming and inclusion effects serial position effects are another interesting cognitive phenomenon that can play a crucial role in the design of product comparison pages in recommender systems. This result generalizes beyond the dialog of knowledge-based recommenders and can be applied to a wide variety of product and service descriptions ranging from product fact sheets, package leaflets, motivational campaigns for the participation in health promotion or political engagement programs.

Based on the results reported in this paper, several challenges in the design of knowledge-based recommender applications emerge. It seems that long attribute lists are not necessary for users' decisions. Furthermore, algorithms are needed that provide as little information as necessary and as much as needed to not reduce a users' trust in the recommender application. In relation to the latter arguments, it does matter how attributes are ordered on product comparison pages and a corresponding recommendation to developers of recommender applications can be made to actively take into account serial position effects when designing result (product comparison) pages for recommenders.

References

1. Atkinson, R.C., Shiffrin, R.M.: Human Memory: A proposed system and its control processes. In: Spence, K.W., Spence, J.T. (eds.) The psychology of learning and motivation: Advances in research and theory, pp. 89–195. Academic Press, New York (1968)
2. Baddeley, A.D., Hitch, G.: Recency re-examined. In: Dornic, I S. (ed.) Attentional and performance, vol. VI, pp. 647–667. Erlbaum, Hillsdale, New York (1977)
3. Bellman, S., Johnson, E.J., Lohse, G.L., Mandel, N.: Designing Marketplaces of the Artificial with Consumers in Mind: Four Approaches to Understanding Consumer Behavior in Electronic Environments. Jrnl. of Interactive Marketing 20, 21–33 (2006)
4. Berdichevsky, D., Neuenschwander, E.: Towards an ethics of persuasive technology. Communications of the ACM 42(5) (1999)
5. Bettman, J.R., Luce, M.F., Payne, J.: Constructive Consumer Choice Processes. Journal of Consumer Research 25, 187–217 (1998)
6. Burke, R.: Knowledge-based Recommender Systems. Encyclopedia of Library & Information Systems 69(32) (2000)
7. Burke, R.: Hybrid Recommender Systems: Survery and Experiments. User Modeling and User-Adapted Interaction 12, 331–370 (2002)
8. Ebbinghaus, H.: Memory: A contribution to experimental psychology. Columbia University, Teachers College, New York (1913)
9. Felfernig, A., Gula, B.: An Empirical Study on Consumer Behavior in the Interaction with Knowledge-based Recommender Applications. In: IEEE Joint Conference on E-Commerce Technology (CEC06) and Enterprise Computing, E-Commerce and E-Services (EEE06), pp. 288–296. IEEE Computer Society, San Francisco, California (2006)
10. Fogg, B.J.: Persuasive computers: Perspectives and research directions. In: Proceedings of the SIGCHI conference on Human factors in computing systems CHI '98 (1998)
11. Fogg, B.J.: Persuasive Technology. Morgan Kaufmann Publishers, San Francisco (2003)
12. Gasser, R., Brodbeck, D., Degen, M., Luthiger, J., Wyss, R., Reichlin, S.: Persuasiveness of Mobile Lifestyle Coaching Application Using Social Facilitation, Persuasive 2006, pp. 27-38 (2006)
13. Gershberg, F.B., Shimamura, A.P.: Serial position effects in implicit and explicit tests of memory. Journal of Experimental Psychology: Learning, Memory, and Cognition 20, 1370–1378 (1994)
14. Gretzel, U., Fersenmaier, D.R.: Persuasion in Recommender systems. International Journal of Electronic Commerce 7(2), 81–100 (2007)

15. Häubl, G., Murray, K.B.: Preference Construction and Persistence in Digital Marketplaces: The Role of Electronic Recommendation Agents. Journal of Consumer Psychology 13, 75–91 (2003)
16. Herlocker, J.L., Konstan, J.A., Terveen, L.G., Riedl, J.T.: Evaluating Collaborative Filtering Recommender Systems. ACM Trans. on Information Systems 22(1), 5–53 (2004)
17. Hitch, G.J., Ferguson, J.: Prospective memory for future intentions: Some comparisons with memory for past events. European Journal of Cognitive Psychology 3, 285–295 (1991)
18. King, P., Tester, J.: The landscape of persuasion technologies. Communications of the ACM 42(5), 31–38 (1999)
19. Kirckpatrick, E.A.: An experimental study of memory. Psychological Review 1, 602–609 (1894)
20. Komiak, S., Benbasat, I.: Comparing Persuasiveness of Different Recommendation Agents as Customer Decision Support Systems in Electronic Commerce. In: DSS 2004. International Conference on Decision Support Systems, Prato, Tuscany (2004)
21. Lashley, K.S., The, K.S.: problem of serial order in behavior. In: Jeffress, L.A. (ed.) Cerebral mechanisms in behaviour, pp. 112–136. Wiley, New York (1951)
22. Mandel, N., Johnson, E.J.: When Web pages influence choice: Effects of visual primes on novices. Journal of Consumer Research 29, 235–245 (2002)
23. Maylor, E.: Serial position effects in semantic memory: reconstructing the order of verses of hymns. Psychonomic Bulletin & Review 9, 816–820 (2002)
24. Nipher, F.E.: On the distribution of errors in numbers written from memory. Transactions of the Academy of Science of St. Louis 3, CCX-CCXI (1878)
25. Payne, J.W., Bettman, J.R., Johnson, E.J.: The Adaptive Decision Maker. Cambridge University Press, New York (1993)
26. Pazzani, M., Billsus, D.: Learning and Revising User Profiles: The Identification of Interesting Web Sites. Machine Learning 27, 313–331 (1997)
27. Petty, R.E., Zakary, L.T., Hawkins, C., Wegener, D.T.: Motivation to think and order effects in persuasion: the moderating role of chunking. Personality and Social Psychology Bulletin 27, 332–344 (2001)
28. Pinto, A.C., Baddeley, A.D.: Where did you last park your car? Analysis of naturalistic long-term recency effect. European Journal of Cognitive Psychology 3, 297–313 (1991)
29. Sarwar, B., Karypis, G., Konstan, J.A., Riedl, J.T.: Item-based collaborative filtering recommendation algorithms. In: 10th Int. World Wide Web Conf., pp. 285–295 (2001)
30. Sehulster, J.R.: Content and temporal structure of autobiographical knowledge: Remembering twenty-five seasons of the Metropolitan Opera. Memory & Cognition 17, 590–606 (1989)
31. Shih, Y.-Y., Liu, D.-R.: Hybrid recommendation approaches: collaborative filtering via valuable content information. In: HICSS'05. 38th Hawaii International Conference on System Sciences, Big Island, Hawaii, p. 217b (2005)
32. Tversky, A.: Intransitivity of preferences. Psychological Review 76, 327–352 (1969)
33. Tversky, A.: Elimination by aspects: A theory of choice. Psychological Review 79, 281–299 (1972)
34. Young, R.K.: Serial Learning. In: Dixon, T.R., Horton, D.L. (eds.) Verbal behaviour and behaviour theory, pp. 122–148. Prentice Hall, Engelwood Cliffs, NJ (1968)
35. Zanker, M., Bricman, M., Gordea, S., Jannach, D., Jessenitschnig, M.: Persuasive online selling in quality & taste domains. In: Bauknecht, K., Pröll, B., Werthner, H. (eds.) EC-Web 2006. LNCS, vol. 4082, pp. 51–60. Springer, Heidelberg (2006)

Persuade Into What? Why Human-Computer Interaction Needs a Philosophy of Technology

Daniel Fallman

Umea Institute of Design & Dept. of Informatics, Umeå University
SE-90187 Umeå, Sweden
Daniel.fallman@dh.umu.se

Abstract. Persuasive interfaces in a class of interfaces belonging to a trend in contemporary HCI where user experiences matter more than for instance user performance. In this paper, we argue that in this shift there is also a shift in accountability, but that this shift tends to remain implicit in HCI. What makes a good user experience? To deal with these issues, we argue that HCI needs to develop a philosophy of technology. Two candidate accounts of contemporary philosophies of technology are introduced and discussed. First, Don Ihde develops a phenomenology of relations between human users, artifacts, and the world and technologies are seen as inherently non-neutral. Second, Albert Borgmann argues that we need to be cautious and rethink both the relationship as well as the often assumed correspondence between what we consider as useful and what we think of as good in terms of technology.

Keywords: Philosophy of technology, HCI, social implications, culture.

1 Introduction

In traditional Human-Computer Interaction (HCI) a common methodological practice, adopted primarily from the cognitive sciences, has been to perform various kinds of lab-based quantitative experiments to gain empirical insight into some aspects of a particular design's usability, typically in comparison with a different design. This practice continues a long tradition in HCI of empiricism, objectivism, and cognitivism. While few would probably argue against the value of improving the usability of interactive systems, a number of conceptual frameworks and associated methodological approaches have recently been proposed as post-cognitivistic alternative approaches to HCI that would be aimed towards and better suited for capturing various aspects of interactive experiences. These include ethnography and ethnomethodology [15, 3], phenomenology [3, 16], distributed cognition [6], and activity theory [13]. A recent trend in HCI is also to seek inspiration in design methods, theory, and practice [4, 10, 5] rather than in formal methods of evaluation. These researchers tend to be interested in the relationship between user and artifact in terms of for instance that relationship's *affective qualities* rather than efficiency; *meaning* rather than various performance metrics; *fun* and *playability* rather than error rate; and *sociability* rather than learnability, and so on.

Y. de Kort et al. (Eds.): PERSUASIVE 2007, LNCS 4744, pp. 295–306, 2007.

1.1 From Usability to User Experience

Traditional HCI typically relies on the 'five E's' of usability, i.e. that designs should be effective, efficient, engaging, error tolerant, and easy to learn. Among other things, this means that when only usability is concerned, i.e. within the *usability paradigm*, it is quite easy to say whether or not something is 'a good design', as it can be measured, analyzed, debated, and assessed according to a whole battery of methods, practices, and techniques that has been developed within the paradigm. With the shift to issues like user experience, affective qualities, playability, and sociability however also comes a shift in *guarantor* and *accountability*—a shift in 'good'. What makes a good user experience? When is a user experience successful or a failure?

We argue that these issues have the possibility to open up and make explicit a dimension of HCI design which has so far been largely deemphasized. This is the dimension of the nature of the technologies that HCI develop and the human, social, cultural, ethical, and political implications of those technologies—it is a *philosophy of technology* for Human-Computer Interaction. This is obviously of particular concern when it comes to persuasive interfaces. Persuasive interfaces opens up a lot of such social, ethical, and political dimensions: if a web site can persuade you to become an instant buyer, is it ethical for a HCI designer to develop such a web site for anyone? If your mobile phone can motivate you to exercise more, will that increase anorexia among young girls? If instant feedback on gasoline use will change how people drive so they use less gasoline, will that come to slow down the development of electrical and hydrogen-powered cars? If online rating systems inspire people to behave better online, what do we really mean by *better*? What is a good persuasive interface? One that persuades one *more* or one hat persuades one into something *good*? Who is to decide?

If interactive systems are knowingly designed to change human attitudes and behaviors, we would also need a philosophy of technology that provides us the means for revealing, analyzing, and discussing the human, social, cultural, ethical, and political implications of these changes—that helps us understand 'the new good'. In this paper, we have first introduced the idea of a philosophy of technology for HCI. Next, we will provide two examples of some prominent contemporary thinking in the area, and conclude by discussing these accounts in the context of HCI and persuasive interfaces.

2 Philosophy of Technology

The *philosophy of technology* is the field of philosophy dedicated to studying the nature of technology and its implications. What separates a philosophy of technology from other kinds of philosophies is often debatable, but Ihde argues that "to qualify as a philosophy of technology ... the philosopher must make technology a foreground phenomenon and be able to reflectively analyze it in such a way as to illuminate features of the *phenomenon of technology itself*" [9, p. 38]. Understanding the importance of technology in our lives, and thinking about it philosophically, has however a very long history and tradition within Western thinking, dating at least back to the Greeks. Whereas many philosophers before them take great interest in technology, it is not until the 20th century—with John Dewey and Martin Heidegger—that it makes sense to talk about any real philosophies of technology. Both regard technology as central to modern life, where Dewey holds a largely optimistic outlook towards modern technologies, while Heidegger comes to develop a more dystopian view.

This basic utopian/dystopian divide is still visible within the field of philosophy of technology. In *Thinking through Technology* [12], Carl Mitcham distinguishes the engineering strand in philosophy of technology, which seems to assume the centrality of technology in human life, but also the humanities approach, which is more concerned with technology's moral and cultural boundaries. This dichotomy is however becoming increasingly questioned and refined by some of the major contemporary philosophers of technology, including Albert Borgmann, Andrew Feenberg, Donna Haraway, Larry Hickman, Don Ihde, and Carl Mitcham.

In the following sections, we will introduce and discuss two contemporary philosophies of technology that could be said to belong to each of these two strands. First, we will look at Don Ihde's view on the non-neutrality of technology, and second on Albert Borgmann's device paradigm. They appear interesting in the context of HCI for a number of reasons. First, they are contemporary in that they deal with and consider the technologies of today, the technologies that surround us and with which we live. Second, while being contemporary there are still apparent connections and legacies between their thinking and that of Heidegger and Dewey. Third, while they are two very different kinds of philosophies of technology—showing the breadth of the field—there are still a number of common denominators that render the two philosophies complementary to each other rather than excluding.

2.1 Ihde's Non-neutral Technology

In *Technics and Praxis* [7], Don Ihde brings to light the way science is related to technology as well as praxis. Focusing on optical technologies, he shows how the early use of telescopes and microscopes helped reveal worlds which until then had been inaccessible. The optical magnification did not simply provide scientists with access to previously unknown territories; it irreversibly oriented scientific inquiry towards the macro and micro worlds that these technologies exposed. This, according to Ihde, transformed not only what was seen but also the scale of what was seen, i.e. how it was seen in relation to technologically un-aided vision. From his analysis, Ihde proposes a magnification/reduction transformation to be a structural feature: "For every enhancement of some feature, perhaps never before seen, there is also a reduction of other features. To magnify some observed object, optically, is to bring it forth from a background into a foreground and make it present to the observer, but it is also to reduce the former field in which it fit, and—due to foreshortening—to reduce visual depth and background" [9, p. 111].

He argues that this kind of transformation is a structural element that belongs to all kinds of technologies, not only optical, and what is more: that the transformation is non-neutral. In his perhaps most influential work, *Technology and the Lifeworld: From Garden to Earth* [8], Ihde takes this argument further by arguing that even seemingly unobtrusive and ubiquitous technology, such as eyeglasses, have this non-neutral mediating character. Ihde argues that even though the changes brought by wearing eyeglasses—i.e. to transform what appear as blurry objects into clear and distinct ones—are typically appreciated by their user, the change does not come without a price. First, the user needs to care for the mediating technology itself. Although most people would consider this as a small price to pay for what is gained, it is for instance possible that wearing eyeglasses may come to affect how people behave in certain situations. Eyeglass-wearing children, for instance, may chose not to enter into certain kinds of play in order not to be in danger of breaking their glasses. Second, Ihde suggests that by using eyeglasses, the world comes to one as enframed. By the back glares that occur and the dust and water spots that appear on the glasses, their user develops a fringe awareness that the world as it appears through the eyeglasses is intruded upon, mediated by a technological in-between: "for every revealing transformation there is a simultaneously concealing transformation of the world, which is given through a technological mediation. Technologies transform experience, however subtly, and that is one root of their non-neutrality" [8, p. 49].

While all technologies are non-neutral, according to Ihde, optical technologies—such as eyeglasses, telescopes, and microscopes—seem to belong to a group of technologies which enhance (and by their non-neutrality also transform) our perceptual, experiential, and bodily experiences of the world. Other kinds of technologies, such as speedometers, clocks, and the buttons on a telephone, seem not to have this enhancing or amplifying character. They do not in the same way seem to directly enhance their user's perception, but rather hold another mode of reference to observed objects; one which relies on different kinds of interpretation. If looking through a telescope is a matter of sensory perception—amplified 'seeing' in some sense—using speedometers and clocks may be better thought of as a matter of 'reading'. A world object is still being referred to—i.e. in the case of the speedometer the referred-to object is typically the speed of the vehicle—but the way it is referred to is not perceptual but rather translated into some form of hermeneutic representation. According to Ihde, this kind of technology is also non-neutral. First, the translation that must occur between the signifier and the signified abstracts and hence reduces the referred-to object, where for instance the experiential concept of speed becomes reduced to a number of miles per hour. Second, the speedometer requires that the user has previously acquired the skill to interpret—i.e. read—the instrument, in order for it to be meaningful. Hence, the speedometer is highly dependent on the context in which it is designed and used; it is a culturally embedded piece of technology whose meaning is constructed.

2.1.1 Human–Technology Relations as Analytical Units

Ihde argues that technologies "insofar as they are artifactual (in a range from simple entities to whole complexes of systems), are developed, used, and related to by humans in distinct ways" [8, p. 26]. By giving prominence to the relations between technology, world, and human beings, he is able to distinguish between such issues as technologies and techniques. Ihde, who has "repeatedly insisted that the materiality of technologies be maintained" [8, p. 26], holds that if one absorbs techniques—as certain ways of practice and thought—into technology that tends to yield technology as an overly general and abstract term. If in such a way everything is thought of as technology, we become increasingly prone to make metaphysical claims [8]. Techniques may hence come with or without technology, but a technique is not in itself a technology—while techniques may still be closely related to technology.

By revealing the relations between technology and people, it also becomes possible to overcome the often suggested and presumed neutrality of technologies, where technology is seen simply as chunks of isolated, dead matter. While a gun, as an example, does nothing on its own the picture changes when the world is approached from a perspective in which the human-technology relation is the primitive unit of analysis: "[it] becomes immediately obvious that the relation of human–gun (a human with a gun) to another object or another human is very different from the human without a gun. The human–gun relation transforms the situation from any similar situation of a human without a gun" [8, p. 27].

A third advantage of giving prominence to human–technology relations has to do with the possibility of preserving in one's analysis the dynamic and actional nature of that relationship. Even though technologies are artificial, it is nevertheless important to realize that they are part of human praxis; used, designed, developed, repaired, discarded, and so on. As Ihde notes, connecting to the thinking of Heidegger and Merleau-Ponty, "humans are what they are in terms of the human–world relation, but this relation in existence is actional" [8, p. 27]. Studying technology by drawing on human–technology relations means that one does not have to abandon the world in favor of just studying the artificial.

2.1.2 A Phenomenology of Human–Technology Relations

What possible human-technology relations are there to be found? Although not perceived as exclusive poles but rather as items along a continuum, Ihde makes a distinction between three basic kinds of relations between humans, technology, and world, namely between the embodiment relation, the hermeneutical relation, and the alterity relation [8]. First, in the discussion on the non-neutral and mediating role of optical technologies it is noticeable that eyeglasses for instance allow their users to embody their praxis through the technology, which is a relationship that Ihde thinks of as fundamentally existential. This is to say that the wearer embodies her eyeglasses in the sense that the technology in question gets in between the wearer and her world, and that she sees the world through the optical lenses of the eyeglasses: i.e. wearer–eyeglasses–world.

The embodiment relation is however not a collective name for all kinds of technologies appearing in between the user and the world. For a technology to hold an embodiment relation it must also be technically transparent—its material or physical characteristic must be such that it allows 'seeing through'. For eyeglasses, this would imply that if the actual glass is not transparent enough, they become impossible to embody from a technical perspective. But the embodying of technology is also dependent on the human being, since it is something that has to be acquired or constituted. For someone not familiar with eyeglasses, there is typically a short period of time in which one notices their weight, possibly experiences some eyestrain, finds the back glares annoying, and perhaps one even has to make some small adjustments in spatial motility. But once the skill of wearing eyeglasses, both in terms of carrying them physically and seeing through them, has been acquired they may become almost fully transparent, or as Ihde suggests: "taken into my own perceptual-bodily self experience" [8, p. 73]. They then become part of the way in which the world is ordinarily experienced; they withdraw into an embodied relation with their user.

The embodiment relation is not limited to optical technology, it may occur for any sensory dimension; for instance in tactile motility, through Merleau-Ponty's [11] examples of the blind man's cane and the woman's feathered hat, but also through hearing aids and the like. Neither is the embodiment relation set aside for or specific to simple or complex technologies, nor is it a matter of whether these are mono- or multisensory. Ihde argues that for example the pleasure and whole body involvement in driving owes to the user experiencing an embodiment relation: "One experiences the road and the surroundings through the driving of the car, and motion is the focal activity. In a finely engineered sports car, for example, one has a more precise feeling of the road and of the traction upon it than in the older, softer-riding, large cars of the fifties. One embodies the car, too, in such activities as parallel parking: when well embodied, one feels rather than sees the distance between car and curb—one's bodily sense is 'extended' to the parameters of the driver-car body" [8, p. 74]. According to Ihde, the embodiment relation between a human user, technology, and the world can be formalized as: *(Human—Technology)—>World.*

Second, speedometers and clocks have earlier been proposed as two technologies requiring interpretation. However, at one level these technologies hold a similar relation to their users as do for instance telescope and eyeglasses: the speedometer also appears in between a human user and the world: i.e. driver–speedometer–world. What is different between the mediating role of eyeglasses and that of a speedometer is that in the latter case, the user's perceptual focus is not on the world but on the technological instrument itself. Perceiving the speedometer is in this sense something one does instead of perceiving the world, as one cannot see the world in the same sense through the speedometer as one sees the world through one's eyeglasses. The seeing of the world that takes place in the first case must be understood as interpretive rather than experiential. The speedometer does not enhance any of its user's innate capabilities or senses in the way technologies do which hold embodied relations to their users; it does not become transparent but rather is itself the object of focus whereas the world tends to withdraw. The speed of the car is in this way something that has to be 'read' out of the appearance of the speedometer, hermeneutically interpreted, and not something that is experienced through it. Although the driver may experientially 'feel' speed simultaneously, for instance through vibrations, sounds, and wind, the speedometer itself does not mediate this. It is rather an abstraction and a reduction of speed into a number on an agreed upon scale.

In the case of technology which shows an hermeneutical relation to its user, the actual perceptual experience is however of less importance, as it operates primarily as a kind of text (for instance, "-10° C") that hermeneutically delivers its world reference (i.e. various levels of coldness, depending on whether one's system is Farenheit or Celsius) to the user by means of the user reading the text and understanding its implication. The hermeneutical relationship is hence referential, in that it places the user's immediate perceptual focus on the technology in between the user and the world. In some circumstances, the user might not be able easily to experience the object of reference experientially at all—such is the case when checking the temperature of some distant city on the Web or when an operator is monitoring the temperature at the core of a nuclear power plant—but is forced to be dependent on hermeneutical instruments. This dependency is hence both on one's own reading of the instrument (that one knows how to read the instrument) as well as a dependency on the proper functioning of the instrument itself, as there is often no way of experientially confirming that the instrument is operating properly. Even in the case of the speedometer, one has to be dependent on one's knowledge of reading the instrument (a European driver, used to kilometers per hour, may find little meaning in an American speedometer displaying miles per hour), as well as dependent on the proper operation of the speedometer (if not impossible, it is at least very difficult to know whether the speedometer is operating properly or whether it slightly exaggerates or understates the speed of one's car). As noted, what characterizes the hermeneutical relationship is not that the technology is in between the user and the world—which is also the case with the embodiment relation—but rather that the immediate focus of attention is the technological instrument itself. The instrument is only transparent in a hermeneutical sense if the user has acquired the skills necessary to be able to read it. This relationship may thus, according to Ihde, be formalized as: *Human—>(Technology—World)*.

Third, Ihde makes a case for what he terms alterity relations. The difference between this human–technology relation and the two previously introduced is that it is not a mediated relation with the world or with a referenced object in the world. Rather, it is primarily a relation to or with technology. Ihde argues that this is a relation between a human being and some otherness, although an otherness generally weaker than the one we find in our relation to other people and animals. But it is on the other hand an otherness which is stronger than our usual relations to objects. The alterity relation is hence, according to Ihde, a form of quasi-otherness relation to technology that in at least some limited way seems to take on a life of its own: "A widely cross-cultural example is the spinning top. Prior to being put to use, the top may appear as a top-heavy object with a certain symmetry of design ... but once 'deistically' animated through either stick motion or a string spring, the now spinning top appears to take on a life of its own. On its tip (or 'foot') the top appears to defy its top-heaviness and gravity itself. It traces unpredictable patterns along its pathway. It is an object of fascination" [8, p. 100]. Ihde also sees some aspects of the alterity relation in people's relations to computers, for instance when playing computer games or using ordinary desktop applications. Even though some of the relations involved in for instance playing a computer game could be understood along the embodiment–hermeneutical continuum, there yet seems to be a kind of otherness, a quasi-autonomy, involved in playing the game: "there is the sense of interacting with something other than me, the technological competitor. In competition there is a kind of dialogue or exchange. It is the quasi-animation, the quasi-otherness of the technology that fascinates and challenges. I must beat the machine or it will beat me" [8, p. 100–101].

The computer seems to be one of the strongest examples of a technology entering into an alterity relation. The argument is that this is not only the case for computer systems that consciously seek to place and involve the user in some kind of virtual environment—such as VR systems, MUDs, chat rooms, online computer games, etc.—but it is also something which may occur when using more traditional, tool-like applications such as word processors. When working with a word processor, the application (and the whole computer system) functions as an almost transparent tool for manipulating the document. However, in the case of a serious breakdown—for instance if a much-needed feature cannot be found or the application crashes and one loses one's work—the ongoing flow and the transparency of the tool, "the quasi-love relationship" (Ihde, 1990, p. 106), is lost and the relationship transforms into frustration and rage which is directed towards the computer system. The relationship is now better thought of as one of "quasi-hate" [8, p. 106], it is a kind of alterity human-technology relation. A quite similar notion of on-going flow, where the user's attention is on the content of the work being carried out, versus breakdowns, where attention becomes directed at the tool itself, is partly derived from Heidegger and has also been developed within the computer field by Winograd & Flores's *Understanding Computers and Cognition* [16].

Obviously, the idea of autonomy or otherness of computers and robots has come to influence a number of science fiction movies, including Robocop, Terminator, 2001: A Space Odyssey, The Matrix, and I, Robot—which are often somewhat pessimistic in their character. Dystopian outlooks like these are however not new, but in fact only continue a far-reaching strand of thinking in which any potential signs of otherness of technology is considered as negative and unwanted, supported by for instance philosophers such as Heidegger, Marcuse, and Ellull [12]. One of the interesting characteristics of the alterity relation is however that the world remains a deemphasized context or background, as the relationship is primarily a relationship to or with technology. Ihde formalizes the alterity relation as: *Human—>Technology—(—World)*.

2.2 Borgmann's Focal Things and Practices

Albert Borgmann's philosophy of technology works with the concepts of meaning, value, and ethics in relation to technological development and use, with substantial connections to Heidegger as well as to Merleau-Ponty. At times—like Heidegger—he is seemingly dystopian when it comes to modern technology. In *Technology and the Character of Contemporary Life* [1], Albert Borgmann outlines a style of thinking in relation to technology and human life that in some respect appears very different from that of Ihde. If Ihde may be characterized as strict, practical, almost engineer-like in his approach to technology, and perhaps first and foremost by having a positive attitude towards technology and technological development in general, then Borgmann stands for a more romantic outlook, which echoes some of Heidegger's neo-classical preferences.

Where much of contemporary technological development is focused on issues surrounding the 'usefulness' of different kinds of technology, for instance the usability tradition within HCI, Borgmann suggests that we need to be cautious and rethink the relationship—and the often assumed correspondence—between what we consider as *useful* and what we think of as *good* in terms of technology: "One the one hand, ambulances save lives and so are eminently useful; on the other hand, cars save us bodily exertion and the annoyances of fellow pedestrians or passengers and are thus, at least in part, a threat to the goods of community and our physical health in the form of exercise" [14, p. 21].

This junction between the useful and the good—that some technologies may be both useful and good, while some technologies that are useful for some purposes might also be harmful, less good, in a broader context—is at the heart of Borgmann's understanding of technology. Through his concept of *focal things*, Borgmann addresses that which: "of themselves have engaged mind and body and centered our lives. Commanding presence, continuity with the world and centering power are the signs of focal things [2, p. 119]. As a primary example of a focal thing, Borgmann draws on the hearth. In a traditional, fairly romanticized depiction of what life 'used to be like' in a country house, Borgmann points out that the heart for the inhabitants of this house, be it settlers, farmers, or ranchers, used to be its fireplace. It was a natural gathering point around which most activities were either centered or in some way related to. To keep the house warm, trees had to be cut down, split into wood and dried, the fire had to be built and maintained, and it was here food preparation naturally took place. In this way, the fireplace as a focal thing was inseparable from our involvement and engagement with the thing in the context in which it appeared. This context, or 'world', is made possible and brought into being only by the appearance of the focal thing [1]. The fireplace, as hearth, hence assembles a set of focal activities; it becomes the center of what inhabiting that house means: "Thus a stove used to furnish more than mere warmth. It was a focus, a hearth, a place that gathered the work and leisure of a family and gave the house a center. Its coldness marked the morning, and the spreading of its warmth the beginning of the day. It assigned to the different family members tasks ... It provided for the entire family a regular and bodily engagement with the rhythm of the seasons that was woven together with the threat of cold and the solace of warmth, the smell of wood smoke, the exertion of sawing and carrying, the teaching of skills, and the fidelity to daily tasks" [1, p. 42].

Focal things seem to be characterized by commanding presence. A focal thing such as the fireplace puts demands on us—to cut down trees, to chop and dry wood, and to keep the fire burning—requiring patience, endurance, skill, and some amount of resoluteness. Keeping the fire alive is also a continuous activity; it is something which connects us with our other activities and with the larger context of life, one's community, one's place. In this way, "a focal thing is not an isolated entity; it exists as a material center in a complicated network of human relationships and relationships to its natural and cultural setting" [14, p. 23]. Focal things also have centering powers, in which the fireplace comes to affirm the place where one lives and the direction of one's life; the fireplace provides a centering experience, a kind of long-term, growing insight that this is the right thing to do and the right way of living [14]. Hence, a key characteristic of focal things, according to Borgmann, is that they tend to unify means and ends. Achievement and enjoyment are brought together; so are individual and community; mind and body; and body and world.

2.2.1 The Device Paradigm

Nevertheless, according to Borgmann, the understanding and appreciation of the role of focal things and practices seems to have disappeared from modern technology. It seems that the latter is rather guided by another kind of promise: "Technology ... promises to bring the forces of nature and culture under control, to liberate us from misery and toil, and to enrich our lives. [...] implied in the technological mode of taking up with the world there is a promise that this approach to reality will, by way of the domination of nature, yield liberation and enrichment" [1, p. 41].

Borgmann argues that this promise has led society to believe that the good life should be technologically mediated and supported. While Borgmann does not reject the possibility of technological good—as was the case with the fireplace—he is however highly skeptical about the conventional view that technology frees us to attend to other, more stimulating pursuits [14]. He argues, on the contrary, that we are typically not freed up at all by technology but rather made passive—and if we are freed up it is only to have time for more technology. In this downward spiral, we become consumers, increasingly disengaged from things and from each other. Technology tends to seduce us toward a focus upon material goods, quantitative thinking, commodities, and disposability, where any kind of guidance from considering issues of the good and the excellent is left out. Borgmann envisions that a particular technology could be placed along a continuum, in which a focal thing would become placed on the one end while what he calls a device would be placed on the opposite end. Devices are hence the opposite of focal things; they are disposable, often mass-produced, discontinuous and detached from any larger context, and appealingly glamorous. Devices, in their effort of being useful, are often disengaging in their attempt to do things for us; without us having to lift a finger, requiring very little of us in terms of skill, patience, effort, and attention [14].

Borgmann's point is that modern technology, propelled by the advances in information technology, tends to operate to deconstruct things and reconstitute them into devices, which contributes to the style of modern life being short of a natural center, a hearth, because of which it is short of a larger and richer social and ecological context: "In this rising tide of technological devices, disposability supersedes commanding presence, discontinuity wins over continuity, and glamorous thrills trump centering experiences" [14, p. 24].

A key characteristic of a device is that it typically only provides what Borgmann calls a commodity, only one aspect of the original thing the device replaces. His most well-known illustration of this is the shift from wood-burning fireplaces to central heating systems. His argument is that a central heating system (a device) provides a single commodity (warmth), which in Borgmann's view is only a small part of the role and meaning of the replaced fireplace (the thing, as discussed earlier). Hence, in the switch from things to devices, the quality, context, texture, and involvement in our relationship with the thing disappear and we are left with merely a number of disengaged commodities.

A device such as the central heating system that gives us the commodity of warmth also has the character of hiding the mechanisms by which commodities get produced. While there is a strong and obvious connection between the number of wood blocks one puts in the stove, the corresponding boost in the size of the fire, after which an increase in warmth follows, the machinery that comes into operation from handling a knob on one's thermostat and the warmth produced by the central heating system is much more unclear and unfamiliar; perhaps even to such an extent that the relationship transforms into an alterity relation, where the central heating system becomes a kind of unknown 'otherness'. In this, it is obvious that the commodity of warmth as generated by the central heating system results in division between the commodity as a technological foreground and the commodity's background machinery. According to Borgmann, the resulting distance is how devices tend to split means and ends, whereas things tend to connect means and ends [14]. This implies that we can have ends without knowing, caring for, or getting in any way involved with the means. One way of interpreting this is to say that although we can have the commodity of warmth without effort, the metaphorical and literal warmth that comes from the effort itself and its social character becomes lost.

2.2.2 The Irony of Modern Technology

Borgmann uses the notion of the device paradigm to put emphasis on the ongoing transformation of things into devices and the technologization of our lives and our society that follows. This also involves what Borgmann calls the irony of technology: "The good life that devices obtain disappoints our deeper aspirations. The promise of technology, pursued limitlessly, is simultaneously alluring and disengaging" [14, p. 31].

Borgmann's prophecy seems to be that we have become mesmerized by the promises of modern technology—"to bring the forces of nature and culture under control, to liberate us from misery and toil, and to enrich our lives" [1, p. 41]—whose devices demand less and less of our own skills, efforts, patience, and risk. But in this shift from engagement with focal things and practices to disengaged consumption of devices, his fear is that we have come to disappoint our own, deeper aspirations. Rather than the promise of technological enrichment and consumption, we have come to find ourselves disengaged, diverged, and distracted, and—ultimately—lonely.

3 Towards a Philosophy of Technology for HCI

In this paper, we have argued for why we see a need for a philosophy of technology to emerge within HCI design. HCI as a field has a strongly rooted tradition of empiricism and cognitivism, and the notion of usability is very 'neutral'. Because of this, HCI has a tradition of being morally ignorant of its consequences. While this is common in many empirical sciences, it seems that current trends in HCI toward an increased interest in issues like user experience, affective qualities, and meaning demands HCI to become more aware in terms of its human, social, cultural, ethical, and political implications. To continue to be relevant, it is important for HCI to understand that it is also leaving the comforting moral aimlessness of traditional usability. Persuasive interfaces bring these matters to a head. Can HCI be purely 'scientific' in developing persuasive interfaces? Does it not matter *into what* our interfaces persuade us?

Our fear is that if HCI as a field does not start to deal with these questions—that many disciplines within the social sciences and the humanities are doing already—its perceived relevance towards users, companies, and the society may be lost, and more relevant fields of research will take over HCI's role. In this process, the two philosophies of technology that have been introduced in this paper could be starting points for such a discussion within the field as to the role of 'the new good' in HCI design. Borgmann's point that information technology tends to deconstruct things and reconstitute them into devices, making modern life even shorter of a natural center, is one such starting point for analysis and discussion. Ihde's distinction between embodiment, hermeneutical, and alterity relations to technology is another.

To summarize this paper, we have argued that when HCI was primarily concerned with issues of usability, the question of what was a 'good design' could be defined clearly; the time it took to complete a task, the error rate, or the learning curve. When it comes to the new HCI however, 'good' is a much more complex issue that we argue can neither be neglected nor treated implicitly. To understand what makes a 'good user experience', HCI will need a philosophy of technology.

References

1. Borgmann, A.: Technology and the Character of Contemporary Life. University of Chicago Press, Chicago, IL (1984)
2. Borgmann, A.: Crossing the Postmodern Divide. Univ of Chicago Press, Chicago, IL (1992)
3. Dourish, P.: Where the action is: the foundations of embodied interaction. MIT Press, Cambridge (2001)
4. Fallman, D.: Design-oriented human-computer interaction. Proc. CHI2003, CHI Letters 5(1), 225–232 (2003)
5. Gaver, B., Dunne, T., Pacenti, E.: Design: Cultural probes. In Interactions 6(1), 21–29 (1999)
6. Hutchins, E.: Cognition in the Wild. MIT Press, Cambridge, MA (1995)
7. Ihde, D.: Technics and Praxis: A Philosophy of Technology. Reidel Publishers, Dordrecht, Germany (1979)
8. Ihde, D.: Technology and the Lifeworld: From Garden to Earth. Indiana University Press, Bloomington, IN (1990)
9. Ihde, D.: Philosophy of Technology: An Introduction. Paragon House, New York, NY (1993)
10. Jordan, P.W.: Designing Pleasurable Products: an introduction to the new human factors. Taylor and Francis, London, UK (2000)
11. Merleau-Ponty, M.: Phenomenology of Perception, Transl. Smith, C., London, uk: Routledge (Orig. Phénoménologie de la Perception, 1945) (1962)
12. Mitcham, C.: Thinking through Technology: The Path between Engineering and Philosophy. University of Chicago Press, Chicago, IL (1994)
13. Nardi, B.A. (ed.): Context and consciousness: activity theory and human-computer interaction. MIT Press, Cambridge, MA (1996)
14. Strong, D., Higgs, E.: Borgmann's Philosophy of Technology. In: Higgs, E.S., Light, A., Strong, D. (eds.) Technology and the Good Life?, Univ of Chicago Pr., Chicago, IL (2000)
15. Suchman, L.: Plans and situated actions: the problem of human—machine communication. Cambridge Univ. Press, Cambridge, NY (1987)
16. Winograd, T., Flores, F.: Understanding computers and cognition: a new foundation for design. Ablex Publishing Corporation, Norwood, NJ (1986)

Classical Rhetoric and a Limit to Persuasion

Anne-Kathrine Kjær Christensen and Per F. V. Hasle

Department of Communication and Psychology, Aalborg University, Denmark
{akch03,phasle}@hum.aau.dk

Abstract. Classical rhetoric was the first discipline concerned with persuasion and in fact still has a lot to offer. This is exemplified by a short discussion of the persuasive appeals known from classical rhetoric as well as the so-called '*aptum*-model'. It is suggested how these sets of rhetorical concepts may be developed into guidelines for persuasive design. Moreover, classical rhetoric can be related to social psychology in an interesting and informative way. This combination of classical and modern disciplines of persuasion however also suggests that there is an inherent limit to the power of persuasive strategies.

Keywords: Rhetoric, persuasive design, social psychology, persuasive appeals.

1 Introduction

The very idea of persuasion – and indeed, the term itself – as a crucial component of communication was brought into the world by classical rhetoric. For obvious reasons, modern studies of persuasion are informed by other disciplines too, notably social psychology, anthropology, marketing and advertisement studies, usability and IT-design etc. Yet in our view we can still be informed on crucial points by rhetorical theory, modern as well as classical. Moreover, rhetoric has been related to social psychology in a striking manner which may help elucidate both – and in particular, draw attention to a possible limit to persuasion.

2 Rhetoric and Persuasive Design

First of all, let us take a brief look at the potential of rhetoric in Persuasive Design (PD). Rhetoric and its role in persuasion has been developed by some of the best minds of Western thought for a period of 2500 years. So it is no wonder that a huge body of relevant material for PD can be found. Let us illustrate this with one set of fundamental rhetorical concepts, namely the persuasive appeals known as *logos*, *ethos*, and *pathos*.

Aristotle (384-322 B.C.) systematically observed speakers and speeches and thus identified the persuasive appeals. Broadly speaking, *logos* is the appeal to rationality, *ethos* is the appeal meant to establish plausibility, and *pathos* is the appeal to emotions. Cicero (106-43 B.C) later described these appeals as the task of informing (*docere*), the task of establishing the speaker's personal credibility (*conciliare*), and the task of involving the feelings of the listeners (*movere*) [2]. The crucial point for

Y. de Kort et al. (Eds.): PERSUASIVE 2007, LNCS 4744, pp. 307–310, 2007.

both of them was that these three parameters had to be brought into an appropriate balance according to the situation, if the presentation was to stand any chance of persuading an audience. It should be noted in passing that the roots of persuasive technology in rhetoric were noted from early on. Thus in [3], Fogg wrote:

> For example, Aristotle certainly did not have computers in mind when he wrote about persuasion, but the ancient field of rhetoric can apply to captology in interesting ways [3 p. 230-231].

The need for the right balance between informing, involving and being credible leads us directly into the concept of *aptum* and the concomitant rhetorical model of communication known as the *aptum*-model. This model comprises five elements developed by Cicero. In Scandinavia the model is often depicted by a pentagon:

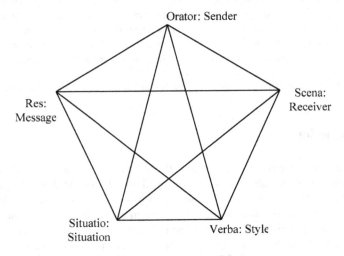

Fig. 1. The aptum-model

The point about the persuasive appeals as well as the *aptum*-model is in both cases that certain parameters have to be adjusted properly.

Thus both the persuasive appeals and the *aptum*-model have analytical as well as constructive uses. They are concepts which aid in analyzing communication as well as suggestions of how to create communication meant to persuade. We illustrate this by figure 2 below (comprising just these two sets of rhetorical concepts, although many more examples could be given; for a more detailed account, see [4]). Obviously, these guidelines need to be made more specific, but it should give a fair idea of the analytical as well as the constructive uses of rhetoric in PD.

3 Rhetoric and Social Psychology

Classical rhetoric has been systematically related to social psychology by Michael Billig [1]. The central tenet of Billig's *Arguing and Thinking* [1] is that we can gain

Rhetorical concepts	Analytical use (e.g. for an existing website)	Constructive use (e.g. for a future website)
Persuasive appeals: Logos Ethos Pathos	Which appeals are used, how are they balanced or adjusted to each other, are they used consistently etc.	Consciously choose balance between persuasive appeals. Make sure chosen balance is used consistently.
Aptum Orator / Sender(s) Scena / Receiver(s) Situatio / Situation, context Res / Message, content Verba / Style, expressive means	How are the *aptum*-relations implemented: orator-scena, orator-verba, res-verba etc.? Does the site seek an apt balance? If so, has it been achieved?	Throughout development, ensure that the *aptum* parameters are well adjusted – such that the expressive means befit the case and the sender, that a suitable relation between sender and receivers (users) is achieved etc.

Fig. 2. Uses of rhetorical concepts

considerable insight into thinking by studying argumentation and especially by studying what classical rhetoric has to say on the subject. Billig observed that social psychology had had a tendency to identify thinking with rule-following.

From classical rhetoric he learned, however, that while arguments and thought may well be based on rules, rules themselves arise from arguments, and indeed, may be disputed by arguments. That is to say that while rules do exist, they are not deterministic. One should not rely on the assumption that following certain rules will always yield the desired results. Any rule may be challenged in some circumstances. Moreover, there is always more than one side to any matter, or argument. Billig attributes great importance to the thought of Protagoras in this respect:

> From all Protagoras's innovatory ideas, it is those relating to the two-sidedness of human thinking which primarily concern us here. According to Diogenes Laertius, Protagoras was "the first person who asserted that in every question there were two sides to the argument exactly opposite to one another". [1 p. 71].

Now in thinking human beings follow the same patterns as in argumentation – we weigh the pros and cons and the relevant arguments when deciding how to act and what to believe – i.e. when making decisions crucial to our *attitudes and behaviour*.

In the Protagoras-quote there is a focus on exact opposites. But classical rhetoric in fact says that there are not just two but many sides to any subject matter. A subject matter of which some understanding is sought is called the *quaestio* in Roman rhetoric. Quintilian says:

> "Question" [quaestio], in its more general sense, is taken to mean everything on which two or more plausible opinions may be advanced. [6]

So an argument – and by extension, any concept or image – may evoke not just its exact opposite but any number of different images, which may be contrary, competing, supplementary or merely introduced as an association.

Comprehension is a dynamical process, since any argument, concept or image may produce counter-examples, often in an unpredictable manner. The conditions of the persuasive designer are in this respect subject to the same limitations as were those of the classical speaker:

> Being author ... does not mean, however, that the [author] owns or otherwise may copyright the image he has created ... having once performed and presented his role, he will have to put up with the fact that a new creative process, however erroneous its products may seem to the original author, has started to circulate and spread its images. [5 p. 35-36]

Similarly, the persuasive designer can hardly expect that the results of her endeavours are entirely safe and predictable. Rather, she must put up with the fact that having done her job "a new creative process ... has started to circulate and spread its images".

4 Conclusion

The way Cicero, Quintilian and many other classical rhetoricians describe persuasion indicates a dynamics of persuasion which makes the whole process partly indeterministic or unpredictable. This insight is *inter alia* supported by Billig's work within social psychology and Nielsen's work on rhetoric as comprehension. On the other hand, classical as well as modernized rhetoric incorporate a large number of concepts and a huge body of experience which should be systematically investigated for the purposes of PD. For one thing, this will be a supplement to principles of and guidelines for PD. For another thing, it is an indispensable part of the historical and systematic foundations of PD and hence should be an important part of the development of the entire field.

References

1. Billig, M.: Arguing and Thinking – A Rhetorical Approach to Social Psychology, 2nd edn. Cambridge University Press, Cambridge (1996)
2. Cicero: De Oratore. Loeb Edition, London (1942)
3. Fogg, B.J.: Persuasive Computers – Perspectives and Research Directions. In: CHI 1998 Papers (1998)
4. Hasle, P.: The Persuasive Expansion - Rhetoric, Information Architecture, and Conceptual Structure. In: Schärfe, H., Hitzler, P., Øhrstrøm, P. (eds.) ICCS 2006. LNCS (LNAI), vol. 4068, pp. 2–21. Springer, Heidelberg (2006)
5. Nielsen, K.H.: An Ideal Critic: Ciceronian Rhetoric and Contemporary Criticism. Peter Lang Verlag, Bern (1995)
6. Quintilian, Institutio Oratoriae. Loeb Edition, London (1921), www2.iastate.edu/~honeyl/quintilian/3/chapter11.html

Persuasion Theories and IT Design

Marja Harjumaa and Harri Oinas-Kukkonen

Department of Information Processing Science, University of Oulu
Linnanmaa, FIN-90570 Oulu, Finland
{Marja.Harjumaa,Harri.Oinas-Kukkonen}@oulu.fi

Abstract. A growing number of information technology systems and services are being developed for persuasive purposes, i.e. to change users' attitudes or behaviour or both. This paper proposes a taxonomy of general persuasive approaches, with interpersonal, computer-mediated and human-computer persuasion as the key types. It also recognizes and briefly describes related theories from social psychology, namely information processing theory, cognitive consistency theory, the elaboration likelihood model and Cialdini's influence techniques.

Keywords: Design, human factors, persuasive technology, persuasive systems, information systems, human-computer interaction.

1 Introduction

Persuasion may be defined as an attempt to change attitudes or behaviours or both without using coercion or deception [3]. Attitude has been described as the single most important concept in social psychology [5], and as one of the fundamental concepts of persuasion. Theories basically suggest that a person's attitudes towards behaviour and subjective norms indicate how that person will act in a situation [4].

A key element in *attitude change* is *persuasion*. Persuasion has traditionally been regarded as a communication process in which a persuader sends a persuasive message to a persuadee or audience with the intention of changing the recipient's attitudes or behaviour, although always leaving the persuadee with the power of decision [4]. The most intensively studied aspects of traditional persuasion have been the source, message and receiver features that are likely to bring about such a change in the receiver's attitudes. The persuasion process can lead to three possible behavioural outcomes [5]: a response-shaping outcome, a response-reinforcing outcome, and a response-changing outcome. It is important to recognize these outcomes, because different goals may imply the use of differing persuasion strategies, although this source-oriented research tradition has been criticized as being too simple and narrow [6].

As persuasion tries to alter the way others think, feel, or act, it is a form of attempted *influence*. There are also other forms of attempted influence, however, like material *inducements* and *coercion* (see Fig. 1), which differ from *persuasion*. Material inducements are exchanges of money or other such things for actions by the person being influenced [4], while coercion implies force and economic sanctions,

Y. de Kort et al. (Eds.): PERSUASIVE 2007, LNCS 4744, pp. 311–314, 2007.
© Springer-Verlag Berlin Heidelberg 2007

whereas persuasion relies on the power of verbal and non-verbal symbols and allows people voluntary participation in the persuasion process [3], [5]. Pop-up windows that always lead to the same outcome (e.g. downloading a file) whether you choose "ok" or "cancel" can be considered coercive rather than persuasive.

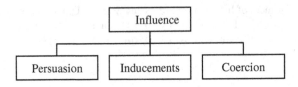

Fig. 1. Forms of influence

Since persuasion is defined as changing the attitudes and/or behaviour of others, the persuader is often trying to convince the persuadee of something. Drawing the line between convincing and persuasion may be difficult in practice. A rule of thumb is, however, that persuasion relies primarily on symbolic strategies that trigger *emotions* in persuadees, while conviction relies primarily on strategies based upon logical proof that appeal to persuadees' *reason and intelligence* [5].

2 Types of Persuasion

There are differences between interpersonal persuasion, computer-mediated persuasion and human-computer persuasion (see Fig. 2).

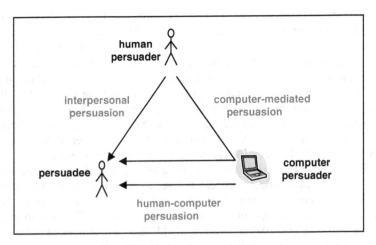

Fig. 2. Three types of persuasion.

Interpersonal persuasion occurs when two or more people interact with each other. Interpersonal communication involves verbal and non-verbal forms of behaviour, personal feedback, coherence of behaviour and an intent to change the attitudes and/or behaviour of other(s) [7].

People may persuade also others through e-mail, instant messages, or other computer technologies, i.e. through computer-mediated communication, so that this may be called *computer-mediated persuasion*. Social scientists have been particularly interested in studying the impact of the Internet and other computer technologies on social behaviour [8]. An example of this would be if someone reads a blog (weblog) and is persuaded by arguments that it presents.

Persuasive technology is not about computer-mediated communication, but rather about human-computer interaction, defined as the study of how people are persuaded when interacting with computer technology [3]. This is referred to here as *human-computer persuasion*. Human-computer persuasion also differs from other persuasion types in that it is not always clear who is the persuader. As computers do not have intentions of their own, those who create, distribute, or adopt the technology have the intention to affect someone's attitudes or behaviour. These intentions can be described as endogenous, exogenous or autogenous [3]. Although computers cannot communicate in the same way as humans, recent studies suggest that some patterns of interaction similar to social communication are possible in human-computer interaction [9], [10]. For example, the interaction between a personalized Web agent and a user can be considered persuasive communication [1]. However, as persuasive technology products are purposely designed in order to persuade [3], the use of e-mail and instant messages, which may well be involved in computer-mediated persuasion, is not part of human-computer persuasion.

3 Related Theories

According to McGuire [11], the basic approaches to the persuasive communication process are information processing theory, consistency theory, the perceptual approach and the functional approach, of which the first two have given rise to many studies and theoretical advancements. Information processing theory treats the persuadee as an information processor, and the basic idea is that to be persuaded, a person has both to receive and understand the message and to accept or yield to it [6]. The key idea of cognitive consistency is that people like their views about the world to be organized and consistent, while psychological inconsistency disturbs people and they feel obliged to reorganize their thinking and restore consistency [4], [6].

In addition to the information processing and cognitive consistency theories, the Elaboration Likelihood Model and the influence techniques suggested by Cialdini belong to promising approaches. Elaboration Likelihood Model [2] is a general theory of attitude change, in which the fundamental idea is that there are two routes to persuasion, a central and a peripheral route. An individual who carefully evaluates the content of the persuasive message may be persuaded by the central route, while an individual who is less thoughtful and uses a simple cue (e.g. the source or length of the message) or a rule of thumb (e.g. "more is better", "experts can be trusted", "consensus implies correctness") for evaluating the information may be persuaded through the peripheral route. Cialdini [12] identifies six influence techniques that explain people's tendencies to comply with a request: reciprocation, commitment and consistency, social proof, liking, authority and scarcity.

4 Conclusions

This paper has proposed a taxonomy of persuasion approaches. In addition to traditional interpersonal persuasion, two types of computer-based persuasion are described: computer-mediated and human-computer persuasion. Persuasive technology refers to the latter. We have also recognized attitude change theories from social psychology which can be applied to information systems design, including information processing theory, cognitive consistency theory, the Elaboration Likelihood Model and Cialdini's influence techniques. The application of theories from social psychology to systems design seems a very promising research area, but directly applicable theories and conceptualizations will be needed.

References

1. Tam, K.Y., Ho, S.Y.: Web Personalization as a Persuasion Strategy: An Elaboration Likelihood Model Perspective. Information Systems Research 16(3), 271–291 (2005)
2. Petty, R.E., Cacioppo, J.T.: Communication and Persuasion: Central and Peripheral Routes to Attitude Change. Springer-Verlag New York Inc, New York (1986)
3. Fogg, B.J.: Persuasive Technology: Using Computers to Change What We Think and Do. Morgan Kaufmann Publishers, San Francisco (2003)
4. Simons, H.W., Morreale, J., Gronbeck, B.: Persuasion in Society. Sage Publications, Inc, Thousand Oaks London, New Delhi (2001)
5. Miller, G.R.: On Being Persuaded: Some Basic Distinctions. The Persuasion Handbook: Developments in Theory and Practice, edited by Dillard, J.P., Pfau, M.(2002)
6. Fraser, C., Burchell, B., Hay, D.: Introducing Docial Psychology. Polity, Cambridge (2001)
7. Wilson, E.V.: Perceived Effectiveness of Interpersonal Persuasion Strategies in Computer-Mediated Communication. Computers in Human Behavior 19(5), 537–552 (2003)
8. Guadagno, R., Cialdini, R.: Online Persuasion and Compliance: Social Influence on the Internet and Beyond. In: Amichai-Hamburger, Y. (ed.) The Social Net: Understanding Human Behavior in Cyberspace, Oxford University Press, Oxford (2005)
9. Nass, C., Steuer, J., Tauber, E.R.: Computers Are Social Actors. In: Proceedings of the SIGCHI Conference on Human Factors in Computing Systems: Celebrating Interdependence, Boston, Massachusetts, United States, April 24-28, pp. 72–78 (1994)
10. Fogg, B.J., Nass, C.: Silicon Sycophants: the Effects of Computers that Flatter. International Journal of Human Computer Studies 46(5) (1997)
11. McGuire, W.J.: Persuasion, Communication, language, and meaning. Psychological Perspectives, edited by Miller, G.A. Basic Books, New York (1973)
12. Cialdini, R.B.: Influence - Science and Practice. HarperCollins Publishers, New York (1988)

Author Index

Lecture Notes in Computer Science

Sublibrary 3: Information Systems and Application, incl. Internet/Web and HCI

For information about Vols. 1– 4473
please contact your bookseller or Springer